B2B Integration

Springer
Berlin
Heidelberg
New York
Hong Kong
London
Milan
Paris
Tokyo

Christoph Bussler

B2B
Integration

Concepts and Architecture

With 165 Figures and 4 Tables

 Springer

Christoph Bussler
Oracle Corporation
500 Oracle Parkway
Redwood Shores, CA 94065
USA

Library of Congress Cataloging-in-Publication Data applied for

Die Deutsche Bibliothek - CIP-Einheitsaufnahme
Bibliographic information published by Die Deutsche Bibliothek
Die Deutsche Bibliothek lists this publication in the Deutsche
Nationalbibliografie; detailed bibliographic data is available in the
Internet at <http://dnb.ddb.de>.

ACM Subject Classification (1998):
D.2.11, D.2.12, H.4, J.1, K.4.3, K.4.4

ISBN 3-540-43487-9 Springer-Verlag Berlin Heidelberg New York

Springer-Verlag Berlin Heidelberg New York
a member of BertelsmannSpringer Science+Business Media GmbH

© Springer-Verlag Berlin Heidelberg 2003
Printed in Germany

Cover Design: KünkelLopka, Heidelberg
Typesetting: Computer to film by author´s data
Printed on acid-free paper   45/3142XT 5 4 3 2 1 0

Preface

The fundamental basis of successful e-commerce is the ability of trading partners to communicate business data securely, reliably and consistently. This transmission occurs over both public and private networks, according to the external or public processes as well as the internal or private business processes of the trading partners. Only then is it possible to exchange purchase orders, invoices, forecasts or payments as dependable messages that enterprises can rely on to conduct business with each other efficiently. The exchange of messages between trading partners is called business-to-business (B2B) integration.

The ability to exchange messages is necessary, but not sufficient for successful e-commerce. Messages received by an enterprise from a trading partner have to be processed. This means in general that received messages are inserted into one or several back-end application systems like enterprise resource planning systems (ERPs) or customer relationship management systems (CRMs). In addition, business data in back-end application systems that need to be communicated to trading partners have to be extracted and sent to them. Sometimes, data have to be communicated between back-end application systems before they are sent to trading partners. The insertion of messages into back-end application systems, the extraction of messages from back-end application systems and the communication of back-end application systems through message exchange between them is called application-to-application (A2A) integration.

A recent development in the service provider industry is application hosting. An application service provider (ASP) is an enterprise that installs and runs back-end application systems on behalf of its customers. These installed applications are called hosted applications. Customers' employees access these applications through Web browsers over the Internet as if they were installed locally in their own data center. Customers are called subscribers in this context and pay a fee to the ASP to access hosted applications. Since the applications are hosted, a subscriber's data are stored remotely at one or several ASPs. ASP integration is defined as the subscriber accessing its own data hosted by an ASP over public or private networks with synchronous invocation or asynchronous messages.

Because messages have to be inserted or extracted from back-end application systems, B2B integration implies A2A integration. Since the back-end application systems can be hosted, A2A integration further implies ASP integration. In general, an enterprise has all three types of integration at the same time. Therefore, enterprises require technology that implements these three types of integration. This technology is called B2B integration technology throughout this book.

The Integration Problem

The three types of integration, A2A, B2B and ASP integration, constitute the integration problem addressed in this book. The integration problem can be characterized as follows:

- **Many endpoints**. An enterprise might have many back-end application systems as well as many trading partners. The number might easily go into the hundreds or thousands. For example, a large manufacturing company might interact with hundreds of suppliers, or a marketplace connects to thousands of buyers and sellers. Therefore, B2B integration technology has to support the management of a large number of endpoints easily.
- **Many different data formats**. In the worst case, each endpoint requires its own data format for message exchange. That might easily result in a large number of data formats that need to be supported by B2B integration technology. In reality, many endpoints share the same data format since they follow the same public B2B protocol standards.
- **Many different B2B protocols**. Analogously, every endpoint might require a different B2B protocol for exchanging messages. Different B2B protocols define different message exchange sequences. This requires the B2B integration technology to support all of them. Again, in reality many endpoints follow the same B2B protocols or conventions, leading to a far less but still significant number of B2B protocols.
- **Business processes**. In the simplest form of integration, the endpoints are connected directly with each other without any business logic between them. A message that has been received is inserted into a back-end application system. However, in more advanced cases business logic must be executed between receiving the message and inserting it into one or more back-end application systems. This business logic is expressed as business processes. Process definition languages for specifying these business processes have to be very expressive to support real applications.
- **Complete history and business intelligence**. Once trading partners and back-end application systems (hosted or not) are integrated, it is possible to look at or analyze the history of messages. For example, it is important for enterprises to determine the average time to execute a purchase order process. Comparing the average time to the fastest might give insight into improvement possibilities. Only if the B2B integration technology provides a complete history of messages and business processes is it possible to do business analysis or business intelligence.

In order to define B2B integration technology that solves the integration problem, a holistic approach is followed in this book. It implements all three types of integration, A2A, B2B and ASP integration, in one set of integration concepts and one complete homogeneous architecture. The integration concepts provide common abstractions across the three types of integration and support the complete integration functionality required to integrate any number of endpoints, independent of their type.

Goals of the Book

The goals of this book are to:

- Provide a solid educational foundation for A2A, B2B and ASP integration
- Describe the fundamental A2A, B2B and ASP integration principles and integration concepts
- Discuss an integration architecture realizing these integration concepts
- Show how existing and future B2B standards and backend systems are integrated into the integration architecture

It is not a goal of the book to:

- Define B2B protocol standards. B2B protocol standards are developed by many standardization groups or industry consortia in their respective application domains. Instead of developing standards, the book shows how B2B protocol standards are integrated into the B2B integration technology architecture.
- Compare integration products that are available today. A large number of integration products are available today, which implement very different sets of integration concepts. This situation alone makes it almost impossible to compare those products directly with each other. In addition, products develop and change rapidly in this field, so that a comparison becomes quickly outdated. The integration concepts that are defined in this book are a solid foundation for comparisons of integration products.
- Define an academic research agenda. A2A, B2B and ASP integration is not a well-researched field at all. There is no academic field of "integration" like there is for database management systems or operating systems. Therefore, it would be very difficult to define a research agenda for A2A, B2B and ASP integration from a holistic viewpoint. Instead, the academic researcher interested in this field or the challenging problems thereof will find many interesting topics throughout this book that are subjects for further research.
- Define an implementation blueprint for a B2B integration technology product. Implementation of integration can take many forms and, unlike other areas in computer science, there is as yet no standard architecture that is commonly accepted as "the" way to implement integration. An integration technology implementation blueprint would be a separate book altogether, since great care

is required to derive to a scalable and reliable implementation. However, at the end of Part III some fundamental implementation principles are discussed.

Content of the Book

Part I of the book introduces the problem of B2B integration by revisiting the history, providing a classification and introducing the integration architecture as discussed in this book. Part II defines the integration concepts in detail, uses these in several examples and discusses the fictional situation of an ideal integration world as justification for the introduced integration concepts. Part III outlines the components and layers of a B2B integration architecture and their dynamic behavior and gives a glimpse of implementation-related issues. Part IV focuses on deploying and managing integration in detail, including change management processes. Part V finishes by reviewing integration standards, research activity, commercial product offerings and speculates on the future of integration.

Suggested Reading Paths for Different Audiences

Several different audiences for this book are recognized, and reading paths are suggested for them in the following. The audiences are:

- **Novice.** Novices need to learn all about integration because they are, for example, studying integration for education purposes, were assigned the task to select an integration product or changed their professions. A novice needs to read the entire book in order to get an impression and a good understanding of the complete field of integration.
- **Expert.** An expert knows about integration from past experience using an integration product or past responsibility for integration. However, the expert realizes that there is no uniformly accepted standard set of integration concepts or integration architecture and wants to see how this could be accomplished.
- **Guru.** A guru knows all there is to know about integration and therefore must also know the contents of the book, in order to maintain this knowledge. Because of this background, the guru can choose what sections to read.
- **Interested amateur.** The curious amateur does not have a mandate to know about integration, but is in general interested and wants to have some insight. This reader wants to get an overview of B2B integration to satisfy his curiosity. It would be great if this would make him a novice, or later on an expert or even guru.

The following diagram shows the different reading paths that are recommended for the different audiences. The path for the novice is not fully shown since it is recommended that a novice reads all chapters. The path for the guru is not shown either since the guru knows best what to look for and what to read.

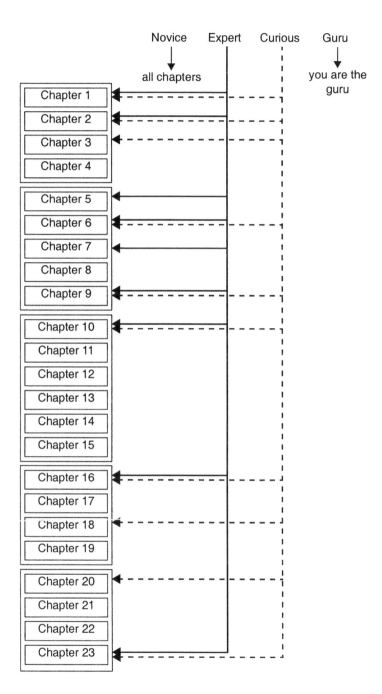

Suggested reading paths

Acknowledgments

Everything should be made as simple as possible, but not simpler.
Albert Einstein

Business-to-business integration is a facinating field currently best characterized by its contradictions:

- Almost every enterprise has been facing business-to-business integration problems for quite a while, but still no conceptual model of integration is available, let alone widely accepted.
- The software industry has been busy building a significant set of complex integration products for a long time, but academic research has not yet picked up on the area on a broad basis as a research field in its own right.
- Integration solutions in enterprises are in reality extremely complex, and difficult to plan and implement based on currently available integration products, but still the perception prevails that integration is very easy to accomplish.
- Businesses at their core rely on integration in order to maintain consistent business data, but integration is very often seen as a low-level programming task on top of low level software components and the hardware infrastructure.

This book addresses these contradictions and contributes to the field of integration in many ways:

- It outlines the complexity of all aspects of business-to-business integration based on a large set of case studies.
- It puts forward a complete and holistic conceptual integration model addressing aii types of integration scenarios as a foundation for dependable business-to-business integration technology.
- It provides insights for researchers who wish to select interesting research problems from the field of integration in order to contribute to its progress.

No book is written in isolation. Business-to-business integration is a multidisciplinary field that requires background and experience in many areas. I would like to acknowledge many colleagues who over the years introduced me to many real integration problems and contributed to my appreciation of the many different aspects of business-to-business integration.

During my time at The Boeing Company I learned about the huge dimension integration solutions can have and what is required to provide solid enterprise application integration. Walt Beck, Pamela Drew, George Engelback, Gary Hess, Steven Poltrock and Mike Uschold were influential in introducing me to real integration problems as well as to real integration solutions.

At Netfish Technologies, Inc. a business-to-business integration product was built, and Igor Balabine, Wei Chen, Ravi Iyer and Glenn Seidman as well as Netfish's customers were instrumental in introducing me to the world of business-to-business integration.

A new form of integration has been built at Jamcracker, Inc. in context of Application Service Providers. KB Chandrasekar and David Orchard gave me the opportunity to learn about and to contribute to Jamcracker's Application Service Provider Aggregation product.

The Oracle Corporation gave me the great opportunity to establish the foundation of a new integration product that provides Enterprise Application Integration, business-to-business integration, and Application Service Provider Aggregation. Roger Bodamer, Kirk Bradley, Matthieu Devin, Dieter Gawlick, Bart van der Hoeven, Janaki Krishnaswamy, Bhagat Nanaimi, Alvin Richards and Shashi Suravarapu gave me the opportunity to establish a comprehensive conceptual integration model and product architecture. A special thanks to Thomas Kurian who made himself available anytime for the discussion of new ideas and who supported me continuously.

The professional dialog with Brian Blake, Mike Brodie, Boualem Benatallah, David Bennet, Fabio Casati, Dieter Fensel, Paul Grefen, Alexander Maedche, Charles Petrie and Amit Sheth was a great way to explore and to test ideas and I am looking forward to continuing our discussions for many years to come.

Ralf Gerstner from Springer-Verlag was very helpful, not only in managing the whole writing process from start to end but also in providing valuable feedback.

The most important continued support I received from my family Barbara and Vernon who moved together with me from place to place over the years. They missed me for weekday breakfasts as well as many evenings but kept encouranging me all the time. Thank you for your wonderful never ending support!

Half Moon Bay, California, March 2003   Christoph Bussler

Contents

Part I Introduction to Business-to-Business Integration 1

1 History 3

   1.1   Why Integration? 4

   1.2   Evolution of Business-to-Business Integration Technology 5

        1.2.1   Homegrown Integration 5

        1.2.2   Point-to-Point Integration 6

        1.2.3   Hub-and-Spoke Integration 10

        1.2.4   Process-Based Integration 12

        1.2.5   Naive B2B Integration 15

        1.2.6   ASP Integration 16

        1.2.7   Mature B2B Integration Technology 17

   1.3   Business Need for B2B Integration Technology 19

        1.3.1   Early B2B Integration 20

        1.3.2   Early A2A Integration 20

        1.3.3   Early Combination of A2A and B2B Integration 22

        1.3.4   Hosted Application Integration 24

        1.3.5   Mature B2B Integration Technology 24

   1.4   Summary 26

2 Introduction to Business-to-Business Integration Technology 29

   2.1   Requirements for Integration Concepts and Functionality 29

        2.1.1   Endpoint 29

        2.1.2   Hosted Trading Partner 30

        2.1.3   Data Format and Event 30

        2.1.4   B2B Protocol 31

        2.1.5   Back-end Application System Adapter and Behavior 31

        2.1.6   Business Process 32

        2.1.7   History 32

        2.1.8   Business Intelligence 33

   2.2   Integration Concepts 33

        2.2.1   Message 33

        2.2.2   Event 35

        2.2.3   Transformation and Translation 37

        2.2.4   Business Event 40

        2.2.5   Business Process and Endpoint Behavior 46

2.2.6   Advanced Business Process 55

2.2.7   Trading Partner and Back-end Application System 57

2.2.8   Endpoint Attribute, Capability and Agreement 57

2.3   Integration Technology Architecture 58

2.3.1   User Interface 60

2.3.2   Integration Logic 62

2.3.3   Connectivity 63

2.3.4   Persistence 65

2.3.5   Layer Component Invocation Model 66

2.3.6   Summary 66

2.4   Integration Technology Deployment 66

3 Types of Integration **69**

3.1   Point-to-Point Back-end Application System Integration 70

3.2   Multipoint Back-end Application System Integration 70

3.3   Back-end Application System Metadata Synchronization 71

3.4   Supply Chain Integration of Two Trading Partners 72

3.5   Supply Chain Integration of Several Trading Partners 73

3.6   Remote Back-end Application System 74

3.7   Marketplace Integration 75

3.8   Hub 76

3.9   Interactive Application 78

3.10 Intra-Enterprise Integration 79

3.11 Application Service Provider 81

3.12 ASP Aggregation 84

3.13 ASP Aggregator Aggregation 85

3.14 Hosted Integration 87

3.15 Reverse Hosting 88

3.16 Business-to-Consumer Integration 89

3.17 Summary 90

4 Classification **91**

4.1   A2A, B2B and ASP Integration 91

4.2   Classification of Integration 92

4.2.1   Business Data Awareness 93

4.2.2   Integration Instance Representation 93

4.2.3   Hosting Paradigm 93

4.2.4   Definition Paradigm 94

4.2.5   Endpoint Specificity 94

4.2.6   Homogeneity 94

4.2.7   Endpoint State Awareness 95

4.2.8   Endpoint Behavior Awareness 95

4.2.9   Invocation Paradigm 96

4.2.10 Data Integration 96

4.2.11 Process Integration 96

4.2.12   User Interface Integration 97
4.2.13   Batch Integration 97
4.2.14   Reliability 97
4.3   Classification of Selected Integration Technologies 97
4.3.1   Streaming Query 98
4.3.2   Publish/Subscribe Technology 99
4.3.3   Remote Procedure Call 100
4.4   Classification of Mature B2B Integration 101
4.5   Summary 102

Part II Business-to-Business Integration Concepts 103

5 Preliminaries 105
5.1   B2B Integration Boundary 105
5.1.1   Event and Process Boundary 105
5.1.2   Integration Logic Boundary 107
5.2   Instance, Type and Metatype 108
5.2.1   Instance 109
5.2.2   Type 109
5.2.3   Metatype 110
5.2.4   Early and Late Binding 110
5.2.5   Dynamic Type Change 111
5.2.6   My Instance is Your Type 112
5.3   Version, Variant and Configuration 114
5.3.1   Version 114
5.3.2   Configuration and Change Propagation 115
5.3.3   Dynamic Change 118
5.3.4   Singular Version 120
5.3.5   Variant 121
5.4   Public and Private Behavior 121
5.4.1   Public Process 121
5.4.2   Private Process 123
5.4.3   Process Binding 124
5.4.4   Schematic Overall Process Layout 125
5.5   Interaction Between Enterprises 126
5.5.1   Synchronous vs. Asynchronous Invocation and Behavior ... 126
5.5.2   Immediate and Delayed Behavior 127
5.5.3   Conversation 128
5.5.4   Direct vs. Indirect Communication 128
5.5.5   Interaction Scope 128
5.6   Interaction Within Enterprises 129
5.6.1   Function Integration 130
5.6.2   Data Integration 131
5.6.3   Event Integration 131

5.7   Summary 131

6 The Ideal Integration **133**
6.1   Single Secure and Reliable Network 133
6.2   Trusted Communication 134
6.3   Single Semantic Data Model and Integration Behavior 134
        6.3.1   Data Model 135
        6.3.2   Integration Behavior 136
6.4   Ideal Integration World 137
        6.4.1   What's Left to be Done for Integration? 137
        6.4.2   Ideal Integration Concepts 137
6.5   Characterization of Integration Concepts 138
        6.5.1   Making Networks Reliable and Secure 138
        6.5.2   Establishing Trusted Communication 138
        6.5.3   Bridging Semantic Differences: Uniform Semantics 139
        6.5.4   Achieving Homogeneous Integration 139

7 Concepts **141**
7.1   Event 141
        7.1.1   Message 141
        7.1.2   Event and Data Type 144
        7.1.3   Event Life Cycle 146
        7.1.4   Event Addressing 148
        7.1.5   Wire Event, Translation and Clear Text Event 151
        7.1.6   Clear Text Event, Transformation and Business Event 155
        7.1.7   Business Event Type Change Management 165
        7.1.8   Event and Vocabulary 167
        7.1.9   Business Event and Business Object 171
        7.1.10 Event Correlation 174
        7.1.11 Event Validation and Data Type Validation 177
        7.1.12 Summary 180
7.2   Process 180
        7.2.1   Hierarchical Decomposition 181
        7.2.2   Data and Data Flow 183
        7.2.3   Context-Dependent Event Validation Rule 190
        7.2.4   Control Flow 192
        7.2.5   Further Aspects 195
        7.2.6   Static and Dynamic Process 195
        7.2.7   Patterns 197
        7.2.8   Life Cycle and Execution Model 198
        7.2.9   Transactions 201
        7.2.10 Compensation 202
7.3   Interface Process 204
        7.3.1   Data 205
        7.3.2   Instantiation Model 205

7.3.3   Data Flow 208
7.3.4   Interface Process-Specific Process Steps 211
7.3.5   Execution Model 215
7.3.6   Batch Processing and Complex Event Relationships 217
7.3.7   B2B and A2A Protocols 219
7.4   Business Process 220
7.4.1   Data 221
7.4.2   Event Address Resolution 221
7.4.3   External Execution Logic 223
7.4.4   User Interactions 224
7.4.5   Business Rule 224
7.5   Binding Process 225
7.5.1   Data and Data Flow 225
7.5.2   Intermediate Storing of Events 227
7.5.3   Instantiation Model and Dynamic Process Binding 227
7.5.4   Behavior Transformation 229
7.5.5   Concurrent Processes and Process Coordination 229
7.6   Process Layout Revisited   230
7.7   Endpoint 231
7.7.1   Type 231
7.7.2   Trading Partner Community 232
7.7.3   Property 233
7.7.4   Organization Modeling 234
7.7.5   Endpoint Relationship 236
7.7.6   Capability 236
7.7.7   Hosting 237
7.7.8   Versioning 238
7.8   Endpoint Agreement 238
7.8.1   Agreement 238
7.8.2   Unilateral Agreement 240
7.8.3   Bilateral Agreement 240
7.8.4   Multiendpoint Agreement 241
7.8.5   Trading Partner Community Agreement 242
7.8.6   Agreement for Anonymous Endpoints 242
7.8.7   Multi-Interface Process Agreements 242
7.8.8   Agreement Conflict Resolution 243
7.8.9   Interface Process Instantiation Revisited 244
7.9   Error Handling and Compensation 245
7.9.1   Error Types 245
7.9.2   Dynamic Instance Modification 248
7.9.3   Compensation 249
7.9.4   Abort 250
7.10 Complete Integration Model 250
7.10.1   Completeness 250

7.10.2 Correctness 251
7.10.3 Semantic Correctness 251
7.11 Summary 252

8 Additional Functionality **253**
8.1 History 253
8.2 Consistency and Reliability 255
8.3 Security 256
8.3.1 Requirements 256
8.3.2 Identification 256
8.3.3 Authentication 256
8.3.4 Authorization 257
8.3.5 Integrity 257
8.3.6 Confidentiality 258
8.3.7 Nonrepudiation 258

9 Recursive Application of Concepts to B2B Integration **261**
9.1 Graphical Notation 261
9.2 Trading Partner Agreement Negotiation 261
9.3 Endpoint Identifier Synchronization 263
9.4 Endpoint Definition Update 265
9.5 B2B Protocol Change Management 266

Part III Business-to-Business Integration Technology Architecture **267**

10 Architecture Overview **269**
10.1 Layered Architecture 270
10.2 Component Structure 271
10.2.1 Component Interface 271
10.2.2 Component Parts 271
10.3 State-Based Architecture 272
10.4 Coordinated Architecture 272
10.4.1 User Interface Invocations 273
10.4.2 Invocations Processing Incoming Events 273
10.5 Integration Example 274

11 User Interface **275**
11.1 Overview 275
11.2 Modeling Environment 277
11.2.1 Modeling Component 277
11.2.2 Testing Component 277
11.3 Management Environment 278
11.3.1 Endpoint Management Component 278
11.3.2 Error-Handling Component 279
11.3.3 Monitoring Component 280
11.4 Analysis Environment 281

11.5   End User Environment 282
11.6   System Administration Environment 282

12 Integration Logic **283**
12.1   Overview 283
12.2   Integration Logic Component Coordinator 284
12.3   Initiating Event Processing 285
12.4   Interface Process Execution 286
12.5   Binding Process Execution 287
12.6   Business Process Execution 287
12.7   Outbound Binding and Interface Process Execution 288
12.8   Outbound Wire Event Processing 288
12.9   Summary 289

13 Connectivity **291**
13.1   Overview 291
13.2   Receiving a Message 291
13.3   Security Verification 292
13.4   Endpoint Agreement Verification 293
13.5   B2B Protocol Execution 293
13.6   Outgoing Wire Event 294
13.7   Back-end Application System Adapter Execution 295

14 Persistence **297**
14.1   Database 297
14.2   Persistent and Transactional Queues 298
14.3   Transactions and Distributed Transactions 298

15 Implementation Principles **299**
15.1   Metamodel and Integration Execution Interpreter 299
       15.1.1   Metamodel 299
       15.1.2   Integration Execution Interpreter 300
15.2   Centralized and Transactional Architecture 300
15.3   Integration Testing and Monitoring 302
15.4   External Program Integration 302
       15.4.1   Application Adapters 303
       15.4.2   External Data Format Interpreter 303
       15.4.3   And Then There is Integration Reality 304

Part IV Business-to-Business Integration Technology Deployment **305**

16 Modeling Methodology **307**
16.1   Overview 308
16.2   Business Behavior 308
       16.2.1   Business Process Modeling 309
       16.2.2   Business Event Definition 309

16.3   Business Partner and Endpoint Definition 310
    16.3.1 Trading Partner Definition 310
    16.3.2 Back-end Application System Definition 312
    16.3.3 Summary 313
16.4   Endpoint Agreement Definition 313
16.5   Modeling Traps 314
    16.5.1 Point-to-Point Integration 314
    16.5.2 Split of Round-trip Behavior 315
    16.5.3 No Business Process 315
    16.5.4 No Real Business Events 316
    16.5.5 Inclusive Interface Processes 316
16.6   Deployment 316
16.7   Integration Project Management 317

17 Advertisement, Discovery and Agreement **319**
17.1   Advertisement 319
17.2   Discovery 321
17.3   Agreement 322

18 Monitoring and Business Intelligence **323**
18.1   Status Monitoring 323
18.2   Business Intelligence 324
    18.2.1 Querying the Correct Integration Concepts 325
    18.2.2 Taking Event Behavior into Account 326

19 Change Management **327**
19.1   Reasons for Change 327
    19.1.1 Internally vs. Externally Caused Changes 327
    19.1.2 Compatible and Incompatible Changes 329
19.2   Business Behavior 329
    19.2.1 Business Process Type Change 329
    19.2.2 Business Event Type Change 330
19.3   Business Partner and Endpoint Definition 330
    19.3.1 Endpoint Definition Change 330
    19.3.2 Interface Process Type Change 331
    19.3.3 Binding Process Type Change 332
    19.3.4 Connectivity Change 332
19.4   Endpoint Agreement Definition 332
19.5   Deployment 333
19.6   Self-Service Changes 334

**Part V Integration Standards, Products, Research
and the Future of Integration** **337**

20 Standards **339**
20.1   Standards in Today's World 339

20.1.1 Portability and Interoperability Standards 339
20.1.2 Current Situation in Context of B2B Integration Standards . 340
20.1.3 Elements of Interoperability Standards 341
20.1.4 Domain-Specific and Domain-Neutral Standards 342
20.1.5 And Where Does XML fit? 343
20.1.6 Standards Compliance 343
20.1.7 Standards Organizations 344
20.2 Process Standards 347
20.2.1 BPEL4WS 347
20.2.2 DAML-S 347
20.2.3 ebXML BPSS 348
20.2.4 RosettaNet 348
20.2.5 Other Process Standards 349
20.2.6 Future Process Standard? 349
20.3 Payload and Vocabulary Standards 349
20.3.1 ACORD 349
20.3.2 EDI 350
20.3.3 EPISTLE 351
20.3.4 HL7 352
20.3.5 OAGI 352
20.3.6 RosettaNet 353
20.3.7 SWIFT 353
20.3.8 Other Payload Standards 354
20.3.9 Vocabulary Standards 354
20.4 Security Standards 356
20.4.1 SAML 356
20.4.2 SSL 357
20.4.3 XACML 357
20.4.4 XKMS 357
20.4.5 XML Encryption 357
20.4.6 XML Signature 358
20.5 Endpoint and Agreement Standards 358
20.5.1 CPP 358
20.5.2 CPA 359
20.5.3 ebXML Registry 359
20.5.4 EDI 838 360
20.5.5 UDDI 360
20.6 Packaging and Transport Standards 361
20.6.1 ebXML MSS 361
20.6.2 EDIINT 362
20.6.3 FTP 362
20.6.4 HTTP 363
20.6.5 MIME 363
20.6.6 SMTP 363

   20.6.7 SOAP 363

   20.6.8 WSDL 364

  20.7 Transaction Standards 364

   20.7.1 BTP 364

   20.7.2 WS-Coordination and WS-Transaction 365

  20.8 Complete Standards 365

   20.8.1 ebXML 365

   20.8.2 RosettaNet 366

   20.8.3 SWIFT 366

   20.8.4 Web Services Architecture 366

  20.9 Adapter Standard J2EE Connector Architecture 367

  20.10 Application of Standards in B2B Integration Architecture 368

21 Products **371**

  21.1 BEA's WebLogic Integration 372

  21.2 IBM's CrossWorlds 373

  21.3 Microsoft's BizTalk Server 375

  21.4 Oracle's 9iAS Integration 377

  21.5 Further Products 378

22 Research **379**

  22.1 Event Definition and Transformation 379

  22.2 Web Services and Web Service Composition 380

  22.3 Quality of Service 382

  22.4 Process 383

  22.5 Adapter 384

  22.6 Ontology 384

  22.7 Integration Architecture 385

  22.8 Business Process Monitoring 386

  22.9 Agreements 386

23 The Future of Integration **387**

  23.1 Why Integration? 387

  23.2 Integration, Quo Vadis? 388

  23.3 The Grand Challenge 388

  23.4 The Grander Challenge: Self-Forming Virtual Enterprises 390

Part VI References and Index **393**

References **395**

Index **403**

Part I Introduction to Business-to-Business Integration

Part I introduces the field of business-to-business (B2B) integration. The history of integration is discussed as a starting point from two different viewpoints: integration technology development and business needs. The history discussion is followed by an introduction to B2B integration technology as defined and discussed in this book. Afterwards, a comprehensive list of different integration scenarios is discussed that shows the spectrum of functionality a B2B integration technology server has to be able to cover. A classification and definition of B2B integration follows in order to categorize integration in general.

1 History

Business-to-business (B2B) integration is a buzzword that has been widely used in the past several years and with large variety of meanings. Its meaning ranges from the simple transmission of XML-formatted messages over the Internet to the automated integration of complex dynamic multinational supply chains based on the exchange of electronic business messages. In addition, B2B integration encompasses direct peer-to-peer exchange of messages between enterprises (without intermediary) as well as their interaction in marketplaces as sellers or buyers (where the marketplace is an intermediary). In this broad sense, B2B integration refers to all business activities of an enterprise that have to do with electronic message exchange between it and one or more of its trading partners.

In addition to this all-encompassing meaning, there is a narrower definition of B2B integration in the context of software technology that is followed in this book. In this narrower sense, B2B integration refers to software technology that is the infrastructure to connect any back-end application system within enterprises to all its trading partners over formal message exchange protocols (also called B2B protocols) like EDI [ASC][1] or RosettaNet [RosettaNet]. In this sense B2B integration is the enabling technology and the necessary infrastructure (referred to as B2B integration technology) to make automated supply chain integration possible, to send XML-formatted messages over the Internet, to send messages in a peer-to-peer pattern to trading partners or to exchange messages with marketplaces. Section 1.2.7 provides a brief definition, and Chap. 2 provides a more elaborate introduction of this narrower definition of B2B integration.

Describing history is, in general, a selective and subjective task. In the following the history of B2B integration is approached from two different viewpoints:

- **Historical evolution of integration technology**. This historical discussion shows how B2B integration technology evolved over time from a purely technical perspective.
- **Historical evolution of business needs**. This historical discussion shows how the requirements for integration developed over time from a business perspective requiring more and more sophisticated B2B integration technology over time. Not suprisingly, the development of the B2B integration technology and the changing requirements are closely related to each other.

---

1. References in "[ ]" refer to Internet resources, and references in "( )" refer to printed articles, reports or books.

Before the two historical discussions, a brief introduction to the need for integration is given to introduce and motivate the basic assumptions underlying this book.

1.1 Why Integration?

Enterprises use different back-end application systems that need to exchange data. The number of back-end application systems in any enterprise can vary from a few up to several hundred. The need for B2B integration technology arises because the back-end application systems are designed and built to operate in isolation. When installed side by side the only way to exchange data between them is by manually re-entering them into the different back-end application systems. However, since this approach is error prone, software technology is necessary in order to transfer data automatically without manual intervention. This software is B2B integration technology.

In addition, enterprises exchange data such as purchase orders between each other. Again, the only way to exchange data without B2B integration technology is by manually extracting and sending the data through means like fax or e-mail and re-entering them manually. In this case, too, B2B integration technology can automate this exchange, eliminating manual intervention.

Fundamentally, back-end application systems and enterprises themselves are heterogeneous, autonomous and distributed systems. B2B integration technology has to play the role of the coordinator between them, addressing these three properties. The systems are heterogeneous since each uses a different conceptual model for expressing the business semantics. When integrating two or more a data transformation task has to be performed that maps the representation and meaning of one system into the equivalent representation and meaning of the other system in order to not change the semantics.

The systems are autonomous since each system changes its state without consulting the other systems it is integrated with. Therefore, B2B integration technology must be able to observe state changes in order to do the coordination instead.

The systems are distributed since each system maintains its own state separate from the other systems. These systems do not share data or state at all. B2B integration technology therefore must transport data between the systems in order to enable the sharing of data.

An interesting question is if it is necessarily the case that the systems (back-end application systems and enterprises) are heterogeneous, autonomous and distributed. While philosophically this is not the case, practically it has to be. Philosophically one could argue that all systems must agree on all concepts in exactly one way. That would make them homogeneous. Furthermore, all systems could share the same data and the same states. This would make them nonautonomous and nondistributed. However, this would require one big database that implements every concept, and stores every single piece of data and state. All systems worldwide would operate against that. And this is where the practical aspects come in. In reality, this is not desired by enterprises since they want to be in control of their data. And that makes them autonomous and distributed. For competitive reasons, back-end application systems develop their own concepts. And this makes them heterogeneous.

The remainder of this book assumes a world of heterogeneous, autonomous and distributed systems. The B2B integration concepts and the architecture are therefore constructed based on this fundamental assumption.

1.2 Evolution of Business-to-Business Integration Technology

Integration technology developed over time in several stages. The most important steps of this evolution are discussed next to show how integration technology, especially in the context of B2B integration, developed over time.

1.2.1 Homegrown Integration

Early on when enterprises discovered that they needed integrate their back-end application systems with each other to enable data exchange between them, they had to implement the integration functionality themselves since no integration products were initially available to solve the integration problem. Integration was not yet considered a profitable market by software vendors. Without going into too much detail, the main approaches of the implementation of integration were the following:

- Back-end application systems called each other synchronously to exchange data. This meant that the back-end application systems had to be modified in order to call each other at the right stage of processing.
- An intermediate storage, such as a file system, database system or queuing system, was used to pass data between back-end application systems asynchronously. One back-end application system stored business data in a location, and another back-end application system picked it up from there. Both back-end application systems agreed up front on the intermediate storage location. If more than three back-end application systems were involved, each pair had its own agreed-upon location where the messages were stored.

The main characteristics of these approaches are that back-end application systems had to know about each other so they could send the data to the correct recipient. Furthermore, back-end application systems had to do data transformation themselves. Either a back-end application system had to produce the data in the format that the recipient expected, or the data were stored in the sender's format and the recipient had to transform the data to its format before reading it. In summary, back-end application systems not only did the internal business data processing but also had to implement and manage the integration between them.

It became clear over time that many enterprises solved their integration problem themselves, indicating that there was a market for integration products. An integration product provides integration functionality without requiring back-end application systems to be aware of the integration. Integration products appeared with varying functionality over time. The most prominent approaches are discussed in this section.

1.2.2 Point-to-Point Integration

Point-to-point integration refers to the pairwise integration of back-end application systems. For each pair of back-end application systems to be integrated, a direct data transfer is established that transports messages between the two back-end application systems. The integration software extracts business data from back-end application systems, transports it to the other back-end application system and inserts it there. Sometimes this is referred to as, extract–transform–load (ETL). There are several different approaches to the implementation of data transfer:

- **Synchronous communication.** In this case the integration software extracts the business data from a back-end application system and synchronously invokes the other back-end application system in order to insert the business data into it. Any data transformation that is necessary is done after extraction of the business data and before it is inserted into the receiving back-end application system. Figure 1.1 shows the architecture topology.

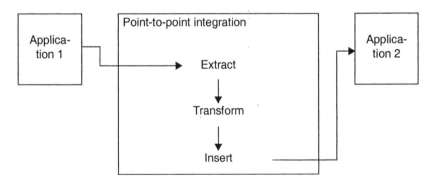

Fig. 1.1. Synchronous point-to-point integration

- **Asynchronous communication based on an intermediate storage.** Instead of synchronously invoking the receiving back-end application system after the business data is extracted, the integration software stores the data in an intermediary storage, like a file system or a database system. The integration software then retrieves the data and inserts it into the receiving back-end application system.

This scheme means that the extraction process and the insertion process are independent of each other. The intermediate storage acts as an integration buffer mediating the extraction or insertion speed. It also isolates the back-end application systems from each other, allowing both back-end application systems to operate independently. For example, if one back-end application system is off-line, the other one can still continue to operate. If the sending back-end application system is unavailable, the receiving back-end application system can still receive data until the storage is empty. Conversely, when the receiving back-end application system is off-line, business data can be extracted and stored in the intermediate layer.

Transformation of data can happen at three stages: (a) after the business data is extracted and before it is stored in the intermediate storage; (b) after the data is retrieved from the intermediate storage and before it is inserted into the receiving back-end application systems; or (c) as a separate process that retrieves the data from the intermediate storage, transforms the data and stores the transformed data back in the intermediate storage. In this case the extraction or insertion of data from and into back-end application systems does not have to deal with data transformation itself. Figure 1.2 shows the architecture topology of the third case.

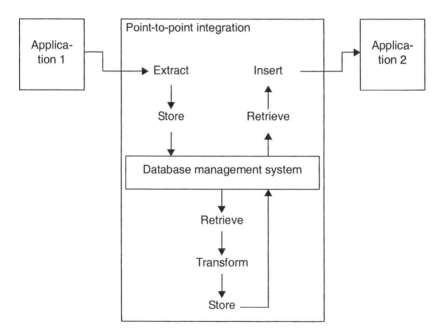

Fig. 1.2. Asynchronous point-to-point integration with a database system as intermediate storage

Figure 1.3 shows the architecture topology for several applications. It is very clear that two storages are required for each pair of back-end application systems that need to be integrated, one for each direction of integration. The specific integration steps like extract, insert and transform are omitted for clarity.

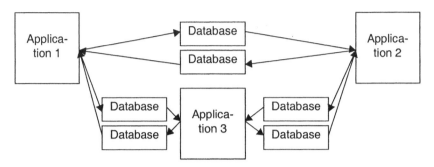

Fig. 1.3. Point-to-point integration of several back-end application systems based on database systems

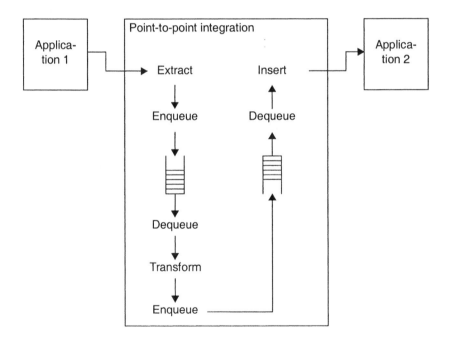

Fig. 1.4. Asynchronous point-to-point integration based on persistent queues

- **Asynchronous communication based on dedicated queues**. Persistent queues provide an alternative to file systems or databases as intermediate storage. Queues have a particular behavior whereby it is possible to dequeue messages in the order they were entered (enqueued) into the queue. However, with appropriate retrieval statements this behavior is also possible in the case of a database or a file system. The isolation of the back-end application systems from each other as well as the different possibilities of data transformation are the same as in the previous case with databases or file systems as the intermediate layer. Figure 1.4 shows the architecture topology with transformation independent of the extraction and insertion activities.

  Figure 1.5 shows a full queue deployment for three applications. The queues for both integration directions are shown between each application. The transformation activities are indicated by having two queues in each direction as shown in Fig. 1.4.

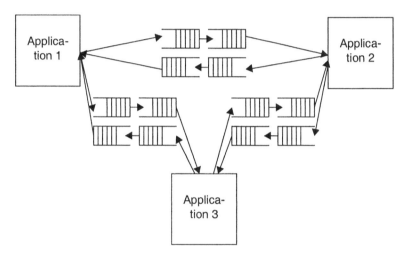

Fig. 1.5. Point-to-point integration of several back-end application systems based on queues

While point-to-point integration software provides the basic integration functionality, it has limitations that are relevant in more complex integration scenarios. The following limitations assume the general case that each back-end application system has to be integrated with every other back-end application system of an enterprise. First, for each new application to be integrated, two data transfer links have to be established to each existing back-end application system, one for each direction of data transfer. In addition, data transformations that transform data between the new back-end application systems and each of the existing back-end application system have to be defined.

Second, status queries determining the state of business data sent between applications have to access all intermediate storages. This means that the status queries have to understand all the different data formats of all the back-end application systems in order to search for specific business data. For example, if a status query would like to find out all purchase orders in transit in order to list them, all storages have to be accessed and each message in each storage has to be queried to determine if it is a purchase order.

Third, more complex message sequences cannot be defined. For example, a three-step integration like the following cannot be achieved: purchase order business data are extracted from a back-end application system and are passed to a second system for processing (for example, determining line item availability). After the processing, the processing result as well as the initially extracted purchase order have to be passed on to a third back-end application system (for example, deciding on approval). This cannot be achieved because point-to-point communications between back-end application systems are direct message transfers between only two back-end application systems. It is not possible to establish relationships or dependencies between two point-to-point data transfers that together make up the three-step process from the example. However, that would be required to implement the example. The various forms of hub-and-spoke integration approaches discussed next address some of these limitations.

1.2.3 Hub-and-Spoke Integration

Basic hub-and-spoke integration changes the topology of the intermediate storage. Instead of having different intermediate storages for each pair of back-end application systems, a central and common storage for all is available. The data transfer is no longer between each pair of back-end application systems, but between each back-end application system and the central hub. Each back-end application system (spoke) only communicates with the central hub. The central hub in turn transfers the data to the target spoke. Data transformation needs to be done in the hub-and-spoke architecture, too. Like in the point-to-point case, the data transformation can happen before the data is sent to the hub, before the data is given to the target spoke or in a separate process that operates independently of the data transfer between the hub and the spoke. Figure 1.6 shows the architecture topology for the latter case. In this representation a database system is used as the storage mechanism, which could also be a file system or a persistent queuing system. Figure 1.6 also shows that all messages of all back-end application systems are stored in a single database system.

In the basic hub-and-spoke architecture, the sending spoke determines the target spoke. It identifies the target spoke in the header of the message sent to the hub. The hub reads the message header and forwards the message to the target spoke after the transformation. This means that each spoke is aware of all the other spokes in order to be able to address them when sending messages to them through the central hub.

One further step to achieving independence of the spokes is the idea of the publish/subscribe addressing scheme instead of the direct addressing scheme. In this more elaborate addressing scheme, the spokes no longer directly determine the target spoke. When a spoke sends the data to the central hub, it does not define any target spoke at all. Instead, the central hub manages rules that determine based on the business data content to which of the spokes the message must be directed. These rules are called subscriptions. An example subscription could be that business data has to be sent to a target spoke whenever the purchase order amount is less than US $100. When a spoke sends data to the central hub (called publication), the subscription rules determine to which spoke the business data must be sent. It could be that the business data is sent to one target spoke if only one subscription applies, to several target spokes in case several subscriptions apply or to none at all.

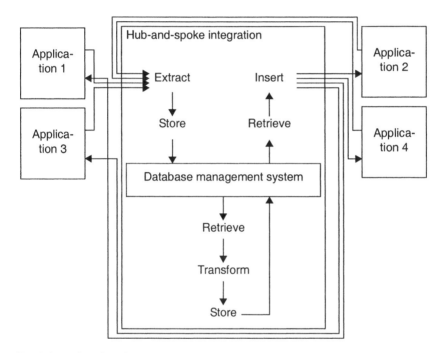

Fig. 1.6. Basic hub-and-spoke integration

If the subscription rules can access not only the message header but also the message body, then the addressing can be accomplished based on message content. This is called contents-based routing.

The benefit of the hub-and-spoke architecture over the point-to-point architecture is that adding a new back-end application system only requires te addition of one data transfer between the back-end application system and the hub. The other already integrated back-end application systems are not affected by the addition. Furthermore, publication/subscription-based addressing allows the dynamic addition of more rules to the hub in order to ensure that messages of the new back-end application system are directed correctly. Using the publish/subscribe addressing scheme it is possible to send a message to more than one target spoke.

Since a central storage stores all messages from all back-end system applications reporting is a lot easier since any report can be created based on the central storage. The report generation need no longer take several storages into account.

The number of data transformations remains the same as in the point-to-point case. Furthermore, multistep integration, as discussed in the context of the point-to-point architecture, is also not possible in the hub-and-spoke architecture.

1.2.4 Process-Based Integration

The point-to-point as well as the hub-and-spoke solutions have several major drawbacks:

- **No multistep integration**. Each message is sent from one back-end application to one or more of the other back-end application systems. However, if a message is sent to one back-end application system and it returns a result that has to be forwarded to a third back-end application system based on a value in the first message, this cannot be achieved using the point-to-point or the hub-and-spoke solution since the first message is no longer available in order to determine the value.
- **No business logic**. Each message is sent between back-end application systems; however, no additional logic like notifications or authorization activities can be added between the data extraction and the data insertion.
- **Only one-way integration**. Each message is sent from one back-end application system to another back-end application system. If it returns a result message that has to be sent back, the result message is treated as an independent message itself. Neither the point-to-point solution nor the hub-and-spoke solution is aware of the fact that the two messages are related to each other following a request/reply pattern or an even more complex pattern.

In order to address these severe limitations, the hub-and-spoke architecture is extended with process management functionality in the form of a workflow management system. Instead of storing messages directly in the database when they are received, they are given to a workflow management system. The workflow management system can start a new workflow instance in order to process a message, or it continues a workflow instance that was waiting for the message in order to continue. A workflow instance determines the processing of received messages, and it sends the messages to the appropriate target spokes.

In process-based integration the workflow instance determines to which target spokes messages are sent. Direct addressing or publish/subscribe addressing no longer applies in this case since the sending spoke does not determine the target spoke, but the workflow instance performs the address resolution instead. The workflow instance has to decide to which spoke the message is sent when te message is ready to be sent.

A consequence of the changed addressing scheme is that data transformation can no longer be performed independently of the workflow instance on the storage itself as in the previous cases because at that point in the processing the target spoke has not yet been determined. Therefore the target spoke format is not yet known. Only if a workflow instance has determined where the message has to be sent does transformation happen accordingly in order to transform the data into the format required by the target spoke.

Figure 1.7 shows the architecture topology for process-based integration. First, messages are given to the workflow management system once they have been extracted. The workflow management system stores messages and retrieves messages as required by the workflow instance. Messages can be retrieved and stored without being sent out. An example is an approval step that needs to retrieve a message, have a user approve it and stores the approved message again. Once the message is ready to be sent out to a target spoke the workflow management system sends the message. Only then transformation takes place before the insert happens.

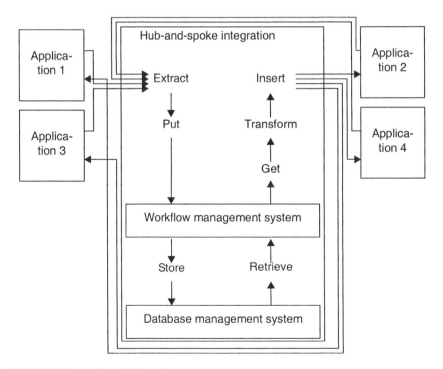

Fig. 1.7. Process-based integration

This architecture addresses all the major drawbacks from the previous approaches. Multistep integration is possible because a workflow instance can have several steps that send messages to back-end application systems and that receive messages from back-end application systems. Since the workflow management system is in control of storing and retrieving messages, it can "remember" messages for more complex scenarios.

Business logic can be built into a workflow definition between the sending and receiving of message steps. For example, this allows for conditional branching based on message content or authorization steps for users to authorize messages.

Integration patterns can be defined that go beyond the one-way or request/reply integration. A workflow definition can implement any pattern between any number of spokes. Figure 1.8 shows a workflow that receives one message. An authorization step requests approval from a user. Afterwards, based on the message content (in this case, the amount denoted in the message), the message is sent to one of two trading partners TP1 or TP2.

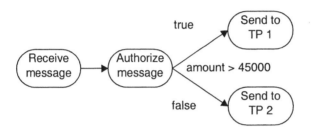

Fig. 1.8. Example workflow

Even though the process-based integration solution addresses many of the shortcomings of earlier approaches, it still does not address all problems that need resolution in more advanced integration scenarios. One problem is that business data from different back-end application systems follow a different format. This means that workflows have to be able to deal with all the different formats. This might result into a high number of workflows if each workflow is designed to deal with one format of a spoke only. If a workflow deals with several formats, the internal workflow logic is quite complex since different parts of a workflow definition have to deal with different formats of the data at the same time.

The workflow in Fig. 1.8 would need to have a conditional branch expression for each format since each format has the amount in a different position or in a different field. Only then would one workflow instance be able to interpret the different formats of the spokes.

Another problem is that B2B protocols as well as back-end application systems define their own message exchange protocol. It might very well be the case that one back-end application system deals with message acknowledgments, but another does not. In this scenario there must be different workflows dealing with the different message exchange formats. The same workflow can no longer be reused across different back-end integration systems or B2B protocols.

Finally, sometimes the business logic within a workflow depends on who the particular trading partner messages are received from or sent to. For example, the authorization amount differs from trading partner to trading partner. In this case, for each trading partner there must be a different workflow encoding the business logic. Alternatively, a case statement must be in the workflow that distinguishes all the trading partners. Either way, the maintenance becomes rather complex if there is a high number of trading partners or if the rules change frequently. All these advanced requirements are addressed in Parts II and IV.

1.2.5 Naive B2B Integration

Compared to the process-based integration functionality, the naive B2B integration technology products were a step backwards. Fundamentally, early B2B integration technology products connected one back-end application system with trading partners. They were not concerned about integrating applications with each other. In that sense they followed the Electronic Data Interchange (EDI) translator approach that connects one back-end application system with trading partners (Sherif 2000). Figure 1.9 shows the architecture topology. The translator connects a back-end application system, does the data transformation required from the format of the back-end application system to the EDI syntax and uses the communication software to send the message to a trading partner.

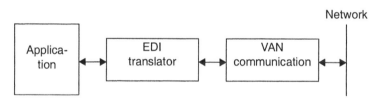

Fig. 1.9. Naive B2B integration

Other B2B standards can be implemented following the same architecture. For each standard a translator can be implemented that facilitates the data transformation as well as the communication requirements of the particular B2B standard like RosettaNet, ebXML [ebXML] or SWIFT [SWIFT]. RosettaNet is a B2B standard used in supply-chains of the High Tech Industry, SWIFT is used in the financial domain whereas ebXML is an emerging standard suitable across multiple industries.

The main contribution of the early B2B integration technology products was that they recognized that an enterprise might have to support more than one B2B protocol to connect to its trading partners. With the recent increase in the number of B2B protocols (Bussler 2001), this contribution is significant.

However, the fact that early B2B integration technology products could not integrate more than one back-end application system limited their applicability and they had to be installed and always managed in conjunction with an application-to-application (A2A) integration product like a hub-and-spoke or process-based integration product. Only such a combination was able to address both the application-to-application integration functionality as well as the business-to-business integration functionality. The downside of this approach is immediately apparent: two products have to be integrated to provide the complete integration functionality.

1.2.6 ASP Integration

A very recent development is the practise of "renting" software to customers. In this scenario an enterprise, called an application service provider (ASP), installs back-end applications systems. However, the enterprise does not install these systems for its own use, but rather to rent access to them to other enterprises (its customers), called subscribers. In this sense, the back-end application systems are hosted by an ASP on behalf of the subscribers, which is called a hosted application system. Subscribers can access the back-end systems over the Internet and pay a monthly or yearly access fee to the ASP.

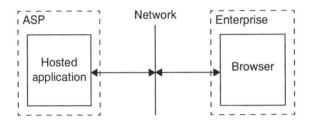

Fig. 1.10. General application service provider topology

As shown in Fig. 1.10 users access the hosted back-end application systems through browser technology over the Internet. For users there is no difference between accessing a hosted back-end application system or one that is locally installed in their company.

The hosted back-end application systems are part of an ASP, whereas the users are part of a subscriber. Since the hosted back-end application systems are part of an ASP, the data of the subscriber also reside at the ASP. If a subscriber needs to integrate locally installed back-end application systems with hosted ones, the integration solution must reach the ASP across the Internet.

Figure 1.11 shows the overall topology in which a so-called ASP connector connects a local and a hosted back-end application system. The important observation here is that this integration (like the B2B integration) crosses the boundaries of two companies. Therefore, both the subscriber and the ASP must have an ASP connector that manages the connection with the back-end application system as well as the communication across the Internet.

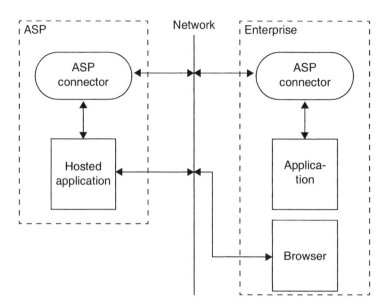

Fig. 1.11. Integration of hosted and local back-end application systems

The difference from B2B integration is that the subscriber does not integrate with the ASP itself, but with its own data in a back-end application system hosted by the ASP. When the ASP receives a message, it needs to determine if this message is coming from a subscriber to connect to one of the hosted systems that hosts the subscriber's data. In this case, the ASP realizes that the message is not about the ASP's business, but about the hosted data of one of its subscribers.

1.2.7 Mature B2B Integration Technology

The various phases of integration technology can be differentiated by the type of integration they support. There are three major types:

- **A2A integration**. A2A integration provides the functionality to integrate back-end application systems with each other within an enterprise.
- **B2B integration**. B2B integration provides connectivity to trading partners over networks like the Internet, following B2B protocols like EDI, RosettaNet or SWIFT.
- **ASP integration**. ASP integration gives a subscriber access to its data hosted by an ASP for integration purposes.

In general, enterprises have the need for all three types of integration at the same time. The average enterprise has more than one back-end application system installed, has several trading partners and subscribes to hosted back-end application systems more and more often. Mature B2B integration technology therefore has to address all three types of integration equally well and at the same time. Section 1.3 discusses the business needs and how they evolved over time in more detail.

B2B integration technology as defined in this book takes a holistic approach in providing the integration concepts and the integration architecture that addresses the three forms of integration in a single set of integration concepts and in one single architecture. Figure 1.12 shows an overview of the B2B integration technology architecture on an abstract level.

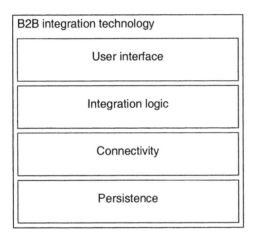

Fig. 1.12. Overview of B2B integration technology architecture

The B2B integration technology architecture is layered and provides the "classical" structure as follows. The user interface layer provides all user interfaces that are required to define the integration, to manage the architecture and to obtain various reports like the current status or the history of processed messages. A modeling user interface provides all the modeling concepts that are necessary to model how business data are defined and passed between applications, trading partners and ASPs. A management user interface provides all necessary controls to manage the architecture at run time when real business data are exchanged. A business intelligence user interface provides reporting functionality as well as monitoring functionality.

The integration logic layer contains a run-time engine that executes the defined processes. It receives business data from adapters or the B2B protocol engine and processes them accordingly. During processing or at the end of the processing, the business data are sent through adapters to back-end application systems, or through the B2B protocol engine to trading partners or ASPs.

The connectivity layer contains back-end application system adapters (or just adapters) that are the means to connect to the interfaces of back-end application systems. They receive and send business data from and to applications. A B2B protocol engine provides B2B as well as ASP connectivity.

The persistence layer stores the business data in their various states of execution in a run-time repository. It makes sure that the processing is consistent and recoverable at any time. A design-time repository contains all the definitions of the processes that define how messages should be processed.

This holistic B2B integration technology architecture, which is founded on a single set of integration concepts, is the last step to date in the evolution of integration technology. Chapter 2 gives a more detailed introduction of the B2B integration technology as presented in this book.

1.3 Business Need for B2B Integration Technology

If enterprises have used EDI for over 30 years to connect to their trading partners, why do they still require sophisticated B2B integration technology? The answer lies in the increasing information technology complexity enterprises face today and will face in the future, where more and more trading partners as well as back-end application systems that follow different formats and process standards have to be integrated. In the following, the most important phases of the history of integration and their requirements are presented from a user perspective. At the same time, the increasing needs of enterprises over time are discussed. These needs result in the different phases of development of integration technology. The phases of integration an enterprise goes through and the development steps of integration technology are tightly related. Therefore, this chapter will refer to integration technology as described in the Sect. 1.2 at the appropriate points. Specific enterprises might skip a phase or might not require certain functionality. However, in general, the different phases can be observed throughout many industries.

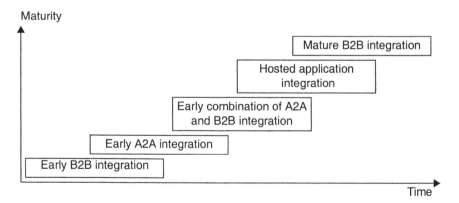

Fig. 1.13. Phases of integration

Figure 1.13 shows the different phases graphically. The different phases overlap with their adjoining ones. The overlap represents that the increased requirements are recognized and built into the new products that go along with the phases. It is a difficult and most likely impossible task to find out which enterprise was first in implementing early B2B integration and early A2A integration. Since it is impossible to say which came first, B2B or A2A integration, early B2B integration arbitrarily appears first on the time line in Fig. 1.13.

1.3.1 Early B2B Integration

Initially, enterprises had one back-end application system storing the critical business data to be exchanged with their trading partners. Each industry had its predominant standard. Many enterprises used EDI for business message exchange as the only B2B protocol standard and the only network they connected to were value-added networks (VANs). In the financial industry SWIFT was the predominant standard. Fundamentally, the complexity was modest. The general architecture topology for EDI is shown in Fig. 1.14.

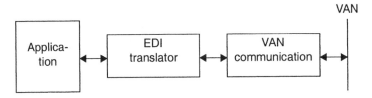

Fig. 1.14. Early business-to-business integration

The only back-end application system that stored data was connected with an EDI translator (Sherif 2000). The EDI translator received the business data from the back-end application system's interfaces, transformed it into the EDI syntax and sent it to a trading partner over the VAN using a communication package. Conversely, the communication package received messages from trading partners using the VAN and handed it over to the EDI translator. It in turn transformed the message into the representation required by the back-end application system and inserted it into the back-end application system. The topology shown in Fig. 1.14 was able to send business data in messages to all trading partners, as well as to receive messages with business data from all trading partners following the EDI standard message layout.

1.3.2 Early A2A Integration

Over time, however, enterprises installed more and more back-end applications following the "best-of-breed" approach. They selected and installed the best back-end application systems they could buy from their viewpoint, for example, an enterprise resouce planning (ERP) system along with a customer relationship management (CRM) system along with a manufacturing resource planning (MRP) system. The best-of-breed approach usually means that the different back-end application systems are supplied by different software vendors. In turn, this results in a heterogeneous environment since the back-end application systems of the different software vendors exposed different interfaces to access their internal data for message exchange. Furthermore, each back-end application system has its own representation in form of document types of the business data exchanged. In addition, enterprises built back-end application themselves ("home-grown applications" or "legacy applications") in those areas for which back-end application software vendors did not provide any software at that point in time.

The consequence of this development is the architecture topology as shown in Fig. 1.15. Since all the back-end applications not only had to exchange business data with trading partners but also between themselves, application-to-application (A2A) integration had to be implemented. As discussed in Sect. 1.2 it could be a point-to-point solution or a hub-and-spoke solution. Figure 1.15 shows the latter. Once it received data from a back-end application system it forwarded it to one or more of the other back-end application systems so that the business data exchange happened successfully.

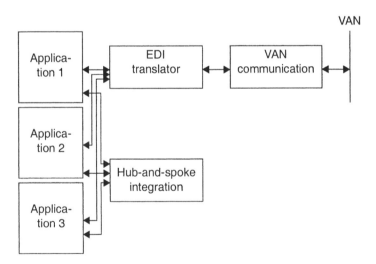

Fig. 1.15. Early application-to-application integration

Figure 1.15 shows that two forms of integration happen concurrently. First, back-end application systems exchange business data with each other through the hub-and-spoke solution, and second, each application potentially exchanges business data with trading partners through the EDI translator (combined with the VAN communication component). Since more than one back-end application system has trading partner connectivity, the EDI translator has to connect to each of them individually. As can be seen, the hub-and-spoke solution is not aware of the B2B connectivity at all.

In more advanced variations of this topology, the integration broker connects to the EDI translator instead of each back-end application system individually connecting to it. In this case the EDI translator is like a back-end application system from the hub-and-spoke solution's point of view (Fig. 1.16). In this architecture topology the integration broker is aware of the B2B connectivity since all messages are routed through it. This means that the integration broker can give accurate reports on the message traffic.

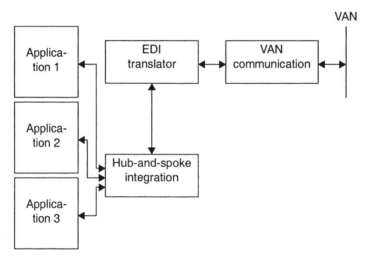

Fig. 1.16. EDI translator as single integration element of integration broker

1.3.3 Early Combination of A2A and B2B Integration

Recent developments in B2B protocol standards like the Open Applications Group Integration Specification (OAGIS) [OAGIS], RosettaNet [RosettaNet] or ebXML [ebXML] pose a new challenge to enterprises. These new B2B protocol standards, if widely adopted, will in general force each enterprise to support more than one B2B protocol standard at the same time. The reason for this additional support requirement is that different enterprises will chose different standards for their trading partner interactions. In order for two enterprises to cooperate, both have to agree on one standard. For an enterprise that is highly connected with many other enterprises this will result in the need to support multiple B2B protocols. Consequently, in addition to the already existing EDI translator, similar software components for other standards have to be installed and maintained.

This development results in an architecture topology as shown in Fig. 1.17. Basically, for each B2B protocol that is required for trading partners, an additional component is added that provides the implementation of the B2B protocol. In order to keep the naming convention, these components are also called translators. Different B2B protocols use different formats to capture the business data. The EDI format is no longer the only one. This is the reason for the additional translators that can translate back-end application system-specific formats into the format required by the B2B protocol. Since additional networks like the Internet are used by B2B protocols, additional communication software is required that supports different forms of transport like the fiile transfer protocol (FTP) [FTP], the hypertext transfer protocol (HTTP) [HTTP] or the simple mail transfer protocol (SMTP) [SMTP].

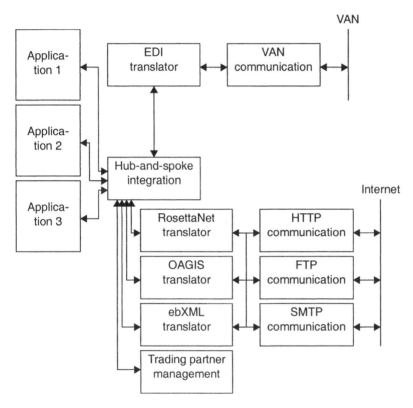

Fig. 1.17. Early combination of business-to-business and application-to-application integration

Furthermore, since all B2B protocols need different data about trading partners like network connectivity or security keys, a separate trading partner management component has to be added in order to manage trading partner information centrally and consistently. The different translators access the trading partner management component to retrieve trading partner information through the hub-and-spoke integration technology. In this way, the trading partner management component is treated as a back-end application system and fits the integration paradigm.

It is apparent that the topology as shown in Fig. 1.17 is quite complex and its management requires careful attention to keep all components consistent with each other. This is especially important for any business rules that might be implemented in the different translators. For example, if an enterprise does not want to receive purchase orders with an amount less than US $1,000, the rule would have to be implemented in all B2B protocol translators. As soon as the same business rule has to be implemented in several places, its consistent implementation has to be ensured manually since the different components do not share a common data infrastructure.

1.3.4 Hosted Application Integration

In the hosted application model the data of an enterprise is also automatically hosted at the ASP, since the back-end application system's database is located at the ASP. This means that enterprises that need to integrate their own hosted data with their back-end application systems have to integrate it over the Internet. This requires an ASP protocol between a subscriber and an ASP in order for subscribers to gain access to their hosted data. The protocol is called an ASP protocol instead of a B2B protocol because the messages sent from the enterprise to the ASP are not about ASP's business data, but about the business data of the enterprise that are hosted by the ASP. This requires slight extensions of B2B protocols to implement the difference. Figure 1.18 shows the architecture topology.

As Fig. 1.18 shows, the complexity of the architecture topology increased again through the addition of the ASP protocol component (ASP connector), which implements the connectivity and the data transfer to and from ASPs. Only one component is added. In reality, it might require as many ASP connectors as the enterprise has subscribed-to ASPs, since in general different ASPs implement different ASP protocols.

In general, an enterprise has therefore to cope with three forms of integration: A2A integration, B2B integration and ASP integration. The fundamental approach of B2B integration technology as described in this book is to support all these three forms of integration with one consistent set of integration concepts that are implemented in one consistent software architecture.

1.3.5 Mature B2B Integration Technology

In the general case, an enterprise has to deal with A2A integration between its installed back-end application systems, with B2B integration to connect to its trading partners and with ASP integration to connect to its hosted applications, all at the same time.

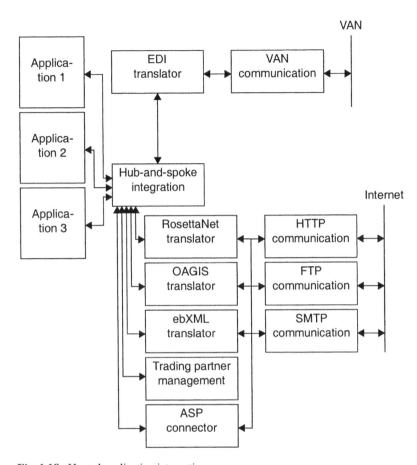

Fig. 1.18. Hosted application integration

The complexity of these three forms of integration has to be managed. Figure 1.18 clearly shows that the complexity of managing all the individual components is very great. Ideally, all the different components would be integrated into one coherent B2B integration technology architecture, following one coherent set of integration concepts according to the mature B2B integration technology architecture shown in Sect. 1.2.7. This removes the complexity of managing an environment with a large number of independently developed software components.

Figure 1.19 shows how the architecture topology changes for a customer if it is based on the mature B2B integration technology architecture. There are three different adapters for the three different back-end application systems required. They are intentionally not shown since they are part of the architecture and are not visible as separate components that require individual management. If the back-end application systems have the same interfaces and the same business data formats, one adapter is enough to handle all three at the same time. Another component not shown is the B2B protocol engine that executes all the different B2B protocols. Like the adapters, it is not a separate component that requires management. The B2B engine connects to VANs as well as to the Internet. Chapter 2 discusses all components in more detail.

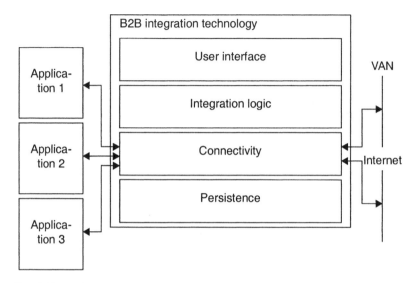

Fig. 1.19. Architecture topology with B2B integration technology

Figure 1.19 shows that the number of connections required between back-end application systems and trading partners is significantly reduced because one component deals with all required connectivity. Compared to the topology in Fig. 1.18, all components that are specific to a back-end application system or a B2B protocol are no longer necessary as separate components, since the B2B integration technology architecture combines the functionality with its implementation.

1.4 Summary

The technical development of B2B integration technology over time and the corresponding increase in business needs for integration caused a huge variety of integration approaches in terms of functionality and architecture (Sects. 1.2 and 1.3). This variety of integration architectures is difficult to compare and, in complex cases, difficult to manage. Enterprises looking for an integration solution are confronted with a fractioned landscape of integration technology.

This clearly demands a new, holistic approach that takes all developments and business needs as the basis for a set of consolidated integration concepts as well as a new and comprehensive B2B integration technology architecture. Chapter 2 introduces such an advanced B2B integration technology architecture, which consolidates all requirements and provides a holistic set of integration concepts, as well as a comprehensive B2B integration technology architecture. A survey of the types of integration and a classification of integration technology follow in Chaps. 3 and 4, respectively. These two chapters provide the foundation to classify both the integration situations at hand and the existing B2B integration technology.

2 Introduction to Business-to-Business Integration Technology

Integration concepts as such are very important, but without an architectural foundation it would be difficult to understand the behavior that the integration concepts are intended to implement. Therefore, this chapter introduces integration concepts and integration architecture in more detail than initially done in Sects. 1.2.7 or 1.3.5. Sections 2.2 and 2.3 define these concepts in even more detail. This definition explains the rationale for the choice of the integration concepts. Finally, a brief discussion gives an insight into B2B integration technology deployment aspects that are of interest. Part IV discusses various aspects of deployment in more detail.

2.1 Requirements for Integration Concepts and Functionality

The integration scenarios discussed in Chap. 1 have in common that the endpoints to be integrated are heterogeneous in their data as well as in their behavior. In addition, the networks are heterogeneous in the sense that any network might be used to connect the endpoints like back-end application systems and trading partners. The particular deployment of the B2B integration technology server used to manage the integration is also heterogeneous. Sometimes the B2B integration technology server is installed locally in an enterprise; sometimes the installation is remote.

These different forms of heterogeneity translate into the high-level integration concept requirements discussed in the following sections. Even more detailed requirements than those discussed next are addressed in the context of the discussion of integration concepts as well as integration architecture in Sects. 2.2 and 2.3.

2.1.1 Endpoint

There can be many different types of endpoints. First of all, back-end application systems are one type of endpoint. Trading partners are another type of endpoint. Furthermore, divisions within enterprises can be endpoints, as can individual employees. The latter type of endpoint becomes relevant when user interaction is required during the execution of integration. All these different types of endpoints have to be supported in order to support the integration scenarios as discussed above.

Endpoints are interrelated. For example, a trading partner has a list of trading partners with whom it exchanges messages, has several divisions, each with several employees. This potentially highly complex structure must be modeled, maintained and accessed at run time to decide where business data has to be sent.

2.1.2 Hosted Trading Partner

A special endpoint is the one that installs and runs the B2B integration technology server. This special endpoint is called a hosted trading partner, and it, from its viewpoint, integrates with all the other endpoints like applications or other trading partners. The enterprise that installs and runs the B2B integration technology server is usually the hosted trading partner. The other trading partners are called remote trading partners or nonhosted trading partners. The terms remote or nonhosted are used to indicate that they are endpoints to be connected to.

In many integration scenarios, there is not one hosted trading partner but many. For example, consider an enterprise that allows its divisions to run their own B2B integration technology servers. In this case there are as many installations as there are divisions. Alternatively, each division could be a hosted trading partner in the same B2B integration technology server installation. A feature of hosted trading partners is that integration definitions made in their context are not shared between them but are completely separated. This means that each division can set up its own integrations without interfering with any of the others. The benefit is that only one B2B integration technology server has to be installed and maintained, while the different divisions can define their integration in isolation without getting in each other's way.

Not all hosted trading partners have administrative rights to the installation. For example, disk allocation, number of operating system processes or other configuration settings are only to be done by the hosted trading partner that has the administration rights for this and who, in many cases, originally installed the B2B integration technology server.

2.1.3 Data Format and Event

In general, each endpoint expects data to be exchanged with it in the data format it understands. The data format of a back-end application system might be very different from that of a trading partner (Chap. 1). A B2B integration technology architecture must be able to support any data format required by the endpoints to which it connects. Received messages or messages to be sent have to be stored within the B2B integration technology. The internal representations of messages are called events.

The support for different data formats implies data transformation capabilities in order to transform between data formats when data is sent from one endpoint to another that does not share the same data format. Transformation of data formats must ensure that business data can be transformed from one data format into another without changing the semantics of the business data content. This is called semantic-preserving transformation. This requires domain value map support that allows replacement of values during transformation. For example, a domain value map would relate "CA" with "California." If transformation requires that the target event uses the long name and the source event uses the short form of a US state, then the corresponding domain value map can be used to look up the long name based on the short name.

Dynamic domain value maps implemented through database lookup are required if domain value data change frequently or are already available. In the latter case the domain data and their mapped values are stored and managed external to the B2B integration technology.

2.1.4 B2B Protocol

Some endpoints (typically remote trading partners) follow B2B protocols to achieve integration. This means that a B2B integration technology server must implement the particular B2B protocol of an endpoint when this endpoint is integrated. In general, endpoints can follow B2B protocol standards like those discussed in Chap. 20, implement their own variations of these or use completely proprietary ones. However, it is also the case that back-end application systems implement B2B protocols as their integration interface instead of using programming interfaces or queueing interfaces. For a B2B integration technology architecture this means that any B2B protocol, be it public standard or proprietary implementation, must be supported. Furthermore, it must be possible to associate any endpoint with any B2B protocol to specify which endpoint supports which B2B protocol (if at all).

2.1.5 Back-end Application System Adapter and Behavior

Some endpoints do not implement B2B protocols as their interfaces. Instead, they expose integration points through mechanisms like application programming interfaces (API), persistent queues, database tables, file system directories or screens as integration points. In these cases the B2B integration technology architecture must be able to connect to those mechanisms. The particular functionality can differ significantly from endpoint to endpoint, so that a B2B integration technology architecture has to be able to deal with a huge variety of functionalities.

Back-end application system adapters help in dealing with this heterogeneity in that they provide an abstracted interface that hides the specific variations of these integration mechanisms. A B2B integration technology architecture should be able to interface with back-end application system adapters in order to benefit from their abstractions.

Back-end application systems or their adapters do not explicitly define the behavior they expose. None of these explicitly specifies, for example, that a purchase order acknowledgment has to be inserted for each purchase order extracted. This behavior has to be obeyed by the B2B integration technology, although not explicitly specified.

Adapters can be transactional or nontransactional. Transactional adapters ensure that the messages from or to the back-end application system are sent exactly once. They use transaction management software to achieve this (Sect. 14.3). Nontransactional adapters have to implement exactly-once semantics like B2B protocols with retry limits and duplicate checks (Sect. 7.3.4).

2.1.6 Business Process

As soon as two or more than two endpoints are involved, the integration might require more than just transforming and forwarding of business data. Complex routing rules might "steer" the business data to specific endpoints. For example, a rule might be that a shipper is selected based on the location of the factory of the trading partner where goods have to be sent. This requires that for each trading partner the locations of their factories are recorded, and that each shipper is assigned to a location. Based on this data the complex rule can be defined.

Communication between endpoints is not necessarily one-way. In many cases a "conversation" takes place between endpoints. An example is the purchase order exchange. This usually involves purchase order acknowledgments that refer to purchase orders. A business process can be defined in such a way that all related business data are handled by the same business process so that the overall conversation between the trading partners is visible within one business process.

2.1.7 History

As long as the integration works without any problems or failures, no specific interest exists, in general, in the history of the business data flowing through the B2B integration technology server. However, as soon as an error or inconsistency occurs, the history that led to the point of failure becomes of immediate interest. It is important that a complete history is available so that every single action in the B2B integration technology server that led to the failure situation can be reviewed.

Another use of history is auditing. An audit reviews the history of changes, like business data flowing through the B2B integration technology server, or changes in the definitions of the integration. Sometimes not only are the changes interesting, but also the read access to data. For example, in the health care industry it must be possible to audit who accessed a specific piece of data at any point in time in addition to updates, insertions and deletions.

2.1.8 Business Intelligence

Long-term trends are important to enterprises. It is important to obtain statistics about past and ongoing integration, like how many message were exchanged with trading partners, or how long it takes for a trading partner to respond. This aggregation of data for the purpose of analysis is important. A B2B integration technology server must make all data and their history available so that data aggregation for analysis purposes can be accomplished.

2.2 Integration Concepts

Even thought the different types of integration discussed in Chap. 1 and in more detail in Chap. 3 look very different from each other, they can be implemented with the same integration concepts. The integration concepts outlined in Sect. 2.1 are introduced here in the form of an overview. The rationale for specific choices of integration concepts is given in order to explain the particular choice. Part II discusses the complete set of integration concepts in more detail without repeating the rationale again.

The rationale for advanced transformation functionality as well as behavior-oriented business processes is discussed in great detail in order to provide an extensive background in these two extremely important areas. Sections 2.2.3–2.2.5 accomplish this.

2.2.1 Message

From an enterprise perspective, data received from a trading partner undergo changes in several stages until they are given to a back-end application system for further processing. The stages of change can be identified precisely. For example, the following stages can be identified for the case where a B2B message is sent to one back-end application system:

- **B2B wire message**. This message is the representation of the data as transmitted, containing not only the business data content, but also any additional data for transmission purposes, like transport headers or packaging data. In the general case, an incoming messages is encrypted and/or signed. The B2B wire message, however, is already decrypted.
- **B2B clear text message**. A clear text message results from processing the wire message, where any transport specific data like transport headers or transport trailers are removed. This clear text message is in the format defined by B2B protocols, including the attachments, B2B protocol headers or other elements.
- **Application clear text message**. This clear text message contains all data in precisely the format required by the back-end application systems.

- **Application wire message**. This message is the representation of the application clear text message on the wire, when all transport specific data have been added, like header or trailer data. The applicaton wire message will be encrypted and/or signed as required by the back-end application system before it is sent. Usually back-end application systems are within the firewall of an enterprise and the common assumption is that this does not require further security precautions. However, more and more enterprises are afraid of internal security attacks, that is those from within enterprises, not from the outside. In this case, even interenterprise communication must be secured through signatures or encryption. Therefore a B2B integration technology architecture must also be able to secure the connection to back-end application systems.

The question remains of how the B2B clear text message is transformed into the application clear text message. If the data format required by the back-end application system is exactly the format as received through the B2B protocol, then the B2B clear text message is the same then the application clear text message. A simple copy operator on the messages is sufficient to get the application clear text message from the B2B clear text message (Fig. 2.1). Figure 2.1 does not yet show how these different messages relate to B2B integration technology. This will be done in the following.

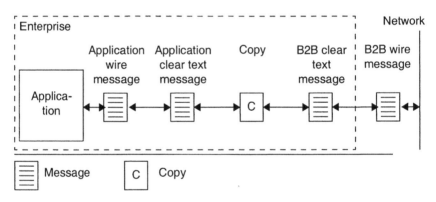

Fig. 2.1. Messages and their processing stages with copy operator

In the general case, the B2B clear text message and the application clear text message are not in the same data format. More complex operations than the copy operator are generally required to create the application clear text message from the B2B clear text message. These more complex operations are called transformation, and the next section will discuss this case in more detail. Figure 2.2 shows message processing with transformation instead of copy as the general case.

The data types of business data transported in messages have to be specified so that the B2B integration technology can interpret them. A data type system is necessary for this purpose and needs to be provided by the B2B integration technology. Document format is used synonymously with data types. Expressed in terms of data types, the copy operator to achieve the transformation is only possible if the B2B clear text message and the application clear text message are of exactly the same data type or document format.

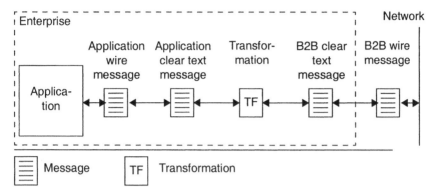

Fig. 2.2. Messages and their stages of processing with transformation

2.2.2 Event

Messages that are received "over the wire" either from trading partners or back-end application systems have to be stored in the B2B integration technology. In order to manage these additional messages, metadata have to be added. Examples of metadata include the date received or the endpoint from which the message was received. The additional metadata along with the message content have to be stored and managed. The integration concept that achieves this is called event.

Events are typed by data types. Each message coming in or going out has to have a corresponding event type. Otherwise, it cannot be represented or processed within the B2B integration technology. At run time, actual messages are represented in event instances. Each incoming or outgoing message has an event instance representation.

Event types are classified according to the processing stages they undergo. Messages that are received are stored in wire events after decryption. Messages that are ready to be sent are wire events, too. Once required checks, like whether the sender is who it claims to be take place, the wire event content is represented as a clear text event. Figure 2.3 shows the overall event processing, including the event classes within the B2B integration technology.

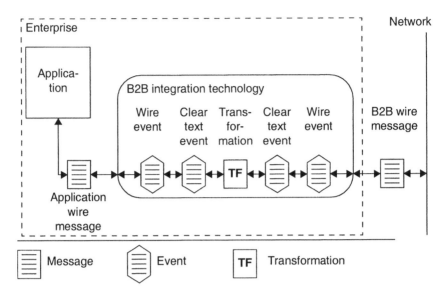

Fig. 2.3. Events and their processing stages

As Fig. 2.3 indicates, events are no longer named according to "application" or "B2B," since event type definitions are not tied to the type of the particular endpoint (i.e., back-end application system or trading partner). Different endpoints can produce or consume clear text events of the same event type independent of whether these are back-end application systems or trading partners. This allows the reuse of event types across endpoints. If event types were tied to endpoints, reuse would no longer be possible and duplicate event type definitions would result.

Each message received by an endpoint or sent to an endpoint that participates in an integration has a wire event as well as a clear text event representation after its receipt or before it is sent. The wire event contains precisely the data that an endpoint expects or sends, whereas a clear text event represents the same data independent of the transport-specific data. Even if two endpoints share the definition of clear text events, each endpoint will have a representation of "its" clear text event instance in the B2B integration technology.

Clear text events can be transformed into each other either by the copy operator if the clear text events of the endpoints are the same, or by a more complex transformation if the clear text events are different. Since the copy operator is a specific form of transformation, a distinction is no longer made from here on.

The stages of event processing are exactly the same if data are passed between back-end application systems. Instead of B2B messages, two or more types of application messages are involved. Figure 2.4 shows the integration of two back-end application systems from the viewpoint of the messages and their stages of change.

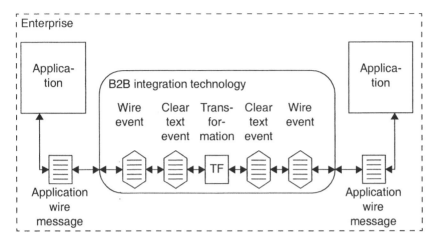

Fig. 2.4. Event processing for two integrated back-end application systems

For clarity of the presentation as well as the architecture, all the events of the different event classes are explicitly represented (and later "stored") in the architecture. For optimization purposes, this explicit representation might be omitted, but this is not the concern of the book. Therefore optimization does not receive special attention.

2.2.3 Transformation and Translation

In the general case where the data types of the B2B protocol and the back-end application system are different, a more complex operator is necessary to obtain the application clear text event from the B2B clear text event. This operator is called transformation.

Before actual messages (message instances) can be processed, a transformation of how to obtain one clear text event from another clear text event (and vice versa) has to be defined. A transformation definition contains a set of transformation rules that extract values of one event (the source event) and insert those into the other event (the target event). This is not necessarily only copying of values. More complex transformations are required, like concatenating values or aggregation of values. For example, an address might be in one long string in the source event. However, the target event needs to have the different parts of an address in different fields like street name, street number or city name. A transformation rule or a set of transformation rules needs to be in place to extract the different elements of an address from the source string and to insert them into the equivalent fields in the target event.

As discussed in Sect. 2.2.1, the events have to be specified using data types in order to interpret their content. The data type system is implemented by the B2B integration technology. When events are defined, then they refer to data types that are defined in the data type system. Data types can be reused across event definitions. For example, an address data type can be defined containing a street name, a street number, city name and zip code, county name and country name. Whenever an event refers to an address, this data type can be reused for its definition. For example, a purchase order event contains a bill-to and ship-to address both, of type address.

A consequence of the data type system is that the B2B integration technology server implements a specific syntax of how to represent the data types. One example is the Extensible Markup Language (XML), another would be a normalized representation in a database. Incoming messages, however, might use a different syntax. For example, an incoming message might be in a delimited representation with a delimitation character like in the case of EDI. In this case a mismatch exists between the syntax used in the message and the syntax used in the B2B integration technology for representing events. This in turn requires a mechanism to convert from any incoming syntax into the B2B integration technology-specific syntax. This conversion is called translation. Figure 2.5 contains an example whereby the endpoint-specific format is delimited by "*" and the event syntax is XML.

Fig. 2.5. Translation example

One approach is to translate incoming messages before they are represented as wire events. However, as said before, the wire event is the exact image of the incoming message (except encryption) and should not be modified at all. Later this becomes very significant for nonrepudiation, where messages must be stored exactly as received in order to reproduce them without modification.

This means that translation must happen between the wire event and the clear text event. The wire event is not only put into clear text format, but is also translated into the syntax defined by the B2B integration technology. Figure 2.6 shows the additional translation steps.

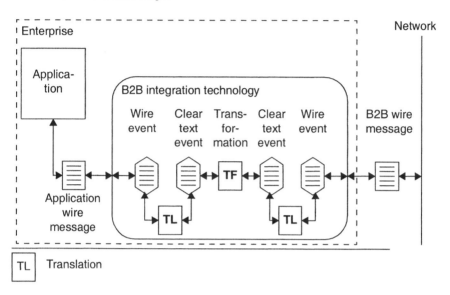

Fig. 2.6. Event processing with translation

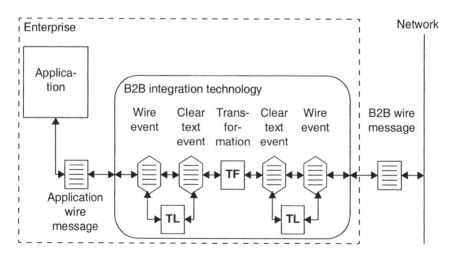

Fig. 2.7. Event processing with optional translation

In the general case, translation has to happen for each of the endpoints because each endpoint can use a different syntax for message content representation. However, in specific cases the syntax might match precisely so that translation is not necessary. Figure 2.7 shows this by indicating that clear text events can be derived from wire events without necessarily executing translation.

The integration concepts introduced so far allow messages to be sent from any endpoint to any other endpoint. Every message is represented as an event, and transformation allows the representation of a clear text event from one endpoint into a clear text event from another endpoint.

We could stop here and declare victory, since we have achieved perfect point-to-point integration functionality. However, as shown in Sect. 1.2.2, there are several limitations to point-to-point functionality. More elaborate integration approaches like hub-and-spoke (Sect. 1.2.3) or process-based integration (Sect. 1.2.4) still have many limitations. Therefore, we will introduce more integration concepts in the following sections to overcome these limitations.

2.2.4 Business Event

One limitation is the high number of transformations that a point-to-point solution introduces. If every message of every endpoint has to be transformed into an equivalent message of every other endpoint, then $n*(n-1)$ transformations are necessary between the clear text events representing the messages of n endpoints. For example, if four endpoints exchange purchase orders and purchase order acknowledgments, and if each of the four endpoints follows a different document format, then each purchase order clear text event has to be translated into every other purchase order clear text event. In total this requires 12 transformations [$4*(4-1)$] for purchase order clear text events and another 12 for purchase order acknowledgment clear text events. In total, there are 24 transformations.

It seems that there is no possibility to reduce the number of transformations, since every message format has to be transformed into every other message format so that every endpoint can integrate with every other endpoint. However, luckily, there is a possibility. The fundamental idea is to construct an event that is the superset of all related clear text events of all endpoints. This is called a business event. For example, if four endpoints exchange purchase orders with each other, then a business event purchase order would be introduced that can capture the contents of each of the four message formats of the four endpoints. The business event has to be defined in such a way that each clear text event can be transformed into it and extracted from it. In that sense, it is a superset of all the purchase order clear text events of the endpoints involved. Another business event would be introduced for purchase order acknowledgments.

The "trick" is to no longer transform clear text events directly into each other, but to transform the clear text events into the corresponding business event first. From there another transformation takes place to transform it to the necessary clear text event. Initially, this sounds like twice the number of transformations, but this is not true. Instead of $n*(n-1)$, only $2n$ transformations are necessary. Figure 2.8 shows the direct transformation approach, and Fig. 2.9 shows the transformation approach with business events.

For the example above, this means that only eight transformations are necessary for purchase orders, and only another eight are necessary for purchase order acknowledgments. In total, there are 16 instead of 24 transformations.

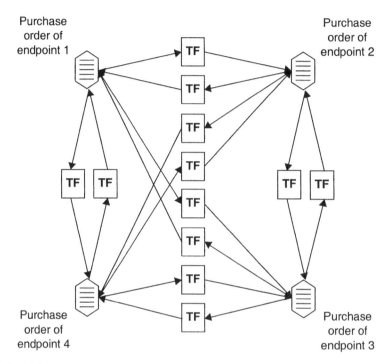

Fig. 2.8. Transformation without business events

An example is in order here to show how a business event works. Continuing with the address data type as before, it is assumed that the first endpoint stores all address information in one long comma-delimited string. The second endpoint has several comma-delimited strings called "address line 1," "address line 2" and "address line 3." The third endpoint has address information completely factored out, i.e., each address element has a separate field. Finally, the fourth endpoint has street, street number and city in one structured record, and the zip code, state and country in another structured record. The business event approach could be the following: for the business event the address is fully factored out, i.e., there is one field for each address element like street, street number, city, zip, state and country.

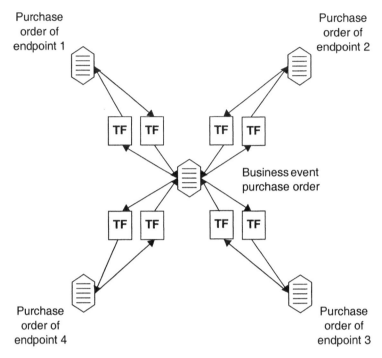

Fig. 2.9. Transformation with business events

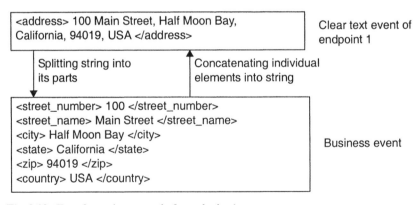

Fig. 2.10. Transformation example for endpoint 1

The transformation for the first endpoint must transform between one string and the fully factored-out representation of an address. Transforming to the business event means "taking the string apart" and identifying all the individual address elements. Once identified, they can be stored in the normalized representation. Most

of the elements are separated by commas, except the street number. In the opposite
direction, the fully factored -out address values have to be concatenated into one
big string. Figure 2.10 shows the example, with XML being chosen as the event
representation.

The transformation for the second endpoint is similar to the first one, except that
it has to deal with three strings instead of one string (Fig. 2.11).

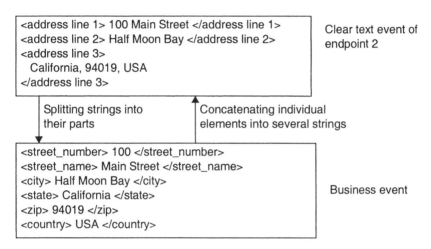

Fig. 2.11. Transformation example for endpoint 2

The transformation for the third endpoint is a copy since the clear text representation and the business event representation are precisely the same. Transforming
to and from the business event are a copy (Fig. 2.12).

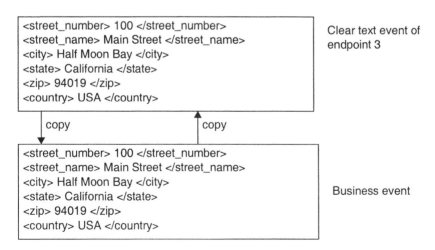

Fig. 2.12. Transformation example for endpoint 3

The fourth endpoint represents the information in two structured records. The transformations have to access the elements of the structured records and store the values in the business event, and vice versa. Fundamentally, the two records hold individual address elements so that the transformation is only concerned with the access to the structured record elements (Fig. 2.13).

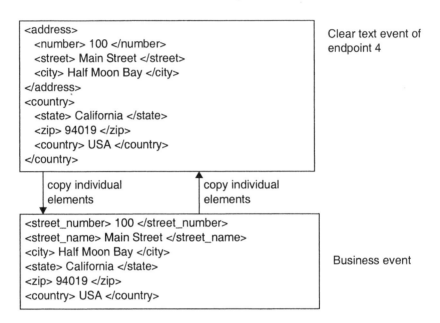

Fig. 2.13. Transformation example for endpoint 4

The approach using business events does not look like a big difference for small numbers of endpoints, but for large numbers the difference is significant. As Fig. 2.14 shows, the approach using business events pays off starting at three endpoints and more. At three endpoints the number of transformations is equal, and at two endpoints the number of transformations is higher. For example, at 10 endpoints, the difference is 70 transformations. Since each transformation is a significant piece of specification work plus is subject to maintenance, the difference is significant.

From an event-processing viewpoint, a business event is another class of event that is introduced and needs to be processed. Figure 2.15 shows the overall event-processing scheme, including the optional translation.

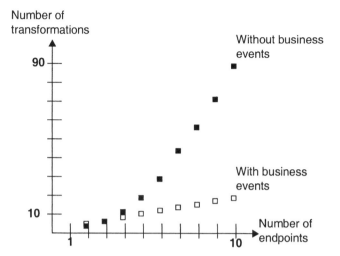

Fig. 2.14. Number of transformations for various numbers of endpoints

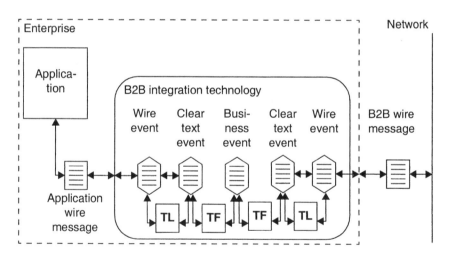

Fig. 2.15. Event processing with business events

As discussed earlier, if the clear text events of the endpoint to be integrated are the same, transformation reduces to a copy operator. In this case going through a business event does not make sense at all. Also, if direct transformation between the clear text events is sufficient, the business event should be bypassed. Figure 2.16 shows the "shortcut" bypassing the business event scheme by providing transformation directly between the clear text events.

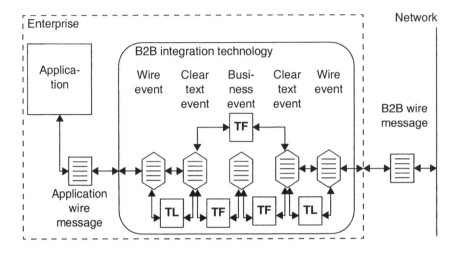

Fig. 2.16. Event processing with and without business events

2.2.5 Business Process and Endpoint Behavior

Messages exchanged between back-end application systems or trading partners are, in many cases, not isolated transmissions in the sense that each message is independent of every other message. Instead, many message are related, like a purchase order and the corresponding purchase order acknowledgment or purchase order acknowledgments if line items are acknowledged individually.

A B2B integration technology can either ignore the fact that some messages are related or it can provide integration concepts to express and implement the behavior of several related messages. The approach taken in this book is to make the behavior explicit in the integration concepts so that a B2B integration technology is able to implement and manage behavior in addition to data. The benefit is that message exchange sequences can be supervised by the B2B integration technology, behavior errors can be detected and compensated, and behavior status can be obtained in order to track the message exchange progress between endpoints.

The naive way to define the behavior is to define a business process that specifies the overall message behavior as well as the related event behavior. In the following, this idea is used to some extent in order to show the major deficiencies.

The example of two endpoints is extended as outlined below. Two endpoints exchange purchase order messages. One endpoint (back-end application system) sends a purchase order and receives a purchase order acknowledgment. The other endpoint (trading partner) receives a purchase order and sends a purchase order acknowledgment. Furthermore, each message transfer of the second endpoint has to be acknowledged by a message acknowledgment. In addition to the message exchange, the business process that connects the two endpoints has to have an approval step for the outgoing purchase order. The purchase order is only sent if an approval happens. The purchase order acknowledgment is passed through without any further processing. Figure 2.17 shows the overall process on a high level from a buyer perspective, i.e., the endpoint sending the purchase order and receiving the purchase order acknowledgment.

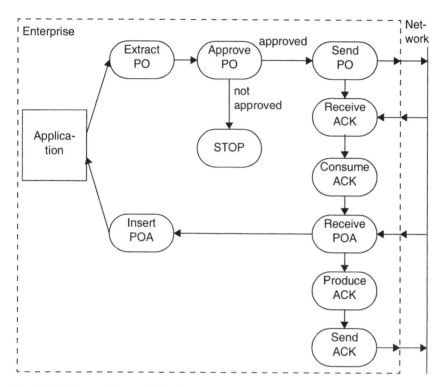

Fig. 2.17. Naive purchase order business process

The rounded rectangles in Fig. 2.17 are business process steps, or steps for short. Steps specify processing that has to happen inside the business process. The first step in the business process extracts a purchase order (PO) from the back-end application system. An approval step follows with two possible results, approved and not approved. In case the PO is approved, the PO is sent out to the trading partner. If not, the whole business process is stopped. In the successful approval case the business process waits for an acknowledgment (ACK) to come back. Once the ACK is received, it is consumed because there is no further use for it. Then the business process waits for the purchase order acknowledgment (POA). Once the POA is received it is inserted into the back-end application system. In parallel, an ACK has to be produced because it has to be sent to the trading partner through the final step.

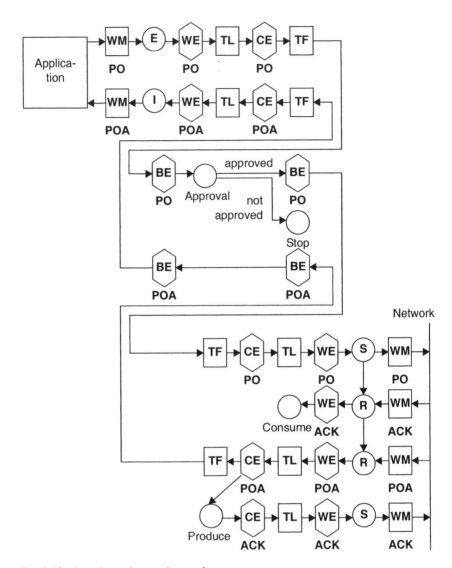

Fig. 2.18. Complete naive purchase order process

The high-level representation in Fig. 2.17 is abstracted from the detailed representation of messages and events. The business process including all the details regarding events is shown in Fig. 2.18. This business process shows the events, including translation and transformation. Furthermore, the integration concept of business events is used. It is very apparent from the representation that the event flow is complex when viewed at this level of detail. In Chap. 7 more abstract symbols are introduced that make the representation of processes much more readable and abstract, while preserving the same semantics.

In order to make the representation more economical in terms of space, the process steps are represented as circles from now on, following a naming convention to allow for brief step names: S stands for send, R stands for receive, I stands for insert, E for extract, C for consume and P for produce. Send and receive are used in the context of trading partners, whereas insert and extract are used in the context of back-end application systems. Steps that implement real business logic like the approval step are annotated for convenience. Event names and message names are abbreviated as follows: WM stands for wire message, WE for wire event, CE for clear text event, and BE for business event. The type of event is annotated underneath the event or message, e.g., PO for purchase order.

The representation in Fig. 2.18 is intentionally informally subdivided into three parts. The upper third of the process deals with the events and messages related to the first endpoint (back-end application system). The middle third deals with the business process, and the lower third with the events and messages related to the second endpoint (trading partner). This subdivision is chosen for clarity of representation.

The processing of the messages and events of the first endpoint does not exhibit anything specific beyond standard behavior. Wire messages are extracted and inserted, and the necessary translations and transformations are specified. Since the concept of a business event is used, the business event is the result or the origin of the message translation and transformation for the first endpoint.

In contrast, the second endpoint behaves differently. In this case acknowledgment have to be specified in addition to the PO and POA messages. The incoming acknowledgment is consumed once it is available as wire event. The consumption is necessary since it is not further required by any other part of the process. The outbound acknowledgment is generated from the incoming clear text event representing the POA. It is not produced from the wire event since, in this case specific endpoint syntax would have to be understood. Instead, the clear text events are in defined data types and therefore are accessible to generate the acknowledgment out of it.

The business logic in the middle third precisely matches the one outlined in Fig. 2.17. An important observation is that the business logic operates on business events. This is very relevant since the business event is an abstraction from the endpoint-specific representation of business data (Sect. 2.2.4). This will later support the reuse of business processes across endpoints.

Error handling has not been defined in Fig. 2.18, even though there are plenty of error possibilities. For example, if no ACK comes back then the process will wait forever for an ACK. This situation has to be dealt with in a complete business process definition. Error handling would have added more modeling elements, but for clarity reasons this is not done here.

As Fig. 2.18 shows, the complete business process can be specified for the complete message exchange behavior. However, several deficiencies can be observed.

First, several different functionalities are modeled at the same time. One part of the business process is concerned with business logic, like the approval step and the subsequent actions, depending on the outcome. The two other parts are concerned with modeling the endpoint behavior in terms of message exchange. For one endpoint the message-passing sequence is defined, whereas for the other endpoint the additional acknowledgments have to be implemented.

Second, none of the three parts can be reused in other integration definitions. For example, if the message exchange of one of the endpoints should be reused in another business process, the business process steps have to be copied (or newly specified). While this is certainly possible, maintenance soon becomes a big problem, since any change has to be repeatedly implemented in several business processes.

These two major deficiencies justify the search for a more appropriate set of integration concepts related to specifying the behavior of events. Therefore the "divide-and-conquer" approach is taken. The "divide" is done at the boundary of the endpoint-specific event processing and the business logic. This means that the endpoint-specific processing is a separate process from the business logic. The example in Fig. 2.18 would be specified as three processes: one for the behavior of the back-end application, one for the behavior of the trading partner and one for the business logic, the approval. The interface of the business logic process, from now on called the business process, is business events. It expects as well as provides business events. Figure 2.19 shows the business process "PO_approval_BP." One of its characteristics is that it operates on business events and therefore it is independent of the clear text representation of particular endpoints.

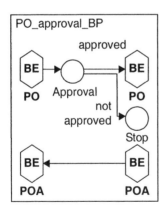

Fig. 2.19. Business process example

The process for the first endpoint, the back-end application system is called an interface process. It's interface are wire events and clear text events, respectively (Fig. 2.20). The wire messages are not part of the interface process since wire messages exist outside the B2B integration technology server (Fig. 2.16).

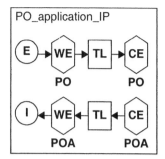

Fig. 2.20. Back-end application system interface process example

Figure 2.20 contains the interface process of the first endpoint, "PO_application_IP." The transformation into business events is not included in the interface process, since from a pure interface perspective it is not known into which business event the clear text events will be transformed. Later, this will become very relevant because this abstraction allows the reuse of interface processes in the context of different business processes.

For the second endpoint, the trading partner, a separate interface process is defined (Fig. 2.21). Like the interface process for the first endpoint, this interface process does not contain the transformations.

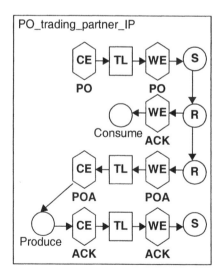

Fig. 2.21. Trading partner interface process example

So far, the overall process shown in Fig. 2.18 has been split into three processes: a business process and two interface processes. This constitutes the "divide" part of the divide-and-conquer approach. The "conquer" part ties these three processes together. None of the three processes contains the transformation between business events and the clear text events. The concept of process binding is introduced for binding the processes together. Process binding defines which clear text events and which business events are transformed into each other. By defining this transformation the binding between the processes takes place. A business process together with all its bound interface processes is called an integration or an integration process. Figure 2.22 shows how the interface process of the first endpoint is bound to the business process.

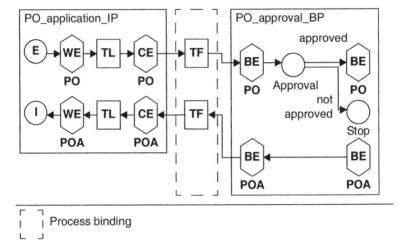

Process binding

Fig. 2.22. Process binding of a back-end application system interface process to a business process

As Fig. 2.22 shows, the event that is produced by the interface process is used by the business process, and vice versa. The number and direction of events match perfectly and require one transformation for each pair. Figure 2.23 shows how the business process is bound to the interface process of the second endpoint. Later an example is provided in Fig. 2.24 showing that additional interfaces can be bound to the business process in the same way by means of additional process bindings.

This divide-and-conquer approach addresses the two major deficiencies of a single process approach: First, the different aspects are modeled in different concepts. The endpoint-specific behavior is specified in interface processes, while the business logic is defined in business processes. Second, these concepts are units of reuse. The business process can be reused for other endpoints, too. The means of binding the different units of reuse is process binding.

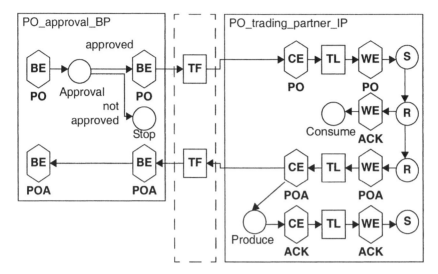

Fig. 2.23. Process binding of a trading partner interface process to a business process

In addition, the interface processes can be reused by binding them to other business processes. Figure 2.24 shows how a third endpoint can be bound to the business process if this endpoint also participates in the exchange of purchase orders and purchase order acknowledgments. This third interface process is for a trading partner that also exchanges purchase orders and purchase order acknowledgments as well, but without the acknowledgments that the second interface process requires.

When to use each interface process depends on the trading partner to which the event must be sent. The events have information in their header about the addressee in terms of a unique trading partner name or identification. Based on this identification the correct interface process is determined and chosen at run time. Once the interface process has been determined, the appropriate process binding is executed.

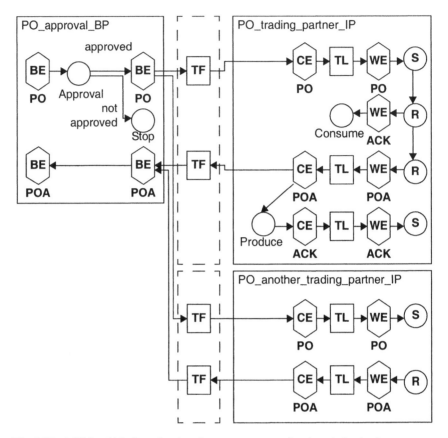

Fig. 2.24. Additional binding of an interface process to an already-existing business process

If no business logic is required for an integration where the clear text events can be transformed into each other directly, the business process can be omitted and the interface processes can be bound to each other directly. Figure 2.25 shows an example.

Process binding so far is explained and introduced as binding those events together that are related to each other in order to achieve the overall integration. In Sect. 7.2 the notion of a formal process interface with formal process input and output parameters is introduced that allows a more precise definition of process binding.

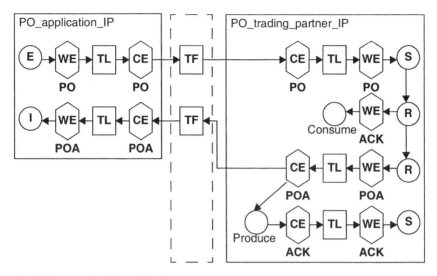

Fig. 2.25. Direct binding of interface processes

2.2.6 Advanced Business Process

Business processes can contain very simple business logic (Fig. 2.18) or very complex logic. Various business process steps need to be available to implement complex business logic in addition to the approval step. More possible process steps are introduced in Chap. 7.

However, at this point two steps should be introduced in the following for a more advanced discussion. The first step is an address resolution step. This step allows a change in the address (receiving endpoint) of a business event if the address given by the sending endpoint is not appropriate. The input of an address resolution step is an event, and the result is the same event except that the addressee is set to a new value. The address resolution step supports various means of defining a new recipient. The most simple one is static addressing whereby the address resolution step directly names an endpoint. This means that no matter which receiving endpoint the sending endpoint indicated, the business events are always directed to the named endpoint. Chapter 7 discuss additional possibilities.

The other step is a transformation step. This allows for the duplication or modification of business events within business processes. For example, if a business event should be sent to two endpoints, a transformation step can be used to duplicate the business event, and two address resolution steps can be used to define where each new business event should be sent. Figure 2.26 shows the scenario with a simple request for quote process (RFQ) where by a request for quote is sent to two different trading partners. The symbol for transformation is used for the transformation step, since from a functionality viewpoint there is no difference from transformations taking place in process bindings.

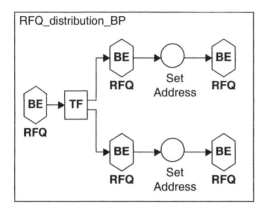

Fig. 2.26. Transformation and address resolution step for business event duplication

This shows an example of how business processes can be used to link two or more endpoints together in order to integrate them. The opposite case is shown in Fig. 2.27 where the events of two endpoints are joined into one business event before sending them to a third endpoint.

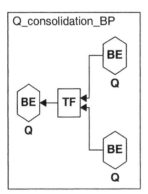

Fig. 2.27. Joining business events

As Fig. 2.27 shows, transformation steps can be used to combine the contents of events into one event. The quotes coming from different trading partners are combined into one quote event that lists all quotes by trading partner. The arcs are from the right to the left since the convention is that trading partner communication is on the right, whereas back-end application system communication is on the left of business processes.

In a real scenario, an RFQ can be sent to any number of trading partners (that is, broadcast), maybe depending on the contents of the request event. In this case the addressees are determined based on business data in the request event. Before run time, the number of trading partners is not known, however, at run time it will be. Broadcast steps that can handle the dynamic determination of endpoints are required and are discussed in Chap. 7.

2.2.7 Trading Partner and Back-end Application System

Trading partners as well as back-end applications are sources and targets of events. Furthermore, employees can be sources and targets of events, for example, when an authorization is required. All the different sources and targets of events are called endpoints. Endpoints are uniquely identified so that addressing is unambiguously possible. Unique identification also guarantees that messages come from exactly one endpoint.

The organization that installs and runs a B2B integration technology server is called the hosted trading partner (hosted by the B2B integration technology). All integration is defined for that hosted trading partner and from its viewpoint. If other trading partners are added then these are remote trading partners defining other legal entities with which the hosted trading partner communicates. However, only those data about remote trading partners have to be collected and managed that are necessary to establish and to maintain the B2B connectivity. For example, remote trading partners need to be uniquely identified. Section 2.2.8 outlines more necessary properties for endpoints.

The hosting scenarios where a B2B integration technology server is deployed to manage the integration require that integration be modeled for different trading partners at the same time. Instead of installing the B2B integration technology in the hosted environment (like an ASP aggregator) once for every subscriber (i.e., trading partner that is hosted), the B2B integration technology server allows several hosted trading partners to be entered at the same time. Integration can be modeled for each of the hosted trading partners concurrently without any interference amongst them.

2.2.8 Endpoint Attribute, Capability and Agreement

Endpoints have identifying attributes (synonymously property) like a name and an unique identifier that is required for processing integration. These two attributes are essential for executing modeled integration (i.e., business processes and interface processes). Since different identification schemes for trading partners exist, it must be possible to add different unique identifiers over time to the trading partner attributes. However, more data has to be available. Public keys of remote trading partners have to be stored in order to decrypt as well as encrypt their messages. Private keys for the hosted trading partners have to be stored for the same reason. All these attributes are necessary for other types of endpoints, too, like back-end application systems.

In addition, endpoint type-specific business information can be stored, including the credit rating, the payment history, a bill-to address, a ship-to address, contact information and other useful data for making business decisions. This list can grow over time, and it must be possible to add this data to endpoint definitions over time. This requires that the definition of endpoints can be extended dynamically. Not all of these additional attributes are relevant for other types of endpoints. For example, a back-end system does not have a ship-to address.

Capabilities of trading partners describe what a trading partner is capable of in terms of B2B integration. For each endpoint the particular B2B protocols have to be stored to know the message capabilities. Any specific modification to standard B2B protocols also has to be noted. For example, these could be modifications of the document definitions or the packaging requirements.

Even if a remote trading partner along with its capabilities or any other type of endpoint is defined, this should not automatically enable the B2B integration technology to exchange messages with that trading partner or endpoint. Otherwise, the start and the stop of sending messages would have to be accomplished by entering and deleting endpoint attributes or capabilities. Instead, a separate concept called endpoint agreement implements this behavior. Only those endpoints can exchange messages for which an endpoint agreement exists and is valid.

An endpoint agreement contains a date range that specifies when the agreement is valid. Furthermore, an agreement refers to a hosted trading partner and an endpoint. This establishes that message exchange is possible between the two defined endpoints. An agreement includes a reference to a B2B protocol or a back-end application system protocol and to messages of that protocol. This establishes that the two endpoints can communicate using this protocol and use the message selected from the protocol. For each message the direction it can be sent must be specified during the validity of this particular agreement. If an agreement is in place then the endpoints can communicate based on the specifications in the agreement. For every single message that is received or is to be sent, there must be an agreement that allows the message to be received or to be sent. If no agreement can be found the receiving or sending must fail.

This concludes the introduction to B2B integration concepts. A complete and detailed discussion of integration concepts follows in Chap. 7 after some fundamental principles are discussed in Chap. 5 and the ideal integration world is outlined in Chap. 6.

2.3 Integration Technology Architecture

The term architecture has different connotations and means different things to different people. In the following, architecture is used in a specific way in order to introduce the abstract software components of an B2B integration technology architecture. Logical is means that abstract architecture components are introduced that would not necessarily be implemented as one implementation component, but may be several. Since implementation strategies and the related details are not the main focus of this book, a fundamental discussion addressiing how architectural components are mapped to implementation components is not included.

Figure 2.28 shows the various layers of the B2B integration technology architecture. This layering is rather "classical" since it can be found in many different architectures of many different software products.

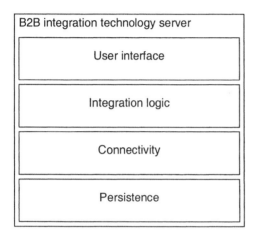

Fig. 2.28. Four layers of B2B integration technology architecture

The four layers are separated according to the different functionality a B2B integration technology server has to provide. Each piece of functionality belongs to one of the four layers and, more specifically, to a component in one of the four layers. The four layers cooperate in order to provide the overall functionality. The invocation relationship between the four layers is a strict top-down invocation relationship. That is, components in upper layers invoke components in lower layers in order to accomplish their functionality, and lower layers cannot invoke components in upper layers. This avoids circular invocation dependencies and ensures that the functionality separation is followed. Components within layers can invoke each other.

The components within these layers are discussed in the following in more detail. The summary section contains the complete representation of all architectural components in Fig. 2.33.

2.3.1 User Interface

The user interface provides several different entry points. Different user interfaces are provided for different tasks that need to be accomplished. Figure 2.29 shows the different components.

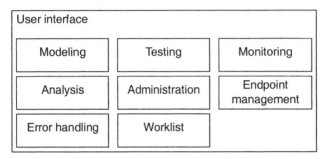

Fig. 2.29. User interface components

The modeling user interface is used to specify integration models using modeling constructs for business process, interface process, process steps, events, data types, transformation and translation. A modeler (a user tasked with specifying integration) uses the modeling constructs provided to him in a graphical form, including drag-and-drop functionality. It is possible to query individual modeled integration in order to select objects for reuse and/or change. Versioning is provided so that modeled objects can be changed without loosing previous states due to updates in place.

The testing user interface follows the idea of a "classical" debugger whereby a modeler can execute the modeled integration with artificial (nonproduction) data in a step-by-step fashion, like stepping through a program instruction by instruction. Along the way messages and events as well as process states can be introspected. The message exchange with back-end application systems or B2B protocols is also available for stepping through. However, the real back-end application system or the real trading partner is only involved on request during testing. If an endpoint should not be involved, a "trading partner mock-up" is necessary for testing purposes that mimics the behavior of the endpoint without involving it. A subcomponent of the testing user interface is simulation where, based on heuristics, different integrations are executed many times, resulting in analysis data of how different integrations perform. Simulations abstract from details like real events with real content and try to give qualitative statements about the integration behavior.

In contrast, performance tests are based on real data that are artificially generated to derive to a real overall system performance profile. Again, performance testing as a subcomponent of the testing user interface may or may not involve the endpoints like back-end application systems or trading partners.

The monitoring user interface allows for the introspection of the running B2B integration technology server during integration execution. The status of events or processes can be retrieved, indicating where in the overall process events are at the time of the status query. The result of a status query is the instance of a business process with all its related interface processes together with an indication of which events are in the integration instance and where they are in terms of the different processes.

Monitoring as part of the monitoring user interface serves a different purpose. The result of monitoring is an aggregation of events or integration processes in the following sense: If a particular type of business process is monitored, then the result returns all event instances in all business process instances in an aggregated representation on the screen. A nonexisting instance of a business process is shown. All event instances of all the real business process instances are displayed at the same time in the nonexisting business process instance representation. From this the user can see where event instances are from an overall viewpoint. The monitoring representation changes according to the changes events go through as part of the processing. The user has the impression of how events progress because of the continued screen update. History is another subcomponent of monitoring, and a history query for one object returns the list of all state changes of this object. For example, the history of an event retrieves a list of all state changes that the event went through according to the business process or interface process. For each event state the context can be queried, i.e., the state of the process at the particular point of the event state change. This allows a user to understand the progress of the event over time in the context of the overall integration process.

The analysis user interface allows for the analysis of the overall B2B integration technology. For example, business intelligence questions like how many purchase orders were sent in the last year fall into this category. Fundamentally, aggregation queries are executed over past and current integration processes. Data warehouse and business intelligence technology is used for this purpose, and the integration data can be aggregated and queried along any dimension imaginable. A subcomponent of analysis is audit, where a complete history for an event or a business process or a trading partner is produced based on history data. This allows official auditing as well as error analysis.

The administration user interface is concerned about the various software components in the B2B integration technology server and their states, not about integration functionality or integration data like event instances. Administration includes backing up the database, monitoring queue sizes, starting and stopping of server processes for throughput and scalability management as well as error handling, like restarting the overall B2B integration technology server after system or power failures.

The endpoint management user interface allows for the management of endpoints, their attributes, capabilities and agreements. After integration processes are modeled, an enterprise wants to put them into production by linking up back-end application systems as well as trading partners. This requires the entry of valid trading partner information and attributes and the definition of their B2B protocols or application protocol capabilities as well as their agreements in order to authorize the message exchange. The endpoint management user interface provides the screens for entering and managing the endpoint data.

The error-handling user interface is concerned with errors in integration processing, not with system failures. System failures like aborted operating system processes are managed in the administration user interface. Integration failures like a failed transformation or a deadlocked integration process are addressed by the error-handling user interface. Various possibilities of error handling are provided to the user in order to handle error situations. For example, a user can modify the event contents in order to continue event processing by resubmitting a changed event. Another example is a failed transformation that requires a change in the transformation rules. Once the transformation has been improved, the user can restart the event processing and try the transformation again. The types of failures that are addressed by the error-handling user interface occur because of modeling errors of the integration processes, or erroneous content in messages, or events that have not been recognized by validation rules.

The worklist user interface allows the B2B integration technology server to notify users about the need for human action. For example, if an event needs to be authorized by a user, the worklist lists this activity and requests the user to approve a given event instance. Users looking at their worklists see all tasks assigned to them including any applicable deadline. Furthermore, the worklist can be used in order to notify a user about processing problems. For example, if an integration process does not continue its execution for a time that is longer than a defined threshold, a user might be notified about this fact. The user can then go into the error-handling user interface to check if an error situation occurred that needs attention.

In summary, various user interfaces are part of the overall integration technology architecture, which allows for the management of all aspects of the complete system. Real integration products might or might not implement this functionality or might group it differently. However, the user interfaces described are all important to establish and to manage integration appropriately.

2.3.2 Integration Logic

The integration logic layer contains the components that implement the integration functionality. Figure 2.30 shows the components of the integration logic layer.

The event management component is responsible for managing the various classes of events (wire event, clear text event and business event). It provides an interface for defining event types and an interface for managing event instances. The type definition interface supports the creation of event types as well as their deletion and their change. The event instance management interface supports the creation of event instances and their state change as well as accessing event contents and updating event contents.

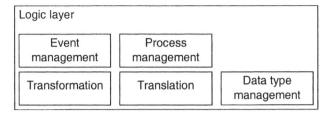

Fig. 2.30. Integration logic layer components

The process management component manages process definitions as well as process execution. The three classes of processes are interface processes, business processes and process bindings. For each of these, a definition interface is provided to define, delete and change types. In addition, process instances have to be created and advanced, interrupted, resumed and sometimes aborted. A process instance management interface is available for these tasks.

The main task of the transformation component is executing transformations at run time in order to transform different event instances into each other. An interface is provided to start the transformation and to obtain the transformation results. A definition interface supports the definition of transformations as well as their modification.

The translation component is very similar to the transformation component. Translation definitions have to be managed and actual translations executed.

The data type management component is very similar to the event management component, whereby data types have to be managed as well as data instances. When an event instance is created then its payloads are represented as data instances. The data instances that constitute the contents of the event instance are created through the data type management component.

All the components of the integration logic layer have to be coordinated in the sense that the components have to be invoked in precisely the correct sequence so that the events and processes are executed according to the integration concept's execution model. This coordination is done by another component (not shown), termed the integration logic component coordinator or coordinator for short. Chapter 12 discusses this component explicitly.

2.3.3 Connectivity

The connectivity layer has all the components relevant for connecting to back-end application systems through adapters as well as to trading partners through B2B protocols (Fig. 2.31).

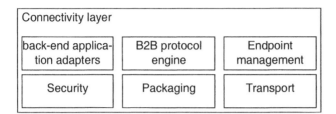

Fig. 2.31. Connectivity layer components

The back-end application system adapters are the software that bridges the interface differences between various back-end application systems and the interface the B2B integration technology provides in order to connect to adapters. Adapters have to be added to the B2B integration technology architecture dynamically on demand, depending on the particular back-end application systems that need to be integrated with each other or with trading partners. In order to allow this adapter "pluggability," the B2B integration technology architecture has to provide a framework that allows us to install, manage and access the adapter at run time. A back-end application system sends messages to an adapter (or an adapter polls for messages), and the adapter passes the message on to the B2B integration technology. Conversely, the B2B integration technology architecture invokes an adapter to insert data into the back-end application system.

The B2B protocol engine provides the analogous functionality to adapters for trading partner integration. A B2B protocol engine can execute any required B2B protocol that is required by a trading partner. A definition interface allows the specification of B2B protocols, whereas at run time the B2B protocol engine can receive as well as send messages to trading partners, according to the B2B protocol definitions. The B2B protocol engine connects through various transports to trading partners.

The endpoint management component manages the attributes, capabilities and agreements of endpoints. It has interfaces for creating, deleting and changing endpoints, associating their capabilities and managing agreements. The latter also have to be created, deleted and managed, for example, extended or terminated.

The security component provides all necessary security services. Encryption and decryption of messages falls in the domain of the security component, as do signature computation and check, nonrepudiation, key management, access rights management, authorization management and authentication management. The latter two are necessary for managing end user access to the B2B integration technology.

The packaging component provides packaging functionality required by B2B protocols or back-end application adapters. If messages are to be sent over a particular transport in particular protocols, their definition might require a specific packaging. Widely used mechanisms are Multipurpose Internet Mail Extensions

(MIME) [MIME 1], Mail Security (S/MIME) [S/MIME] or Simple Object Access Protocol (SOAP) [SOAP].

The transport component implements the functionality required to use network protocols like HTTP [HTTP], SMTP [SMTP], FTP [FTP], MIME Encapsulation of EDI Objects (EDIINT) [EDIINT] and others. Messages are sent or received over these network protocols, and therefore, all networks and network protocols required by trading partners have to be implemented.

2.3.4 Persistence

The persistence component is very important for the reliability of the overall B2B integration technology architecture technology. However, there are no integration specific components, but standard, off-the-shelf components are usesd (Fig. 2.32).

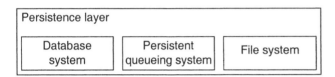

Fig. 2.32. Persistence layer components

The database system stores all data managed by the B2B integration technology architecture. This includes not only messages and events but also processes, transformations and all other configuration data. In the ideal case all data reside inside the database.

The persistent queueing system is available to implement queuing behavior. Like a database system, it provides transactional access to the enqueue and dequeue operations for inserting or retrieving messages, respectively. Queueing behavior in the sense of first-in first-out (FIFO) semantics is difficult to implement on relational database tables, so queueing systems are used for this. Furthermore, persistent queueing systems can extend over several systems and therefore can be used for remote communication. One end of the same queue appears to be on one machine, whereas the other end appears on another machine. The enqueue and dequeue are machine local operations. Through this approach the executables do not have to be aware of the distribution aspects of the communication.

File systems are used to store data in files. From a B2B integration technology viewpoint a file system is necessary to perhaps store configuration information for starting up the B2B integration technology server. However, from a data management viewpoint database systems are by far the preferred technology due to their functionality in terms of transaction support, reliability, backup and restart capabilities, to name a few.

From a distributed system perspective a transaction-processing monitor might be a necessary component to support distributed transactions across the B2B integration technology and any back-end application system that can participate in distributed transactions. However, this is not the state of the art in terms of integration and is discussed in Chap. 13 in more detail.

2.3.5 Layer Component Invocation Model

From an architectural perspective, the invocations between layers are top-down: that is, upper layers strictly invoke lower layers. Since layers consist of components (part-of relationship), this means that components invoke each other. The component invocation model demands that the invocation between components of different layers is top-down: the user interface components invoke the integration logic components. These in turn invoke the connectivity components as well as the persistence components. When messages are received from the connectivity components, these are stored in the persistent components to be picked up by the integration logic components. Following this scheme, the invocation model is strict from higher levels of the architecture into the lower levels of the architecture.

An implementation might deviate from the architectural view. For performance reasons the connectivity components might not only store incoming messages in the persistence layer but also notify integration logic components of the arrival of messages. This means that integration logic components do not have to inquire the persistent layer components for new messages, but receive notifications. This would break the invocation relationships between the layers since a lower layer invokes a layer higher up if notifications are viewed as invocations. However, this change in the implementation strategy might be acceptable because the architecture would work without this optimization effort.

2.3.6 Summary

In summary, all components discussed individually in the previous sections are represented in one architecture representation in Fig. 2.33. Part III describes the functionality as well as the invocation relationship between the components in more detail.

2.4 Integration Technology Deployment

Each enterprise that needs back-end application system integration or trading partner integration is faced with the question of which integration software to use and how to deploy it successfully. The initial temptation is to build integration technology in-house rather than to purchase an integration product like a B2B integration technology server. The integration problem appears easily solved, especially because of the recent popularity of XML and message transport over the Internet by means of HTTP or SOAP. Furthermore, early successes can be accomplished easily when the whole integration problem is perceived as the task of sending XML instances over the Internet.

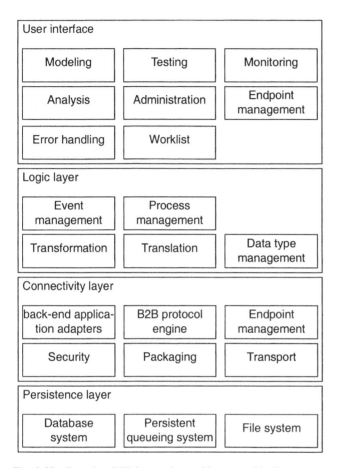

Fig. 2.33. Complete B2B integration architecture with all components

Sections 2.2 and 2.3 clearly indicated that it takes well-defined integration concepts and a well-organized integration architecture to solve all parts of the integration problem. Clearly, sending XML "over the wire" is one of the least difficult areas of B2B integration. Therefore, when discussing B2B integration technology deployment in the following, the use of a B2B integration technology product rather than a home-grown or in-house solution is assumed.

While deployment is not the main focus of the book, a high-level discussion needs to take place in order to have a complete discussion of B2B integration technology. The initial phase is the decision of which particular B2B integration technology server to license or buy. This decision depends to a large extent on the particular integration problem to be solved as well as the already-installed software products and their vendors. The particular integration problem to be solved needs to be clearly and fully specified in an integration requirement specification, at least to the greatest extent possible. Based on this, a selection process will select the particular B2B integration technology product. If the enterprise is following the single software vendor approach, then this vendor's integration product will most likely be the favorite one. If the enterprise follows the best-of-breed approach, then the product with the functionality best matching the integration requirement specification will be favored.

Once the selection has been made, three major deployment phases can be recognized: the preproduction phase, the production phase and the after-production phase or postproduction phase. The preproduction phase requires the set up of the environment that is necessary to put the B2B integration technology server into production. This includes defining the integrations that are to be executed first, the trading partner data of those that are to be integrated as well as the back-end application systems. Careful testing is performed, and the trading partner agreements are put in place to start the production phase.

Once the production phase is ongoing, more integrations will be defined or existing ones modified or deleted. New trading partners will be added, existing ones modified or deleted. Back-end application systems will be added and existing ones will be upgraded, possibly requiring modification of the integrations. The installed B2B integration technology server is a "live" installation that requires continuous careful maintenance. Of course, the B2B integration technology server itself might be upgraded to a newer software version, however, ideally that does not affect the modeled integrations, back-end application systems or trading partner at all (except for a possible downtime).

The production phase might be ongoing "forever," i.e., for the entire life of the enterprise. Or, the B2B integration technology server itself might be retired (e.g., when the enterprise no longer requires integration or there is a need to switch to another B2B integration technology server of a different vendor, typically arising from enterprise mergers). In this last phase of the deployment life cycle, the trading partners have to be deleted one by one and the trading partner agreements with them must be terminated. The connectivity to the back-end application systems need to be deleted so that events are no longer received from them. Once all ongoing integrations are finished and no new ones are started, the B2B integration technology server can be removed from the software infrastructure of the company. While a lot more could be said about B2B integration technology server deployment, no more detail is added here. Instead, the reader is referred to Part IV.

3 Types of Integration

There are many different ways to integrate enterprises with each other, with their various autonomous divisions and with their hosted or nonhosted back-end application systems. In order to derive the spectrum of integration use cases for a generic B2B integration technology architecture it is mandatory to explore and to examine integration scenarios in more detail and in more depth. This chapter reviews an exhaustive set of integration scenarios from an integration technology point of view. The scenarios are described graphically.

This chapter shows the spectrum of integration use cases that a B2B integration technology must be able to solve. The variety of potential integration situations is introduced. Chapter 4 provides a classification of the integration functionality itself in order to classify different integration technologies independent of integration use cases. This allows us to characterize different integration technologies by their functionality. Both this chapter and Chap. 4 provide a frame of reference for concrete integration situations as well as specific integration technology. The integration scenarios are described as well as depicted graphically. Figure 3.1 shows the legend of the basic set of graphical symbols used in the following sections.

Fig. 3.1. Legend of symbols for integration scenarios

The symbol for enterprise depicts the integration boundaries of an enterprise. As is later shown, back-end application systems, B2B integration technology servers and other components are inside the enterprise icon since they are part of the internal software components of the enterprise. The symbol for application represents any type of back-end application system, including legacy systems as well as "out-of-the-box" application systems, that is, systems that are bought instead of built by the enterprise. The symbol for the B2B integration technology server represents the B2B integration technology server used for the specific integration scenarios. The symbol for networks is a line since the widely used cloud representation takes too much space in figures. Where necessary, the graphical symbols are annotated in order to clarify a scenario.

An important note is that whenever two or more B2B integration technology servers are shown inside or outside an enterprise or application service provider, they could be from different vendors, i.e., they are not necessarily the same technology or product. This note is important since the graphical notation does not imply that the same technology from the same vendor has to be used.

The integration scenarios assume that the B2B integration technology provides the functionality required for the scenarios. Any particular type of integration technology as discussed in Chap. 1 could be used in reality, as long as it provides the necessary functionality. Of course, mature B2B integration as specified in Chap. 2 would be fine, too.

3.1 Point-to-Point Back-end Application System Integration

The simplest integration scenario is point-to-point integration between two back-end application systems within one enterprise. This scenario represents the case in which two applications exchange data with each other (Fig. 3.2).

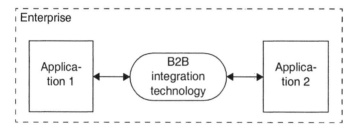

Fig. 3.2. Point-to-point integration

Each of the two back-end application systems is connected with the B2B integration technology server. The B2B integration technology server provides the functionality discussed in Chap. 1 or Chap. 2 in order to connect the two back-end application systems.

3.2 Multipoint Back-end Application System Integration

Multipoint integration refers to the case where three or more back-end application systems are communicating with each other. Figure 3.3 shows the topology with three back-end application systems.

It is not necessarily the case that each back-end application system communicates with every other one. Multipoint integration can fundamentally be of two types. In the first type, each pair of back-end application systems is communicating in a point-to-point relationship (or not at all, if two back-end application systems are not communicating at all). This means that point-to-point functionality as discussed in Sect. 1.2.2 is sufficient.

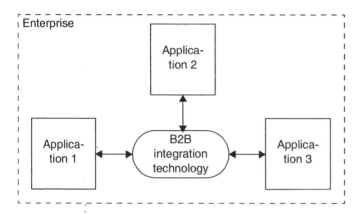

Fig. 3.3. Multi-point integration

In the second type, in addition to pairwise communication three or more back-end application systems are exchanging messages through a business process. For this case business process management functionality as discussed in Sect. 1.2.4 is required.

3.3 Back-end Application System Metadata Synchronization

The "smallest" integration scenario is when a back-end application system communicates with the B2B integration technology server itself to exchange data like trading partner data. This scenario requires some more detailed explanation. Trading partner data contain information about a trading partner's name, unique identification as well as network addresses for communication. back-end application systems manage trading partner data for their purposes so that they can refer to trading partners internally. For example, an Enterprise Resource Planning (ERP) system stores purchase orders, and each purchase order is related to the trading partner that either sent the purchase order or to which the purchase order was sent.

A B2B integration technology server has to do the same for providing its functionality. Each message it processes comes from a trading partner or is sent to a trading partner (in the business-to-business case). In order for a B2B integration technology server to be able to identify trading partners, it uses the unique identifiers that are stored within its trading partner management subsystem.

When a back-end application system sends business data to the B2B integration technology server, it refers to a trading partner's unique identifier indicating the target trading partner of the message. The B2B integration technology server has to send the message to the trading partner with that unique identifier. In order for the B2B integration technology server to interpret the unique trading partner identifier the same way (i.e., refer to the same real trading partner), the trading partner data must be synchronized between the back-end application system and the B2B integration technology server. For example, if a trading partner is added to the list of trading partners in the back-end application system, then the same trading partner needs to be added to the B2B integration technology server's trading partner subcomponent. In order to accomplish the synchronization of trading partner data, the back-end application system needs to be integrated with the B2B integration technology itself. Figure 3.4 shows the topology with one back-end system application. Chapter 9 discusses in more detail how the trading partner synchronization can be accomplished using the integration concepts provided by the B2B integration technology server themselves.

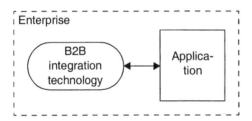

Fig. 3.4. Metadata synchronization

This type of communication is called metadata synchronization since the integration is about data that is necessary to accomplish the regular business data integration, like purchase orders. The messages exchanged contain data about trading partners like their unique identifier or business phone number, not business data like a shipment notice. If more than one back-end application system is connected (the usual case to be expected) then in general each has to be included in trading partner synchronization.

3.4 Supply Chain Integration of Two Trading Partners

This case can be illustrated by the almost "classical" example of two trading partners exchanging a purchase order and a purchase order acknowledgment. Fundamentally, two trading partners exchange business data over a network in order to establish a trading relationship, to exchange business data, notifications or status messages. Each trading partner uses a B2B integration technology server to execute the communication (Fig. 3.5).

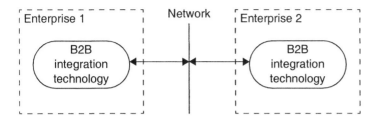

Fig. 3.5. Supply chain integration of two trading partners

Usually, the trading partners store or retrieve the business data from back-end application systems. Therefore the B2B integration technology deployed is integrated with the back-end application systems used by the enterprises. Figure 3.6 shows a more complete supply chain topology.

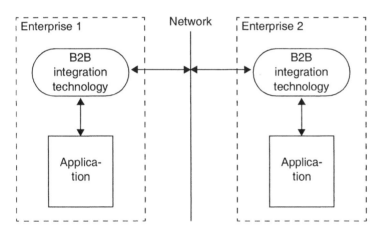

Fig. 3.6. Supply chain integration of two trading partners and their back-end application systems

In the general case each trading partner has different back-end application systems as well as a different number of systems. Also, each trading partner might have B2B integration technology from a different vendor so that both trading partners cannot rely on having any technology in common at all. This requires true interoperability on a B2B protocol level.

3.5 Supply Chain Integration of Several Trading Partners

As soon as more than two trading partners are involved in a supply chain, then it is likely that not every trading partner involved is communicating with every other any more. For example, a transport company communicating with a supplier does not necessarily communicate with the seller. Figure 3.7 shows the communication topology. The back-end application systems of the trading partners are omitted in the graphical representation. Since between each pair of trading partners there can be a different type of network (e.g., Internet or VAN), a separate network is depicted.

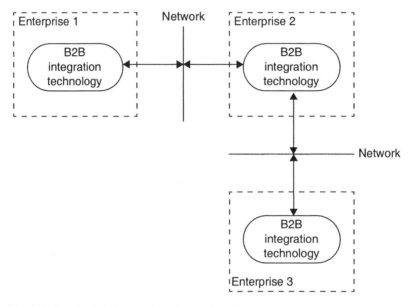

Fig. 3.7. Supply chain integration of several trading partners

Each trading partner involved in this example has bilateral communication relationships, but not every trading partner communicates with every other trading partner. Of course, it is possible that every trading partner in a supply chain is connected to every other trading partner to exchange business data. The B2B integration technology server must be able to deal with all cases.

3.6 Remote Back-end Application System

Small trading partners do not necessarily want to buy, install and maintain a B2B integration technology server in addition to the back-end application systems they already have. In case they have a small number of back-end application systems that do not communicate with each other, they might want to connect to their supply chain directly without running a B2B integration technology server. In this case the back-end application systems need to be "B2B integration enabled."

One way to enable a back-end application system to connect to trading partners is a dedicated B2B protocol back-end application system adapter that implements a particular B2B protocol, but cannot provide any other connectivity (for example, with other back-end application systems). In this scenario the back-end application system can directly connect to trading partners' B2B integration technology servers (Fig. 3.8). From a B2B integration technology viewpoint, the dedicated B2B protocol back-end application system adapter appears like any other B2B integration technology because the adapter implements a specific B2B protocol like any other B2B integration technology server.

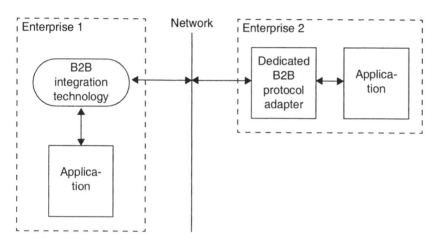

Fig. 3.8. Dedicated B2B protocol back-end application system adapter

3.7 Marketplace Integration

In its simplest form, a marketplace lists suppliers offering their products and allows buyers to access the supplier listings. Once a buyer finds a product they wish to buy, the marketplace has achieved its goal. All subsequent business data exchange, like a purchase order exchange, takes place outside the marketplace and independent of it (Fig. 3.9). A marketplace provides access to a seller and a buyer. Both are also connected directly for subsequent message exchange.

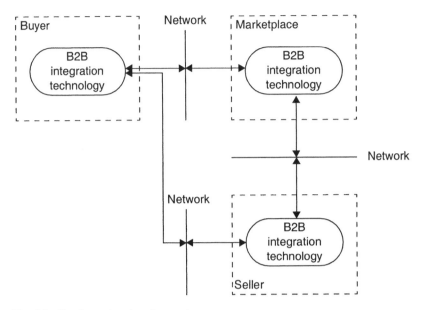

Fig. 3.9. Simple marketplace integration

More sophisticated forms of marketplaces provide automatic buyer/seller matching and might also issue the purchase orders and manage the purchase order acknowledgment as a response. In these cases the business data exchange is also managed by the marketplace. It might or might not be necessary for trading partners connected to a marketplace to exchange business data between themselves in addition to with the marketplace. In the extreme case, the marketplace provides all business data exchanges so that the trading partners do not have to connect with each other directly at all. In the latter case, no direct communication is set up between trading partners. For the example in Fig. 3.9, this means that there is no direct communication relationship between the buyer and the seller.

3.8 Hub

An enterprise with many trading partners in general faces the problem that it has to support many B2B protocols, since its trading partners might have chosen different B2B protocols for B2B integration. An implication of this is that the enterprise has to support all transformations necessary from its internal representation of business data to those of the various B2B protocols. For each business event like a purchase order, one transformation per B2B protocol has to be implemented. If a business event can be sent as well as received, two transformations (one for each direction) are necessary. The total number of transformations is therefore, in the worst case, the number of business events times two (directions) times the number of B2B protocols supported.

A high number of transformations means a significant maintenance effort for an enterprise. Large enterprises might be able to afford the maintenance cost, but smaller enterprises certainly would appreciate not incurring the cost. This problem is addressed by transformation hubs.

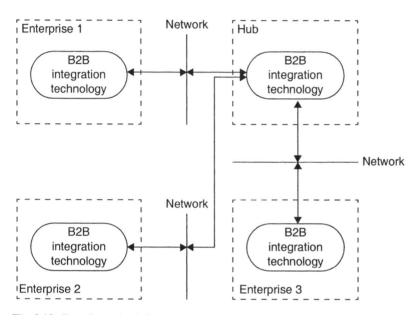

Fig. 3.10. Transformation hub

Transformation hubs implement the transformations between B2B protocols so that the enterprises do not have to do it themselves. Each enterprise communicates with the hub through one B2B protocol over a specific network. This requires that an enterprise only has to transform its internal business data to this one B2B protocol. The transformation hub takes care of implementing the high number of transformations (and most likely charges a fee for it). Once a hub receives a message and transforms it, it is forwarded to the final destination trading partner. Figure 3.10 shows the topology with one hub and three trading partners connected to it.

In addition to transformation, a hub can provide more services. For example, a hub can log the messages as they come into the hub and leave the hub for auditing purposes. At any time a trading partner can access the hub asking for all or a specific subset of messages that it has sent. Furthermore, the hub can provide analysis functionality that a trading partner can use. For example, the hub could analyze how many messages came in for a trading partner sorted by originating trading partner. A hub can also provide time-stamping services so that messages are time stamped according to a single clock in the hub instead of the individual clocks in the trading partners. This might avoid issues in message processing when the clock times are significantly different.

3.9 Interactive Application

The discussion so far has not covered the case where an interactive application accesses the B2B integration technology server. In this case an interactive application like a browser or graphical user interface is integrated with the B2B integration server technology. A user using the interface enters the data as required by the user interface. Once finished with the entering of data upon submission, the interactive application connects with the B2B integration technology server and passes data on to it. An example is an employee procurement application, where employees select products to be purchased for internal use (like pencils). Once all products are chosen, the purchase order is issued through the B2B integration technology.

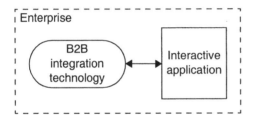

Fig. 3.11. Interactive application integration

Even though this sounds like a new type of scenario, in reality it is not. From the perspective of the B2B integration technology server, the interactive application is a back-end application system. The fact that a user drives the interaction through a user interface is not visible to the B2B integration technology server. The most common case is that the interactive application is inside the enterprise (Fig. 3.11).

The not-so-common case is that the interactive application is outside the enterprise boundaries. In this case there are two possibilities: either it connects to a B2B integration technology server that is also outside the enterprise boundaries (Fig. 3.12) or it connects directly across the network by complying to a B2B protocol that is supported by the B2B integration technology server (Fig. 3.13). In the first case, the two B2B integration technology servers exchange messages as if there were no interactive application. In the latter case, the interactive application is like a remote back-end application system, as discussed earlier.

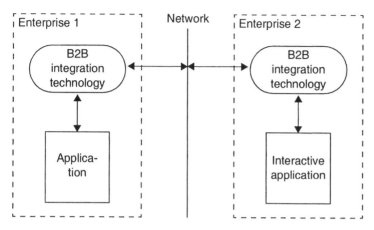

Fig. 3.12. Interactive application connected through remote B2B integration technology server

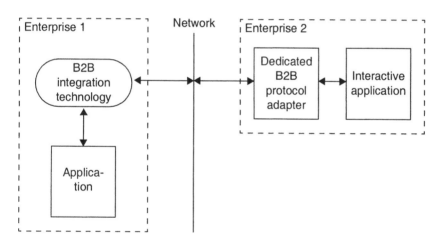

Fig. 3.13. Remote interactive application

3.10 Intra-Enterprise Integration

In addition to the scenario where enterprises connect with each other (like in the supply chain scenario), they can also connect various internal groups like divisions with each other. So far it is assumed that only back-end application systems are internal to enterprises and need to be integrated through a B2B integration technology server. However, larger enterprises consist of several divisions that are, in many cases, geographically distributed. These divisions can have their own set of back-end application systems that they manage and that process division internal business data. In cases when they are comfortable providing access, one B2B integration technology server for the whole enterprise can manage all integration requirements. This server connects back-end application systems within divisions as well as across divisions.

Divisions in many cases feel uncomfortable providing access to their back-end application systems directly to the other divisions of the enterprise. In this case each division can deploy a B2B integration technology server by itself. Each B2B integration technology server integrates the applications of a division with each other. As soon as divisions need to exchange data between themselves, the B2B integration technology servers communicate with each other as if other divisions were external enterprises. Depending on the enterprise, they all follow the same B2B protocol, or different divisions can implement different B2B protocols. Figure 3.14 shows two divisions of one enterprise, each deploying its own B2B integration technology server.

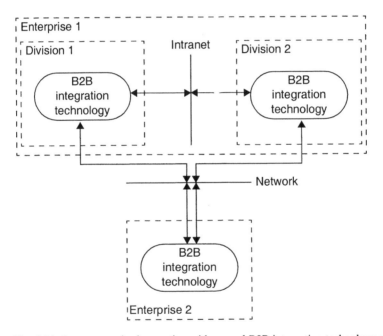

Fig. 3.14. Intra-enterprise integration with several B2B integration technology servers

Since each division has its own B2B integration technology server, each division can connect to external enterprises through B2B protocols individually. This means that there is no longer a single B2B integration technology server that facilitates interenterprise communication. It depends on the particular enterprise to set the policy on external communication. Figure 3.14 shows the case where every division connects to external enterprises individually.

If an enterprise decides to have only one B2B integration technology server connecting to external enterprises then it could be one out of those deployed in divisions. Alternatively, it could be a dedicated B2B integration technology server that does not belong to any particular division but to the enterprise as a whole instead. All divisions connect to this dedicated server in case they require connectivity to external enterprises.

3.11 Application Service Provider

As introduced in Chap. 1, application service providers (ASPs) install back-end application systems in their enterprise and make them available to their customers (hosted back-end application system). In general, customers access the user interfaces of hosted applications through browsers over the Internet.

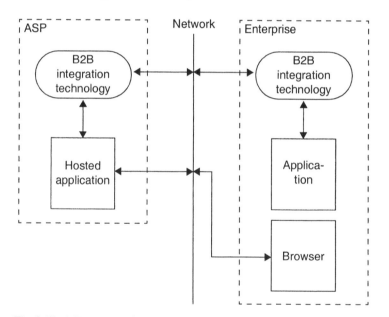

Fig. 3.15. ASP connectivity using a B2B integration technology server

However, in addition to accessing a hosted application through browsers, an enterprise wants to integrate the hosted application with its locally installed back-end application systems. In order to achieve this, it must be possible to access the hosted application systems as if it were locally installed. This is possible if an ASP provides access to the hosted application over a network through a B2B protocol.

Then it is possible that an enterprise can integrate its own hosted data with its own local data. Figure 3.15 shows the topology involving a B2B integration technology server. If an ASP hosts only one back-end application system, a dedicated B2B protocol adapter as discussed earlier might be sufficient to achieve the necessary connectivity with its customers.

An interesting "twist" is the following. If an enterprise 1 exchanges business data with enterprise 2 using a B2B protocol, then it can be that the enterprise 2 does not have any back-end application systems installed at all. Instead, all its back-end application systems are hosted at one or several ASPs. In this case the B2B protocol execution happens between enterprise 1 and an ASP that acts on behalf of enterprise 2 (Fig. 3.16).

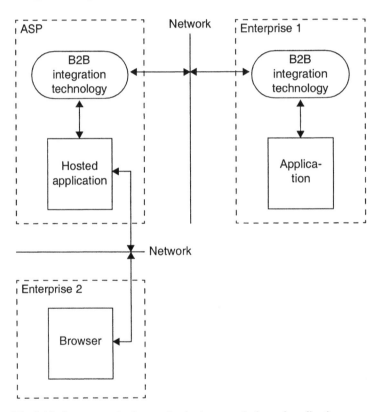

Fig. 3.16. Interenterprise integration in the case of a hosted application

Enterprise 1 integrates with enterprise 2 through a B2B protocol. Enterprise 2 has its back-end application hosted at the ASP. This results in enterprise 1 integrating with the hosted application of enterprise 2 through the ASP that hosts the application. However, enterprise 1 is not aware of this fact, since it connects to the ASP as if it were connecting to enterprise 2 (if enterprise 2 had a local deployed B2B integration technology server).

An even more interesting twist is if an enterprise that has its back-end application hosted connects to another enterprise that also has its back-end application hosted. In this case the two ASPs that host the application on behalf of the enterprises connect with each other on their behalf (Fig. 3.17).

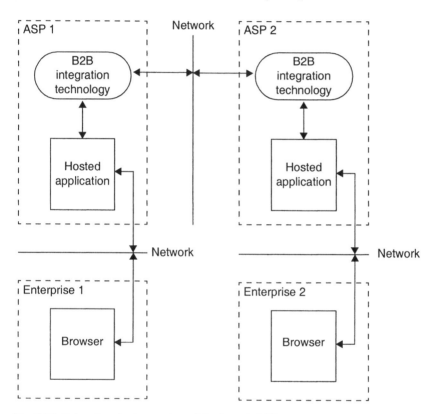

Fig. 3.17. Interenterprise integration solely through ASPs

Enterprise 1 and enterprise 2 both have their application hosted at ASP 1 and ASP 2, respectively. In order for both enterprises to interoperate and exchange business data, the ASPs hosting their applications have to communicate on the behalf of the enterprises.

Fnally, an interesting scenario arises if both enterprises have their applications hosted at the same ASP. In this case the interenterprise integration can be accomplished within the one ASP itself and no communication is required across any network. This requires that the B2B integration technology server is able to communicate with itself. It sends out the business data to itself, and only at this point in time it does become clear that the B2B integration technology communicates with itself. Up to this point it is unaware of this, especially if there is no specific setup or "shortcut" in the B2B integration technology server itself for this case.

3.12 ASP Aggregation

Up to this point it was assumed that an ASP only hosts one back-end application system of a particular software vendor. However, this is not necessarily true. It is very well possible that an ASP hosts several different back-end application systems. All the previous discussions still apply in this case. Furthermore, within an ASP the back-end application systems can be integrated with each other using the B2B integration technology. A customer that subscribes to two back-end application systems within the same ASP can request the ASP to integrate the back-end applications with each other so that the customer's back-end application systems can communicate data between each other.

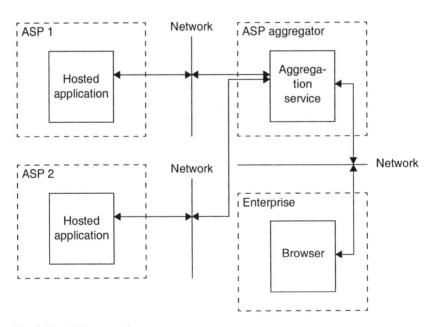

Fig. 3.18. ASP aggregation

More and more often, enterprises face the situation that the back-end application systems that they want to be hosted cannot all be hosted by the same ASP. They have to work with different ASPs. Each ASP hosts some of the back-end application systems. This requires an enterprise to coordinate with different ASPs at the same time in order to integrate their hosted applications as well as the interenterprise integration. However, it would be advantageous for these type of enterprises to have a single point of management for all their hosted applications, no matter how many ASPs host the applications. This is accomplished by ASP aggregators. These are ASPs that are gateways to other ASPs. They provide a single point of contact to enterprises that want to have their applications hosted. In turn, ASP aggregators manage the coordination between the different ASPs for an enterprise so that the enterprise gets the impression that it deals only with one ASP (Fig. 3.18).

In Fig. 3.18 the enterprise connects to the ASP aggregator. The browser of an employee has one point of contact provided by the ASP aggregator. Depending on the task the employee wants to accomplish, the ASP aggregator connects internally to the appropriate ASP that hosts the application. This architecture allows the enterprise to look at all its hosted applications in a homogeneous way as if all are installed at a single ASP.

The application integration problem also exists in the context of ASP aggregation. The various back-end application systems that an enterprise has hosted need to be integrated. In addition, the enterprise might communicate with other enterprises. Since the ASP aggregator knows about all the hosted applications of an enterprise, it can provide the integration functionality with its B2B integration technology server, and it can also provide the interenterprise integration functionality (Fig. 3.19). In this particular topology the various individual ASPs do not have to deal with integration aspects themselves. All integration functionality is provided by the ASP aggregator using its B2B integration technology server.

3.13 ASP Aggregator Aggregation

The ultimate in aggregation is ASP aggregator integration where ASP aggregators are integrated with each other to provide their subscribers with a homogeneous view across all ASPs that they are integrating. This is a necessary scenario when a subscriber's hosted applications are not covered by one ASP aggregator, but require two or more. One ASP aggregator can integrate the other aggregators to provide a homogeneous view. In addition, each ASP aggregator can integrate every other one. In this scenario all ASP aggregators can provide access to all integrated ASPs. Figure 3.20 gives an example topology where two ASP aggregators are mutually integrated with each other. The representation of ASPs in this figure is reduced and does not show the hosted applications in order to be able to fit the representation into one figure.

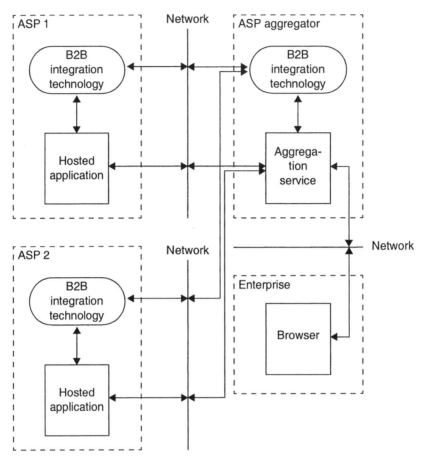

Fig. 3.19. ASP aggregator-implemented integration

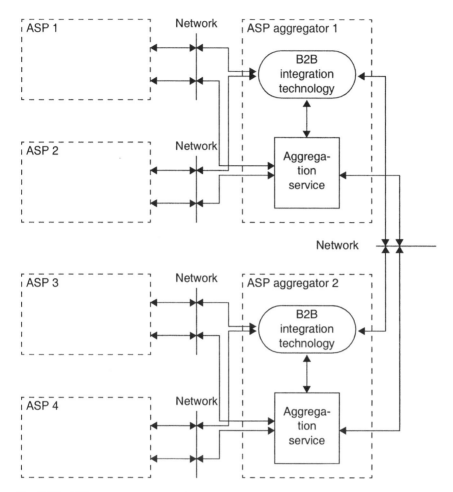

Fig. 3.20. ASP aggregator aggregation

3.14 Hosted Integration

An enterprise might not be willing to host the back-end application systems it requires. It wants its data locally stored. Instead, it would welcome an ASP hosting the integration functionality. In this case, the ASP has to worry about defining and managing the integration. Each of the back-end application systems is connected to the ASP's B2B integration technology server, in this case through dedicated B2B adapters so that the ASP can connect and integrate the back-end application systems (Fig. 3.21).

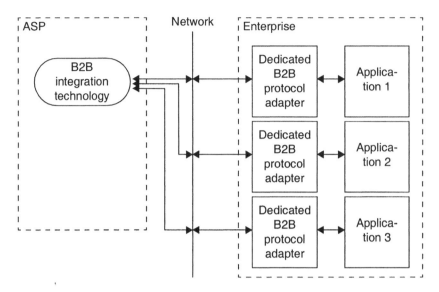

Fig. 3.21. Hosted integration

Compared to an ASP aggregator the back-end application systems are not hosted themselves, but are locally installed with the enterprise. Only the B2B integration technology server is hosted.

If a B2B integration technology server is hosted, then it must be possible to define integration for different enterprises (customers) concurrently on the same installation. If this is possible, then the intra-enterprise integration scenario discussed above can be supported in a different way. Instead of every division having to deploy and run their own B2B integration technology server, the enterprise could host one deployment internally and have the divisions act like customers that host their integration in the one deployment. This would relieve the individual divisions of the need to maintain their own B2B integration technology server installation. Furthermore, this one installation can also perform the interenterprise communication with trading partners.

3.15 Reverse Hosting

In the reverse hosting case an ASP does not install the software in-house, but at the customer's, i.e., subscriber's site. This means that the software and the data that the software manages is under full control of the subscriber; however, the management of the hosted software is performed by the ASP. This means that the subscriber outsources the management of the software to an ASP while still having full control over the hosted software. Figure 3.22 shows the topology of this use case. The back-end application systems integrated by the B2B integration technology at the subscriber's site are not shown.

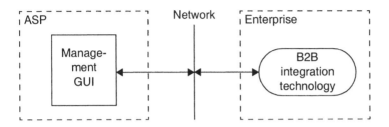

Fig. 3.22. Reverse hosting

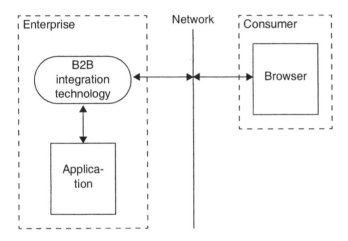

Fig. 3.23. Business-to-consumer integration

3.16 Business-to-Consumer Integration

The business-to-consumer integration scenario is very similar to the interactive application integration case discussed earlier. The difference is that consumers on their desktop or laptop computers cannot be asked to install any dedicated B2B protocol adapter to communicate. Instead, the browser the customer uses to communicate has to be directly connected with the enterprise that is selling goods. This requires the B2B integration server technology to support browser communication protocols like HTTP to be available as B2B protocol. In this case, the B2B integration technology server can directly communicate with browser technology (Fig. 3.23).

3.17 Summary

The discussed integration scenarios cover a wide range of possibilities. Some, like the hosting scenarios, seems far-fetched today, but if predictions are true that in the not-so-distant future more and more applications will be sold in hosted form, these scenarios will become increasingly common and familiar to the integration community.

From the viewpoint of this book all integration scenarios are equally important in terms of the integration concepts and the integration technology architecture. Therefore all integration scenarios will be covered by the integration concepts and the integration architecture.

4 Classification

A classification helps to identify concepts and functionality. Similarly, a classification of integration helps us to understand the difference between the integration concepts followed in this book and other integration approaches or integration problems. A classification can be driven to an extreme very easily by trying to be complete in all details that can be distinguished. In the following this is not done for the sake of clarity; instead, a more pragmatic approach is followed. Only the most important classes are discussed that allow us to classify the integration concepts followed in this book and distinguish it from other approaches.

4.1 A2A, B2B and ASP Integration

A starting point for the classification of integration are the three types of integration discussed so far, A2A, B2B and ASP integration. A2A integration refers to the integration of any number of back-end application systems within an enterprise. B2B integration refers to the message exchange between two or more enterprises, and ASP integration refers to back-end application systems that are hosted and require integration.

Most of the integration scenarios discussed in Chap. 3 can be classified into one of these three types. However, the three types overlap and the classification might not be straightforward. An example is the integration of a back-end application system over a network that resides in a remote division of the enterprise. Is this A2A or B2B integration? Since this integration is over a network, it must be B2B integration. But since a back-end application system of the same enterprise is integrated, it should be A2A integration.

This particular conflict can be resolved by a slight modification of the definition of B2B integration. Instead of using the network as the characteristic, the legal situation would be more applicable. The new definition would be that B2B integration is the case when the boundaries of two legal entities are crossed. A typical example is when two trading partners communicate. Consequently, a back-end application system that is integrated over a network would uniquely fall into the category of A2A integration.

A more detailed classification the three types of integration is not useful since the functionality of these three types overlaps significantly. For example, each of the three types of integration has to deal with data transformation.

Even though B2B integration is one of the three types of integration discussed in the previous section, from now on B2B integration is considered the superset of the three types of integration in this book. The major reason is that B2B integration requires the other two types of integration in order to cover all the integration scenarios introduced in Chap. 3. Without A2A integration and ASP integration it is not possible to talk about B2B integration meaningfully.

4.2 Classification of Integration

Making a classification work requires choosing the appropriate classes to be able to categorize integration concepts and integration technology appropriately. The following classes have been chosen for this purpose. For each class the criteria are provided as well as an explanation. Based on this classification B2B integration is defined as discussed in the book in Sect. 4.3.

Table 4.1. Classes and criteria

Classes	Criteria
Business data awareness	Aware, unaware
Integration instance representation	Instance-based, stream-based
Hosting paradigm	Dedicated, hosted
Definition paradigm	Declarative, programmed
Endpoint specificity	Open, closed
Homogeneity	Homogeneous, heterogeneous
Endpoint state awareness	Aware, unaware
Endpoint behavior awareness	Aware, unaware
Invocation paradigm	Synchronous, asynchronous
Data integration	Yes, no
Process integration	Yes, no
User interface integration	Yes, no
Batch integration	Yes, no
Reliability	Reliable, unreliable

Classifications can be easily criticized by being "wrong" in the sense that certain aspects are not included (for example, performance) or that given classes are not further subdivided (for example, data sources into relational sources and nonrelational sources). The following classification tries to strike a balance between being detailed enough without providing so much detail as to be overwhelming. The goal is to provide enough classes to be meaningful. The classes are chosen for the purpose of the book's definition of integration. Table 4.1 lists all classes and their criteria to give an overview. Each class is discussed separately in the following sections.

4.2.1 Business Data Awareness

Integration can be business data aware or business data unaware. Business data aware integration is able to interpret the business data sent in messages as payloads. This requires a data type system that the B2B integration technology provides and understands in order to interpret the business data content. For example, business data awareness is relevant for content-based routing, where business data is sent to an endpoint based on a specific value in the business data. For example, large purchase orders are sent to a different trading partner than small purchase orders, where the size is defined by the purchase order amount.

Business data unaware integration cannot interpret message contents at all. This prohibits content-based routing of messages to endpoints. Business data unaware integration is limited to forwarding the data based on the header information available in the messages.

4.2.2 Integration Instance Representation

Two fundamental instance representation models are instance-based integration representation versus stream-based integration representation. Instance-based integration representation represents each ongoing integration (like a purchase order processing) as an instance at run time that has state. At any point in time the instance representation can be queried about the state it is in, which denotes the progress it made. If several purchase orders are in the B2B integration technology server at the same time, each purchase order is represented by a separate instance and each instance progresses independently of the other ones.

In the stream-based integration representation, the different integrations are not represented as instances with their own state. Instead, they follow a queueing model whereby each integration is represented as a message in a network of queues. The state of an integration can only be derived by observing its position in the queue network. Similar approaches can be found in other architectures like workflow management systems. Alonso et. al. (1995) describe how a workflow management system can be built around a queueing model instead of an instance model.

4.2.3 Hosting Paradigm

The trading partner model can be a dedicated model or a hosted model. A dedicated integration model assumes that there is one trading partner for which integration is defined and executed. All other trading partners in the B2B integration technology server are remote trading partners to which the dedicated trading partner connects.

In the hosted integration model it is possible to host several trading partners concurrently in one B2B integration technology server. For each of the hosted trading partners integration can be defined independently of any other hosted trading partner. In this situation any number of hosted trading partners can be managed at the same time.

4.2.4 Definition Paradigm

Integration can be defined in a declarative way or in a programmed approach. In the declarative approach the integration modeler defines integration using a declarative language. A declared integration is executed at run time by an interpreter that interprets the declarative statements. Modelers do not have to worry about how the integration is actually implemented. Instead, they only deal with the declarative language that represents the integration concepts.

In the programming approach the language for defining integration is a programming language. In this case the integration "modeler" is required to use a programming language in order to achieve the necessary integration. This means that modellers need to be aware of the inner workings of the integration technology in such a way that they can use a programming language without creating potentially unrecoverable error states.

4.2.5 Endpoint Specificity

Closed endpoint support restricts the integration to a set of fixed types of endpoints like only back-end application systems with a fixed assumption of behavior. Open endpoint support does not restrict the integration to a particular type of endpoint and does not assume certain behaviors of certain types of endpoints. For example, in an open endpoint support it is perfectly possible to communicate with a user through a B2B protocol. In a closed endpoint support situation only trading partners would use B2B protocols for integration.

4.2.6 Homogeneity

Integration can be homogeneous or heterogeneous. Homogeneous integration assumes that all endpoints follow the same data definitions as well as the same behavior definitions. In the narrower sense, this means that all endpoints use the exact same standard definitions. For example, all endpoints agree on one definition of purchase order. In the wider sense this means that all use the same language for defining their data and behavior, while the data and/or the behavior specifications written down in this language possibly mismatch. For example, all use XML schema to define their business data, while each endpoint might vary on the specific definition of a purchase order.

In heterogeneous integration every endpoint is free to choose the standard and the definitions as well as the specific languages it wants to follow in order to achieve integration. The latter case is by far more realistic. However, the former one exists in closed communities, and the former is a special case of the latter.

4.2.7 Endpoint State Awareness

Integration transports business data across different systems. Integration can be aware or unaware of the state the integrated systems have. In the state-aware case the integration itself has state that is linked to the state of the endpoints. This means that any state change either in the integration or in one of the endpoints potentially causes state changes in the other endpoints or in the integration. In state-aware integration, for each state change it must be defined whether this change causes other state changes. The notification of state changes is accomplished through message exchanges between the integration and the endpoints. For example, if a purchase order is sent, the originating endpoint is in state "purchase order sent," whereas the receiving endpoint is in "purchase order received."

In state-unaware integration any state change in the integration or in an endpoint can happen independently of each other. While this is an easier integration paradigm, it can easily lead to inconsistent systems if state matters. An example of state-unaware integration is data integration, where data is extracted from systems. The extracted data (potentially aggregated or modified) no longer has any state dependency with the originals. Any change in the originals is not automatically propagated to the extracted data. Consequently, the extracted data might be different and inconsistent after the first change of any original data.

4.2.8 Endpoint Behavior Awareness

Endpoints expose behavior through sending and receiving messages. Specific messages are related to each other, such as an acknowledgement message for a message containing business data. Behavior-aware integration recognizes that messages are related and keeps track of them. At any point in time the B2B integration technology knows the state of the interaction with the endpoint and where in the overall endpoint behavior the current conversation is.

Behavior-unaware integration treats each message as an individual message that is not related to any other message. Integration does not recognize the fact that messages are related, and, consequently, cannot reason about the state of the endpoint behavior.

4.2.9 Invocation Paradigm

Integration can be executed synchronously or asynchronously in relation to the endpoints. If integration is executed asynchronously in relation to the integrated endpoints, then the interaction with the endpoints is finished before the integration itself is finished. For example, as soon as a message is picked up from an endpoint the interaction with this endpoint is done. Then the B2B integration technology continues processing that message independent of the endpoint.

Synchronous invocation means that all integration functionality is executed synchronously in relation to the integrated endpoints. When an endpoint passes a message to the B2B integration technology, it starts executing the integration in the same thread. This includes passing business data to the receiving endpoints. Only when all endpoints have received their business data does the execution thread finish.

4.2.10 Data Integration

Data integration can be supported or not. Data integration replicates, copies and/or aggregates data from endpoints without modifying the source endpoints of the data. In this sense the extracted data have a life on their own, independent of the data source. The source of the data does not recognize the integration, and any change in the source data is not propagated to the data integration taking place.

A specific form of data integration is the establishment of a homogeneous logical data schema across different heterogeneous data sources. In this case all endpoints contribute to a consistent data schema, and the data integration has to make sure that the translation from the logical schema to the data schema of the endpoint is consistent and complete. This is referred to as the schema integration problem.

Updates in the context of data integration are only discussed if the data integration supports an integrated logical data schema that is perceived to be not only a homogeneous point of querying but also the single point of update.

4.2.11 Process Integration

Process integration can be supported or not. The business logic in process integration is defined as processes that define how a message is processed once it is extracted from an endpoint up to the point where the message is given to one or more other endpoints. The message can be transformed on the way. Possible operations on such a message are split into multiple messages, replication into several identical messages or consolidation with other messages.

If process integration is not supported, then messages are passed directly between endpoints without the ability to execute any business logic in between. The consequence is direct point-to-point integration.

4.2.12 User Interface Integration

User interface integration can be implemented by B2B integration technology or not. Online integration is the integration of user interfaces of various back-end application systems for interactive use by users. In the ideal case users get the impression that all back-end application systems work seamlessly together to the extent that the integrated user interface looks like the user interface from one back-end application system.

4.2.13 Batch Integration

Batch integration can be supported or not by B2B integration technology. Batch integration is the integration of messages between endpoints like back-end application systems or trading partners. No user interface is involved in this type of integration, as it connects the B2B integration technology programmatically to back-end application systems and trading partners. Batch in this context does not mean the transmission of several purchase orders in one message.

Batch integration seems to conflict with user interface integration. This is not the case since it might be that a process representation is chosen to define how user interfaces are integrated as well as their invocation order. For example, it might be that specific back-end application systems have to be accessed in a specific order in order to compose the user interface contents correctly. This can be done by process definitions.

4.2.14 Reliability

Reliability is not automatically a given for B2B integration technology. Reliable integration ensures that all messages passed to or received from the B2B integration technology are reliably processed. This includes ensuring that messages are not accidentally dropped or duplicated. In terms of invocations or transmissions an

"exactly-once" semantics has to be ensured. Transactional processing is a base requirement for reliable B2B integration technology.

Unreliable integration follows a best-effort approach in terms of message handling. This might cause dropped messages, duplicated messages and other potentially unwanted behavior.

4.3 Classification of Selected Integration Technologies

In the following several integration technologies are discussed that illustrate several of the previously introduced integration classes. The list is by far not exhaustive and only looks at a few of the interesting integration technologies. B2B integration as presented in this book is discussed in Sect. 4.4.

4.3.1 Streaming Query

Streaming queries (Babcock et. al. 2002) is an interesting database query technology that changes the behavior of conventional query interfaces. Instead of issuing a query that returns a result before terminating, streaming queries do not terminate at all while continuously returning results. A streaming query, issued once, continues to return results whenever data are inserted or modified that satisfy the query. In terms of the above classification, this technology implements the following criteria:

- Business data awareness: aware because queries can query the content of the data
- Integration instance representation: stream-based because results are streamed out of the database
- Hosting paradigm: dedicated since a streaming query is always executed in the context of a specific database management system
- Definition paradigm: declarative since queries are defined using a declarative language, structured query languagae (SQL) in context of relational database management systems
- Endpoint specificity: endpoint specific since streaming queries work only in context of specific database management systems
- Homogeneity: homogeneous since streaming queries operate against one schema
- Endpoint state awareness: aware since any change in the endpoint results in a reevaluation of the query
- Endpoint behavior awareness: aware in the sense that data changes are observed by the streaming query
- Invocation paradigm: synchronous in relation to the database management system
- Data integration: yes, since the streaming query returns data
- Process integration: no, since queries do not implement a process model
- Interface integration: no, since queries do not provide a user interface
- Batch integration: yes, since queries run directly against the database management system
- Reliable: yes, since streaming queries remember the already-processed data to continue correctly after failure. Furthermore, streaming queries themselves are recovered after a failure so that they do not have to be issued again.

4.3.2 Publish/Subscribe Technology

Publish/subscribe technology is used in context with queueing technology. Different forms of publish/subscribe technology exist for different queueing systems. Oracle Advanced Queuing, IBM MQ and Microsoft MSMQ are some examples [Oracle AQ, IBM MQ, Microsoft MSMQ]. Fundamentally, producers and consumers of data are distinguished. Independently of consumers, a producer produces data in a given place like a queue or database system. A producer can produce any amount of data at any point in time. Consumers that have interest in this data register interest in the data. One inefficient execution implementation would be that a consumer continuously polls the data of the producer by constantly executing queries. Since a producer can also delete data, the consumer might miss data between its queries. Instead, the publish/subscribe paradigm allows consumers to register interest by subscriptions. Subscriptions are like queries, but instead of the consumer issuing them, the producer causes the queries to execute after every change made to the produced data. This way the consumers are guaranteed to get the data in which they are interested. In a clever implementation the queries are only executed if there are data that the query is interested in. In this case no query is executed unnecessarily. The publish/subscribe technology falls into the following classes:

- Business data awareness: aware because subscriptions can query the content of the data to select interesting ones for the consumer
- Integration instance representation: instance-based because the subscriptions are executed every time the producer changes the data
- Hosting paradigm: dedicated since a subscription is specific to a producer
- Definition paradigm: declarative since subscriptions are queries defined using a declarative language in the context of the publication system
- Endpoint specificity: endpoint specific since subscriptions work only in the context of a specific publication systems
- Homogeneity: homogeneous since subscriptions work only in the context of a specific publication system
- Endpoint state awareness: aware since any change in the published data causes reevaluation of the subscriptions
- Endpoint behavior awareness: aware in the sense that data changes are observed by the subscriptions
- Invocation paradigm: synchronous in relation to the publication system. However, the invocation relationship between the publisher as well as the subscriber is asynchronous.
- Data integration: yes, since the subscriptions return data
- Process integration: no, since subscriptions do not implement a process model
- Interface integration: no, since subscriptions do not provide a user interface
- Batch integration: yes, since subscriptions run directly against the produced data

- Reliable: yes, since subscriptions remember the already processed data to continue correctly after a failure. Subscriptions recover themselves automatically after a failure.

It is not surprising that streaming queries and publish/subscribe technology are in very similar classes. This is because a streaming query can be seen as a subscription to a database and the database can be seen as the publication system. In this sense streaming queries can be used to implement a publish/subscribe system.

4.3.3 Remote Procedure Call

Remote procedure calls (RPCs) are a synchronous remote invocation mechanism where one program (client) can invoke a procedure of a remote program (server). The basic idea is to define the procedures a server exposes in an interface definition language (IDL). From this definition two pieces of program code are generated, a client as well as a server piece. The client uses the client piece to invoke a remote procedure, whereas the server uses the server piece to implement the procedure. The two pieces accomplish the remote invocation as well as the parameter marshalling that has to take place in order to serialize the parameters for transmission. The RPC can be classified as follows:

- Business data awareness: unaware because the RPC mechanism does not access the data transmitted
- Integration instance representation: instance-based because each invocation is separately created and executed
- Hosting paradigm: dedicated since two specific programs are involved in the invocation
- Definition paradigm: programmed since the RPC is a programming language concept
- Endpoint specificity: endpoint specific since the client invokes a specific procedure in a specific server
- Homogeneity: homogeneous since both, client and server are implemented in the same programming language (the original definition of RPC is followed here. Brokers like Corba allow the client and the server to be implemented in different programming languages)
- Endpoint state awareness: aware since the invocation is synchronous; if the client or the server is unavailable, no invocation can take place
- Endpoint behavior awareness: unaware since the client does not react to server behavior at all
- Invocation paradigm: synchronous since the client waits for the server response
- Data integration: no, since the RPC does not deal with data per se, it transmits data as determined by the client and the server
- Process integration: no, since the invocation is not defined as a process
- Interface integration: no, since an RPC does not provide a user interface

- Batch integration: yes, since a client and a server communicate directly on a programmatic level
- Reliable: no, since RPCs do not run in a transactional context

It would be a very interesting task to categorize all technologies that are perceived as integration technologies. However, this would not directly contribute to the B2B integration technology as defined in the following section.

4.4 Classification of Mature B2B Integration

The integration scenarios as discussed in Chap. 3 covered the spectrum of integration problems that B2B integration technology addresses. These defined B2B integration technology by presenting the relevant spectrum. In the following B2B integration is defined in terms of the classification of integration as defined in Sect. 4.3.

- Business data awareness: aware because B2B integration accesses the content in order to make decisions, like routing data to particular endpoints. Furthermore, content is accessed in order to achieve transformation from and into endpoint-specific formats.
- Integration instance representation: instance-based since every message exchange is a separate instance in the B2B integration technology in order to provide status reporting, history and manageability of ongoing integrations.
- Hosting paradigm: B2B integration technology can host any number of trading partners to support the hosting scenario. B2B integration technology is aware of the fact that several trading partners might be hosted and therefore ensures that these hosted trading partners do not share any definitions in order to provide a true hosting environment.
- Definition paradigm: declarative since this allows a uniform B2B integration execution semantics aside from other benefits, like a complete representation of integration concepts as data in a database schema.
- Endpoint specificity: B2B integration technology is open so that any type of endpoint exposing any type of interface can be integrated. There is no type of endpoint that cannot be integrated.
- Homogeneity: heterogeneous since B2B integration technology cannot assume at all that different endpoints follow the same data and behavior representation. Any form of data and/or behavior needs to be supported automatically leading to support for heterogeneity.
- Endpoint state awareness: in order to ensure consistency within and across endpoints, the B2B integration technology must be aware of endpoint state. Any state change within an endpoint needs to be recognized by B2B integration in order to react appropriately. Conversely, a B2B integration only can change states when the state change does not lead an endpoint into an inconsistent state.

- Endpoint behavior awareness: B2B integration is aware of endpoint behavior since B2B integration must ensure that messages sent by endpoints or required by endpoints are picked up or sent in the appropriate order. Otherwise the behavior requirements of endpoints would not be fulfilled.
- Invocation paradigm: synchronous as well as asynchronous support has to be provided by B2B integration technology since endpoints can follow both invocation paradigms. With the requirement of supporting all types of endpoints this is a mandatory support.
- Data integration: B2B integration does not deal with data integration.
- Process integration: each B2B integration scenario is modeled as a process.
- Interface integration: B2B integration technology does not provide user interface integration. Portal technology is an example of a more appropriate technology instead. However, portal technology can use B2B integration technology for gathering the data that need to be displayed to users through the user interface.
- Batch integration: B2B integration technology supports batch integration since all endpoints to be integrated are integrated programmatically without any user interface involvement.
- Reliable: since B2B integration technology integrates endpoints that exchange crucial business data like purchase orders, it is absolutely required that B2B integration technology is reliable. No message must be dropped or duplicated, exactly-once behavior must be guaranteed.

4.5 Summary

This classification concludes Part I. The history of B2B integration was given in Chap. 1, and an introduction to mature B2B integration technology discussed in Chap. 2. In Chap. 3 an exhaustive list of integration use cases has been provided that B2B integration technology must implement, and a classification of integration was given in this chapter to be able to classify different integration technologies. Part II specifies the B2B integration concepts in great detail, and Part III introduces the overall B2B integration technology architecture.

Part II Business-to-Business Integration Concepts

The main focus of Part II is to introduce the B2B integration concepts in great detail. As preparation, we discuss preliminaries like versioning that can be treated in isolation and independent of the integration concepts. An ideal integration world is envisioned that allows us to put the B2B integration concepts into perspective from the viewpoint of heterogeneity (which integration concepts bridge heterogeneity), and from the viewpoint of integration functionality (which integration concepts allow us to model integration). Integration concepts independent of functionality are introduced separately, and finally, the integration concepts are applied to integration itself recursively.

5 Preliminaries

The integration concepts presented in this part of the book are based on a set of assumptions and basic decisions that are covered in this chapter. This includes a versioning model, a metamodel as well as various forms of interactions between and within enterprises. The separate discussion creates the perspective in which the integration concepts must be seen. While the different preliminaries seem to be a random collection of statements at first, in fact they reduce the complexity of introducing the integration concepts later on.

5.1 B2B Integration Boundary

Any system definition must include a specification of its boundaries so that at any point it is clear what is "inside" and what is "outside" the system. The distinction is important, since only concepts that are known by the system can be supported by the system. "Outside" concepts cannot be recognized by the system and are therefore not within the system's scope.

The concepts that are recognized by a B2B integration technology are defined by its integration concepts. Consequently, they are available for modeling and execution. Those concepts that are outside the B2B integration technology system boundaries are not available as integration concepts. However, some of the outside components, like back-end application system adapters, are important for the overall understanding of B2B integration technology and later on for a working deployment of B2B integration technology. Therefore they are included in the discussion. There are two boundaries that are discussed separately, the event and process boundary and the integration logic boundary.

5.1.1 Event and Process Boundary

As introduced in Chap. 2, events are B2B integration technology internal representations of data received as messages or to be sent out as messages. The integration concept of events is B2B integration technology internal, and the concept of message is B2B integration technology external.

The interface of the B2B integration technology expects events and makes events available, therefore it is called the event interface. To be more precise, the event interface expects and returns wire events. Messages are not part of the interface definition and are unknown to the B2B integration technology.

Messages, however, are concepts that adapters implement. back-end application system adapters send and receive messages from back-end application systems, and the B2B engine sends and receives messages from trading partners. These adapters (including the B2B engine) have to process messages as part of their functionality. Adapters interface with the B2B integration technology through the event interface. Adapters therefore have to give wire events to the B2B integration technology or have to take wire events from the B2B integration technology and send them to back-end application systems or trading partners. It is their task to convert messages into wire events or to convert wire events into messages.

Messages have the connotation of being asynchronous. If a message is exchanged between an adapter and a back-end application system, then it is assumed to be asynchronous. However, synchronous exchange is also possible. No distinction is made in this book, and messages might be transferred asynchronously as well as synchronously between adapters and back-end application systems.

The B2B integration technology architecture recognizes adapters as components (Chap. 2). Without adapters it is not possible for a B2B integration technology server to actually integrate back-end application systems and trading partners. However, the internals of adapters are unknown to the B2B integration technology. It does not introspect adapters and is not able to interpret any adapter internal data structures. The B2B integration technology strictly complies to its event interface and does not go beyond it. Consequently, the integration model does not contain any adapter internal concepts, while the B2B integration technology architecture itself recognizes adapters as components.

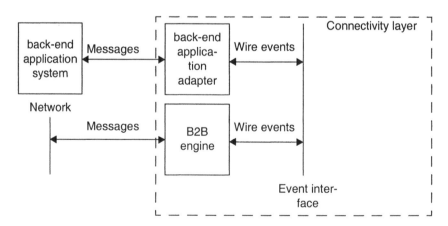

Fig. 5.1. Event and behavior boundary

Events are B2B integration technology internal data that exist and are processed in a process context as shown in Chap. 2. These process contexts are business processes as well as interface processes bound by process bindings. All of these are B2B integration technology internal concepts that can be modeled and executed.

Any processes that are defined and executed within adapters like back-end application system adapters or the B2B engine are not part of the B2B integration technology's integration concepts and are outside the B2B integration technology. This follows the same boundaries as events and messages.

Figure 5.1 shows the boundary graphically with one back-end application adapter and one B2B engine. Adapters are part of the connectivity layer, as shown in Chap. 2, and connect to the event interface within the connectivity layer, which is indicated by the dashed box.

Having defined the event and process boundaries this way does not mean that this is the only way these boundaries can be defined. It is possible to make all adapter internal concepts part of the integration concepts of the B2B integration technology. However, adapters have to deal with such a huge variety of differences in back-end application system interfaces as well as B2B protocol specifics like security and transport that the effort to create integration concepts for this variety is quite significant. The model would probably look more like a programming language than a set of integration concepts. The question arises whether it is more appropriate to implement this variety through a programming language in adapters rather than to define integration concepts for these and build an interpreter that can interpret the integration concepts. Being able to deal with this variety in terms of adapter implementations is by far easier and more appropriate, hence the presented boundary definitions.

5.1.2 Integration Logic Boundary

The other important boundary is the integration logic boundary. This interface is implemented by the integration logic layer as introduced in Chap. 2. It allows the user interface to access the B2B integration technology in order to populate the system with integration definitions. Example integration logic interfaces are creating, updating and deleting process definitions as well as event definitions. In addition, it can access run-time data for various purposes like administration and monitoring. Example interfaces for this purpose are retrieving process instances as well as event instances.

In analogy to adapters, the integration concepts of a B2B integration technology server do not provide concepts that are relevant within the (graphical) user interface itself like screen layout or positions of objects on the screen. However, it recognizes the user interface as an architectural component that accesses the integration interface in order to provide users access to the B2B integration technology.

Figure 5.2 shows the integration logic boundary. The dashed boxes show the user interface layer as well as the integration logic layer or the B2B integration technology architecture. The interface shown is the integration logic interface accessed by the user interface internal logic. Two example operations are shown, one for updating a process definition and one for retrieving event instances.

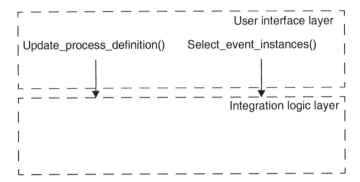

Fig. 5.2. Integration logic boundary

In summary, the integration concepts will not contain adapter internal or user interface internal concepts. It assumes that the internals of those components are invisible to it. The event and process boundary as well as the integration logic boundary ensure this from an architectural viewpoint. The integration concepts that are defined in Chap. 7 therefore focus on the integration concepts within these boundaries.

5.2 Instance, Type and Metatype

All elements within the B2B integration technology follow the instance–type–metatype hierarchy. Instances are instance-of of types, which are instance-of of metatypes. The relationship is called instance-of. Instances represent "real" entities like specific trading partners or ongoing integration processes. Types define the integration model elements in a particular deployment like a PO–POA process of an enterprise. Metatypes implement the integration concepts for defining types and are given by the B2B integration technology in the form of a conceptual model. In contrast, types are defined by the enterprise that deploys B2B integration technology. This ensures that the semantics of each element is clearly defined according to this hierarchy. Figure 5.3 shows the hierarchy as well as an example with process concepts.

The conceptual model of the B2B integration technology is the set of all metatypes. Types as well as instances are dynamically introduced either by user interfaces or by message exchanges. The results of modeling are the types as well as some instances like trading partners. The results of message exchanges are event instances as well as process instances created for processing event instances.

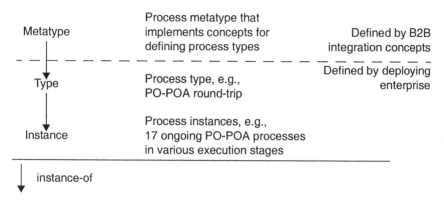

Fig. 5.3. Instance–type–metatype hierarchy

5.2.1 Instance

Instances represent "real" objects like a particular trading partner or a particular business process. Instances are of a particular type. For example, a trading partner instance representing the Oracle Corporation is of type trading partner. An instance representing the purchasing of a Boeing 747 aircraft is of type PO–POA. Any number of instances can exist that are of a type, including none. No instance can exist if there is not a type defined.

Instances fall into two categories. First are those that have to be explicitly created, for example, by a user with the modeling user interface. A prominent example is trading partner instance data like the name, unique identifier and additional attributes of a trading partner. The other instances are those that are created automatically. For example, if a purchase order message arrives in a B2B engine, then the B2B engine needs to instantiate an appropriate wire event instance corresponding to this message. In this case the wire event instance was created by the B2B integration technology without human user involvement.

This distinction is noteworthy for the clarification that instances can come into existence in many ways.

5.2.2 Type

Types are introduced by integration modelers by the deploying enterprise. Integration modelers are user roles that are assumed by employees who are chartered with building an integration model so that the enterprise can start conducting message exchanges to implement integration.

Types specify structure as well as behavior. For example, defining event types results in a structural definition. Based on this structure, event instances can be created. Defining process types results in a structural as well as behavioral definition. A process type builds a structure by defining process step types that build a hierarchical decomposition hierarchy. A process type builds a behavioral definition, since an execution sequence of process step types is defined that has to be obeyed during process instance execution.

As instances are of a particular type, types are of a particular metatype. Types can only be created for the metatypes defined by the B2B integration technology. Furthermore, the metatypes constrain the particular construction of types (see Sect. 5.2.3). This means that the semantics of integration models are defined by the metatypes since no arbitrary types can be introduced but only those allowed by the metatypes.

5.2.3 Metatype

Metatypes define the semantics of the B2B integration technology system. This includes the structural semantics that defines the valid data structures like events, as well as the behavioral semantics that defines valid behaviors like processes.

Metatypes are not introduced dynamically by integration modelers but are fixed as part of the B2B integration technology and cannot be modified (except by the programmers of a particular B2B integration technology implementation for a particular software release). This ensures that all types that are going to be defined by integration modelers are defined according to these metatypes and have the same consistent structural and behavioral semantics.

For example, the process metatype defines the structure of all valid process types. The process metatype defines that process types have a name, that they contain none, one or more process step types that constitute the hierarchical decomposition, and that they have control flow between the process step types, among other parts. A definition of a particular process type like the PO–POA process must follow the process metatype definition and consequently must have a name, none, one or more process step types as well as control flow between them. In this sense a metatype constrains the construction of a type and ensures the intended semantics.

Chapter 7 introduces the metatypes for the integration concepts. Based on these, integration modelers can create the integration model for their enterprise over time.

5.2.4 Early and Late Binding

Types are not created in isolation but refer to each other. In many cases these are part-of relationships, but in addition there are reuse relationships. A reuse relationship is a relationship between two types whereby one type reuses another, already existing type. In order to define a complete type, all its parts and all its reuse relationships have to be specified.

At run time, instances are created according to a type. It is possible to create instances for all parts of a type as well as all reuse relationships for a type at the time when the type is instantiated. For example, when a process instance is created all its process step instances and all the control flow instances are created (among other elements). After all the instances are created, the execution of the process instance starts. This early instantiation is called early binding. All instances are created as early as possible, even if it is not known whether they will ever be used. A conditional branching in a process at this point leaves out those process step instances at run time that are in the path where the condition evaluates to false. While this is a possible binding model, it creates unnecessary instances and is therefore wasting resources. Late binding, however, creates only those instances that are necessary to continue with the execution. For example, when a process instance is created, none of the process step instances are created until the processing of the process instance starts. Only then are process step instances created and then only one by one. This late binding avoids the creation of instance that are unnecessary. Late binding is an important prerequisite for dynamic type changes, as discussed in Sect. 5.2.5.

5.2.5 Dynamic Type Change

Modeling decisions might become invalid at some point in time, and the integration model needs to be changed in order to address the invalidity. For example, an event type has to be changed in order to accommodate two more fields containing business data.

When a new version of an existing type is created, then this is called a static type change. A new version of a type does not affect any already existing instances of that type, since the new version does not affect its prior version. However, this might not be desirable. For example, it might be necessary to change the event type definition to accommodate two more fields and have all existing ongoing process instances use the changed type definition (i.e., the new version of it). With the concept of late binding this is a possibility. The change of a type that is used by ongoing instances is called dynamic type change.

While dynamic type change is desirable in many situations, a dynamic type change can easily compromise the instance consistency of the affected instances. For example, in the opposite case where two fields are removed from an event type, the impact becomes obvious. If the business process includes a conditional branching that accesses one or both of the removed fields, the business process will fail as soon as the condition in the conditional branching is executed. It is very easy to compromise instance consistency.

In the given example it is easy to detect the potential problem. It is possible to check if all fields of an event are available that are going to be accessed by any business logic in the business process. However, such a check (fundamentally based on impact analysis) is not always possible. For example, if the order of two sequential process steps is reversed, it might be the case that ongoing instances will not execute one of the two steps at all, namely those instances that have already executed the first of the two steps but not yet the second. After the reversal, these instances have already executed the first step and continue.

While dynamic type changes are an important functionality in running systems, dynamic change has to be done very carefully by a modeler and can lead into inconsistencies that will not be detected by the B2B integration technology automatically. So the modeler has to be very careful with dynamic type changes.

5.2.6 My Instance is Your Type

While the purpose and the relationship of metatypes, types and instances is very clear and precise, one often hears the statement "my instance is your type." Fundamentally, this says that an instance exposes the same meaning as a type. While in the above description this is by construction not possible (a type and an instance are in the instance-of relationship), the statement exposes some underlying confusion that needs clarification.

The three layers introduced on the conceptual level of integration have to find their equivalence in the implementation of a B2B integration technology architecture. Fundamentally, metatypes, types and instances have to be implemented so that instances can be created after a modeler specifies the corresponding types.

In order to implement a B2B integration technology architecture several implementation technologies like object-oriented programming languages or relational database management systems might be used. Each of these implementation technologies has its own conceptual model. Some of them also follow the metatype–type–instance model. For example, the programming language Java [Java] allows programmers to implement classes that can be instantiated at run time of Java programs.

The construction of Java classes has to follow the way Java defines classes. In order to constrain how classes are defined, there must be the equivalent of a metatype in Java. This ensures that programmers only define classes that conform to the metatype as defined in Java. Metatypes in Java cannot be changed since they define (together with the run-time system of Java) the semantics of this programming language.

If the task at hand is to implement a B2B integration technology architecture, then this means (besides other things) to implement the integration concepts. Since these are defined in terms of metatypes, those have to be implemented. If Java is chosen as a programming language, then the only relevant concept that can be defined in Java are classes. Metaclasses are not a concept defined by Java that can be specified or changed by programmers. One possibility is that an integration metatype will be implemented as a Java class. Here precisely is an occurence of te case stated above, namely, that two seemingly different levels implement the same semantics. A class in Java implements an integration metatype.

However, that is not true because both, the Java class and the integration metatype are not comparable. Instead, the Java class implements the integration metatype. The Java class concept and the integration metatype concept are not comparable since they are concepts of two different systems (the Java language system versus the B2B integration technology system). After this implementation the integration metatype is still an integration metatype, and the Java class is still a Java class. Each has to be viewed in its respective system. The relationship between the two is not an equivalence relationship on a conceptual level, but an implements relationship between two different systems on an implementation level.

The implementation of an integration metatype by a Java class is not all that requires discussion at this point. Integration types also have to be represented (like the PO–POA process), as well as integration instances (like a particular process instance of type PO–POA). If an integration metatype is implemented by a Java class, then the instances of this Java class are the implementation of integration types. An integration modeler who wants to model an integration type will cause an instance of the Java class that corresponds to the integration metatype of the integration type. Once the Java instance is created, it represents the integration type. As the modeler adds details to the integration type (for example, like adding process step types), implicitly the Java instance will be modified to accommodate the details. Once the integration modeler decides that the modeling is done, the Java instance needs to become persistent since integration types are persistent, too.

Once the integration modeler is satisfied with the integration types, they should be ready for instantiation. For example, if a message is received by the B2B integration technology, a process instance gets created that processes the corresponding wire event. However, the question is to which concept in Java does an integration instance correspond like a process instance? It is not possible to instantiate the Java instance that implements the integration process type, since an instance in Java is at the leaf level of the instantiation hierarchy. Obviously, another Java class needs to be created that can be instantiated and allows for creating integration instances like process instances. There could be a Java class for each integration type, but these are already represented by Java instances. Alternatively, one Java class can be created that can execute all integration process instances of all integration types. This latter approach is preferable since this Java class that implements the instantiation of integration instances is fixed and does not have to be modified as integration modelers introduce new integration types.

Figure 5.4 shows the overall situation that was described. An integration metatype is implemented by a Java class. An integration type is implemented by a Java instance. The behavior of the integration type is implemented by another Java class, and an integration instance is implemented by a Java instance.

From here on the implementation strategy is not addressed further.. There might very well be other ways to implement the integration concepts in specific implementation technologies. The fact is that most implementation technologies do not support a one-to-one correspondence between the metatype–type–instance hierarchy of the integration concepts and the implementation technology concepts. Some kind of mapping between these levels has to be accomplished.

In the following, all definitions and discussions take place solely in the three levels of integration concepts. Therefore the mapping problem to implementation technologies is not referred to any more.

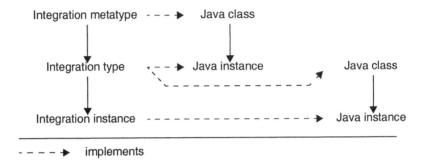

- - - - ▸   implements

Fig. 5.4. Correspondence between Java and the metatype–type–instance hierarchy of the integration concepts

5.3 Version, Variant and Configuration

Changes to existing integration types in an integration model are sometimes necessary because of changed integration requirements. For example, it might be necessary to remove two fields from an event type definition because the corresponding message will no longer carry these two fields because of a change in a trading partner's system. A possibility is to update the integration types whenever necessary. For example, the event type would be updated, overwriting the existing definition with a new one thus removing the two fields. However, there are several problems with this approach. First, there might be instances of integration types created that are still processed. For those instances the integration type would not be consistent any more, hence they would become inconsistent with respect to their event type. Second, a change in an integration type might make another integration type inconsistent. For example, if a business process type refers to one of the two fields that are going to be removed, business process instances of that type are going to fail because the fields that they expect in the event instance are not available.

In order to deal with both problems of integration type modification, i.e., already existing integration instances as well as integration type inconsistencies, the concepts of versions, variants and configurations are briefly introduced and discussed.

5.3.1 Version

Each integration type that is modeled by an integration modeler receives a version number. Version numbers increase so that each subsequent change of an integration type receives a higher version number. Through this approach the order of changes to an integration type can be reconstructed. Not every single change to an integration type necessarily leads to a new version of that type. Modelers who change integration types have to explicitly state when they are finished applying changes. Only then does the new version of the integration type become visible and can be referred to by other types. This means that a major change as well as a minor change can be accomplished within a single version, if necessary. Once a new version is created, the previous version cannot be changed any more. This ensures that there is only one version of a given type in the system that can be modified.

Versions are nonoverlapping, that is, a new version can only be created based on the immediately preceding version. It is not possible to create two subsequent versions from a given one (i.e., no branching is possible).

The concept of versions addresses one of the two integration type modification problems stated above. A change of an integration type leads to a new version of it. The version number becomes an identifying element of integration types. Instances of integration types always refer to an integration type and its version number. This way, a new version will not affect existing instances of integration types.

5.3.2 Configuration and Change Propagation

Different integration types progress in terms of their versions at different paces. Some integration types might change often, while others are more stable. In general, integration types refer to each other. For example, a business process type refers to a business event type that it processes.

In a versioned environment a more precise relationship is necessary. A version of an integration type must refer to a version of another integration type. For example, version 2 of a process type refers to version 17 of a business event type. This is necessary since not every version of one type fits with every version of another type. For example, if a business process accesses a business event element to evaluate a conditional branching, then the business process is no longer consistent once the element is removed from the business event. In this case the version of the business process no longer works with the new version of the event type.

There are two ways to express this more precise relationship. First, a direct version relationship has a version of an integration type refer to a version of another integration type. The type definition internally refers to versions of other integration types. Second, an indirect version relationship is possible. This means that integration types do not refer to versions of other integration types, but only to their names without indicating a specific version. An additional concept specifies the precise version outside the integration type itself. This separate concept is called a configuration. A configuration specifies which particular version of an integration type refers to another version of an integration type, whereas the integration types themselves only refer to each other independently of their versions. Figure 5.5 shows a direct version relationship, and Fig. 5.6 shows an indirect version relationship. Both figures use a pseudolanguage, and the keywords of this language are in bold.

business_process_type PO-POA **version** 2

   ...

   business_event: PO **version** 17;

   ...

end_business_process_type

business_event_type PO **version** 17

   ...

end_business_event_type

Fig. 5.5. Direct version relationship

business_process_type PO-POA **version** 2

   ...

   business_event: PO;

   ...

end_business_process_type

business_event_type PO **version** 17

   ...

end_business_event_type

configuration
  business_process_type PO-POA **version** 2
  business_event_type PO **version** 17
end_configuration

Fig. 5.6. Indirect version relationship

Figure 5.5 shows that the specific version of a business process type refers to a specific version of a business event type. Figure 5.6 shows that neither the business process type nor the business event type refer to versions of each other. The business process type only refers to the name of the business event type, however, without referring to its version. Instead, the configuration relates the specific version of the business process type to the specific version of the business event type.

Every time a new version of an integration type is created, the question arises whether the existing integration types that refer to the previous version of the changed integration type (referring integration type) need to refer to the new version in order to remain consistent. If a referring integration type has to refer to the new changed version, it itself will change since the relationship changes from the old to the new version. This is the case for the direct version relationship since the version number is explicitly included in the referring integration type. Consequently, its version has to change. If it has a referring integration type, then this might have to change, too. Changes might easily lead to a cascading effect until all the changes are accommodated. This is called version change propagation.

In the indirect version relationship approach the behavior might be different. If a referring integration type does not have to change when a referred-to integration type changes, then only a new configuration has to be introduced. This new configuration has the same version of the referring integration type refer to the new version of the changed integration type.

In the direct as well as the indirect version relationship approach these changes have to be accommodated. Figure 5.7 and Fig. 5.8 show the result after a change of the business event type. Both figures show a new version of the business event type and a new version of the business process type. The decision was made that the business process type needs to refer to the new version of the event type, hence the new version of the business process type. First, the business event was changed to version 18. Consequently, the business process type has to refer to the new version in this example and must itself advance to version 3 in order to refer to version 18 of the business event type.

business_process_type PO-POA **version** 3
  ...
  business_event: PO version 18;
  ...
end_business_process_type

business_event_type PO **version** 18
  ...
end_business_event_type

Fig. 5.7. Direct version relationship after a change

business_process_type PO-POA **version** 3
  ...
  business_event: PO;
  ...
end_business_process_type

business_event_type PO **version** 18
  ...
end_business_event_type

configuration
  business_process_type PO-POA **version** 3
  business_event_type PO **version** 18
end_configuration

Fig. 5.8. Indirect version relationship after a change

As discussed before, just incrementing the version number on the business process type might not be sufficient. It might be necessary to change its definition. For example, if two fields are deleted from the event type, then the new version of the business process needs to be changed in such a way that it no longer refers to the two deleted fields. Fundamentally, the involved types have to match to avoid introducing inconsistencies.

Configuration addresses the second of the integration type modification problems. Any change can be accommodated by propagating the change causing new versions of referring types. This means that potential inconsistencies that would arise without change propagation are avoided. Existing versions of types will not become inconsistent because a new version of an integration type is introduced. This is a very desirable property because it guarantees that existing instances that are running will not be affected by a new version.

5.3.3 Dynamic Change

The versioning and configuration approach discussed so far relates the types and their referring types to each other and makes sure that the versions are correct. Every change of a type results into a new version, potentially resulting in a change propagation if the new version of the type needs to be picked up by the referring types.

The dynamic type change discussion in Sect. 5.2.5 suggested that types can be changed for existing instances in order to pick up changes immediately, not only for newly created instances. This in turn requires that existing versions of types are changed in place so that an instance can pick up the changes immediately. This contradicts the very nice property pointed out earlier that new versions (i.e., changes) do not affect existing versions of types. Furthermore, a type change in place might affect all instances of that type, not only those that should pick up the change immediately (which are not necessarily all instances). The question is how to resolve this contradiction. The need for a resolution is apparent since both changes in place as well as changes not affecting existing types are desirable to have.

The fundamental idea is the following. Any change made to types results in a new version, and this might cause change propagation. This approach remains as described before. However, if the new version of a type should be picked up by an existing instance, then the version of the instance's type should not be changed. This can be achieved by an instance-specific configuration using the indirect configuration approach. An instance-specific configuration will be created for those instances that should pick up the change immediately. In those instance-specific configurations, the referring type remains in its version, however, the types that it refers to might be advanced to the version of the changed type. Of course, for this approach to work the execution model must be late binding, as discussed before.

Figure 5.9 shows an example. In this case the business process type remains in its version, however, it refers to the new version of the event type. This should only be applicable for those instances listed in the configuration after the keyword "for_instances." The numbers after the keyword are instance identifiers. Once the instances are finished executing, the instance-specific configuration no longer has any effect.

business_process_type PO-POA **version 2**
　...
　business_event: PO;
　...
end_business_process_type

business_event_type PO **version 18**
　...
end_business_event_type

configuration
　for_instances 3, 7, 14
　business_process_type PO-POA **version 2**
　business_event_type PO **version 18**
end_configuration

Fig. 5.9. Instance-specific configuration

Earlier it became very clear that type changes in place are difficult because of the inconsistencies they can introduce resulting in an inconsistent system state. As the example in Fig. 5.9 shows, the same version of a business process type refers to a new version of a business event type. If this does not introduce an inconsistent type definition, then the approach of an instance-specific configuration is sufficient.

If any mismatch exists, this configuration will lead to an inconsistent state. This means that the business process type itself might require changes in order to address this mismatch. An example for this case was discussed early in Sect. 5.3 where removing two fields from the business event type causes conditions to become inconsistent referring to those fields. In order to achieve this, a copy of the business process can be made specifically for those instances, and it can be modified. This is called an instance-specific integration type. Since this specific type is for specific instances only, it is invisible to all other instances. Furthermore, this specific copy of the type is not available for general use in configurations.

Figure 5.10 shows an example where an instance-specific integration type of the business process type is shown. The same keyword is used as for instance-specific configurations. The instance-specific integration type is for two particular instances. However, the configuration refers to three instances. This means that the business event type is specific to only those two instances mentioned. The third instance continues to use the general version of the business process type.

business_process_type PO-POA **version** 2
  for_instances 3, 7
  ...
  business_event: PO;
  ...
end_business_process_type

business_event_type PO **version** 18
  ...
end_business_event_type

configuration
  for_instances 3, 7, 14
  business_process_type PO-POA **version** 2
  business_event_type PO **version** 18
end_configuration

Fig. 5.10. Instance-specific integration type

In summary, accommodating dynamic type changes for integration instances is achievable by instance-specific configurations and potentially instance-specific type changes. This provides the desirable property that instance-specific changes are scoped by the instances and therefore limited to those instances. Once the instances are finished with execution, the specific changes no longer have any impact. The introduction of the integration concepts will completely abstract from versioning and configuration requirements since all the concepts fit the version and configuration approach as introduced.

5.3.4 Singular Version

Some instances represent real-world entities like trading partners. An interesting question is what it would mean to have several versions of such instances, since they might contain different values for the same property. For example, if the address of a trading partner changes, then this results into a new version of this trading partner. The previous version would not be accurate any more. Fundamentally, two consequences have to follow. First, every type referring to the previous version of the trading partner has to refer to the new version to use the new address. Second, all existing references (through already existing instances like business process instances) have to be dynamically changed so that the running instances immediately pick up the new values.

This category of instances is called singular versions since only one version is valid at given point in time. If a version is marked as a singular version, then the two consequences can be enforced automatically by the B2B integration technology.

An important note has to be made here. The discussion of versioning and configuration took place in the context of integration types. However, there are integration instances like trading partners (or endpoints in general) that are created and managed manually, i.e., not created automatically by arriving events. Those instances can be subject to versioning and configuration, too, as the example just given indicates. All statements made above with respect to versioning and configuration apply to those instances, too.

5.3.5 Variant

In the context of versioning and configuration the notion of variants is sometimes mentioned. Variants of an object are concurrently valid versions of an object that have a common version as their predecessor. This constitutes a branch in the version sequence. Variants are two different and separate changes of the same previous version. In that sense they can be viewed as two separate concurrent specializations of the previous version. In context of B2B integration technology this means that two specializations of integration types (or instances) are created.

This approach has the deficiency that the fact that two versions are variants of each other is not specified in the integration type itself, but has to be derived from the configuration data. This is not very practical since the integration modeler has to keep this in mind.

If specialization has to be supported, a much better approach is to explicitly provide the concept of specialization (or subtyping) for integration types. Sometimes the concept of specialization is called inheritance. In this case the specialization is explicitly modeled as a property of an integration type. Furthermore, the specializations are versioned independently of each other. As a consequence, variants do not have to be supported any more and the integration modeler does not have to remember the variant structure himself. Bussler (2002b) introduces process subtyping, or process inheritance, as one example of how to explicitly denote the subtyping of processes.

5.4 Public and Private Behavior

The integration concepts explicitly distinguish public and private behavior as introduced in Chap. 2. In the following this is repeated to enforce the idea.

5.4.1 Public Process

Endpoints exhibit behavior in the form of sending messages and receiving messages. The processing of those messages that takes place within the endpoint is not visible from the outside the endpoint. In order to establish consistent communication between the endpoints it is essential that both endpoints understand how the other endpoint behaves so that the behavior of both endpoints match.

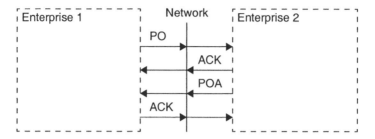

Fig. 5.11. Message exchanges between two endpoints

Figure 5.11 shows four messages exchanges between two endpoints as an example. From each endpoint's view, the opposite endpoint has complementary behavior. If one endpoint expects a message, the other endpoint has to send one, and vice versa. Furthermore, the order of the messages has to match. A specific message has to be exchanged at a specific point in the sequence.

Message exchanges can be modeled as processes. These are referred to as public processes because the endpoints can exchange these in order to let each other know what their behavior is going to be. Public processes are implemented by the integration concept of interface processes. One approach is to model the message exchange in one process; the other is to model the message exchange in two interface processes.

If interface processes are modeled in the form of one process, it must be clearly defined what process steps are to be executed by which of the endpoints. Figure 5.12 shows an example that models the message exchange shown in Fig. 5.11. Each process step is marked with endpoint 1 or endpoint 2 in order to denote which endpoint has to execute the process step.

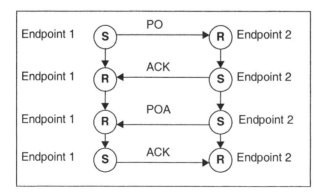

Fig. 5.12. One interface process for two endpoints

Figure 5.13 shows the same example, however, modeled as two different interface processes. The behavior is precisely the same, but the steps are explicitly separated by belonging to either one of the two processes that are marked with endpoint 1 or endpoint 2.

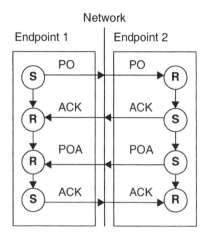

Fig. 5.13. Two interface processes for two endpoints

While the representation in one process is preferable because the behavior of the two endpoints match by construction, the representation as two different interface processes is more commonly used. Therefore the latter case is the one supported by the integration concepts.

At execution time when message are exchanged, it is expected that the endpoints comply to their interface processes. Any deviation would be regarded as error and treated as such. Error handling will be discussed in detail in Sect.7.9 in the context of the integration concepts.

None of the process steps in either case refers to anything other than the message exchange behavior that is publicly visible. Behavior that is private to the endpoint is modeled separately in private processes.

5.4.2 Private Process

Private processes specify the endpoint-internal processing of events (B2B integration technology internal representations of messages). These processes are called private since they are, in general, not exposed outside the endpoint. Private processes are implemented by the integration concept of business processes. In many cases the business processes implement the enterprise's behavior, which is generally considered important competitive knowledge that requires protection.

The integration concepts available to model business processes are the same as those for interface processes. Figure 5.14 shows a simple example (from Chap. 2).

In terms of an analogy with abstract data types and information hiding, interface processes can be seen as an interface description and business processes can be viewed as the implementation of interface processes.

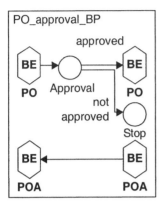

Fig. 5.14. Example of a business process

In programming languages that make the explicit distinction between an interface and its implementation, different language constructs are available to specify both. Through name equivalence, the correct implementation for an interface can be selected. This is where the analogy fails in the context of interface and business processes. Interface processes are bound by an explicit integration concept called process binding rather than through a naming convention, since different business processes can be bound to the same interface process. For example, there might be several business processes specifying different buying processes (like through direct buying, auctions or marketplaces). However, all of them at some point exchange purchase orders and purchase order acknowledgements, i.e., use the same interface process for this activity.

5.4.3 Process Binding

Since business processes and interface processes are independent self-contained type definitions, they need to be bound together so that events obtained from interface processes can be passed on to business processes, and vice versa. The process binding between business processes and interface processes has to fulfill two tasks. First, it needs to relate every event coming from a business process to the equivalent one in the interface process, and vice versa. This is done by either a direct mapping or one that involves transformation between the different event types, as shown in Chap. 2. Second, if events are coming from one of the processes that the other one does not need, the process binding needs to consume those events. The same is true for the opposite case. An event required by a process not coming from the other one has to be generated so that the process is satisfied (Fig. 5.15). Only the events passed between the processes are shown, not the internal process implementations.

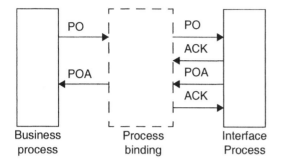

Fig. 5.15. Process binding consuming and producing events

As Fig. 5.15 shows, the interface process produces and consumes four events, whereas the business process only produces and consumes two events. The process binding has to make sure that each of the processes' expectations is met and has to consume the first acknowledgment and produce the second acknowledgment.

5.4.4 Schematic Overall Process Layout

A given private process (business process) that communicates with endpoints has to be bound to an interface process for each endpoint. For each interface process there is a process binding that binds the business process to the interface process. Figure 5.16 shows a general layout that is the pattern that applies to all integration models developed by an integration modeler involving a business process.

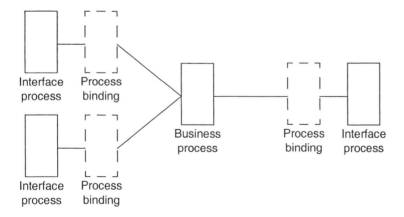

Fig. 5.16. Schematic overall process layout

Figure 5.16 shows the relationships between the different types of processes schematically without showing any events between the processes or any implementation within the processes. One business process and three interface processes are related.

5.5 Interaction Between Enterprises

In business-to-business interactions, two or more enterprises communicate with each other. In the end, the business data needs to be transported over the network and processed within the business processes. Several different characteristics of interenterprise interaction are discussed in the following: synchronous as well as asynchronous invocations and behavior, conversations and direct as well as indirect communication. These three characteristics are orthogonal to each other, and any combination can be found in reality.

5.5.1 Synchronous vs. Asynchronous Invocation and Behavior

Invocation is distinguished from behavior. An invocation example is the message exchange between the B2B engines of the endpoints. For example, the transport of a message over HTTP is an invocation. The sending of a message over SMTP is another invocation. Invocations are the transport of a message over a network protocol like HTTP, SMTP or FTP. Behavior, in contrast, is the representation of an invocation in the interface process. For example, a send step causes a message to be sent. That send step might either wait for the response message to come back (in case there is a response), or does not wait for it. Instead, a subsequent receive step will receive the response. How invocations relate to behavior is discussed in the following.

Synchronous invocations are distinguished from asynchronous invocations. Synchronous invocations establish a direct control flow relationship between the invoker and the invoked component whereby the invoker is blocked until the invoked is done with processing. In the context of B2B integration, both the invoker and the invoked are the B2B engines (or the transport components, to be more precise, see Chap. 2.3.3). During the invocation, a message can be passed from the invoker to the invoked, and the invoked can send a message back to the invoker in the same synchronous invocation. However, this is not necessary. It is possible that the invoked does not send a message back to the invoker at all. This behavior is a client/server behavior whereby the client invokes the server and is blocked until the server is done with processing. HTTP is a popular synchronous invocation mechanism available for invocations over the Internet. FTP is another synchronous invocation mechanism. Only when the files are stored in the receiver's file system is the FTP invoker unblocked.

Asynchronous invocations do not establish a control flow between the invoker and the invoked. Instead, the invoker sends a message asynchronously and does not wait for a response to come back. The transport mechanism forwards messages to the invoked (receiver). The receiver at some point in time receives the message asynchronously to the invoker. SMTP as well as VANs (value-added networks) are popular mechanisms for this. In case the invoked needs to send back a response, it can send it back asynchronously as a separate message.

However, the invoked can also use synchronous invocations to send back a message. In general, an invoker as well as an invoked can use several transports for message exchanges; they do not have to be limited to only a specific one.

Like invocations, behavior can be synchronous as well as asynchronous. A send step in an interface process can be synchronous. This means that it sends a message and waits for a response message to come back. To be precise, interface processes deal with wire events, not with messages. A wire event that is sent by a send step in an interface process needs to be converted to a message, and then the invocation has to take place. A synchronous send step waits for the response event to come back. The underlying transport, however, can be synchronous as well as asynchronous. In the synchronous case the response message comes back in the same synchronous invocation, and the corresponding wire event is handed back to the send step. In the asynchronous invocation case, the transport sends the message asynchronously and waits for an asynchronous invocation to receive the response message. Only then is the response wire event given back to the synchronous send step.

An asynchronous send step sends the message and does not wait for a response. Instead, a subsequent receive step waits for a response to come back (if no response is coming back, no receive step would have been specified). The invocation can be synchronous as well as asynchronous in this case, too.

In summary, synchronous as well as asynchronous behavior is defined in terms of sending and receiving wire events. The sending and receiving of wire events can be accomplished by synchronous as well as asynchronous invocation. Since messages are outside the scope of the integration concepts, the mapping of sending or receiving steps to synchronous or asynchronous transport invocations is not further discussed in the context of integration concepts.

5.5.2 Immediate and Delayed Behavior

Wire events to be sent out can be sent out as soon as possible. This means that as soon as a wire event is raised, it is picked up by the communication layer and sent to the specified endpoint. However, sometimes endpoints specify the time range, such as hours per day or days per week, when they are expecting messages. Outside these time ranges they will not accept messages. Therefore it must be possible to delay the sending of wire events according to the endpoints' requirements.

The same is true for the opposite case. If wire events are received they do not need to be processed immediately. Instead, they can be left unprocessed until a specific time arrives. The hosted trading partner can configure this. Alternatively, messages can be rejected instead of received. This is the case where the hosted trading partner is very strict about the times it is willing to accept incoming wire events.

Of course, in the synchronous invocation approach the synchronous invocation cannot be held until the endpoint is willing to receive the data. In this case an error message must be returned if the endpoint is not willing to receive the data at this point in time.

5.5.3 Conversation

Invocations caused by sending or receiving steps of interface processes are singular one-way invocations or request/response invocations involving two messages. In most B2B scenarios, several related invocations take place that have to be executed in a specific order. Interface processes support the specification of these multiple related invocations by being able to sequence sending as well as receiving steps within one interface process.

An interface process that causes several invocations with another endpoint is sometimes called a conversation. Both endpoints' behavior is specified as an interface process. This is in contrast to client/server invocations, where only the server is defined in terms of the interface it provides. The interface is usually defined through an interface definition language. The client's behavior, however, is not explicitly represented through any interface definition language.

5.5.4 Direct vs. Indirect Communication

Two endpoints can directly communicate with each other through invocations that are composed to conversations by interface processes. Direct communication means that there is not another endpoint like a hub between the two communication endpoints. This is commonly referred to as peer-to-peer communication.

Indirect communication means that there is a hub. If one endpoint sends a message to a hub, the hub in turn forwards the message to the final destination, i.e., the other endpoint. Both endpoints are aware of the hub and have to specify the addressing of messages accordingly. From an interface process viewpoint, however, the hub appears like an endpoint. This is the case because both the endpoint and the hub have to execute invocations according to the interface processes. From an integration modeler viewpoint the hub is treated as an endpoint.

5.5.5 Interaction Scope

Implicit in all discussions about communication between endpoints is the assumption that there is no need for introspecting the endpoint itself beyond the publicly exposed behavior. In most cases there is no ability or authorization, either. Endpoints usually make sure that only the public process is visible to other endpoints, but not how the public processes are implemented. Consequently, no public process provides an introspection message that would allow inquiries about the state of the business process or any subsequent endpoint to which the business process is connected.

In general, this means that in a supply chain scenario, the supply chain partners only communicate with their direct neighbors in the chain, and not beyond. It is therefore impossible to inquire about the overall supply chain status. However, in principle, it is possible to define inquiry messages and to provide public processes that support the sending and receiving of inquiry messages.

For the B2B integration technology this does not have any impact. If an enterprise decides to support inquiry messages, then those have to be specified, and the public processes have to support their sending and receiving. From a B2B integration technology viewpoint, there is no distinction from messages containing business data.

Alternatively, a set of interoperating trading partners could agree on a centralized communication model wherein one of them is the central coordinator (like a hub). In this case all communication between any two trading partners is done through the hub. Therefore the overall status of the invocation is available at any time since the business processes in the hub can expose their state. For example, any trading partner involved in a supply chain can inquire about the overall state at any time (provided that the inquiry messages are implemented by the hub).

Continuing this thought, it might possible that one trading partner communicates with several hubs. In this case it knows about several hubs without the hubs necessarily knowing about each other. This situation only supports the inquiry of the overall communication status in context of one hub, not across hubs. If the hubs are aware of each other, they could exchange inquiry message themselves and could give an overall status of the overall communication.

5.6 Interaction Within Enterprises

Fundamentally, there is no difference between the communication between enterprises (interenterprise communication) and the communication within enterprises (intra-enterprise communication). In both cases invocation and behavior have to be distinguished.

A slight difference, however, exists in the transactional behavior of communication with endpoints that are within enterprises. Intra-enterprise communication can be transactional, in contrast to interenterprise communication, where the communication cannot be transactional due to the nontransactional networks. It is possible to invoke back-end application systems under transaction control (if they provide a transactional interface). Since this is a possibility, transaction boundaries have to be managed in interface processes that connect to back-end application systems. Furthermore, several invocations can be grouped within one transaction.

5.6.1 Function Integration

When several back-end application systems are invoked under transaction control and are under the control of one transaction, then all of the invocations succeed or none of them succeed. This is called function integration. Since function integration relies on transactions, an all-or-nothing effect is achieved at the back-end application systems as well as at the B2B integration technology.

Normal atomar, consistent, isolated and durable (ACID) database transactions are, in general, not sufficient since the back-end application systems have their own databases and as does the B2B integration technology. This requires distributed transactions that allow the coordination of several resource managers such as databases (Gray and Reuter 1993).

Function integration is a very handy way to call back-end application systems, since this reduces the amount of compensation effort compared to the case where the back-end application systems are called sequentially in separate transactions. As soon as one fails in the latter case, all the already committed transactions have to be compensated through additional invocations since issuing aborts is no longer possible.

Figure 5.17 shows function integration graphically. The box around the extraction integration process steps indicate that those are to be executed as one transaction across back-end application system invocations. This is, of course, only possible if the back-end application systems can be invoked under transaction control. If they cannot, then the interface process has to be specified without the function integration box.

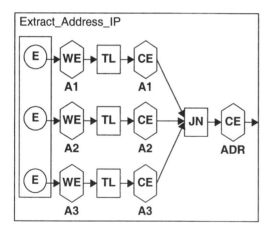

Fig. 5.17. Function integration

Figure 5.17 shows three steps that extract address information. Each extraction results in a wire event (A1 to A3) that is translated into a clear text event. The three clear text events are composed into one that contains the address. The composition step is called "JN" for join.

5.6.2 Data Integration

Data integration is a data-centric integration approach. Data integration is also known as schema integration over heterogeneous data sources, which means that the schemas of the various data sources are different. The main problem of data integration over heterogeneous data sources is the schema integration problem. When a query has to be executed over data sources, then the query has to be formulated against one schema, the so-called global schema, which is composed of the schemas of the data sources, also called local schema. Schema transformation has to take place in order to derive to the global schema based on the local schemas. This transformation can be done explicitly by transformation rules, or implicitly by rewriting queries that are formulated against the global schema, but have to be executed over the local schema.

An important observation is that data integration makes query execution across heterogeneous data sources possible. The queried data are independent of their sources, i.e., any change in the source no longer affects the already queried data. Furthermore, changes in the data sources are only observed when a query gets executed. Otherwise, changes are unnoticed.

Since data integration is not part of the integration concepts, no further discussion takes place. An extensive body of research literature exists about data integration (Bouguettaya et al. 1998; Elmagarmid et al. 1998).

5.6.3 Event Integration

Event integration is at the center of the B2B integration concepts. Discrete events taking place at endpoints are recognized by the B2B integration technology in the form of messages. The B2B integration technology realizes the messages as events and, based on process models (interface, binding and business processes), the integration of endpoints is achieved.

Messages that originate from endpoints are considered discrete and cause the execution of integration functionality. Messages that are sent to endpoints are considered endpoint external events that have to be processed by the endpoints, and in most cases lead to a state change within the endpoints. The integration concepts introduced in Chap. 7 enable event integration.

5.7 Summary

This chapter introduces some fundamental preliminaries that provide the context of the B2B integration concepts that are introduced in Chap. 7. However, an interesting question that is discussed next is, how would the ideal integration world look? Chapter 6 addresses this question since it puts the integration concepts of Chap. 7 into perspective, separating them into those that are required to bridge heterogeneity and those that are required to model integration.

6 The Ideal Integration

How would an ideal integration world look? We can construct an ideal integration world and, based on these results, determine what would remain to be done in integration if there were an ideal integration world. Therefore the discussion is specifically and intentionally carried to the extreme in order to explain the main intent of the presented conceptual model in this book and to clearly identify the integration concepts presented in Chapt. 7.

From an enterprise viewpoint, a B2B integration technology server should provide the illusion of an ideal integration world in the context of the real integration situation. Only then can an enterprise concentrate on its real core competencies and strengths, namely, its internal business processes representing competitive knowledge.

6.1 Single Secure and Reliable Network

One area that receives much attention and requires a great deal of work to implement is the transport layer, which needs to support secure and exactly-once message transmission over unreliable and insecure networks. Message duplicates, message losses, message injection, message modification, message reordering or message introspection must not happen during message exchange. If this happens, it has to be detected and compensated for.

In order to achieve secure exactly-once message transmission, complicated protocols have to be implemented that are based on message duplication detection, message receipt time-out, message resending, message resend retry counters, message resend upper limits, acknowledgment messages, sequence numbers, message signatures and message encryption. All this functionality is necessary to implement secure and exactly-once message transmission.

Messages can be lost during transmission. This is detected by acknowledgments not coming back to the sender of the original message in time. The message receipt time-out specifies how long an acknowledgment can take before it is regarded as being lost. Once the message receipt time-out is exceeded, the same message is sent again. The resend happens up to the resend retry counter value. Once this value is reached the exchange is regarded as failed. However, it might be that the acknowledgments are only delayed. In this case, the message was received and an acknowledgment was generated every time. However, since the time-out happened, the message was sent several times. Message duplication detection makes sure that the multiple resending of the message is detected and that it does not get processed every time, but only once.

In the other case, the message was never received by the recipient. In this case acknowledgments are never generated. This means that duplicate checks will never be performed because fundamentally no message exchange takes place.

In order to detect if a third party takes messages from the network, sequence numbers are added to messages. Messages have to contain sequence numbers, which are increasing and dense. This means that the recipient can detect a missing message if a sequence number is missing. In case a system failure happens, each of the B2B integration technologies involved knows which of the messages was the last message they processed, since the sequence numbers are stored once a message is successfully sent or received. After a failure the B2B integration technology can compare the message sequence numbers and start from the last successfully transmitted message.

In the ideal integration world, there would be one single network that connects all endpoints and that provides this capability at the network interface. A message sent to an endpoint (be it a trading partner or a back-end application system) would be guaranteed to be secure and delivered exactly once.

Of course, a message transmission would also be transactional in the ideal integration world, so that the sending of a message would immediately succeed or fail from a sender's viewpoint. This would avoid the asynchronous failure handling necessary in the nontransactional case if the receiver has to reject the message (event though it would have been delivered once).

6.2 Trusted Communication

Mutual trust and reliable relationships are important aspects of B2B integration to achieve trusted communication. In an ideal integration world agreements between trading partners, once established, would be unambiguously interpreted and 100% complied to by the endpoints. Messages sent would not be repudiated. That is, an endpoint could rely on the fact that if it receives a message, it is coming from the endpoint who sent it, and the endpoint does not deny ever having sent that message.

6.3 Single Semantic Data Model and Integration Behavior

If all data definitions are done once, with exactly one meaning and with every endpoint in the world agreeing and complying to it, then the data definition and the meaning of data would be homogeneous. In this case no effort would be required to bridge any differences in the structure or the interpretation of data.

If public processes were defined once, with exactly one meaning and with every endpoint agreeing and complying to it, then the public behavior would be homogeneous, and no effort would be required to bridge any differences in the structure and the interpretation of public or interface processes.

6.3.1 Data Model

In an ideal integration world, each and every business concept is defined exactly once, with one meaning that every endpoint agrees on and complies with at any time. This includes trading partners as well as back-end application systems. This would be the equivalent to a single shared and agreed-upon world ontology. Furthermore, every endpoint uses the same document exchange format (syntactical representation) for the communication between endpoints, and each business concept has exactly one representation in the document exchange format that is unambiguous.

Within endpoints for the purpose of persisting data, different storage formats might be used that are different from the document exchange format. While this is perfectly acceptable, a lossless and unambiguous conversion from the storage format to the document exchange format is required. This ensures that the business concepts are uniquely represented without any possibility of misinterpretation.

In this ideal integration world, translation and transformation are no longer necessary, since all business data exchanged are represented in the same format and have a unique meaning. The message representation and content would be the same as the wire event representation and content, and in turn that would be the same as the clear text event representation and content, which again would be the same as the business event representation and content. In summary, only business events would be defined and exchanged. Figure 2.16 would change dramatically and would look like Fig. 6.1.

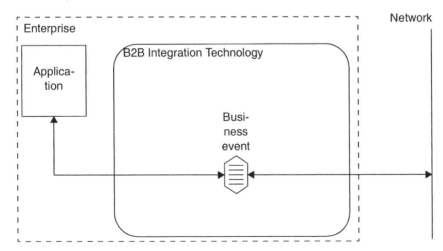

Fig. 6.1. Events in an ideal integration world

6.3.2 Integration Behavior

In perfect analogy to business concepts and document exchange formats, business behavior, also known as interface processes (public processes), would be defined, too. For each business behavior that exists, like a purchase order and purchase order acknowledgment message exchange, there would be one definition of the interface process that implements that behavior. All the interface processes would be part of a world ontology of business behavior that every endpoint agrees upon and that every endpoint interprets precisely identically.

There would be one way to define interface processes through one process specification language (analogy to the document exchange format). The interface process definition language would have one agreed-upon semantics that every endpoint would comply to and execute identically. This avoids any misinterpretation of the interface process behavior.

Business processes that are internal to an endpoint can be defined in any process language the endpoint chooses. Even more, the interface processes can be mapped to that language for processing at run time. However, if this internal process language differs from the interface process definition language, a conversation must happen in such a way that no ambiguities or misinterpretations are possible. This is in analogy to the persistence data model in te case of document exchange formats.

Based on this discussion, there would be only one interface process for a given business behavior, and the processes in Fig. 2.24 would look like that shown in Fig. 6.2. As shown, there would only be one interface process for all endpoints; transformation is no longer necessary. The events all represent business events because of the data homogeneity. The process binding is reduced to a direct binding of events (dashed lines). In summary, all business data and interface processes are defined only once and are syntactically as well as semantically equivalent across all endpoints.

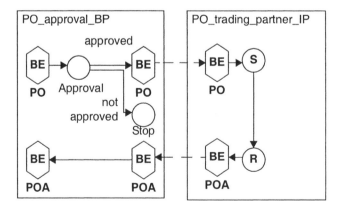

Fig. 6.2. Interface processes in an ideal integration world

6.4 Ideal Integration World

6.4.1 What's Left to be Done for Integration?

At this point the ideal integration world looks ideal, indeed. It appears that by "just" agreeing on one business concept world ontology and one business behavior world ontology all integration issues go away.

However, this is not the case (luckily, some might say). The only major problem that would go away would be the heterogeneity in terms of business data and public business behavior (interface processes). However, the core competency of enterprises, namely their internal business processes, would not be part of the world ontologies.

Rather, the opposite is the case since enterprises see business processes as one of their most valuable competitive assets. They would not contribute their processes to a world ontology at all, since it would allow an enterprise to analyze the competitions' processes and improve its own along the way.

And this is precisely the focus of ideal integration: providing an infrastructure that allows enterprises to specify and to execute their own and proprietary business processes in any way they need in order to maintain their competitive advantage, or to increase it in order to challenge their successful competitors. Different enterprises need to operate differently inside to be able to compete effectively.

What's left to be done in ideal integration is to develop the best process definition language possible, since this will support the only distinguishing part of enterprises, namely their internal business processes.

6.4.2 Ideal Integration Concepts

In the ideal integration world all endpoints expose a homogeneous integration behavior that is reliable and trustworthy based on the previous discussion. Heterogeneity would be completely eliminated from communication and interoperability functionality. Whatever business data need to be exchanged can be looked up from the business data world ontology. The same applies to interface processes, which would come from the interface process world ontology.

The ideal integration concepts would be reduced to business events, business processes and interface processes. These three concepts are sufficient in order to specify enterprise internal processes representing the competitive knowledge in the ideal integration world.

Business processes vary over time to gain competitiveness. Successful enterprises constantly improve their internal business processes. New insights into the execution of business processes triggers continuous process developments that will change existing processes.

6.5 Characterization of Integration Concepts

Homogeneous communication and interoperation are very desirable. Unfortunately, the ideal integration world does not exist any time soon. Therefore integration concepts have to be available that deal with the heterogeneity and have the heterogeneous world appear to be homogeneous.

6.5.1 Making Networks Reliable and Secure

Since there is no single secure and reliable network, the B2B integration technology architecture has to provide the illusion that there is one. The transport component in conjunction with the B2B engine and the adapters has to provide at its interface the behavior that would be equivalent to a single secure and reliable network.

The interface's implementation uses security functionality like encryption, signatures and sequence numbers to achieve the security required. It uses message duplication detection, message receipt time-outs, message resend retry counters, message resend upper limits and acknowledgment messages to achieve exactly-once delivery semantics.

Transactionality cannot be achieved since networks are not resource managers that can participate in distributed transaction processing. Therefore the transport layer (in conjunction with the B2B engine and the adapters) has to deal with asynchronous error handling when messages are sent back by the receiver, indicating a failure.

In summary, the transport layer together with the B2B engine and the adapters provide at their interface the abstraction of a secure and reliable network. There are integration concepts that allow the achievement of this abstraction. Therefore the B2B integration technology architecture can give the illusion of a secure and reliable network.

6.5.2 Establishing Trusted Communication

Trust is established electronically to the extent possible in order to achieve a trusted and reliable relationship between endpoints. The concept of endpoint capabilities and endpoint agreements supports the characterization of endpoints and their behavior. Endpoint capabilities support the specification of endpoints, their attributes and their behavior. Each endpoint within its B2B integration technology specifies the attributes and behavior of all the other endpoints it is communicating with. This allows each endpoint to keep track of the specifics of other endpoints from its viewpoint.

The integration concept of endpoint agreement supports the specification of the expected behavior between two or more endpoints. Endpoint agreements specify the message exchanged, their definition, their direction, their behavior in terms of exchange sequence, the period an endpoint agreement is valid and many other attributes. An endpoint agreement is agreed upon by the endpoints, and consequently, it allows all endpoints involved to verify that messages sent are according to the agreement. Reliable endpoint relationships can be built through endpoint agreements because the endpoint agreements allow the verification of the message exchange consistency, which is the basis for reliability.

Mutual trust is not established in the positive sense, but through control mechanisms. First, nonrepudiation of messages is implemented, which prevents an endpoint from denying ever sending a message that it sent. Through nonrepudiation each endpoint can prove that a message it received was sent by the endpoint indicated by the message. Technically, this is achieved by storing incoming messages as received, i.e., fully encrypted and signed. This ensures "trust" in the sense that endpoints can rely on the content and on the intention of a message that was sent by an endpoint. Second, nonrepudiation in conjunction with secure and reliable message transmission provides the necessary infrastructure to enforce trust together with the legislation. The nontechnical part, i.e., enforcing contracts in court based on endpoint agreements and nonrepudiated messages, is not discussed here, even though this is a very important element of the trust component.

6.5.3 Bridging Semantic Differences: Uniform Semantics

Differences in data exchange format are removed by translation. The translation accepts any data exchange format and transforms it into the chosen representation of the B2B integration technology architecture. Transformation makes sure that the semantic interpretation of incoming data adjusts to the B2B integration technology established semantics in the form of business events. Outgoing, the transformation engine allows for the production of the semantics as required by the endpoint. Differences in behavior are mediated through process bindings that adjust the interface behavior of endpoints to the business process behavior.

6.5.4 Achieving Homogeneous Integration

Once the semantic differences are bridged, the networks are made reliable as well as secure and trust is established between endpoints, then a homogeneous integration is possible in the sense that the private processes of an enterprise look like in an ideal integration world. This is because any endpoint-specific data exchange format, semantics and behavior are abstracted from them. All business processes operate on business events that are the same for all endpoints and have one endpoint-independent behavior.

Figure 6.3 is an abstraction layer representation that visualizes the homogeneous integration based on heterogeneous endpoints. The different layers achieve bottom to top different levels of abstraction, contributing more and more to the homogeneous integration layer. In each layer some of the important integration concepts are mentioned that achieve the abstraction.

Homogeneous integration	Business process
Uniform semantics	Translation, transformation, clear text event, interface process, process binding
Trusted communication	Nonrepudiation, trading partner capability and attributes, trading partner agreement
Reliable and secure transport	Encryption, signature, sequence number, message duplication check, message retry, upper sending limits, message time out, wire event

Fig. 6.3. Homogeneous integration based on heterogeneous endpoints

7 Concepts

The basic integration concepts required to define and execute integration between an arbitrary number of endpoints are discussed in this chapter. These integration concepts are independent of a particular implementation architecture or of particular implementation technologies. All approaches from academic research, standards organizations, industrial research and industrial products define and implement these concepts in one form or another implicitly or explicitly. Since B2B integration is not yet an established discipline (like relational database management systems), the terminology around the presented integration concepts varies significantly from case to case. Furthermore, different approaches propose alternative integration concepts that might look different albeit all address the same functionality. However, in general they can all be mapped to those presented in the following.

7.1 Event

Without exception , all business data that are passed through the B2B integration technology architecture are represented and managed as events. Event is the only concept that deals with the data to be passed between endpoints. In Sect. 7.2 processes are introduced as the only way to specify the business logic that processes events. Events and processes are the two cornerstones of concepts for integration.

7.1.1 Message

According to the integration boundary discussed in Chap. 5 messages are outside the B2B integration technology architecture boundary, and each message is represented as wire event within the B2B integration technology architecture. Consequently, the message format is not under the control of the B2B integration technology architecture. It has to deal with any message format of any endpoint that needs to be integrated. It needs to be able to interpret the message format as well as to produce the message format with the help of translation.

Messages represent one of two occurrences. One occurrence is the representation of a state change, and the other one is the representation of a query. In the former case, a message coming from an endpoint communicates a state change within the endpoint. The state change within the endpoint occurs and the message represents a notification about the state change. For example, once a piece of equipment has been manufactured and is ready for shipment, a shipper has to be contacted to pick up the equipment and ship it to the buyer. A user working with the back-end application system selects a shipper and signs off a request to this shipper. A message to this shipper indicates that a request was established in the back-end application system. The message therefore represents the state change in the back-end application systems that causes the request to be sent to the shipper. The shipper receiving the message has to react either accepting the shipment request or denying the shipment request. The acceptance or denial is done within the shipper's back-end application system. This is again a state change and is communicated back to the manufacturer as a separate message (again indicating a state change, this time in the shipper endpoint).

The latter case, the message representing a query, does not indicate a state change at all. A query is used for exactly that: to obtain data based on a search criterion or predicate. For example, a product query might ask for all router models that have a specific performance profile. Such a message causes the recipient's back-end system to search for the requested data and send them back to the sender. This does not cause or communicate a state change.

Messages carry discrete pieces of data values as compared to programming language pointers. A message is self-contained in the sense that all data that are required in order to process that message are contained within the message. The sender and the recipient of messages agree on the content of the messages, and both make sure that they can populate the message with the data required and that the data contained in the message are sufficient for processing it. If data are missing, the recipient cannot process the message and must ask the sender for additional data. This additional message exchange, while possible, is inefficient, and it is preferable that the additional data are included in the first message immediately.

It is possible that messages contain references to previously communicated data. For example, if a purchase order contains an engineering drawing that gives the specification of the product, then this has to be communicated only once. Any subsequent message exchange, for example, ordering three additional pieces of the product, does not require the drawing to be sent again. The purchase order that orders the additional number can refer to the already-sent engineering drawing. However, this requires that both the sender as well as the receiver agree on a naming scheme as well as the fact that the drawing is available for reference as long as the sender can order more pieces.

An alternative type of reference is a reference into the sender's endpoint. For example, a message that has an attachment containing a photograph does not contain the photograph itself, but an address within the sender's endpoint, like an FTP address. The sender keeps the photograph in this location so that the recipient of the message can retrieve the photograph whenever it needs it. In this case the photograph is only transmitted when required and not necessarily at the time of the first message exchange. As soon as the photograph is obtained by the receiver of the message, it becomes part of the receiver's history so that it can be nonrepudiated.

Messages, like events, have a structured content according to some data type that defines the message structure. Message structures are formally defined. For example, a message might consist of three parts: a header, a body and an attachment. The header contains the sender's identifier, the recipient's identifier, the date and time transmitted as well as the message type, like product definition update. The body contains a description of the product, and the attachment an engineering drawing of the product. This structure is defined by a data type within the endpoints so that both know how to parse the message. However, the individual components are of their own data types. For example, the description of the product could be an XML instance. While an XML instance is well defined by its type (e.g., through an XML schema definition), it could contain text that is unstructured.

While messages are self-contained, it might be that several messages belong together, and together they contain a complete set of business data. Without all messages received, the recipient cannot make sense out of the message exchange. For example, large purchase orders can be transmitted in pieces, and the header of the purchase order is transmitted in a separate message from the line items. Similarly, each line item in turn is also transmitted as a separate message. Only if the message containing the purchase order header as well as all messages containing the line items are transmitted can the recipient start processing the purchase order. In this case the recipient needs to know the number of line items that it needs to receive. Otherwise, it would not know how long to wait until all line items are received. There are several possibilities to find out the number of line item messages. The header might contain the total number of line items. Or, the header contains the purchase order amount and the recipient has to add up the individual amounts of the line items until the whole amount is reached. Or, each line item has a line item number that is increasing, and the last line item has a flag indicating that it is the last line item. However it is done, the recipient needs to figure out the number of line items. Once all line items are received, the recipient has to decide if it processes the messages as individual events or if it combines all messages into one event for processing. The interface process can combine the individual message or the process binding or the business process. The decision lies with the integration modeler.

The opposite case exists, too, where one message contains several pieces of business data. This case is called a batch. For example, a batch could contain 17 purchase orders. The 17 purchase orders are complete purchase orders in their own right, but are transmitted together in one message, maybe for transmission efficiency. This is equivalent of sending the 17 purchase orders individually. A difference is that the batch is acknowledged with one acknowledgment instead of 17. This in turn requires an agreement between the endpoints about how the acknowledgment encodes the case that some of the purchase orders are valid and consistent, whereas other contain errors and how the sender should react in this case. For example, it could resend those purchase orders that had errors with the errors fixed.

In the discussion of interface process concepts in Sect. 7.3, the different examples given here are modeled as different processes that show how the various cases can be achieved.

7.1.2 Event and Data Type

Since events are objects internal to the B2B integration technology architecture, they have to have a defined structure. In general, events have an event header and event elements. The event header contains data that are required by the B2B integration technology architecture in order to manage the events. This includes the identifier from the sender as well as the recipient, the date and time when the event was created, the type of event, like a purchase order or a patient record, and other information discussed as needed in the following. The event header is not part of the business data content, but is solely required for management purposes of the event within the B2B integration technology architecture.

Data Type

The event elements contain business data like engineering drawings or the elements of a shipment order. Since the content might be accessed by the business process, it needs to be represented in a form that the B2B integration technology architecture can interpret. This is achieved through a data type system. Each event element must be of a data type, which can be a complex data type, of course.

The more expressive the data type system is, better complex data can be represented. No new data type system shall be invented here. Instead, one that is at least equivalent to XML schema is assumed. This is because more and more B2B protocols are defined in XML schema, and so this automatically becomes a requirement because of this reality.

Event Type

An event can have as many event elements as required. There is, in principle, no upper limit. Not every event element has to be interpretable by the B2B integration technology architecture. For example, an event element might contain a spreadsheet that details a cost structure. The spreadsheet software can interpret the spreadsheet, but the B2B integration technology architecture cannot. However, the event element containing the spreadsheet is of a data type, in this case it might be of type binary. Therefore, the event element is typed by a data type as required, but the contents of the data type cannot be interpreted by the B2B integration technology architecture. The same is true for representing message attachments containing drawings, photographs, video, sound or other data that require specific software for access.

In the following a pseudolanguage is used to illustrate the different event concepts. This language is a pseudolanguage because it is not formally defined, however, at the same time this is a very effective way to convey concepts and details. XML is not used as syntax for this pseudolanguage because of the enormous space the tag structure requires.

Figure 7.1 shows a specification of an event type. An event type has a name (address_update) as well as event elements. Event elements have names, too, that are unique within an event type definition (new_address). This is important for the unique addressing requirements. The event element is of a defined type (address). The event header is not explicitly defined, but is implicitly instantiated at run time in event instances. Since the event header is management data of the B2B integration technology architecture, it is an internal data structure that is predefined by the run time system.

```
event_type address_update
  event_element new_address
    address;
  end_event_element
end_event_type
```

Fig. 7.1. Example event type specification address_update

The data type address is defined in Fig. 7.2. Data types are specified separately so that they can be reused in different event elements. No more-specific constraints are defined in the data types like the fact that the zip code has to be a value out of the list of valid zip codes. This is done by event validation, which is discussed later in Sect. 7.1.11.

```
data_type address
  street: string;
  street_number: positive;
  city: string;
  zip: positive;
  state: string;
  country: string;
end_data_type
```

Fig. 7.2. Example data type address

Basic data types not only need to include string, integer, positive, boolean but also binary, text and other more specific ones. Again, no new data type system is invented here and it is assumed that the fictive data type system proposed has all primitive data types and all constructs for building complex types as needed.

Events have properties that are important later on to understand the overall B2B integration technology architecture execution behavior. First, events are reliable. Once an event instance is created, it is created reliably, surviving any system failure. This ensures that a created event exists under any circumstances.

Second, event instances are unique. It is impossible to create another event instance with the same event identifier. Even an event copy does not create the same identifier but rather a new, unused one. This ensures that events are unique and references to event instances can exist and are consistent forever.

Third, event instances are immutable. This means that no event instance can be updated. Every required update causes a new event instance to be created that is a copy of the event to be changed. The updated event has a new identifier and contains the change. Also, the new event has a reference to the former event so that it is clear that one event is the descendant of the other one. This ensures that every reference to an event instance can rely on the fact that the event is not changing its contents unrecognized. Furthermore, the history of events does not have to deal with the fact that there are two entries for the same event instance. Through the references events have between themselves (if they are modifications of each other), the history of changes can be retrieved easily. Another benefit is that different parallel branches of parallel processing of events become isolated from each other since no two parallel branches can update one event instance concurrently.

7.1.3 Event Life Cycle

Events are objects with state that undergo a life cycle from creation until consumption. Events are never deleted and can be referenced forever. This might not be possible in reality due to storage space limitations, however, the integration concepts assume this.

Event States

The life cycle of event instances consists of several states and several possible state transitions. The states are

- **Non_existent**. This is an artificial state in which the event instances do not yet exist. It is helpful as a starting point later on regarding state transitions.
- **In_creation**. The creation of an event instances is not instantaneous. The event instance has to be created and all event headers as well as event elements have to be filled in. This might take several operations on the event instance, whereas header fields or element fields are set one by one. Only after the last field value is set has the event instance been created.
- **Created**. An event instance in this state is completely created and all header as well as element fields are set. Even though it is created, it is not yet ready for processing. It has to transition to the next state in order to be processed.
- **Raised**. An event instance that transitioned into this state can be processed. This means that the B2B integration technology architecture picks this event, finds out what the next processing step is and causes the processing to happen. An example is transformation, where an event is transformed into another event.

- **In_consumption**. Once an event instance is picked up for processing, it transitions into this state. This makes sure that it is not picked up again for processing. It remains in this state until the processing is finished. For example, while a transformation is ongoing, the source event instance is in this state while the target event instance is in state in_creation.
- **Consumed**. Once the processing of an event instance is finished, the event instance is transitioned into the consumed state. This means that the event instance is still available as history, but cannot be accessed any more for processing.
- **In_error**. If an event instance has an error or is in an error situation, the event instance is transitioned into the in_error state. This makes sure that event instances that have errors can be detected. This state is transitory in the sense that error handling has to transition the event instance from the error state back into a normal nonerror state.

Once an event instance is consumed, the question is why is it not deleted at this time. The reason is that event instances in general must stay as history. Any analysis of history or any auditing requires that the event instances are available.

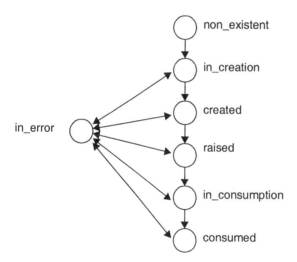

Fig. 7.3. State and state transitions of event instances

Event State Transitions

The state transitions are shown in Fig. 7.3. Starting at non_existent, the event instance transitions in the normal case through the states as shown. During any normal state transition an error can happen, and the event instance is transitioned into the error state. Depending on the error handling for the situation, the event instance is transitioned back into a normal event instance state. In addition, while being in in_consumption or in in_creation, errors can happen. In this case the event instance also transitions to the in_error state waiting for the error handling.

7.1.4 Event Addressing

An event instance has an origin endpoint and a target endpoint to which it is addressed. The origin or source endpoint is the one that is sending the event instance. For example, this can be a back-end application system or a trading partner. The B2B integration technology architecture then knows the origin of the event instance. It can leave the origin unmodified or modify it. For example, when back-end application systems are integrated, the origin address is left unmodified because the receiving back-end application system might make internal decisions based on the origin of the event instance. Figure 7.4 shows this case, where an event is sent from back-end application system A1 to the back-end application system A2.

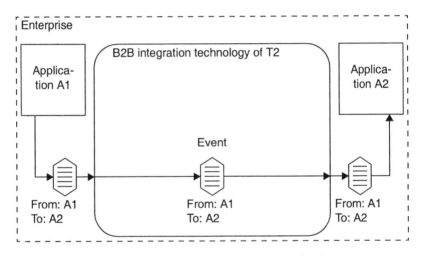

Fig. 7.4. Addressing of event instances between back-end application systems

When the event instance is received from a back-end application system and is to be sent to a remote target trading partner, then the origin endpoint is modified. In this case the back-end application system is no longer the origin, instead, the trading partner itself that sends the event instance is the origin. The reason for this modification is that the remote trading partner does not know and, in general, should not know about the back-end applications of the source trading partner. Instead, the trading partners only know each other as endpoints (and not their back-end application systems), and they are sources and targets of event instances in interenterprise communication. Figure 7.5 shows this case, where an event is sent from back-end application system A1 to trading partner T1. The business process (not shown) modifies the source address from A1 to T2, whereby T2 is the sending trading partner.

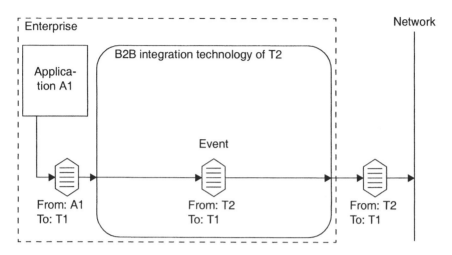

Fig. 7.5. Readdressing of event instances sent to trading partners

The target address in an event instance is set by the sending endpoint. The B2B integration technology architecture processes the event instance according to a business process. That business process examines the target endpoint address and decides, based on this, where to send the event instance. For example, if the target is another back-end application system, the business process will send the event instance to it. The same applies if the event instance is addressed for a trading partner. However, the business process can decide to overwrite the target address and send the event instance to another endpoint. This decision can be based on business logic. For example, the sending endpoint sends a shipment request to a particular shipper, but the business process determines that another shipper would be more appropriate in this case. So it overwrites the target address with the more appropriate shipper. Figure 7.6 shows this case, where a back-end application system decides to send an event to shipper S1. However, the target address is overwritten by the address of shipper S2.

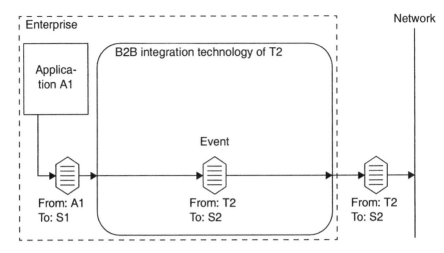

Fig. 7.6. Address overwrite by business logic

If an event is coming from a remote trading partner, it addresses the event instance to the receiving trading partner. The B2B integration technology architecture processes the incoming events with business processes. The business process has to determine to which back-end application system the received event instance must be sent. This is necessary since the incoming event instance is addressed to the receiving trading partner, not to a back-end application system (because the remote trading partner does not know the internals of the receiving trading partner). Once the back-end application system is determined, the event instance is given to it as the new target endpoint. Figure 7.7 shows the case where an event is sent from trading partner T3 to trading partner T2. The B2B integration technology architecture of T2 decides to send the event to back-end application system A1.

So far event instances were addressed to exactly one endpoint. However, it is possible that an endpoint wants to send an event instance to several other endpoints. For example, a request for quotation is to be sent to all suppliers that can deliver the product in the request for quotation. In one scenario the endpoint sends as many event instances as there are endpoints that should receive that event instance. Alternatively, the endpoint can send one event instance, but puts a list of endpoints in the target address. At some point in the processing of the event instance this is detected. At this point the event is copied as often as there are endpoints in the target address. In each copied event the target address is set to one target endpoint, and then it is sent out. Instead of the endpoint managing multiple event instances, the B2B integration technology architecture does it. The details are discussed in the context of binding processes in Sect 7.5.

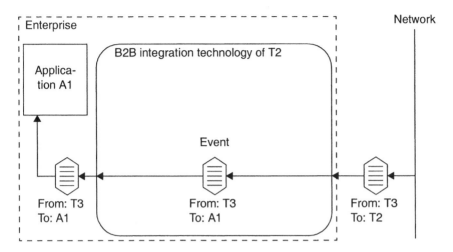

Fig. 7.7. Readdressing of event instances received from remote trading partners

7.1.5 Wire Event, Translation and Clear Text Event

Up to this point the discussion of the different aspects of the event properties applied to all event classes: wire event, clear text event or business event. This section goes into more detail and specifically addresses wire events, clear text events and the translation between both.

Wire Event

Messages are represented as wire events within the B2B integration technology architecture without modification of their contents. For each type of incoming message there is a corresponding wire event type. When a message is received, it is stored in one wire event element instance of the corresponding wire event type. If the incoming message is a MIME-packaged message that has several MIME parts, the whole message is still stored in one wire event element. This ensures that the incoming message is not modified, which is a very significant property. In addition, the incoming message are stored as-is (fully encrypted) to provide support for nonrepudiation. This requires that incoming messages as well as outgoing message can be reproduced as-received or as-sent.

Incoming or outgoing messages can be in any format, most likely encrypted. They are stored in decrypted form in the wire event. In the general case this requires that the wire event element is of data type binary. This allows for storage of any incoming message, no matter what its format. Figure 7.8 shows a wire event type definition. The wire event element called message is of data type message.

The data type message has one element of type binary. An instance of this element type contains one message at run time.

```
data_type message
   original_message: binary;
end_data_type

wire_event_type create_purchase_order_RN
   event_element message
      message;
   end_event_element
end_wire_event_type
```

Fig. 7.8. Wire event type definition

For each incoming message type there must be a corresponding wire event type. This is necessary since interface processes refer to wire event types and assume that the contents of a wire event type are as intended by the wire message. For example, if there is a wire event type that represents the create purchase order message of the B2B standard RosettaNet, then the interface process assumes that instances of this wire event type contain create purchase order messages of RosettaNet.

When a message is received, it is analyzed to the extent that the corresponding wire event type can be determined. This is achieved in two steps. First, the message header of the message is analyzed for any protocol information. If the message header does not contain enough data, then the rest of the message is examined. Theoretically, it still might not be possible to determine the protocol information. In this case, manual help would be required. However, all B2B protocols (or back-end application system protocols) are designed in such a way that protocol information can be easily determined from messages. Therefore, this case is assumed in the following.

Once the protocol information for a message is known, the corresponding wire event type has to be determined. This is achieved by a lookup that relates the message type and the wire event type with each other. The architectural components that execute the lookup are the back-end application adapter or the B2B engine. Once the wire event type is determined, an instance of this wire event is created, the wire event element is populated with the message and the wire event instance is handed over to the event interface of the connectivity layer (Sect. 5.1.1). The lookup is discussed in more detail in the architecture chapter.

The outbound processing happens analogously. An instance of a wire event is sent by an interface process. This wire event instance is then given to a B2B engine or a back-end application system adapter through the event interface of the connectivity layer. Through a lookup the message type can be determined and the message can be sent out.

Translation

A consequence of storing messages in wire event elements of type binary is that the wire event element contents cannot be interpreted directly. They must be reformatted into the data type system defined by the B2B integration technology architecture. This step is called translation. The translation can interpret the particular format of the message (after decryption) and can represent the content in the data type system of the B2B integration technology. Translation is therefore specific to the different formats defined by the different B2B protocols. Translation is achieved by a separate architectural component that allows for the addition of translation functionality to the B2B integration technology architecture over time to handle all possible protocol formats that might occur. Usually, translation is a piece of executable code that is specifically written to interpret the message format and produce data types in the data type system of the B2B integration technology.

Clear Text Event

The result of translation from a wire event instance is a clear text event instance that contains the message content in the data type format defined by the B2B integration technology architecture. For each wire event type, there is a corresponding clear text event type.

Figure 7.9 shows a clear text event type definition corresponding to the wire event type definition in Fig. 7.8. The data type purchase_order is defined consisting of two parts, a header and the line items. The header is of data type header (not further defined here), and the line items are of data type list_of line item (not further defined here). The clear text event type has one element with the name payload that is of type purchase order.

```
data_type puchase_order
  header: header;
  line_items: list_of(line_item);
end_data_type

clear_text_event_type create_purchase_order_RN
  event_element payload
    purchase_order;
  end_event_element
end_clear_text_event_type
```

Fig. 7.9. Clear text event type definition

At run time, when a wire event instance is created, the wire event instance is translated into a clear text event instance. The binary element of the wire event instance is read by the translation, and the element payload of the clear text event instance is created. The header as well as the line_items part are populated accordingly.

At type definition time when the wire event types and the clear text event types are defined, their relationship is established, too. This relationship defines which clear text event type and which wire event type correspond to each other, and which translation has to happen between the two. There has to be one translation for each direction, i.e., from wire event type to clear text event type, and vice versa. At run time, with a given wire event instance or a given clear text instance, the translation is determined to create the other event.

Some messages have multiple parts. For example, they are MIME packaged and each part of the message corresponds to a MIME part. In such a case, a decision has to be made by the integration modeler whether the different parts of the message should translated into different clear text event elements or into one. The examples in Fig. 7.8 and Fig. 7.9 are the case when a message is translated into one clear text event element. If the message that is represented by the wire event according to Fig. 7.8 has several parts, then those are not translated into different clear text event elements, but into one.

Figure 7.10 shows a different clear text event type definition. In this case the header and the line items are in two different event elements. The translation in this case has to make sure that the header data are translated into the event element named payload header, and that the line items are translated into the event element payload_line_items.

```
data_type puchase_order_header
  header: header;
end_data_type

data_type purchase_order_line_items
    line_items: list_of(line_item);
end_data_type

clear_text_event_type create_purchase_order_multielement_RN
  event_element payload_header
    purchase_order_header;
  end_event_element
  event_element payload_line_items
    purchase_order_line_items;
  end_event_element
end_clear_text_event_type
```

Fig. 7.10. Multielement clear text event type definition

There is no uniform terminology around translation and transformation. Even though translation is used in natural languages when one is translated into another, transformation is often used in the context of B2B integration instead. Analogous to transformation, the term mapping is used. Syntax conversion (translation) is sometimes explicitly called out; sometimes it is not. In summary, translation is used in this book when one syntax has to be represented in another syntax (from wire event to clear text event, and vice versa) and transformation when the contents are re-represented (from clear text event to business event, and vice versa).

7.1.6 Clear Text Event, Transformation and Business Event

Business events are a separate event class in which all clear text events from the various endpoints can be uniformly represented. Business events were introduced in Sect. 2.2.4. For all clear text event types of the different endpoints that implement the same endpoint-specific message with the same meaning, one business event type is defined. Business event types are a common representation schema for all the corresponding clear text event types. Business event instances are derived from clear text event instances through transformation. All business event instances look alike, no matter which endpoint the event instance data came from originally. That is the goal and purpose of business events.

Business Event

For example, if different endpoints have different clear text event types for creating purchase orders, then there is one business event type for creating a purchase order. Each of the instances of the different clear text event types is represented in an instance of the corresponding business event type. As discussed in Sect. 2.2.4, the number of transformations are significantly reduced by this approach.

The various clear text event types of the endpoints contain different business data, depending on the B2B protocol standard they use. The corresponding business event type must be able to represent all of them in such a way that every clear text event can be represented as a business event, and vice versa. In this sense a business event is a semantic superset of the clear text events it represents.

What is the best approach to actually define a business event type? First of all, all clear text event types of the various endpoints that represent the same event have to be collected. Examples are creating purchase orders, requesting quotations, notifying about lab results, and so on. Once the corresponding clear text event types are determined, the business event type has to be created. There are several difficulties to overcome at this point. First, the business event type has to be defined. Second, the transformations from the clear text event types to the business event type have to be specified, and vice versa. Third, semantic mismatches have to be addressed.

First, we discuss how to construct a business event type with the assumption that the business data in each of the instances of any clear text event types are complete, so that each instance of a clear text event type can be represented in an event instance of any other clear text event type. This means that no instance carries more data than another instance, and no mismatches are present. Afterwards, mismatches are discussed separately.

Naive Business Event Design

Given all the clear text event types of the various endpoints, the easy way out for constructing the common business event type is to have different event elements for the different clear text events. This approach is straightforward, easy and always works. The following example shows this in detail.

Figure 7.11 shows a clear text event type for reserving a hotel room. It is defined in the context of trading partner 1. The address data types are borrowed from Sect. 2.2.4.

```
Trading partner 1:

data_type address
  string;
end_data_type

data_type reservation
  /* this specifies the length, dates, etc., of the stay */
end_data_type

clear_text_event_type reserve_hotel_room
  event_element address
    address;
  end_event_element
  event_element reservation
    reservation;
  end_event_element
end_clear_text_event_type
```

Fig. 7.11. Clear text event type of trading partner 1 for reserving a hotel room

Figure 7.12 shows a clear text event for reserving a hotel room of trading partner 2. The naming conventions of trading partner 1 are different from those of trading partner 2.

Trading partner 2:

data_type guest_address
  address: address;
  country: country;
end_data_type

data_type address
  number: positive;
  street: string;
  city: string;
end_data_type

data_type country
  state: string;
  zip: positive;
  country: string;
end_data_type

data_type hotel_reservation
  /* this specifies the length, dates, etc., of the stay */
end_data_type

clear_text_event_type reserve_room
  event_element guest_address
    guest_address;
  end_event_element
  event_element hotel_reservation
    hotel_reservation;
  end_event_element
end_clear_text_event_type

Fig. 7.12. Clear text event type of trading partner 2 for reserving a hotel room

Both clear text events have different data types for storing address information. Figure 7.13 shows a business event type that simply specifies one business event element for each clear text event's elements. Since each clear text event type has two event elements, the business event type specifies four event elements. It reuses the data types used in the clear text event types. The transformation from the clear text event to the business event is straightforward. The contents are copied into the business event elements that correspond to the clear text event elements.

```
business_event_type reserve_hotel_room
  event_element address
    address;
  end_event_element
  event_element reservation
    reservation;
  end_event_element
  event_element guest_address
    guest_address;
  end_event_element
  event_element hotel_reservation
    hotel_reservation;
  end_event_element
end_business_event_type
```

Fig. 7.13. Initial business event type for reserving a hotel room

This looks almost like the ideal approach. The business event type definition is a noncreative task where the already defined clear text event elements are copied into the business event type definition. Furthermore, the transformation required to transform between the clear text events and the business events is a mere copy. This is too good to be true, and the downside of this approach is discussed next.

First, the concept of business events in its original idea made sure that the number of transformations is reduced dramatically because it avoids the point-to-point pairwise transformation between clear text events. With the above design, however, this is no longer the case. There is no common representation and de facto it requires that each clear text event is transformed directly into another. This is the case since a source clear text event is re-represented identically in a business event type element. From there it has to be transformed into the target clear text event. This means that a point-to-point pairwise transformation took place.

Second, a not-so-visible downside is that there is no longer a homogeneous representation of all clear text events representing reserving hotel rooms. Any analysis tool must be able to differentiate the business event elements. For example, if the number of reservations in a specific city has to be determined, the analysis algorithm has to access each business event instance and determine, which of the business event elements is populated. Since the naming scheme is different, it has to know all the different schemes. In one case it can access the city directly (element corresponding to trading partner 2), whereas in the other case it has to analyze a string and extract the city (element corresponding to trading partner 1).

Third, if more endpoints are added that have their own clear text event specification, more business event elements have to be added, and all functions accessing the business events have to be updated to reflect the new event element definitions. This includes not only the analysis tools, but also conditional branchings in business processes.

All in all, the initial approach, which looks straightforward and easy, is not advantageous at all. Therefore, a better approach is discussed next that does not have the discussed downsides.

Advanced Business Event Design

Business event types should be designed in such a way that the data types involved are most specific with respect to business data. Each identifiable business data value should be a separate data type. The data types and their structure need to ensure that all data types in the clear text events can be transformed into the data types the business event uses. Furthermore, the business event should be a superset of the business data of the individual clear text events. No data value in a clear text event should be dropped during the transformation into the business event. This ensures that there is no data loss when going from the clear text event to the business event. In total, this ensures that the business event represents the clear text event completely and with the most specific representation. This cannot always be accomplished, and the different types of mismatches are discussed at the end of this section separately.

```
data_type address_details
   street_number: string;
   street_name: string;
   city_name: string;
   city_zip: string;
   state_name: string;
   country_name: string;
end_data_type

data_type reservation_details
      /* this specifies the length, dates, etc., of the stay */
end_data_type

business_event_type reserve_hotel_room
   event_element address_details
     address_details;
   end_event_element
   event_element reservation_details
     reservation_details;
   end_event_element
end_business_event_type
```

Fig. 7.14. Final design of the business event type for reserving a hotel room

Figure 7.14 shows the business event type for hotel room reservation following the appropriate design rules. With the new specification of the business event the mentioned downsides can be avoided. Each of the two clear text events can be transformed into the business event. The clear text event of trading partner 1 can be transformed into the business event by decomposing the address string. In the opposite way, the business event address elements can be concatenated. The clear text event transformation for the clear text event of the second trading partner is easier, since in this case the values are already decomposed.

Any analysis algorithm accessing the business events no longer has to understand that there are two different event elements representing the same data, since all business events look alike, independently of the endpoint from which the data comes from. Furthermore, any new endpoint can be added, and its clear text event can be transformed without affecting the business event. None of the algorithms accessing the business event have to be changed because of a new endpoint.

Since some clear text events might have data values that others do not have, not every clear text event can populate all data values in the business event. In case a data value is not populated, it must be specified that the value is not populated, e.g., through setting a flag or inserting the value NULL.

Transformation

Without going into too much detail, a transformation specific discussion should take place at this point. So far only string operations like copy, concatenation or split were mentioned. Fundamentally, functions for all data types have to be available as well as data type conversions if the data types between clear text events and business events mismatch. Sometimes conversions are necessary that are more complex than just data type conversions. For example, the clear text event might specify a distance in miles, whereas the business event does so using kilometers. In this case a function has to be defined that converts miles into kilometers, and vice versa. All these operations and functions have in common that they are idempotent, i.e., derive to the same result if executed again.

Sometimes transformation rules access nonidempotent functions like retrieving the current time. The time value is different at different invocation times. Retrieving the time might be necessary to record when transformation took place. The same is true for date values. When retrieving the date or time it is important to include the time zone or to retrieve the date for a given time zone so that later on the reference is clear.

Application events might already have time values, for example, representing the time when a message was originally sent. If this time value is in a different format than the one of the business event, then it needs to be converted, too. European data formats differ from those used in the US and Japan.

So far we discussed only transformations that go from one or more single values from the source event to one or more single values in the target event. The example used was the case where an address is contained in a single string and has to be decomposed for the business event. Conversely, the individual values of a business event have to be concatenated to one string when going to the clear text event.

In addition to single-value transformations, there is the case where an event contains so-called repeating fields. Repeating fields are best characterized as dynamic arrays where the type definition defines the array element data types, but the dimension of the array (i.e., its size) is unspecified. At run time when an array is instantiated it contains a number of array elements and that number can be different from event instance to event instance.

Given that a source event has an array, each array element has to be transformed into a target event representation. The simplest scenario is where the target event has an equivalent array and each array element from the source event has to be transformed to an array element in the target event.

A slightly more complicated case is when the source array elements have to be aggregated in the target event. In this case several source array elements have to be combined into one target event array element. For example, a purchase order ordering several sizes of paper cups for a coffee chain might have a line item for each size of paper cup. If there are three sizes of cups, then there are three line items each indicating the size and number. The target event might only have one line item for all the three sizes and several sub-line items, one specifically for each size. In this case an array element from the source event needs to be transformed into a sub-line item in the same line item array element of the target event.

A more complicated case is when complex re-sorting has to take place according to different sorting criteria. For example, in the textile industry a purchase order might come in for T-shirts in different sizes and colors. The source event might have a line item for each color and within this line item there is a sub-line item for each size. The target event might be sorted the other way around. It requires a line item for each size, whereby each line item has a sub-line item for different colors. The transformation for this case must read all source array elements, re-sort them and write the target element fields.

To complicate matters, the target event might require also sub-line items for those colors for which no T-shirt is ordered in order to indicate an explicit no-order. This means that there are target event fields that do not have a corresponding source event field. For this case the transformation rules must know all possible colors and check for each size of the T-shirt if there are sub-line items for all colors. If there is no order in the source event, an empty sub-line item has to be created. Of course, this example can be extended for sizes, too, to indicate explicit no-orders for certain sizes. The transformation rules would then have to know all sizes, too.

There is not always a one-to-one relationship between the business concepts that have to be mapped into each other. Without going into too much detail, it is possible that a business concept in a clear text event is represented as two or more concepts in a business event, and vice versa. Going from one to several concepts requires that the transformation rules "split" the attributes into several concepts, whereas in the opposite case the transformation rules "join" the concepts into one.

Transformation Map

Several transformation rules are, in general, required to transform a clear text event to a business event, a business event to a clear text event, a clear text event to a clear text event or a business event to a business event. The transformation rules that together are required to accomplish a transformation completely are called a transformation map. A transformation map consists of the set of required transformation rules, the source events as input parameters and the target events as output parameter. At run time, an instance of the transformation map is created, the input or source event instances are supplied to it, and it returns the set of output or target event instances.

Transformation Mismatches

Transformation mismatches exist because of semantic heterogeneity of business concepts. In general, it cannot be expected that the source and target fields match precisely so that all transformation rules are one-to-one copies of fields. If the business concepts are the same and if they are represented alike in the source and target events, a business concept equivalence exists. The transformation is therefore a copy. If the business concepts are the same, but their values are represented differently, the business concepts are still equivalent. The transformations are slightly more complex and were discussed in Sect. 2.2.4. A field has to be split or fields have to be concatenated in order to get from a source to a target field.

In addition, there are more types of mismatches between source and target fields. One type of mismatch is business concept abstraction/subsumption. A business concept might be a specialization of another business concept. For example, the source might use normal date as the data type for delivery date, whereas the target uses working day date as data type for delivery date. Working day date is a special case of date since not every date is a working day (Sundays do not fall under this category). When mapping from normal date to working day date the problem arises how to map non-working day dates to working day dates. One solution is to take the normal date from the source event, find out the next working day from that and put that as the value in the target event. The mapping from a more general business concept to a more specialized business concept requires that the values of the general concept be "narrowed down" to the possible values of the specialized concept, as shown in the date example. However, as can be seen, the actual date might have been modified and so the values of the two business concepts of delivery date are not the same. This can possibly cause problems later on when the delivery is on time from the perspective of the source event and "early" from the perspective of the target event.

The opposite case, i.e., mapping from a more special concept to a more general concept, does not pose the problem as described. A more special concept exhibits the same behavior as the more general concept and can be represented as such. For example, a working day date can always be represented as normal day date without any problem. No problem arises since the actual value of the date is the same in both cases.

Where does this discussion about the business concept abstraction/subsumption leave us in relation to the design of business events? Business concepts used in business events can either be more abstract or more specific than those in clear text events. In order to propose a general approach the goal needs to be clearly defined. Ideally, going from a clear text event instance to a business event instance and from there to another clear text event instance should not change the semantics of the event instance content at all. The semantics of the content of the two clear text events should stay precisely the same. If we were to transform from a first clear text event to a business event to a second clear text event, where the type of the two clear text events is precisely the same, the contents must be exactly the same in both clear text event instances. This means that the business event should have the more abstract version of a business concept, and the clear text events should have the equal or more specific concept. In terms of the date example, the business event would contain the normal date, since every working day date can be expressed as normal date and the two clear text event instances would have the same date values after the transformation.

However, sometimes the more specialized concept has more attributes than the general concept. For example, a hotel room might have specializations like standard room and deluxe room. The deluxe room has an attribute called special feature that describes what makes the room a deluxe room. If the business event would contain the more abstract concept, in this case hotel room, the special feature attributed could not be transformed and would be lost (in addition to the fact that the room was a deluxe room). Since the goal is to not change the semantics through transformation but ensure the equivalence, the idea to have the more abstract business concepts in the business event does not work.

Based on this observation, the approach of designing business event types has to be modified to the following. The superset of meaning as well as structure has to be constructed for all business concepts as part of a subsumption relationship. For example, in the working day example, the structure of both the normal date and the working day date is the same, that is, both have a date value. The superset of the meaning is normal date since working day dates are normal days. In order to be able to distinguish normal from working day dates in the business event, a concept classifier needs to be introduced that can indicate if the date is a normal date or a working day date. In case of the hotel room example, the superset of the structure is the deluxe hotel room structure since it contains all fields of a normal hotel room plus one more attribute storing the special feature. A concept classifier can indicate if the room in the business event instance is a normal or a deluxe room. In the case of storing a normal hotel room, the special feature field can either be without value (e.g., NULL) or empty with the meaning that there is no special feature.

In summary, loss of information (business concept abstraction) should be avoided by transforming from clear text events to business events. Only then can the business concept equivalence be achieved for all clear text events that are transformed to and from business events.

It was assumed up to this point that the clear text event that is transformed into the business event and the clear text event that is derived from the business event have equivalent business concepts and not an abstraction/subsumption relationship. Since this might also be possible, the approach of designing business events has to be verified for this case.

Two subcases have to be distinguished. First, going from a more specialized business concept in one clear text event to a more abstract business concept in a clear text event. For this case the above approach for business event type construction applies. The business event contains the more specific business concept. From there, it must be mapped to a more abstract business concept in the clear text event. This might or might not incur loss of information. However, since the transformation is to a more abstract business concept, in general, this cannot be avoided. For example, mapping from a working day date to a normal date looses the information that the original date was a working day date. Transforming from a deluxe room to a normal hotel room looses the fact that it was a deluxe room as well as the particular special features.

Second, the originating clear text event might have the more abstract business concepts compared to the target clear text event. In this case the above approach for designing business event types also applies, since the business event can store the more abstract business concept. Transformation from the business event to the more specialized clear text event poses a problem (that is in the nature of the situation when going from a more abstract to a more specialized concept). Information might have to be added in order to satisfy the more specialized business concept. For example, a normal hotel room might have to be transformed to a deluxe hotel room. Even though a normal hotel room does not have a special feature, when transforming to a deluxe hotel room a special feature has to be provided. In this case, it might have to be set to empty. The semantics might also change. For example, transforming from a normal date into a working day date requires a rule about what to do in case the normal date is not a working day date. A possibility is to go back to the last previous date or the next following working day date.

Also possible are data type mismatches between the attributes' data types of related business concepts. For example, in one case the zip code might be represented as a positive, whereas in another case it might be represented as a string. A typecast for both ways (positive to string, and vice versa) has to be built into the transformation rules to deal with this situation.

Clear Text Event Transformation

As discussed in Chap. 2, transformation between clear text events without going through business events is possible. In this case business concepts are transformed into each other too, but directly, without going through business events. All the discussed transformation issues as well as transformation mismatches can occur, too.

Not going though a business event does not eliminate the transformation mismatches at all since business concepts and their representation are still transformed into each other.

A Note on Lossless Transformation

Lossless transformation is not always possible due to abstractions or mismatches, as discussed above. In order to minimize the amount of unavoidable loss, loss should occur at the transformation from the business event to the clear text event (lossful transformation). This ensures that business events always contain the complete set of data of the concepts contained in clear text events.

In addition to the benefit of having the complete set of data in the business events, this approach also makes sure that concepts can be restored in a round-trip integration scenario. For example, while sending a request event from one endpoint to a second endpoint, address data might get lost because the second endpoint does not require any address data at all. However, when the second endpoint sends back the reply event to the first endpoint, the address information has to be fully contained. Since the second endpoint does not deal with address data at all, it has to be retrieved from somewhere else so that the reply event targeted for the first endpoint contains the full address information. The full address information is contained in the business event representing the request (if the integration modeler followed the recommendation to include the full data set into the business event), and from there the full address data can be obtained. In this sense the business event also served as an "intermediate" storage of the address data. Section 7.2.2 shows the example in the context of a process specification.

7.1.7 Business Event Type Change Management

Business events are central to B2B integration when direct transformation between clear text events is not chosen. Once all the transformation rules between clear text events and business events are established, the integration of the various endpoints' events is established.

A change management problem arises if another endpoint has to be integrated and its events have to be transformed into the already existing business events. Further business event change management issues arise if endpoints change their event definition or if endpoints are removed. In the following these change management issues around business events are discussed.

Adding a Clear Text Event Type

When a new clear text event type has to be mapped to an existing business event type, the following changes to the business event might be necessary in order to accommodate the additional clear text event type.

- **Additional attributes.** A new clear text event might contain a business concept that is equivalent to that in the business event except for an additional attribute (or several). In this case the additional attribute has to be added to the business event in order to be able to capture the data at run time. All existing clear text events have to be revisited in order to determine how the new attribute is mapped to those, if at all. This might require changing some of the transformation rules from the business event to the existing clear text events, and vice versa. If the new attribute is not used by transformation rules, a lossful transformation occurs.
- **Additional concepts.** The new clear text event type might have a new concept that has not been captured in the business event type. In this case the business event has to be extended, and the corresponding transformation rules have to be built. However, most likely the new concept is not used to derive the already existing clear text events, since the transformation rules for those have already been established. This indicates a lossful transformation whereby the business event might contain data for a concept that is not mapped to all clear text events.
- **Additional domain values.** New clear text events might define domain values that have not been defined before. For example, if distance ranges are different in a new clear text event, e.g., [0..10[, [10..30[, [30..50[and [50..] then introducing this additional domain data type in the business event would not be advisable, since it is possible to map this to an already existing data type consisting of [0..10[, [10..50[and [50..] without any problems. If it would be introduced to the business event type, additional transformations would be required for all the other already existing clear text events.
- **Additional concept classifier.** For example, a new hotel room type, suite, might be introduced. The recommended change would be to change the existing classifier from standards and deluxe to standard, deluxe and suite. The existing transformation rules that refer to this classifier have to be revisited to make sure that they use the new element suite, if appropriate, to achieve a semantically correct transformation.

New or different abstractions as well as subsumption relationships might be introduced through new clear text event types, too. Those will result in additional attributes, concepts, domain values or concept classifiers.

There is a temptation to just add additional concepts, attributes or concept classifiers and not to change existing ones. This temptation exists because any change to existing concepts, attributes or concept classifiers affects the existing transformation rules, which have to be adjusted to accommodate the changes. However, not making a change even though it would be appropriate to do so compromises the values of a business event and should be avoided if possible. The example of the additional concept classifier for hotel room types shows this. If an additional and separate concept of suite were introduced instead of a concept classifier change, then this would not change the existing transformation rules. However, it would make any later access to the business event less uniform because any access would have to deal with a concept classifier for hotel rooms in addition to a new concept suite.

Removing an Existing Clear Text Event Type

Removing an existing clear text event type is very easy and straightforward because this does not have to impact business event types at all. In the worst case, some concepts or some attributes of concepts are used no longer since they were specific to the removed clear text event type. Therefore, removing an existing clear text event type does not change the corresponding business event type at all.

However, if an integration modeler wants to have a business event type be minimal in the sense that all concepts and all attributes of concepts of a business event are used, then the removal of a clear text event type might change the business event type. All concepts or attributes of concepts that are used no longer have to be removed. Any concept classifier that was introduced to distinguish concepts might have to be changed and may no longer contain the removed concepts. Domain values might have to be changed to no longer have values that were specific to the removed clear text event type.

As a consequence, transformation rules that access the concepts or attributes of concepts have to be changed or removed. Any reference to a removed concept classifier has to be changed, too. Domain-value aware transformation rules have to be revisited so that they do not refer to those values any more that have been removed.

Changing an Existing Clear Text Event Type

Changing an existing clear text event type can be reduced to the removal of the old version and the addition of the new version of the clear text event. Fundamentally, no management problem specific to the change of existing clear text events is introduced.

7.1.8 Event and Vocabulary

Each endpoint defines its own set of business concepts. Since business concepts are represented by data types and their corresponding domain values, each endpoint implicitly defines its own vocabulary. A vocabulary in this context is the set of all permissible values for a given data type. The values for a data type can either be intentionally or extensionally defined. Intentionally defined data types are those where no explicit list of values has to be specified. For example, the data type positive can contain any positive number. When using this data type the list of all positive numbers does not have to be explicitly defined (which would be impossible). Restrictions are possible, too. For example, a shop might define that no product costs more than US $499. In this case the data type price might be of type positive with a restriction that restricts the contents to less than 500.

Not all data types are intentionally defined. Sometimes it is necessary to extensionally define the possible values. The values for extensionally defined data types can be a list of constants that is predetermined, like the list of the names of all US states. This is a static list of domain values (static domain value list). In addition, the values can be dynamic, like the list of product identifiers for the products a company sells, or the list of customer identifiers for the customers of a company or its trading partners. Such a list is finite at any point in time and the values can be enumerated, but the list might change over time (dynamic domain value list).

Since each endpoint has a vocabulary, the transformation rules transforming an endpoint's clear text events to business events and vice versa have to deal with transforming vocabularies. Since the business events are defined through data types, they too have their own vocabulary. Transformation has to deal not only with the concept mismatch issues as discussed before, but also with transforming intentionally as well as extensionally defined data types.

Transformation rules that access intentionally defined data types have either to copy the values, to type cast values or to split or concatenate values adhering to any restriction. All transformation rules and examples introduced so far dealt with this case only. In addition, a formula-based transformation has to take place, like mapping between temperature in degrees Fahrenheit and temperature in degrees Celsius. This mapping takes place through a formula. All these transformations are idempotent, i.e., a repeated transformation gives the same transformation result.

Transformation rules that access extensionally defined data types have to make sure that they adhere to the explicitly listed values. In these cases it is not possible to automatically infer which value for the source data type corresponds to a given value of the target data type. In order to provide the correspondence, the concept of a so-called domain value map is introduced. A domain value map relates a value of one domain value list for one data type to a value in another domain value list for another data type. Different domain value maps have to be distinguished, and each is discussed separately in the following.

Static and idempotent domain value maps are those that relate values of a static domain value list to a value in another static domain value list. In the case when clear text events are transformed into business events and vice versa, the domain value map has to map between values of clear text and business event data types. In the case when a clear text event is transformed into another clear text event, the domain value map has to map between data types of clear text event types. An example is the map of the names of the US states. "CA" is mapped to "California" or "WA" is mapped to "Washington." This is a direct map since one value is directly related to another value. If one business event is potentially transformed into different clear text events with different vocabularies, several domain value maps are necessary to map from the business event vocabulary to the different clear text event vocabularies, one for each vocabulary that has to be mapped into.

These types of domain value maps are idempotent since the mapping from one value to another value always results in the same value. This is important, since it ensures consistency in vocabulary transformation. It is necessary that one value is always mapped to one other value. Otherwise, the domain value map would be ambiguous. It might be that in special cases the direction of the mapping in the domain value map plays a significant role. This means that when mapping from one domain value list to another domain value list the same domain value map cannot be used for the opposite mapping direction. Instead, two domain value maps are necessary. If this is the case, the transformation rule that looks up a domain value has to select the correct domain value map for the mapping direction at hand.

These domain value maps are attributed static because they do not change unless the underlying domain value lists change. Such a change only happens if the data types are changed, i.e., the meaning changed or adjusted. In general, this is rarely the case.

In addition to static and idempotent domain value maps, there are dynamic and idempotent domain value maps. A dynamic and idempotent domain value map changes often compared to static domain value maps. In addition, they mostly contain identifier data from event exchanges at run time. Identifier data come into existence at run time and they have to become part of dynamic domain value maps at run time. Hence the continuous change of the dynamic domain value maps. For example, if a back-end application system issues a purchase order, the purchase order has a unique identifier. That unique purchase order identifier is used without change in the corresponding business event. When the purchase order is sent to the trading partner, the trading partner creates its own representation of the purchase order in its system and consequently uses its own identifiers. The receiving trading partner therefore has its own identifier for the purchase order as well as the identifier from the sending trading partner. In order to be able to relate any subsequent message from the sending trading partner to the internal purchase order, a map has to be established from the sending trading partner's purchase order identifier to the receiving trading partner's identifier. This is done with a dynamic domain value map. Once the receiving trading partner's internal identifier is related to the external identifier of the purchase order, any subsequent transformation of incoming events can be accomplished by looking up the corresponding identifier. Another example is a dynamic domain value map for customer identifiers. The identifiers used in a back-end application system might be different from those used for identifying endpoints in the B2B integration technology. The same applies for all other types of trading partners like suppliers, shippers and so on.

Another form of domain value map is a dynamic and nonidempotent domain value map. These types of maps change often, and a repeated lookup might result in a different value. For example, if currency conversion has to take place so that all hotel reservations are shown in euros then any reservation request coming in that is not in euro has to be converted to euros. In order to achieve this, a currency converter has to be invoked with the currency and value from the clear text event, with the destination currency, in this case euro, and the day of conversion to indicate which day's currency exchange rate to use. When the transformation takes place then the external application like the currency converter is invoked in order to transform the values. Currencies are extensional defined data types since a finite number of currencies is available. The domain value maps between currencies are dynamic since the currency exchange rate changes daily. Instead of updating the metadata of the B2B integration technology daily with a new version of the currency domain value map, it is possible to invoke a back-end application system that manages the currency conversion instead. In this approach the transformation rules accessing currency data do not look up the domain value maps, but invoke a program for obtaining the values. While this is an implementation detail, it is relevant here since it shows that the implementation of domain value maps can assume different forms.

So far, the discussion was about transforming vocabularies into each other for the data types that define the contents of the different events. However, metadata of the events, i.e., the management data necessary to deal with event instances themselves, might also be subject to transformation. For example, event addressing is of this nature (Sect. 7.1.4). A back-end application system sending out an event uses its internal format of the endpoint addressing identifier to indicate where the event should be sent. The identifier, however, might not match with that used by the endpoint management of the B2B integration technology to identify the same endpoint. Once the event is received from the back-end application system, the identifier that specifies the target endpoint has to be transformed into the one used by the B2B integration technology to identify the same endpoint. This is accomplished by a dynamic and idempotent domain value map that relates the endpoint identifiers that correspond to each other. This precisely fits the concept, since this domain value map maps the identifier from the clear text event to the business event, and vice versa.

As discussed in the transformation mismatches, lossful transformation between vocabularies is a reality, too. This happens if there is no possibility to uniquely relate domain values from one list into domain values in another domain value list. For example, local deliveries might be categorized as near and as far in one clear text event type, but according to ranges in another clear text event type, like [0..10[(between 0 and 10 miles), [10..50[(10 and 50 miles) and [50..] (50 miles and more). In this case the domain values of distance are incompatible in the sense that there is no formula possible to derive a domain value of the one (e.g., near) from the other (which range is considered near?). In this case the two domain values near and far are more abstract then the more specific ranges. Transforming from the two domain values near and far to the more specific ranges loses information, i.e., is a lossful transformation. However, this situation has to be dealt with. Therefore the ranges should be used in the business event type. The transformation rules from and to clear text events have to make sure that the two domain values are transformed the same way in both directions. For example, near might be mapped to the first range and far to the second range. The caveat is that far never gets mapped to the third range, even though the actual distance might fall into this range. Therefore, the interpretation of the clear text event must accept that the actual range might not be accurate. If this is not possible, then the business event needs to be defined in such a way that both the two domain values as well as the ranges are available in it so that the transformation can be more accurate.

An interesting problem is posed by synonyms and homonyms. For example, if two values in one domain are synonyms, either could be used in a domain value map. And both could be used in different domain value maps, since they are synonyms. However, the fact that the two values are synonyms has to be known by all systems involved so that they do not flag this as an inconsistency, for example, when a back-end application system receives events that have both values since two different maps are used. Of course, it would be better to avoid this situation and settle on only one of the two values.

Homonyms, in contrast to synonyms, should not pose a problem since the context in which a data type is used should clarify which meaning of a value is assumed. For example, if a price is used it needs to be clear from the context whether this includes or excludes taxes.

7.1.9 Business Event and Business Object

Business events in general refer to business data, like a purchase order or a health care record. A complete purchase order or a health care record has a finite set of fields that can be described through one or several data types. A complete purchase order or a complete health care record is called a business object. A business object contains all fields that belong to it and that define it completely.

A business event that indicates the creation of a purchase order or the creation of a health care record usually contains the complete business object. If it is sent from one endpoint to another, it needs to contain all fields so that the receiving endpoint can create the complete business object.

However, not all business events carry the complete business object. For example, if a health care record needs to be deleted, only the health record's unique identifier has to be transmitted because it uniquely identifies one record. More data from that record is not necessary for its deletion. Another example is the update of a purchase order. If only one line item has to be changed, then only this line item needs to be transmitted. Again, it is a subset of the data of the business object purchase order.

Usually several different business event types are related to one business object. For example, related to a purchase order (a business object) are the event types create purchase order, get status of purchase order, update purchase order or delete purchase order. Business events express the intent of the sender of what the receiver is asked to do, like create, update, delete, get status. So that the modeler need not encode this intent as a naming convention of event names, it can be separately defined as an action name in the event type definition. Figure 7.15 shows a business event with the action name.

```
data_type PO_header
  header: header;
end_data_type

data_type PO_line_items
  line_items: list_of(line_item);
end_data_type

business_event_type purchase_order
  action create;
  event_element header
    PO_header;
  end_event_element
  event_element line_items
    PO_line_items;
  end_event_element
end_business_event_type
```

Fig. 7.15. Business event type definition with action name

Each business event related to the same business object contains a different subset of the fields of the business object. This subset must be consistent with the definition of the business object. If business objects were defined as types and if event types referred to the business object they are concerned with, an automatic consistency check could be performed if the event carries a consistent subset of the business object fields. In order to formally support the consistency, business objects can be defined as separate integration concepts. Based on the business object, a business event is defined.

```
data_type puchase_order_header
  header: header;
end_data_type

data_type purchase_order_line_items
  line_items: list_of(line_item);
end_data_type

business_object_type purchase_order
  actions create, update, delete, get_status;
  header: purchase_order_header;
  line_items: purchase_order_line_items;
end_business_object_type
```

Fig. 7.16. Business object type purchase order

Figure 7.16 shows the definition of the business object purchase order. It has two parts, a header and line items. Furthermore, it lists the possible actions of the business object.

Figure 7.17 shows the business event type related to the business object. It contains a reference to the business object to which it is related. Furthermore, it reuses the data type definitions of the business object. This ensures the consistent definition of the business event type.

```
business_event_type purchase_order
action create;
business_object purchase_order;
event_element header
  purchase_order_header;
end_event_element
event_element line_items
  purchase_order_line_items;
end_event_element
end_business_event_type
```

Fig. 7.17. Business event type definition with reference to business object

Another way to express the fact that events are subsets of business objects is to look at business events being views on business objects. This way the consistency is almost guaranteed, since views are defined as restrictions on objects.

Since business events carry data values, the question arises whether business object instances should be created and maintained within the B2B integration technology. This would be in contradiction to back-end application systems since back-end application systems usually manage business object instances. Business object instances within the B2B integration technology would duplicate the representation. However, they would not be stored in order to execute any business logic, since this is the domain of back-end application systems. Instead, the business object instance is a way for the B2B integration technology architecture to remember the contents if it is needed for the business logic at some later point in time. This is necessary and is discussed in Sect. 7.5. Therefore, events that carry business data will cause the creation of business object instances within the B2B integration technology architecture.

It cannot be excluded that a business event contains data from several business objects. For example, a business event might not only contain a shipment request but also the complete address of the customer to whom the goods should be delivered. The shipment request contains part of the customer business object, namely the complete address. In this case the business event type definition has to refer to all the business objects involved as well as the specific data types from those business objects (Fig. 7.18). The business event refers to two business objects. In the business event element definitions, the data types used are qualified by the business object. This mechanism defines which data type and which element of a business object is used in this business event type definition.

```
business_event_type shipment_request
  action create;
  business_object shipment;
  business_object customer;
  event_element payload
    shipment.shipment_request;
  end_event_element
  event_element customer
    customer.customer_address;
  end_event_element
end_business_event_type
```

Fig. 7.18. Business event type referring to several business objects

It is advisable to specify business events as views on business objects because this enforces specification consistency by having event types refer to data types specified in business objects. However, this dependency is not mandatory. An event type can be specified independent of any business object type.

7.1.10 Event Correlation

Events can be processed synchronously with respect to the endpoint to which the events are sent. This means that response events are returned in the same synchronous invocation (if at all). The interface process step receives the result and the interface processing continues. The synchronous invocation ensures that the response event is available in the correct interface process in case there are several instances of the same interface process type in the system at a given moment. That seems to be an obvious observation, however, in the asynchronous event exchange case, this is no longer straightforward.

In the asynchronous case of exchanging events with endpoints, the situation is different. In this case the response event is received asynchronously to the interface process that sent the original request event. This in turn means that for a given response event, the appropriate interface process instance has to be determined. In the synchronous invocation situation, the synchronous connection automatically ensures that the response event is received by the correct interface process instance. In the asynchronous case, an alternative way of determining the interface process instance has to be found.

For example, if 100 purchase order event instances are sent to different endpoints, then 100 purchase order acknowledgment instances are expected back from those endpoints (assuming no errors). For each of the 100 purchase orders, there is a separate interface process instance waiting for the purchase order acknowledgment event instances as the response event instance. For a given purchase order acknowledgment event instance, it must be determined to which interface process instance it belongs, so that it matches up with the corresponding purchase order instance.

For a given event instance that is a response event instance to an original event instance and that has to be received by the same interface process instance that sent the original event instance, the correct interface process instance has to be determined. The concept that allows for the determination of the correct interface process instance is event correlation.

Event correlation is based on a correlation predicate that determines if two event instances are related. For example, a purchase order event instance and the corresponding purchase order acknowledgment event instance both refer to the same purchase order identifier. The predicate that relates the two event instances has to test whether the two data values that represent the purchase order identifier are equivalent. If this is the case, the two event instances are related. If not, the two event instances are not related.

To continue the example, for each incoming purchase order acknowledgement event instance the correlation predicate is executed for each purchase order. For one of the purchase orders the predicate will return true, which indicates the two corresponding event instances. Once the purchase order event instance is determined, the interface process instance can be determined easily, since interface process instances refer to the event instances they processed. Once the correct interface process instance is determined, the purchase order acknowledgment event instance can be given to the process step that is waiting for it. In a real implementation, most likely not all purchase orders are tested until a correlated purchase order acknowledgment event instance is found. Instead, the correlation predicate is interpreted as a query for the purchase order instance with the particular purchase order identifier.

The general mechanism for event correlation is a correlation predicate over event instances. A correlation predicate can refer to several data values in event instances and can use arbitrary comparison operators to compare the data type values. When event types are designed the correlation predicates have to be defined between the event types that will need to be correlated during run time.

Figure 7.19 shows the definition of two business objects, a purchase order and a purchase order acknowledgment. Both contain a purchase order identifier and a correlation predicate that specifies that the product identifier has to be the same in order for two event instances to be correlated.

```
data_type puchase_order_header
  header: header_type;
end_data_type

data_type header_type
  purchase_order_identifier: integer;
  buyer: integer;
  seller: integer;
end_data_type

data_type purchase_order_line_items
    line_items: list_of(line_item);
end_data_type

business_object_type purchase_order
  actions create, update, delete, get_status;
  header: purchase_order_header;
  line_items: purchase_order_line_items;
  correlation purchase_order.header.header.purchase_order_identifier =
    purchase_order_acknowledgement.header.header.purchase_order_identifier;
end_business_object_type

business_object_type purchase_order_acknowledgement
  actions create, get_status;
  header: purchase_order_header;
  line_items: purchase_order_line_items;
  correlation
    purchase_order_acknowledgement.header.header.purchase_order_identifier =
    purchase_order.header.header.purchase_order_identifier;
end_business_object_type
```

Fig. 7.19. Example correlation predicate

As Fig. 7.19 shows, both business objects have the same correlation predicate associated with them. However, that does not necessarily have to be the case. Each business object can define from its viewpoint what correlated events are, and therefore the correlation predicates can be different.

More than two event instances can be correlated. For example, if a purchase order header and all the purchase order line items are sent in an event each, then all of them have to be given to the same interface process instance for processing. In this case the correlation predicate ensures that all event instances are correlated and consequently given to the same interface process.

However, it might be the case that event instances cannot be related, since it is not possible to define correlation predicates. This would be the case if two related event instances do not share at least one business data element that has the same value. This means that it is impossible to automatically determine the correct interface process instance for the event instances that are responses. This can be resolved in two ways. One way is that the design of the interface process has to be changed to a synchronous invocation. This would ensure that the response event instance goes directly back to the correct interface process instance. Another way is that instead of one interface process, two interface processes are specified. Since both are independent of each other, it makes correlation unnecessary. If still one interface process is required, alternatively a human user can be involved to point out the correct interface process instance. However, this approach does not really scale if many event instances are received.

7.1.11 Event Validation and Data Type Validation

Events in general contain business data that are subject to consistency. Consistency in this context means that the values themselves have to be consistent in that they must have values of the appropriate data type domain. For example, a date field needs to contain a valid date, or a price field cannot be negative. In addition, combinations of fields have to be consistent, too. If the zip code of a city is used in combination with the wrong city name, then the combination is inconsistent, while each of the fields taken by itself is consistent.

One approach that can be taken is to assume that the business data that are communicated are already consistent because it is assumed that each endpoint only communicates consistent business data. In addition, any change within any process like translation or transformation will produce consistent events.

While this approach is possible, it cannot address the case when an endpoint does not always produce consistent data, or when it is not known if an endpoint produces consistent data. In this case a consistency check is in order, and validation rules for this have to be specified and subsequently executed at run time for the appropriate event instances.

Furthermore, an architecturally sound B2B integration technology ensures that only consistent event instances are processed and therefore enforces validation of event instances. If validation rules are enforced before event instances are processed, then the integration modeler can assume that only consistent event instances (according to the defined validation rules) are in the system. This means that translation, transformation or any other access can assume consistent event instances.

Where would validation rules be executed to enforce consistency before event instance processing begins? The appropriate place is after the creation of the event instance occurs (state created) and before the event is in state raised. Event instance validation takes place when the event instance transitions from created to raised. If the validation succeeds, then the event succeeds transitioning to raised. If the validation fails, the event instance state transitions to the in_error state. This approach ensures that only consistent events are in raised state and inconsistent events end up in the in_error state. Error handling has to deal with events in the error state and "un-error" them. This is discussed in Sect. 7.9.

In general, consistency rules (or synonymously, validation rules) can implement various types of checks. These are checks for mandatory fields that have to contain values as well as optional fields that might or might not contain values. Field contents can be checked, and those rules ensure that values in fields are of a certain data type domain. This can be based on dictionaries or external function accesses like the current day of the year. The combination of fields can be checked to ensure that a set of fields together, like an address are consistent. Some checks are defined on correlated events. For example, a purchase order and a purchase order acknowledgment have to refer to the same products in their line items and to the same prices. These types of consistency rules are across events. Validation rules that only apply in specific process states are discussed in Sect. 7.2.3.

There are several places where validation rules can be defined. First of all, business objects are subject to consistency, and so their specification can contain consistency rules. In addition, business event types can contain consistency rules. In the case a business event type is a view on a business object, the question is whether the business event type specification inherits the validation rules as specified in the business object. This is the case for validation rules that are related to an individual data type that is completely contained in the business event type definition. The specification of the business event type can decide in this case if the validation rule is overwritten or not by specifying a replacement. If a validation rule of the business object spans several data types that are not all contained in the business event, inheriting the validation rule into the business event type only makes sense if all data types are in the business event type, too. Otherwise, the validation rule would refer to data types that are not available in the business event type. In the case when a business event type is specified independently of a business object, its validation rules are specified without any relationship to any business object type.

Wire events as well as clear text events can have their own validation rules, of course. Since both classes of event types are defined independently of business objects, their validation rules are specified independently of any other object in the system.

Validation rules can also be defined in the context of data types, independent of their use in any business object or event type. In this case every business object or event type that uses that data type inherits the validation rule automatically. If this rule does not apply, the rules has to be replaced by another more appropriate one.

The replacement of validation rules is achieved as follows. Each validation rule has a unique name, and each validation rule is defined in the context of the data types it validates. If a data type is used then the validation rules apply automatically (they are inherited). However, if the validation rule is changed, then a validation rule with the same name as the inherited one can be specified. This then means that instead of the inherited rule, the newly defined rule applies.

Figure 7.20 to Fig. 7.22 show an example. Figure 7.20 shows a data type that has two validation rules, r1 and r2, associated with it. The data type is an address, the rule r1 defines that the city name is mandatory and the rule r2 defines that the city name and the zip code have to correspond. Both rules are functions that return the data type Boolean. When event instance validation takes place, both validation rules are executed and only if both return true does the event instance validation succeed. If there are additional rules they have to result into true, too.

```
data_type address_details
    street_number: string;
    street_name: string;
    city_name: string;
    city_zip: string;
    state_name: string;
    country_name: string;
    validation
        r1: is_mandatory(city_name);
        r2: correspond(city_zip, city_name);
end_data_type
```

Fig. 7.20. Data type definition with two validation rules

Figure 7.21 shows a business object type that refers to the data type defined in Fig. 7.20. Two more validation rules are added: one for making sure that the reservation dates are correct and another that validates that the room is either a standard or deluxe room. The data type reservation_details is not further specified.

```
business_object_type hotel_room
    action reserve, unreserve, get_status, change;
    event_element address_details
        address_details;
    end_event_element
    event_element reservation_details
        reservation_details;
    end_event_element
    validation
        r1: reservation_details.from_date < reservation_details.to_date;
        r2: reservation_details.room_type = standard | deluxe;
end_business_object_type
```

Fig. 7.21. Business object type with validation rules

Figure 7.22 introduces a business event for reserving a hotel room, and this definition overwrites some of the validation rules.

```
business_event_type hotel_room
  action reserve;
  event_element address_details
    address_details;
  end_event_element
  event_element reservation_details
    reservation_details;
  end_event_element
  validation
    address_details.r1: is_mandatory(city_name) AND is_US_address(city_name);
    hotel_room.r2: reservation_details.room_type = standard;
  end_business_event_type
```

Fig. 7.22. Business event with validation rule overwrites

The first validation rule overwrite of rule r1 of the data type makes sure that the address is a US address. The second validation rule overwrite of rule r2 of the business object makes sure that only standard rooms are reserved.

Validation might be context-dependent, i.e., specific validation rules should only be executed at a specific point in the business process or interface process, and not whenever the event instance is raised. Then the business process defines these rules at the appropriate point (Sect. 7.2) and only at this point are the rules applied to the event instances.

7.1.12 Summary

The integration concept event is one of the fundamental concepts that are necessary to accomplish B2B integration. This section of the current chapter discussed all aspects of events including translation, transformation and vocabularies. With this powerful B2B integration concept available, the second very fundamental concept, processes, is introduced next in all its aspects.

7.2 Process

As important as the B2B integration concept event is the concept of a process. Processes are the means to define the processing of events within the B2B integration technology architecture. Each event that has been received always is processed by a process and each event that has been sent to an endpoint is always sent by a process. No event can be processed without being part of a process. In this sense processes and events are mutually dependent and complementary concepts, since one cannot exist without the other during execution. Processes implement behavior, whereas events implement data.

As discussed in Chap. 2, three classes of processes are involved in B2B integration, interface processes, business processes and binding processes. In the following sections, these will be introduced in detail. This section discusses the aspects of the concept of a process that apply to all process classes. Section 7.3 discusses interface-specific aspects; Sect. 7.4 business process-specific aspects and Sect. 7.5 binding process-specific aspects. In the following the different aspects of the process concept are introduced step-by-step in detail. Initially, basic process aspects are introduced that form the structure of processes, and later process behavior is discussed that defines the behavior of process instances at run time.

7.2.1 Hierarchical Decomposition

Processes are prescriptions for execution. In general, during execution different data are manipulated. In the context of B2B integration, the data are event instances (and later data instances defined by data types). The data aspect of processes is introduced in Sect. 7.2.2. Most processes are stepwise executions (Sect. 2.2.5). The execution steps are defined by process step types that are part of a process type. The order of the process step execution is defined by data flow rules (introduced in Sect. 7.2.2) and control flow rules (introduced in Sect. 7.2.4). This section focuses solely on the hierarchical decomposition that allows process steps to be defined as part of process types.

A process type is a uniquely identifiable object (by its name) that defines a scope for its decomposition. The decomposition is accomplished by making other existing process types part of the process type. These process types are process types in and of themselves, however, they are referenced by the process type they are part of. The mechanism that allows for referencing of the process types is called a process variable. It is analogous to a local variable in an object-oriented programming language that contains object instances at run time, but is of a particular object class (its type) when defined. Figure 7.23 shows a first example.

```
process_type PO_approval
   ...
end_process_type

process_type PO_POA
   decomposition
      approval_process: PO_approval;
end_process_type
```

Fig. 7.23. Two process types, where one is part of another

Figure 7.23 shows that both process types (PO_approval, PO_POA) are defined independently of each other, and one references the other one through a process variable called approval_process. This means that not only is the decomposition defined, but also that the process type that is referenced is reused. It could be reused in other process types, too, and can itself reuse other process types. The reuse is possible because the process type is defined independently and not in the scope of the referencing process type. This reuse is called process type reuse.

A process type that is decomposed but is not part of a decomposition itself is called a top-level process type. A process type that is part of a decomposition is called a sub-process type in the context of the process type of which it is a part. In Fig. 7.23 PO_POA is a top-level process type and PO_approval is both a top-level process type as well as a sub-process type (in the context of PO_POA). The decomposition hierarchy can be arbitrarily deep because a sub-process type can have process variables itself that reference other process types. There is no limit to the depth of the decomposition.

Process types only reference other process types (and later on are the mechanism that allows us to define the order between the process variables as well as the data flow). However, as discussed already, it must be possible to define execution logic in addition to decomposition. For example, transformation as well as translation of events has to take place. Other examples are authorization by users or notification of users. The concept that supports execution logic instead of decomposition is called a process step type. A process step type defines which execution logic has to be executed. Different process step types are available for implementing execution logic. For example, in order to achieve transformation, a transformation process step type is available that can invoke and execute transformations. The term execution logic is used to indicate that programs are executed that implement specific functionality like transformation, translation or authorization.

Process step types cannot stand alone like process types. They always have to be part of a decomposition in order to be executable at run time. However, process step types cannot be further decomposed themselves. They are "simple" in this sense.

```
process_step_type transformation
    ...
end_process_step_type

process_type PO_approval
    ...
end_process_type

process_type PO_POA
    decomposition
        approval_process: PO_approval;
        po_transformation: transformation;
end_process_type
```

Fig. 7.24. Process type referring to a process step type

Figure 7.24 shows an example that uses a process step type. Process step types are referred to by process variables as are process types. The process step type transformation is specified and referred to by the process type PO_POA. As Fig. 7.24 indicates, a process type can reference other process types as well as process step types at the same time and in any number.

The decomposition of a process type can be empty. In this case the process type does not have any process step inside that can define any execution logic. Such a process type could later be used in order to provide a synchronization point in the data flow or control flow of a process type in order to synchronize different execution paths. It is like a no-operation (NOOP) process type. The equivalent is a process step type without any execution logic, a NOOP process step type.

7.2.2 Data and Data Flow

The data and data flow aspect of processes in the context of B2B integration consists of three different parts. One is process parameters, which pass event instances or data to processes and obtain results from processes in the form of event instances or data instances. The second is local process data variables that can store instances of events as well as data. The third part is data flows, which connect parameters with each other as well as with local process data variables.

Process Parameter

Process parameters define the data interface of processes. Process parameters can be uniquely defined within a process through a unique name. Process parameters are analogous to formal parameters in programming languages. A process type and process step type, for that matter, can have any number of process parameters (all rules for parameters apply to both, process types and process step types in the same way).

Each parameter is of a specific type and is either an input parameter or an output parameter. The type of a parameter can either be an event type or a data type. At run time, instances of either event types or data types are passed to the process instance or process step instance or are obtained from them. In the case of an input parameter, event or data instances are given to the process from outside it. In the case of an output parameter, an event or data instance is given from the process to its outside.

Process parameters can be either mandatory or optional. Mandatory means that a parameter has to have an event or data instance passed to it at run time. The process will not finish unless all mandatory parameters have received an instance. An optional parameter might or might not have an event or data instance at run time. In either case, the process can execute.

Specifying parameters as mandatory or optional parameters is, however, not enough to express the necessary semantics in B2B integration. Sometimes it is necessary to define that either of two parameters must be present at run time because the business logic within the process needs exactly one of the two. This can be achieved by parameter constraints that are predicates over formal process parameters. There is one parameter constraint for all process parameters that have to be put into relation with each other. Parameter constraints refer only to those that are related. For example, if a purchase order is sent out, either an acknowledgment or an error message is expected. In this example both the acknowledgment and the error message are optional parameters and are both contained in a parameter constraint defining that either but not both must be returned. The parameter constraint could look like XOR(acknowledgment, error) if acknowledgment and error are the two parameter names.

All process types as well as process step types have a default output parameter called error_status. This output parameter will contain an error status (for example, of type integer) in case an error happened, or status 0 if no error happened. One example is that if a parameter constraint is violated, then the error_status contains an equivalent error status. Based on this error status error handling can take place.

Input parameters might have an associated precondition, and output parameters might have a postcondition associated with them. The process can only succeed if both the preconditions as well as the postconditions are fulfilled. For example, the precondition of a parameter called acknowledgment might be that the value in the sender field needs to be the same as the value in the target field of a previous output by parameter purchase order. If any preconditions or postconditions fail, the error_status field contains an appropriate error status.

A subset of the input parameters has to be supplied when the process is instantiated to allow the instantiation to succeed. These are called initiating process parameters. If the initiating parameters are not available, the process cannot be instantiated and executed. For example, a purchase order must be present for the selling process to start.

Unlike in conventional workflow management system models, input parameters do not necessarily have to be supplied at process creation time. It is possible that input parameters can be supplied concurrently to the execution of a process instance or a process step instance. The same applies to output parameters. Results in output parameters can be available long before the process instance or process step instance is finished.

This type of concurrent parameter binding is necessary, since in long-running processes it is not possible to supply all parameters at start time. Some of them are the consequence of the processing itself. They are by construction only available at some later point. For example, if a purchase order has not been processed, it is not possible to obtain a purchase order acknowledgment. Later, it will become clear that concurrent parameter handling allows different processes that are bound by binding processes to execute concurrently while they are synchronized by connecting their input and output parameters.

Figure 7.25 shows a process type definition that has several process parameters, where IN or OUT denotes input or output parameters, respectively. The parameter constraint defines that one of two parameter sets are possible (i.e., parameters that have to contain instance data or event instances). In case 1 a PO came in and either an out_ACK or an out_ERROR was returned. In case 2 a PO came in, an out_ACK was returned, a POA was returned and either an in_ACK or an in_ERROR came in. The second case only happens if the PO was acknowledged successfully through an out_ACK. Any other combination leads to an error_status that is different from 0. This parameter combination is similar to the behavior of a seller in the B2B standard RosettaNet. A precondition and a postcondition are modeled as examples. The precondition specifies that the incoming acknowledgement must be from the same endpoint to which the POA was addressed. The postcondition specifies that the outgoing acknowledgment needs to go to the same endpoint from which the purchase order came. The pre- as well as postcondition syntax refers to the name of the parameter to which the predicate belongs. The PO is defined as the initiating parameter. None of the event types are defined in the example.

Figure 7.26 introduces a graphical notation for the various constructs. It will be extended with additional graphical symbols over time throughout this chapter.

process_type PO_POA_seller
  parameter
    IN mandatory initiating PO: purchase_order;
    IN optional in_ACK: acknowledgement;
    OUT optional POA: purchase_order_acknowledgment;
    OUT optional out_ACK: acknowledgment;
    IN optional in_ERROR: error;
    OUT optional out_ERROR: error;
    OUT mandatory error_status: status;
  parameter constraint
    XOR (
      (PO **AND** (out_ACK **XOR** out_error))
      (PO **AND** out_ACK **AND** POA **AND** (in_ACK **XOR** in_error)))
  parameter pre_conditions
    in_ACK: in_ACK.sender = POA.target;
  parameter post_conditions
    out_ACK: out_ACK.target = PO.sender;
  end_process_type

Fig. 7.25. Process type specification with process parameters

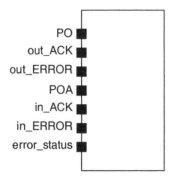

Fig. 7.26. Graphical representation

In order to check whether a parameter is set, a test function is available that takes the name of a parameter and returns true if the parameter has an instance assigned to it, otherwise it returns false. This allows the business logic to check for the status of a parameter, if necessary. This applies to optional and to mandatory parameters as well as to input and output parameters.

Parameters can have constant values assigned at definition time. This means that the constant values are available at run time and no dynamic binding of parameters takes place. For example, a transformation step requires the particular transformation map that needs to be used at run time. This can be specified as a constant at definition time, and at run time the transformation process step will use the constant to select the corresponding transformation map. Through constant parameters the configuration of process step types or process types can be made explicit.

Local Process Data Variable

In case it is necessary to store event instances or data instances for later use within a process, then local process data variables can be used. If an event instance or a data instance is assigned to a local process data variable, the instance is available for the lifetime of the process. Not only parameters can be stored and made available this way but also intermediate results of computations. A local process data variable is typed and can be set and read as often as necessary within the lifetime of a process instance or process step instance. An example is that an incoming event like a purchase order is stored so that all subsequent process steps or sub-processes can refer to the same purchase order identifier.

Data Flow

With process parameters and local process data variables defined, not much can be achieved unless assignments between theme are specified. For example, where should an instance in a top-level process input parameter go? Should it be assigned to a local process data variable or to an input parameter of one of the subprocesses or to an output parameter to the same top-level process (i.e., no processing at all)?

The concept of data flow is the means to specify the "flow" of the data within a process. The data flow constructs link the different parameters with each other and with the local process data variables. Table 7.1 shows the possible combinations of parameters and local process data variables that data flow constructs can combine.

Table 7.1. Possible data flow combinations

To \ From	Process type input parameter	Process type output parameter	Subprocess input parameter	Subprocess output parameter	Local process data variable
Process type input parameter	(Not possible)	Parameter contents passed through without processing	Parameter is passed directly to subprocess for processing	(Not possible)	Parameter is passed to local process data variable for intermediate storage
Process type output parameter	(Not possible)	(Not possible)	(Not possible)	(Not possible)	(Not possible)
Subprocess input parameter	(Not possible)	(Not possible)	(Not possible)	(Not possible)	(Not possible)
Subprocess output parameter	(Not possible)	Parameter contents passed directly into an output parameter of the top level process	The output of one subprocess becomes the input of another subprocess	(Not possible)	The output is stored in a local variable for later reference
Local process data variable	(Not possible)	The value of the local variable will be the value of the output parameter	The value of the local variable will be the input of the sub-process	(Not possible)	One local variable is assigned to another local variable

Data flow can only be defined within one level of a process type, i.e., only between its parameters, its process data variables and the parameters of the process variables. Data flow cannot go across levels since the process type and the subprocess types define different scopes.

process_type PO_approval
  parameter
    in mandatory initiating PO: purchase_order;
    out mandatory approval: boolean;
    ...
end_process_type

process_type PO_POA_seller
  parameter
    IN mandatory initiating PO: purchase_order;
    IN optional in_ACK: acknowledgement;
    OUT optional POA: purchase_order_acknowledgment;
    OUT optional out_ACK: acknowledgment;
    IN optional in_ERROR: error;
    OUT optional out_ERROR: error;
    OUT mandatory error_status: status;
  parameter constraint
    XOR (
      (PO **AND** (out_ACK **XOR** out_error))
      (PO **AND** out_ACK **AND** POA **AND** (in_ACK **XOR** in_error)))
  parameter pre_conditions
    in_ACK: in_ACK.sender = POA.target;
  parameter post_conditions
    out_ACK: out_ACK.target = PO.sender;
  local process data variable
    authorized: boolean;
  decomposition
    approval_process: PO_approval;
  data flow
    PO -> approval_process.PO;
    approval_process.approval -> authorized;
end_process_type

Fig. 7.27. Data flow within a process type

Figure 7.27 shows an example of data flow constructs within a process type. The data flow shown connects the parameters of the subprocess authorization_process, which is of type PO_approval. This subprocess has an input parameter and an output parameter. A local variable authorized is defined that will contain the result of the subprocess. The data flow constructs defined that the PO that initiates the whole process is directly flown to the subprocess. The result of the subprocess is flown to the local process data variable. It is mandatory that the data types match. Figure 7.28 shows the corresponding graphical notation. The square represents the local variable and the circle represents the subprocess.

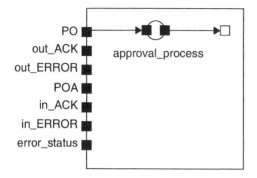

Fig. 7.28. Graphical representation

It is possible that several data flows originate at a parameter or local variable. In this case the instances are passed-by value, i.e., they are copied "along the way" before being given to the destination parameter or variable of the data flow. The destination parameters or local variables are therefore independent of each other in processing the instances.

It is also possible that several data flows end up in the same destination parameter or local variable. Since a parameter or local variable can hold only one instance at a time, the repeated writing will overwrite the contents. While local variables are meant to be overwritten several times to reflect changes in their values, parameters are not. The first attempt to overwrite a parameter results in a run-time error and the error status is set appropriately. This is because the parameter might have been read and a repeat overwrite would not be processed any more. If several data flows go to the same parameter, then the modeling must make sure that only one of the data flows will happen at run time, by setting the origin parameters appropriately.

An easy way to deal with this situation is to have the different data flows not go directly to the parameter, but to a transformation subprocess step and have one data flow from the transformation step to the parameter. The transformation step can have a parameter constraint on its input parameters that is an XOR across all input parameters. This makes sure that only one input parameter is received. Alternatively, the transformation step could reconcile all input instances in case more than one is received.

Queued Parameters

In most cases it is possible to precisely define the input and output parameters of a process type, since the possible event or data instances are known up front. However, in some cases the number of event instances that have to be passed is unknown at the time the process type is designed. In this case it must be possible to pass more than one event or data instance in a parameter. This can be accomplished by a list or an array data type that can contain an arbitrary number of event or data instances. At design time an array or list defines that there might be more than one event instance or data instance that needs to be processed. At run time the list or array is taken, and the processing has to iterate over all the list items or array fields.

Using an array or list assumes that all data instances or event instances are available at the same time for processing. However, a B2B-specific property is that in many cases not all of them are available at the same time, but only over time. In addition, they should be processed immediately after they arrive and the processing should not wait until after all have arrived.

This is addressed by input and output parameters that have a queueing behavior, i.e., their contents are made available as soon as they arrive and it is possible to repeatedly receive their contents. The parameter behaves like a queue with enqueue and dequeue operations whereby the business logic inside the process can dequeue and enqueue at its discretion. It is possible that not all events on a queued parameter are processed if not necessary. Figure 7.40 shows such an example, where only the first acknowledgment is processed, but not any subsequent ones.

7.2.3 Context-Dependent Event Validation Rule

Event validation rules as introduced in Sect. 7.1.11 are defined on a single business object, single event or single data type. As it is defined until this point, it is possible to check the consistency of a single event instance or a single data instance. However, since one process type or one process step type can have several input parameters, it is possible that there is a constraint across the instances in these input parameters. For example, if a process type receives two event instances, like a purchase order header event and a purchase order line item event, both events must be related and must refer to the same purchase order identifier to make sure that the header and the line items fit together, i.e., represent the same order. Otherwise, the line items might belong to a different header, most likely resulting in inconsistent processing of these event instances.

This requirement demands validation rules across input parameters and across output parameters in addition to the validation rules that are already defined for events and data instances individually. These validation rules can be specified in the process type definition itself. Figure 7.29 shows an example. The section validation shows two validation rules that affect two parameters. Since the process structure has not changed, no graphical representation is given; it is the same as in Fig. 7.28.

process_type PO_POA_seller
  parameter
    IN mandatory initiating PO: purchase_order;
    IN optional in_ACK: acknowledgement;
    OUT optional POA: purchase_order_acknowledgment;
    OUT optional out_ACK: acknowledgment;
    IN optional in_ERROR: error;
    OUT optional out_ERROR: error;
    OUT mandatory error_status: status;
  parameter constraint
    XOR (
      (PO **AND** (out_ACK **XOR** out_error))
      (PO **AND** out_ACK **AND** POA **AND** (in_ACK **XOR** in_error)))
  local process data variable
    authorized: boolean;
  validation
    in_ACK: in_ACK.sender = POA.target;
    out_ACK: out_ACK.target = PO.sender;
  decomposition
    approval_process: PO_approval;
  data flow
    PO -> approval_process.PO;
    approval_process.approval -> authorized;
end_process_type

Fig. 7.29. Validation rules across parameters

The validation rules across parameters within a process type or process step type are applied independently of how the process type or process step type is reused as a subprocess. However, additional constraints might come up in the context of the reuse of a process or process step type. For example, several event instances are processed in parallel, whereby each instance represents an individual line item. The line items were split earlier on from a single event that contained all line items. At the end of the parallel processing, all event instances end up in an array parameter. The purchase order header is received in a second parameter. At this point a check is in order to make sure that all line item events arrived. However, the receiving process has no way to validate this constraint, and therefore the validation rule must be defined elsewhere.

A validation rule for this case must have access to the original event that contains all line items in order to find out how many line items there are in total. In addition, the same validation rule must have access to the array parameter containing all processed line items in order to see if the number of array elements is equal the number of original line items. This validation rule is best specified within the process type itself that defined the business logic of splitting the original event and joining the individual line items back into an array parameter.

Figure 7.30 shows the example in detail. The process PO_POA receives a complete purchase order. It is split along the way (not shown), and the subprocess stock_check receives the purchase order header as well as the purchase order line items in two input parameters, where the parameter receiving the line items is an array parameter. This process has a very simple structure and so no graphical notation is shown.

```
process_type stock_check
  parameter
    IN mandatory initiating PO_header: purchase_order_header;
    IN mandatory initiating PO_line_items: array of purchase_order_line_item;
    ...
end_process_type

process_type PO_POA_seller
  parameter
    IN mandatory initiating PO: purchase_order;
    ...
  decomposition
    stock_check_process: stock_check;
  validation
    PO.number_of_line_items = stock_check_process.PO_line_items.size;
end_process_type
```

Fig. 7.30. Context-dependent validation rules

These rules are called context-dependent validation rules since they only apply in the context of a process type and do not belong to the definition of business objects, event types or data type. They do not implement constraints across parameters. Like all validation rules that address event instance validation, they are executed when the event changes its state to raised. If the validation rule refers to several event instances that are not yet raised, the last that is raised causes the validation rule to be executed.

7.2.4 Control Flow

The control flow aspect of processes is concerned with the ordering of the subprocess execution within a process. This includes process types as well as process step types as subprocesses.

Whenever two subprocesses must be executed in a specific order (i.e., they cannot be executed independently of each other), a control flow construct can be used to order them. Several control flow constructs are available; the most basic ones are as follows:

- **Sequence**. The most basic control flow construct is the sequence that defines the execution order of two subprocesses. If two subprocesses are sequenced, then as soon as the first subprocess is finished executing, the second subprocess is able to start.

- **Conditional branch**. If two subprocesses should be executed conditionally, then a conditional branch is used to specify this. A conditional branch requires a predicate that evaluates to true or to false. Depending on the outcome, one or the other of the two subprocesses is enabled for execution.

  Sometimes a whole set of subprocesses requires alternative execution. In this case not only are two subprocesses specified within the conditional branch, but two sets of subprocesses are specified where one set or the other is executed depending on the outcome of the predicate.

- **Parallel branch**. If subprocesses are independently executable, a parallel construct can be used to specify the two subprocesses that are to be executed in parallel. Like in the conditional branching case, sets of subprocesses can also be executed in parallel, if those sets are specified with the parallel construct.

- **Loops**. In some situations it is necessary to iterate through a number of subprocesses repeatedly. The loop control flow construct is used to specify under which conditions a set of subprocesses must be repeatedly executed. The "while" as well as the "repeat until" loops are two of the available loop constructs.

More control flow constructs exist, like delay or time-out. They are introduced later on as required. The list of control flow constructs can become quite lengthy. However, many of those are described in detail in Jablonski and Bussler (1996), Leymann and Roller (1999) and van der Aalst and van Hee (2002).

As discussed in the previous section, data flow defines which values of the parameters are passed on to specific other parameters. This implicitly defines a dependency between the process and its subprocesses as well as a dependency between the subprocesses. A receiver of a parameter is executed after the sender of the parameter value.

Control flow constructs themselves specify a dependency, too. This dependency is defined on the subprocesses themselves, not on the parameters. However, since data flow implicitly also defines a dependency on the subprocesses, it is possible to specify a conflict.

Figure 7.31 shows an abstract example of a conflict. The data flow implicitly specifies that B needs to be executed before C since the output parameter of B is flown to the input parameter of C. However, the control flow defines that C is executed before B. This is an inconsistent specification, since both dependencies conflict in the order of the subprocess execution they define (Figure 7.32 shows the conflict graphically; the dotted lines represent the control flow). It is therefore important that the integration modeler who specifies the subprocesses avoids any conflicting specification in the data flow as well as the control flow between the subprocesses. One possible strategy is to not specify any control flow rule when a data flow rule is already established. Another strategy is to specify for each data flow rule a corresponding control flow rule so that both define the same dependencies and therefore do not conflict.

```
process_type B_type
  parameter
    OUT mandatory result: boolean;
end_process_type

process_type C_type
  parameter
    IN mandatory initiating result: boolean;
end_process_type

process_type A
  decomposition
    B: B_type;
    C: C_type;
  data flow
    B.result -> C.result;
  control flow
    sequence(C, B);
end_process_type
```

Fig. 7.31. Conflicting data and control flow specification

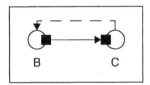

Fig. 7.32. Graphical representation

Since both data flow and control flow specify execution dependencies, why have control flow in the first place? There are multiple answers to this question. First, data flow is just concerned about the data flowing between processes. Sometimes, no data is flowing but the execution order is not arbitrary either. In this case control flow is used to specify the order. Sometimes, data flow indicates that subprocesses can be executed in parallel when they cannot for non-data flow reasons, like execution resource allocation. Control flow can be used to further specify the order or to constrain possible parallelism. Second, data flow is not conditional, nor can it specify loops. However, sometimes this is a necessary execution order, and so control flow can be used to specify it.

If both control flow and data flow specify dependencies and can conflict, why not unify both integration concepts into one? The answer to this question is that the explicit separation of the two concepts supports the focus on different process aspects separately and therefore allows the integration modeler to concentrate on each separately, too. The modeler can divide the problem and also has appropriate modeling constructs available.

Control flow is still a matter of debate, and in the literature different approaches and underlying formalisms can be found. Examples are in Jablonski and Bussler (1996), Leymann and Roller (1999), van der Aalst and van Hee (2002), Miller et al. (1997) or Muth et al. (1997).

7.2.5 Further Aspects

In Jablonski and Bussler (1996) as well as Leymann and Roller (1999) more aspects of processes are discussed. Besides hierarchical decomposition, data flow and control flow, the additional aspects organization and application are introduced. The organization aspect deals with assigning process steps to resources for execution. For example, an authorization step is assigned to a manager role for authorization. Users are related to roles. At run time the roles are resolved into the related users in order to assign a process step to the appropriate users of the role to which it is related.

The application aspect deals with the assignment of back-end application systems to process steps that are required to execute the process step. In more detail this means that the data passed to a process step are given to a back-end application system for processing, and the result is given back to the step as result data.

As already discussed (Chap. 2), the model of B2B integration has the same two additional aspects, however, not as process aspects. Instead of invoking back-end application systems from within process steps, their invocation happens through adapters that are related to interface processes. The organization aspect is handled precisely the same way. Events can be addressed to endpoints that are users and an adapter implements the communication with the user.

This handling of the two former process aspects is superior since back-end application connectivity as well as user interactions are handheld precisely the same way. In addition, they are removed from the process concept, which in turn makes the process concept a lot simpler and easier to implement as well as easier to define. The benefit for the integration modeler is that the modeler can "worry" separately about the concepts at different stages in the design process.

7.2.6 Static and Dynamic Process

Once a process type is defined, process instances of that process type can be created and executed. Several process instances can be executed concurrently that are of the same process type.

If a B2B integration technology architecture implements a static process model, then process instances, once instantiated, are executed according to their process type definition, and there is no possibility to change their execution. Decomposition, validation, conditions, data flow and control flow are executed as specified in the process type. For example, it is not possible to add or remove a process step (structural process change), change a data flow or control flow construct (behavioral process change).

Why would it be necessary to make structural or behavioral process changes? The answer lies in changing process requirements while a process is executing. For example, a purchase order process might be defined and process instances are executing for some time. It turns out that the payment behavior of the buyers is changing and payments are delayed or even defaulted, which never happened before. At this point in time it is decided that, effective immediately, a payment history is built for each buyer and credit checks of buyers have to be performed. This means two things. First, a new revision of the purchase order process has to be constructed that collects the payment history. As soon as the invoice is issued, a payment history entry is made that the invoice was issued and a time-out process step is started with the payment due date. At that date either the payment happened or not. In either case, the payment history is updated accordingly. Also, a credit check process step is added before the purchase order acknowledgment is sent. Every new process instance will execute according to this new process type revision.

Second, already executing process instances have to be changed so that the new directive is incorporated. For all process instances that did not yet sent a purchase order acknowledgment, a credit check of the buyer is added. For those that have not yet issued an invoice, the payment history steps are added. For those where the invoice was already issued but the due date has not yet been reached, a time-out step is added for the due date as well as the payment history steps. And finally, for those process instances that are beyond the due date, a step is added that updates the payment history with an entry that the buyer paid or not, depending on what happened.

This is an example that shows that it is necessary to sometimes not only revise process types but also process instances while they are ongoing. The possibility to change running process instances is called a dynamic process model. Structural process changes as well as behavioral process changes are supported in a dynamic process model. The underlying mechanism is that of versioning, as discussed in Chap. 5.

One of the problems that can arise is that a dynamic change can cause a process instance to become inconsistent. For example, after a change the data flow and the control flow are inconsistent. An integration modeler that applies the change has to do so very carefully, since in general it is not possible to check all modifications for consistency.

An introduced inconsistency shows another reason why dynamic process changes are important. An inconsistency can be introduced by a dynamic change or even by an incorrect process type specification in the first place. Once an inconsistency occurs, a dynamic change method offers the chance to fix the inconsistent process instance. Therefore, dynamic process changes are also an important mechanism for error handling.

7.2.7 Patterns

Process pattern is an important integration concept that allows the repeated definition of equivalent process types without actually specifying them every time individually. An example of such a situation is the B2B standard RosettaNet, which
specifies quite a number of processes. All processes have exactly the same behavior, and the only distinguishing factor is the event types used in these process type
specifications. The process decomposition, the data as well as the control flow are
the same in all processes. What varies across the processes are the event types, pre-
and postconditions as well as the context-dependent validation rules, i.e., event
types and all other concepts that access event type contents like validation rules.

The concept of a process pattern addresses this particular situation. It defines a
complete process pattern without requiring the specification of specific event
types. A separate binding of the process pattern to event types is provided that
binds the same process pattern to different event types. Such a binding results in a
process type.

```
process_pattern request_reply
  [
  event_type event_type_1;
  event_type event_type_2;
  validation_rule validation_1;
  ]
  parameter
    IN mandatory initiating request: event_type_1;
    OUT mandatory response: event_type_2;
  validation
    validation_1;
  ...
end_process_pattern

process_type seller
  as process pattern request_reply [PO, POA, PO.identifier = POA.identifier];
end_process_type

process_type inquiry
  as process pattern request_reply [Inquiry, Inquiry_result, NULL];
end_process_type
```

Fig. 7.33. Process pattern and binding

Figure 7.33 shows an example. A process pattern request_reply is defined. The
angle brackets define the replacement types of the pattern. For example, three types
can be replaced, two event types and one validation rule. The pattern is specified
like a process type, but it uses the replacement types instead of real types like event
types. Later in the binding real types are bound to the replacement types. One

replacement event type is used as the input parameter, the other replacement event type is used as the output parameter. The third replacement type is a validation rule and is used just as in the process pattern definition.

Following the process pattern specification two bindings are shown that cause process types to be defined. The first process type, called seller, binds a PO event type to the first replacement event type, a POA event type to the second replacement event type and a validation rule to the replacement validation rule.

A second process type is defined using the pattern binding an Inquiry event type to the first replacement event type, an Inquiry_result to the second replacement event type and the NULL validation rule to the replacement validation. The NULL will be interpreted as true when the validation section is evaluated at run time. Process patterns are an effective concept especially when an enterprise has many process types that are equivalent except for event types used in the process types.

7.2.8 Life Cycle and Execution Model

Process instances exhibit behavior and this requires the definition of a process execution model. In the following a process execution model for the introduced process concept is provided. First, the process states and process state transitions for processes and process steps are defined. Afterwards, the execution model for the process execution itself is introduced.

Process States

Process states are the states processes can be in during their life cycle. The phases that can be distinguished are creation, execution and retirement. The process states are as follows:

- **Non_existent**. This is an artificial state that allows users to have a complete state transition model.
- **In_creation**. In this state the process instance exists and has a unique identifier. In this state the input parameters have to be set. A process type can have several parameters that are not set at once, but one parameter at a time. Since the operations to set the initiating input parameters are distinct, a separate state is introduced that sets the input parameters as discrete steps.
- **Created**. Once all input parameters are set, the process instance creation is complete, as denoted by this state. Parameters can no longer be set.
- **In_execution**. In this state the process is executing. Noninitiating input parameters can be set and output parameters can be checked for contents and read. Subprocesses are executed according to the data flow and according to the control flow implied order.
- **Interrupted**. A process instance can be interrupted and will be in this state after the interruption is issued. No execution takes place in this state, no input param-

eter can be set and no output parameter can be read. It can be transitioned back to in_execution and then the execution resumes.

- **Executed**. A process instance is in this state when no further execution can take place. All control flow and all data flow happened and no further sub-process is executed.
- **Aborted**. A process instance can be interrupted without ever again getting back into the state in_execution. In this case the process instance did not finish its execution normally. Instead, it will never finish the execution. In this case, the process instance is in the state aborted to indicate this situation.
- **In_error**. When an error occurred the process instance transitions into this state. Error handling can take place in this state and afterward the process instance can be put·back into in_execution or interrupted or aborted, depending on the outcome of error handling.

All states apply to process step types, too. There is no difference in behavior between processes and process steps from a state model.

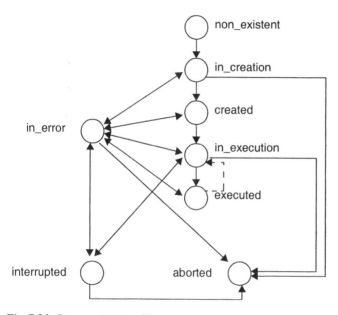

Fig. 7.34. Process state transitions

Process State Transitions

Transitions between process states are necessary to advance a process instance. Figure 7.34 shows the possible transitions between the process states. The normal order of state changes without any anomaly is non_existent, in_creation, created, in_execution and executed.

Any state transition can detect an error and then the process instance goes into error state. From there it can go back to the state where the error was detected in order to retry the state transition that originally caused the error. A process instance can be interrupted once it is in in_execution, and it can transition back to in_execution to continue. However, it can go into an error state instead if resuming from the interruption does not work. It can be aborted, too, from the interrupted state to stop the execution. This is also possible from in_execution directly as well as from in_creation. The latter is the case when a process instance should never be executed. If a process instance is in_error state that is irreparable then it can be aborted directly from there.

Process step instances have the same transitions between their states, and again there is no difference from process instances. One specific transition, going from executed to in_execution, is only present in processes, not in process steps. Therefore a dashed representation is shown in Fig. 7.34. This transition is necessary since it is possible to dynamically change process instances according to the dynamic process model. After a process instance is finished, it is possible to change it, and that change might require execution again. An example is that a step is added that needs to be executed.

Process Execution

Process execution fundamentally means to determine the execution order of the subprocesses of a process once the process is successfully instantiated. The following execution model covers the state in_execution.

It is assumed that the transition from created to in_execution succeeded. This includes checking the preconditions of the initiating, mandatory and optional input parameters that were set during creation. Also, the parameter constraints have been checked to the extent that they are not violated. If a parameter constraint references a parameter that is not yet set then this is evaluated as true at this point because it is possible to set the parameter later on.

Generally, at this point the following happens (called the process execution cycle). Data flow as well as control flow constructs are evaluated and it is determined if both data flow as well as control flow result in common subprocesses. Only those data flows are evaluated where the source parameter is available. For each of these it is found out if at least the initiating parameters of one or more subprocesses can be supplied. Those subprocesses are marked as the data flow candidate set.

For control flow this means determining the next subprocesses that can be executed. Only those control flow constructs are taken into consideration that start at an existing subprocess instance (or that are the first control flow ever), because only those might be done and therefore successors might be executed. The subprocesses resulting from those control flow constructs are marked as the control flow candidate set.

If the intersection of the data flow candidate set and the control flow candidate set is nonempty, subprocess execution candidates have been found. These candidates are checked to see if any context-dependent validation rules apply. The rules that apply refer to the parameters of the subprocess candidates. They are evaluated, and if these result in true, then the subprocesses are created. If one of them results in false, the process instance is put in state in_error, and the default output parameter error_status is set accordingly.

At this point, the execution of the process instance has started and it continues by constantly evaluating data flow and control flow as discussed. Whenever a subprocess is executed or aborted or put in the in_error state, the execution cycle is executed again because these are the only cases when a change occurs that might cause data flow and control flow to evaluate to new subprocesses.

From the second execution of the execution cycle onwards additional evaluations have to take place. Some of the data flows do not result in initiating parameters of subprocesses, but into noninitiating mandatory or optional parameters of already executing process instances. Those parameters are set whenever such a data flow is detected. Data flows having an output parameter as source are evaluated, too, in the same fashion as explained above in the execution cycle.

As soon as a subprocess is created, its internal preconditions, validation rules and parameter constraints are checked. If one of these fails, the process instance is put into the in_error state. Before a sub-process is finished and moves into the state executed, the postconditions are checked. If they do not evaluate to true, the process instance is put into state in_error.

7.2.9 Transactions

Processes in B2B integration are, in general, long-running processes. A long-running process in contrast to a short-running process has persistent intermediary states that are recoverable. A long-running process instance is generally not executed from its beginning to its end within one database transaction. Instead, several database transactions are involved in executing a process instance. Fundamentally, each process state is recoverable. This means that as soon as a process instance is put into a specific state, the transaction that achieved this is committed. The execution cycle therefore has to issue the appropriate transaction commits.

Each successfully committed transaction denotes a recoverable state of the process. While this aspect is not relevant for the conceptual definition of the process concept, it is important for the understanding of the aspects of the process concept in terms of its behavior. If a transaction fails, the process instance is set back to its last recoverable process state. That, of course, sets back all data flows and control flows, too, since all have been changed in the failing transaction. That process state is a consistent state and process execution continues by executing the execution cycle again.

Committing each process state is the default behavior. Several variations of this are possible, which are discussed briefly. One of the very different variations is that all process states are nonrecoverable. In this variation the process instance is executed in one transaction, and no intermediate state is recoverable at all. These processes are sometimes called microprocesses. Microprocesses are executed completely in one database transaction, and any failure results in setting back the process instance to its very beginning.

Microprocesses are useful in integration scenarios where the endpoints have to be called synchronously and the communication is transactional. In this case a tight binding between the process and the endpoint is achieved. Also, if several calls to the back-end application system are necessary to extract the business data, this makes sure that all or none of the business data are extracted.

In addition, several endpoints can be accessed in one transaction, too. The microprocess does not restrict the number of endpoints invoked. Of course, this type of transaction model might require distributed transactions (Gray and Reuter 1993).

However, either using the default or using microprocesses does not cover all integration scenarios. It might be that all those process steps that invoke back-end application systems should be executed in one transaction; however, once the business data is extracted, the processing should continue using the default transaction model. This means that some of the subprocesses of a process are executed within one transaction like microprocesses, but not all of them. Function integration as a separate use case falls into this category (Sect. 5.6.1).

In this case it is necessary to set the transaction model explicitly. This is done by setting a subprocess to be a microprocess. Once a subprocess is set as a microprocess it is completely executed as a single transaction until it is either in state executed, in_error or aborted. This allows an integration modeler to combine subprocess steps in that microprocess that should be executed as one transaction. If there are further subprocesses in that microprocess, then they are automatically executed completely within the same transaction, too.

If a subprocess is not marked as a microprocess, then the default transaction model applies. If a process step is marked as a microprocess, then the process step is executed within one transaction completely, and no intermediary states are recoverable either.

More elaborate schemes of transaction boundaries within process instance execution are discussed in Leymann and Roller (1999), Waechter and Reuter (1992) and Schuldt (2001).

7.2.10 Compensation

The nature of long-running transactions is that intermediary states are committed and therefore externalized in the database or other persistence layer components. This includes not only the process state itself, but also the data (event instances and data instances) that are processed by the process instance. Process instances and their state as well as data and event instances are therefore visible to other process instances in the system or any other program that is able to access the database.

Long-running process instances therefore cause side effects in the database used (or any other persistence component).

Furthermore, long-running processes cause side effects in the endpoints, too. If during a process instance, execution event instances are sent to endpoints, then the endpoint might undergo a state change as result of the event instance. For example, an update of a customer record is sent to all back-end application systems. As soon as the back-end application system receives the event it will update its internal state and commit that update, i.e., externalize its state, too. The process instance has caused a back-end application state change.

If after this state change happened the process instance wants to undo the effect (revert the state of the back-end application system back to the state before the state change), a normal database abort will not achieve this, since the back-end application system state has already been externalized to its persistent component like a database or file system.

The ability to revert back the back-end application system state is called process compensation, see Gray and Reuter (1993) and Waechter and Reuter (1992). A so-called process compensation step has to send another event to the back-end application system, asking it to change its state again. This causes another update that, once committed, externalizes another state change of the back-end application system. The event sent by the process compensation step needs to accomplish the reverting back by an appropriate event. For example, another customer record is sent that contains the previous state of the customer record. With this additional event, the back-end application system processes this state change as any other. However, from a process instance's viewpoint the back and application system's state is reverted back to the state that the process instance saw before the first update.

In general, process compensation works as follows. The integration modeler has to decide which side effects have to be compensated for when compensation becomes necessary. For each subprocess a corresponding compensation subprocess is modeled. Data flow can be defined between those and between compensation subprocesses in order to provide for the necessary compensation data. In the above example, this would be the customer record before the update, so that the compensation subprocess can send the customer record to the back-end application system in order to revert the state of the back-end application system.

Additional business logic might be necessary to achieve correct compensation. For example, an employee booking a trip might receive a payroll advance for trip cost reimbursement. If the trip was cancelled, the travel agency might collect a cancellation fee. That fee has to be paid by the employee. This means that the employee does not have to give back the whole payroll advance, but the advance with the cancellation fee deducted. Payroll deduction to deduct the payroll advance therefore has to be adjusted by the cancellation fee.

This example shows that compensations are not only the inverse operation like cancel trip or deduct payroll advance, but might cause additional processing like paying the cancellation fee and adjusting the payroll deduction. This might require additional compensation subprocesses in order to those defined for the subprocesses. In addition, this example shows that the execution order of the compensation steps might not be the inverse of the subprocess steps that has been executed. Compensation subprocesses can have their own execution order in order, which is needed to achieve consistent compensation.

More advanced topics around compensation are discussed in the literature. For example, as discussed above, process states are externalized. This is true for compensation subprocess states, too. In general, it is possible that several ongoing process instances might access the same externalized data and event instance. If at the same time compensation subprocesses are executed, the question arises whether inconsistencies can arise because of the concurrent access of externalized event and data instances. A discussion around this advanced topic can be found in Schuldt (2001).

Finally, compensation subprocesses might fail, too. For example, a back-end application system might deny executing an event that was meant to be a compensating event instance. In this case compensation failed. The question arises if there should be compensation subprocesses for compensating subprocesses themselves. While this seems to be a possibility, it might cause indefinite compensation if each compensation step can cause another compensation step for it, and so on. The integration modeler therefore has to be aware of this problem and has to make sure that the compensation logic design does not cause an endlessly ongoing compensation. This would be like an indefinitely executing loop, which must be avoided for the obvious reasons.

What is the reason for requiring compensation? Fundamentally, if a process cannot finish its execution successfully because of some error, its effects have to be compensated for in order to leave a consistent state behind in the B2B integration technology and the endpoint. In the simplest case, compensation does not exist, and it is a NOOP. In more elaborate cases, real compensation processing has to be done as discussed.

7.3 Interface Process

Interface processes are processes that implement the message exchange behavior with endpoints (also called public processes). They have to be able to comply to any exchange behavior that an endpoint might require. As introduced in Chaps. 2 and 5, interface processes bind to business processes through binding processes in order to accomplish behavior abstraction. In this way the business process involved does not have to be aware of endpoint-specific properties and behavior.

All properties of the integration concept process as described in the previous section apply, in general, to interface processes. Interface processes have additional specific characteristics compared to processes that are introduced in this section.

7.3.1 Data

Interface process parameters are restricted to specific event types. Input and output parameters of interface processes that connect with binding processes can only be clear text event types (Sect. 5.4.3). Those parameters that represent the messages received from endpoints or sent to endpoints can only be wire event types. This restriction is due to the role interface processes play. Interface processes represent the behavior of an endpoint. Endpoints only send and receive wire events, and therefore the parameters that deal with endpoints can be only of wire event type.

Wire events are translated into clear text events, and this translation is another specific task for interface processes. Therefore, the parameters that connect to binding process parameters can only be of type clear text event. This implies that translation has to take place on the way from an input parameter receiving a wire event to an output parameter returning a clear text event. The same is true for the other direction, from clear text event types to wire event types. Another implication is that events within an interface process are either of type wire event or clear text event.

7.3.2 Instantiation Model

There are two ways to instantiate interface processes. One is in the outbound case, where a binding process results in a clear text event that has to be picked up by an interface process in order to send it to an endpoint. The interface process has to translate the clear text event into a wire event before it is given to the connectivity layer components. As soon as the binding process produces the clear text event a corresponding interface process has to be created. The clear text event of the binding process is given to the initiating input parameter of the corresponding interface process, and therefore is sufficient to create the interface process. The selection of the correct interface process is straightforward, since the parameters of the process binding as well as the interface process are directly related to each other (Fig. 2.24).

The other case, the inbound case, is more complicated. In this case a wire event is received from an endpoint and the correct interface process has to be found. There are two subcases that need to be distinguished. One is that the incoming wire event creates a new interface process instance altogether. The other subcase is that the incoming wire event relates to an already existing interface process instance and has to be given to it for it to continue correctly. Here correlation as discussed in Sect. 7.1.10 is used to determine an already existing interface process. The two subcases are dealt with as follows:

- If a wire event shows up from an endpoint, then first it is checked to see if a correlated wire event exists.
- If there is no existing correlated wire event, then a new interface process that has this wire event as initiating parameter is created. If no interface process is found,

then an error occurred and has to be handled. If more than one interface process is found, then the integration modeler did not make sure that there is only one possible interface process.

The case that several interface processes have a wire event as initiating parameter can be dealt with in several ways. One is to declare this situation an error and to handle the error. Another way is to define this case as an expected case, and flag this case for further resolution. For example, a user could be asked to pick an interface process. A more sophisticated way is to consult a function that selects an interface process based on the wire event content (policy function).

- If a correlated wire event is found, then the interface process instance can be determined that produced this correlated wire event (wire event instances carry references to their respective interface process instances, and vice versa). The next step is to find out if the existing interface process instance can receive the incoming wire event as an input parameter. If there is an input parameter that can receive this wire event, then the wire event is given to the interface process instance input parameter.

  If there is no input parameter that can receive the wire event, then the next step is to find an interface process that is bound to the same business process as the interface process of the correlated wire event and that can take the wire event as the initiating parameter. Figure 5.16 shows this scenario, where two interface processes are related to the same business process through two different process bindings. If such an interface process is found then it is instantiated, and the wire event is given to it as initiating parameter.

  If no such interface process can be found, an interface process is searched for that can take this wire event as initiating parameter without it being bound to the same business process as the interface process of the correlated wire event. This case is then the same as if there were no correlated wire event at all.

It is possible that more than one correlated wire event is found. If these all belong to the same interface process instance or to different interface process instances that are all related to the same business process instance, then this is a perfectly fine case. However, if they belong to different interface processes of different business processes then a more complicated situation exists. That situation is easily resolved if there is only one way to give the wire event to an input parameter. However, if it is possible to give the wire event to input parameters of different interface processes, then an error situation occurred that requires error handling. The situation can no longer be resolved as before. Either it is an error, or a policy function has to be involved.

One could wonder whether it would be better to not define correlation between events, but to associate a correlation predicate to the interface process instead. However, this does not make the instantiation decision of interface processes easier, since in this case, too, several interface processes' correlation predicates might apply to the same event instance.

Figure 7.35 shows an example that resembles the B2B standard RosettaNet. Two interface processes are shown, one that handles the purchase order and purchase order acknowledgment case, the other that handles error messages in a separate interface process. Both interface processes are bound to the same business process.

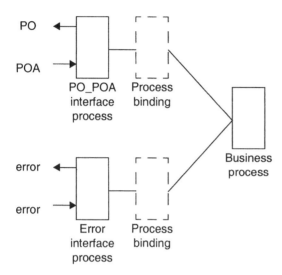

Fig. 7.35. Two interface processes related to one business process

All of the three event types, PO, POA and error, are correlated by the purchase order identifier that is unique and contained in each of them. As soon as the PO is sent, an instance of the PO_POA interface process exists. As soon as a POA is received by an endpoint, all correlated event instances are retrieved. A PO must exist with the same purchase order identifier. As soon as the PO is found, the instance of the interface process is determined. Once the interface process instance is found, the POA is given to it.

Error handling works analogously. As soon as an error event is received, the correlated event instances are retrieved. In case the POA is processed already, two event instances are correlated, one PO and one POA. Both refer to the same interface process instances, i.e., PO_POA. Based on this it can be determined that PO_POA cannot receive the error event instance. But based on the business process that is related to the PO_POA instance, the error interface process is determined, instantiated and the error event instance is given to it.

The selection of an interface process to either instantiate it or to continue an already existing instance is so far solely based on the fact that a wire event can initiate an interface process instance or continue one. The origin endpoint of the wire event was not taken into consideration at all. Later, the initiation algorithm for interface processes will be extended (Sect. 7.8.9) to take endpoint agreements into consideration, too. Otherwise, all endpoints would have to support all interface processes if the origin of wire events does not play a role. This, of course, does not make any sense, since all endpoints would have to have identical behavior.

7.3.3 Data Flow

Data flow as already introduced works perfectly fine for interface processes. The simplest interface process is one that flows its parameters to a translation step and returns the translated event to the output parameters. Figure 7.36 shows such a simple interface process and Fig. 7.37 shows the graphical notation.

```
process_step_type po_translation
  parameter
    IN mandatory initiating we_PO: we_purchase_order;
    OUT mandatory ce_PO: ce_purchase_order;
end_process_step_type

process_type PO_POA
  parameter
    IN mandatory initiating we_PO: we_purchase_order;
    OUT mandatory ce_PO: ce_purchase_order;
  decomposition
    translation: po_translation;
  data flow
    we_PO -> translation.we_PO;
    translation.ce_PO -> ce_PO;
end_process_type
```

Fig. 7.36. Data flows in a simple interface process

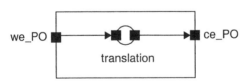

Fig. 7.37. Graphical representation

It is cumbersome for the integration modeler to specify all these data flows to and from translation process steps again and again in the different interface processes. A more efficient refinement of data flow could make the specification much easier. In addition to making translation available as a process step, it can be made part of the data flow specification itself. Figure 7.38, which shows this refinement, demonstrates immediately the positive impact of the simplification.

```
process_step_type po_translation
  parameter
    IN mandatory initiating we_PO: we_purchase_order;
    OUT mandatory ce_PO: ce_purchase_order;
end_process_step_type

process_type PO_POA
  parameter
    IN mandatory initiating we_PO: we_purchase_order;
    OUT mandatory ce_PO: ce_purchase_order;
  data flow
    we_PO -> ce_PO {po_translation};
end_process_type
```

Fig. 7.38. Data flow refinements in an interface process

This data flow definition specifies that a process step has to be invoked during the data flow execution. The types of the parameters can be inferred from the process step definition. The source and target of the data flow are the possible input and output parameters of the process step. If the types match uniquely, the process step can be invoked with the correct parameters.

If the parameters of the translation step cannot be matched uniquely, a matching of parameters has to be specified within the data flow specification. Figure 7.39 shows this case for the same example as shown in Fig. 7.38. The reference to the process step is extended by a signature that lists the actual parameters in the order they must be mapped to the parameters of the process step. The actual parameters in this case are the source and target of the data flow. The order of the parameters is determined by the order the formal parameters are declared in the process step type specification.

```
process_step_type po_translation
  parameter
    IN mandatory initiating we_PO: we_purchase_order;
    OUT mandatory ce_PO: ce_purchase_order;
end_process_step_type

process_type PO_POA
  parameter
    IN mandatory initiating we_PO: we_purchase_order;
    OUT mandatory ce_PO: ce_purchase_order;
  data flow
    we_PO -> ce_PO {po_translation(we_PO, ce_PO)};
end_process_type
```

Fig. 7.39. Explicit parameter assignment in data flow

process_type PO_POA_buyer
  parameter
    IN initiating ce_PO: ce_purchase_order;
    OUT we_PO: queue of we_purchase_order;
    IN we_in_ACK: queue of we_acknowledgment;
    OUT ce_out_ACK: ce_acknowledgment;
    IN we_POA: queue of we_purchase_order_acknowledgment;
    OUT ce_POA: ce_purchase_order_acknowledgment;
    IN ce_in_ACK: ce_acknowledgment;
    OUT we_out_ACK: queue of we_acknowledgment;
  decomposition
    po_translation: po_translation;
    ack_receive: we_ACK_receive (2);
    po_resend: we_po_resend;
    poa_translation: poa_translation;
    ack_translation: ack_translation;
    poa_receive: poa_receive;
    poa_receive_again: poa_receive;
    ack_resend: ack_resend;
  data flow
    ce_PO -> po_translation.ce_PO;
    po_translation.we_PO -> we_PO;
    po_translation.we_PO -> po_resend.we_PO;
    po_resend.we_PO -> we.PO;
    we_in_ACK -> ack_receive.we_in_ACK;
    we_in_ACK -> ack_translation.we_in_ACK;
    ack_translation.ce_out_ACK -> ce_out_ACK;
  control flow
    sequence(po_translation, loop L1);
    loop L1 (
      sequence(
        ack_receive,
        condition(ack_receive.timeout == true,
          po_resend,
          sequence(ack_translation, **loop_end**)
)
)
    );
end_process_type

Fig. 7.40. More sophisticated interface process

The data flow refinement is optional in the sense that an integration modeler does not necessarily have to use it. The only question that arises is that of error handling. What if the translation results in an error? In this case the error_status of the interface process is set instead of the error_status of the translation process step. Otherwise, there is no difference between the two approaches.

7.3.4 Interface Process-Specific Process Steps

More sophisticated endpoint behavior might require process steps that have not been introduced so far. One example is if an endpoint implements a reliable connection with duplicate checks, time-outs and retries. For this case the following additional process steps are required:

- **Time-out**. A time-out step is specified with a time value. Once the time-out step starts, it waits for the set amount of time and then it finishes. The time can either be a duration (like 5 h) or a specific date and time (like 7 p.m. PST on October 30, 2002). If it is a duration, it waits for the duration from the point in time where the transition to its state execution succeeded successfully. In the case when the specification is a date and a time, it waits until that point in time and then finishes.
- **Time-out attribute**. A time-out attribute is not a process step in itself, but can be attached to any process step type. In this case the process step assumes the time-out behavior in addition to the behavior it has without the time-out attribute. So it either executes its normal function, or it signals a time out if the time specified is exceeded.
- **Duplicate check**. A duplicate check step determines for a wire event instance if this wire event instance represents the same wire message as another wire event instance. If this is the case, the wire message was sent twice.

Figure 7.40 shows a more complicated interface process that uses some of these additional process steps. Figure 7.41 shows the graphical notation. The interface process in Fig. 7.40 sends out a wire event purchase order and receives an acknowledgment using the ack_receive process step. A time-out attribute is specified (2 h) for the ack_receive step. This is specified in the decomposition section. In case the acknowledgment is not received within 2 h, a time-out occurs and the wire event purchase order is resent with the po_resend process step. In order to resend the purchase order, the resend step has to have access to the wire event purchase order through data flow. The loop cycles until it receives the acknowledgment. Since the loop can execute a number of times, the parameters have to be declared as queued parameters. Only the first acknowledgment is processed, and any subsequent one is not processed any more. The special process step loop_end indicates that the loop processing is finished and the loop finishes. The control flow that follows the loop is continued.

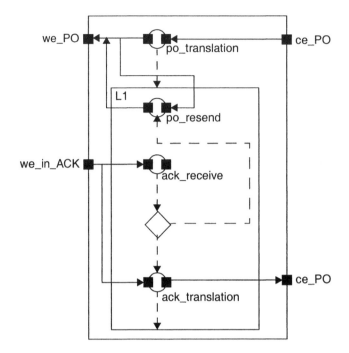

Fig. 7.41. Graphical representation

Figure 7.42 completes the example shown in Fig. 7.40, and only the control flow and data flow parts are shown. Figure 7.43 shows the complete graphical representation.

data flow
  ce_PO -> po_translation.ce_PO;
  po_translation.we_PO -> we_PO;
  po_translation.we_PO -> po_resend.we_PO;
  po_resend.we_PO -> we.PO;
  we_in_ACK -> ack_receive.we_in_ACK;
  we_in_ACK -> ack_translation.we_in_ACK;
  ack_translation.ce_out_ACK -> ce_out_ACK;
  we_POA -> poa_receive.we_POA;
  we_POA -> poa_translation.we_POA;
  poa_translation.ce_POA -> ce_POA;
  we_POA -> poa_receive_again.we_POA;
  ce_in_ACK -> ack_translation.ce_in_ACK;
  ack_translation.we_out_ACK -> we_out_ACK;
  ack_translation.we_out_ACK -> ack_resend.we_in_ACK;
  ack_resend.we_out_ACK -> we_out_ACK;
control flow
  sequence(po_translation, loop L1);
  loop L1 (
    sequence(
      ack_receive,
      condition(ack_receive.timeout == true,
        po_resend,
        sequence(ack_translation, **loop_end**)
)
)
  );
  sequence(loop L1, poa_receive);
  sequence(poa_receive, poa_translation);
  sequence(poa_translation, ack_translation);
  sequence(ack_translation, loop L2);
  loop L2 (

Fig. 7.42. Continuation of more sophisticated interface process

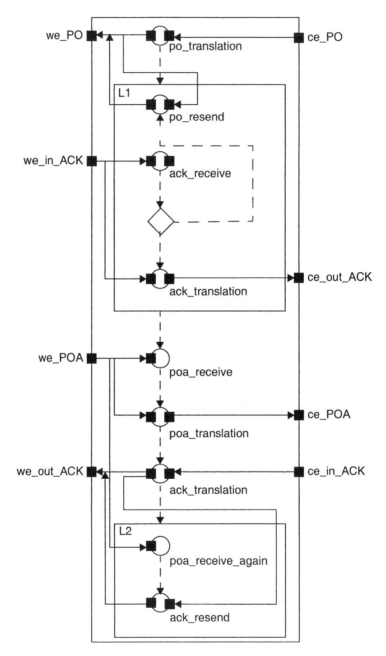

Fig. 7.43. Graphical representation

The second loop of the process requires explanation. After the first we_POA is received, the we_ACK is sent out. However, it might be that the we_POA is resent by the endpoint, maybe because on the endpoint's side the we_ACK timed out. Therefore it has to be assumed that the we_ACK was lost or too late, and the we_ACK has to be sent again. The loop ensures that for each POA coming in one we_ACK is sent out.

The interface process specified in Fig. 7.40 and Fig. 7.42 shows a particular possibility of handling a B2B protocol that might lose messages or might send messages delayed. Many variations of this exist. For example, an endless loop is usually not implemented. Instead, after three attempts to receive an event the loop is stopped, and an error situation occurs.

Sometimes integration modelers do not like to have events in the system that are not processed. In this case the queued parameters all must be processed. Yet other integration modelers do not like queued parameters at all. When they fix the number of acknowledgments to three, they model three distinct input parameters instead of a queued one.

7.3.5 Execution Model

Correlated Events That are Out of Order

If messages are sent using an asynchronous transport protocol like SMTP, it is possible that several correlated message that are sent in order by an endpoint are received out of order by the receiving endpoint. The transport protocol allows messages to pass each other. The question arises what should be done in this case. One possibility is to reject correlated messages received out of order right away, and not even allow those message to be filled into input parameters as wire events.

However, this is not necessary. The business logic inside an interface process determines when input parameters are picked up, and in which order, for processing through data flow and control flow among the process steps. For the business logic inside, it does not matter if the input wire events are received in the order they are processed or not. What matters is that the input wire events are available when needed by the buiness logic. If a wire event is not yet available, the business logic either waits for the input wire event or has a time-out attribute associated that then deals with the missing input event as a time-out situation.

Through this approach, the out-of-order situation that is part of the nature of asynchronous transport protocols can be handled without causing an error situation. Fundamentally, the out-of-order situation is compensated for.

Uncorrelated Events That are Out of Order

In some integration scenarios, the order of received uncorrelated initiating events has to be preserved. In this case, the order of the event arrival has to be the order the interface process instances are started or continued.

The reason is best explained using an example. After a purchase order is sent by a buyer and received by a seller, it is possible that the buyer later cancels it, with the expectation that the cancellation compensates for the order. The seller then has to cancel the purchase order so that no product is produced and shipped to the buyer.

As can be easily seen, the order of the two events is very important, because otherwise the cancellation would come before the creation. This would result in an error situation for the cancellation because there is no corresponding order. The subsequent order would take place and the buyer would receive the product against its intentions.

In general there is a variety of order criteria. The example said that purchase orders and their cancellations have to be processed in order, but not the purchase orders themselves. Also, the example did not specify if this is the case for all endpoints or only for some. Furthermore, the example did not elaborate on how the purchase order acknowledgments have to be handled. A possibility is that the purchase order acknowledgement order has to be the reverse of the incoming purchase order. Possible order criteria are as follows:

- **Within one event type**. In this case, event instances of the same event type have to be ordered.
- **Across two or more event types**. In this case, event instances of several event types have to be ordered.
- **Within one endpoint**. In this case, event instances coming from the same endpoint have to be ordered.
- **Across two or more endpoints**. In this case, event instances coming from several endpoints have to be ordered.
- **Independent of event types**. In this case, a predicate is defined that identifies event instances. The identified event instances have to be processed in order. For example, a predicate could be the employee identifier that defines that all events, independent of their types, have to be ordered if they contain an employee identifier.
- **Independent of endpoints**. In this case, a predicate is specified that defines the endpoints and events coming from those have to be ordered.

Some of the order criteria can be combined to achieve more complex ordering criteria. For example, two event types can be ordered within a single trading partner. This would be the example that ensures that purchase orders and their cancellations from one trading partner are ordered.

So far, the order discussion was limited to incoming events from an endpoint. However, it was implicitly assumed that the corresponding outgoing events, for example, to a back-end application system, are produced in the same order as the respective incoming events. However, sometimes one incoming event might result in three events to three different back-end systems. In this case, the order has to be preserved, too. The number of endpoints that receive the resulting events does not impact the order criteria.

Another important ordering criterion is the pickup of an event according to a preestablished order. For example, if purchase orders are sent out and purchase order acknowledgments are received, the receiving of the purchase order acknowledgments are picked up in the order the purchase orders were sent out. This case ensures that the interface processes that are waiting for the purchase order acknowledgments are continued in the order they sent out the purchase orders.

The ordering of events, although discussed here, is a system property and requires configuration of the B2B integration technology. There are no specific integration concepts for ordering as such.

Adapter Error Handling

Interface processes are at the boundary of the system as described in Sect. 5.1.1. The adapter that receives an outgoing wire event might execute perfectly well or might encounter an error. In the latter case, it might be important to deal with the adapter error as part of the interface process. For example, it might be that the error should cause a resend of the wire event instance.

In order to deal with an adapter error within the interface process, the adapter must return an error code to the interface process so that the business logic internal to the interface process can pick up the error code and react appropriately. Since the only method is to use parameters, the error code of an adapter can be modeled as an input parameter to the interface process. The adapter, upon detecting an error, can set the error code in the input parameter that is related to this particular adapter. The business logic within the interface process can react to it. For example, it can read the error code, evaluate it and then resend the wire event instance.

7.3.6 Batch Processing and Complex Event Relationships

Batch

For network transmission efficiency it is sometimes advantageous to send many purchase orders in one transmission. This reduces the transmission overhead significantly and hence is faster, more efficient or cheaper. Such a message is called a batch message. In terms of B2B integration concept terminology, one batch message (the unit of transmission) is either one or several events, depending on the situation to make the internal structure of the message visible to the processes or not.

In the former case the batch message is represented as one wire event. The interface process processes the wire event as one instance and hands it off to the binding role, which in turn continues to deal with it as one event. The fact that the batch message has an "interesting" internal structure is ignored.

In the latter case, the structure of the batch message is recognized, and it is split into several event instances. Several alternatives exist to split the batch message:

- **Adapter**. If the adapter splits the batch message into its parts, then one wire event instance will be created for each of its parts. Each wire event instance is a separate wire event instance. Therefore, splitting the message might result in as many interface processes as there are parts.

  Since the adapter splits the batch message, it knows that all the resulting wire event instances originate from the same batch. The adapter can assign a unique batch identifier to the batch message and assign the same batch identifier to all wire event instances. This batch identifier ties all wire events together, and the B2B integration technology can therefore find out all wire events that belong together by virtue of being from the same batch message.

  Again, it is possible that each wire event instance initiates a separate interface process instance. However, with the batch identifier it is possible to define an event correlation so that all event instances can be processed by the same interface process. An array or queued input parameter can be used to collect all event instances from the same batch into one interface process.

  In the outbound case, an adapter can collect all wire event instances that belong to a batch and construct a batch message from them before sending it to an endpoint. In this case it is important for an adapter to know how many wire events belong to a batch, so that it knows when it received all wire events. The batch identifier could contain that number.

- **Interface process**. Instead of an adapter splitting the batch message, it could be done by an interface process. In this case the batch message is represented in one wire event instance by the adapter, which initiates an interface process. The interface process will then split this wire event instance into several wire event instances with a split process step type. The split process step type receives one wire event, the so-called batch wire event, and returns an array or a queued parameter that contains wire event instances, each representing a part of the batch wire event. This step can set the batch identifier as well as the number of the elements in the batch. From then on several wire event instances have to be processed by the subsequent process instances, like binding processes and business processes.

  In the opposite case, it is possible that an interface process collects all wire event instances that belong to a batch and composes the batch wire event. This can be achieved by a process step type that is the inverse to a batch split.

- **Binding process**. Instead of splitting the batch in an interface process the split can happen in a binding process itself. In this case the interface process treats the batch as one event, and the business process does not have to split the batch since the binding process achieved it.

- **Business process**. The business process could split the batch itself, requiring neither an interface process nor a binding process to do it.

Where the batch is split is a matter of methodology. If, for the same business process, events are received that are sometimes a batch and sometimes represent individual business objects, then the split should not happen in the business process in order to shield it from the different cases.

Complex Events

Complex events are the opposite to a batch. In this case several messages are received that together result in one event. Each message on its own contains part of the business data that only together define a view of a business object.

For example, a purchase order might be sent in separate messages. The header as well as each line item are a separate message. Only all messages together allow the processing. Each individual message does not contain enough data for its processing.

As in the case of a batch, the question arises where the individual parts are collected and composed. The receiving adapter can accomplish this. In this case all messages that are related are collected by the adapter, and it composes one wire event instance that is an initiating input parameter of an interface process. An interface process, binding process or business process can do it, too. Again, it is a matter of methodology where the composition is done. Like in the case of a batch, the business process is most likely not a good place, since it prefers to deal only with the right abstractions, i.e., complete events.

7.3.7 B2B and A2A Protocols

Some endpoints are back-end application systems, some are trading partners, some are application service providers and some are users. All these endpoints are different in their nature, technically as well as nontechnically in terms of their legal status. Interface processes abstract from all the differences and provide a uniform way to specify the endpoint behavior in terms of wire event exchange sequences that are translated to clear text events. This is a very important achievement of this integration concept, since it makes the modeling activity for the integration modeler a lot easier.

In addition, it makes it possible to replace endpoints with each other. For example, a back-end application system is used in order to maintain enterprise data. The corresponding interface processes make sure that the wire event exchange behavior with this back-end application system is appropriately implemented. If the enterprise decides to no longer have the back-end application system in-house, but to host it instead at an application service provider, then the only the interface process for this back-end application system has to be exchanged with the interface process interacting with the application service provider. This might involve changing the binding process, too. However, the business process remains the same.

This example shows that interface processes provide a mechanism for easily replacing endpoints participating in business processes. This flexibility is important if an enterprise often changes trading partners.

The class of protocols used to communicate with a trading partner as endpoint is called a B2B protocol. In most cases a B2B protocol defines the interaction sequence of the messages, the payload structure and, in many cases, the vocabulary for the payload as well as security. Chapter 20 describes many B2B protocol standards. Since B2B protocols are interoperability protocols between enterprises specifications explicitly exist in the form of standards. It is therefore possible to obtain an extensional representation of B2B protocols. An interface process is the implementation of a B2B protocol for one or several endpoints that conform to that protocol.

The class of protocols to communicate with back-end application systems, called A2A protocols, is in most cases implicit. back-end application system vendors usually do not provide an explicit representation of the protocol to access the back-end application system. Therefore the appropriate interface processes cannot be designed according to an explicit representation. Instead, "tribal" knowledge has to be obtained, for example from the software vendor or consultants, to allow the specification of the interface processes. However, once the interface process is designed, tested and working, an explicit representation of the A2A protocol for a back-end application systems exists. The payload definitions are made available for back-end application systems. This part of a protocol is therefore explicitly represented and available.

Not all B2B protocol standards include the definition of the exchange sequence, but only define the payload structure. For those cases the approach is the same as that for the A2A protocols. The message exchange sequence has to be agreed upon between the two trading partners exchanging messages. Once the agreement is achieved, an explicit representation is available in form of the interface processes.

In summary, B2B protocols and A2A protocols are very similar. Both define endpoint behavior, and both require the explicit representation of the message exchange through interface processes, payload structure definition as well as security specifications. The major difference between both classes of protocols is that B2B protocols are mostly represented explicitly through standards, whereas A2A protocols are mostly represented implicitly, if at all.

7.4 Business Process

Business processes specify the business logic that processes event instances. A business process specifies which business event it needs and which business events it returns in order to achieve a specific functionality. For example, a purchasing business process implements the purchasing business logic of an enterprise. It requires a purchase order business event to be sent out and requires a purchase order acknowledgment event to be received from the selling trading partner.

In business terms, the business processes are an encoding and an implementation of the competitive knowledge of an enterprise that allows it to succeed in a competitive marketplace. From the enterprise's viewpoint, business processes implement the so-called "best practices" (in reality, the currently known practices).

Many business processes only coordinate endpoints by means of binding the corresponding interface processes. In those cases the only value added by a business process is the knowledge of how to route business event instances between endpoints. However, business processes can incorporate additional business logic. Examples are address resolution to determine the endpoints of event instances, authorization steps that require users to authorize specific event instances, notification steps that notify users of noteworthy states in a business process or business rules that implement additional business logic.

The key in specifying business processes is that business processes are specified independent of particular endpoint behavior. Different endpoints behave differently in terms of the message exchanges and payload structures. Interface processes and binding processes abstract from those differences to present all endpoints homogeneously. Business process specifications should make use of this property because it allows for the addition or the replacement of endpoints later on without major business process revisions.

7.4.1 Data

Business processes only operate on business event types and data types. Binding processes make sure that any clear text event received from an interface process is transformed into a business event. This is the only restriction to the process integration concept as defined in Sect. 7.2.

7.4.2 Event Address Resolution

Addressing business events can have many forms. These include direct event addressing, indirect event addressing and event broadcast, which are introduced in the following.

Direct Event Addressing

Direct event addressing is the simplest form of addressing. Direct event addressing specifies the target endpoint identifier in the header of the business event instance to which it is sent. The target address is either specified by the endpoint from which the event is coming or is set by the business process. If it is set in the business process, an event addressing process step is required. This business process step is configured with the endpoint identifier at design time. At run time every business event that is received by this process step will have its target address set to the endpoint identifier that was specified at design time. This is the way the different addressing schemes in Sect. 7.1.4 can be implemented. Furthermore, the event addressing process step can also be used to set the source endpoint, as explained in Sect. 7.1.4.

Indirect Event Addressing

Indirect event addressing derives the target endpoint identifier dynamically at run time. Instead of specifying a fixed endpoint identifier in an event addressing process step, an address resolution rule is specified that derives the endpoint identifier. For example, an address resolution rule could be that if the recipient of goods is located within the USA the shipper UPS is used, otherwise DHL is used. When a shipment request is sent out, it will either go to UPS or DHL, depending on the recipient.

This rule requires the recipient trading partner as input, and it must be able to derive the shipment address from the trading partner, otherwise it would fail. If it cannot be guaranteed that every trading partner has a shipment address, a default could be specified in the rule to use a particular shipper for those cases. It would then be left to the shipper to find out the concrete shipment address, by perhaps contacting the receiving company.

Set of Event Addresses (Event Broadcast)

If one business event has to be sent to several trading partners, then there are different ways to model this. One is to replicate the business event instance as many times as there are trading partners that should receive it. Once the replication takes place, each business event instance is individually set to the target endpoint identifier.

Alternatively, a set of endpoint identifiers can be set on the business event instance. This means that there is one business event instance that contains a list of target endpoint identifiers. In this case the business process does not have to replicate the event instance and set the target address individually.

The question is, however, when does the replication of the event instances take place, since in the end a separate message has to be sent to each target endpoint. This replication takes place automatically before the process bindings are determined. In general, each endpoint can require a different interface process if it conforms to a different A2A or B2B protocol. This means that for each target endpoint a different interface process has to be executed, which in turn means that for each endpoint a different process binding has to be executed. Figure 2.24 shows an example of this case.

Based on this the replication is done automatically when the business event instance is in an output parameter of the business process that binds to process bindings. As soon as the business event instance is available in the output parameter for each target endpoint, a process binding is instantiated. For each endpoint the business event instance is replicated and then is passed to the initiating input parameter of that particular process binding. The target endpoint specification is changed to only this particular endpoint in the replicated business event instance (in this sense it is not a true replica but a modified one). In summary, each target endpoint will receive a separate message and so the event broadcast functionality is achieved.

Each of the business events that are finally sent out as messages can cause a response message to come back. For example, a request for quotation can be broadcast to several trading partners and each can send back a quote as response. How does the "inverse broadcast" work? The goal is to collect all response events and make them available to the business process. Again, this is solved at the boundary of the business process and the binding process. Each of the instantiated binding processes binds the quote to an input parameter of the business process. That input parameter will either be a queued or an array parameter. As the response events are received they are added to the array or appended to the queued parameter.

7.4.3 External Execution Logic

Within the business process, business logic can be implemented that goes beyond managing the event instance flow between endpoints. For example, the sales tax can be computed for outgoing purchase orders, depending on the state or country of the receiving trading partner. Another example is to apply a discount based on published discount offers.

These types of computations are programs that need access to state data like a discount database or a tax regulation database. These programs are not as complicated as an enterprise resource planning (ERP) system and are in many cases rather small. The question arises how these are accessed from within a business process.

From another viewpoint, these programs are like back-end application systems that operate on data. Their size or purpose does not make them different from an integration viewpoint. They remain executables that need to be invoked, and the invocation results need to be obtained. Therefore the same modeling concepts can be used as for other back-end application systems. An interface process has to be defined and it has to be bound to the business process. Adapters are used to access these programs and to establish the connection between the adapter and the parameters of the interface process that exchange wire events with the adapters. This approach applies to all functionality that is implemented in programs or executables that are foreign to the B2B integration technology.

One observation is that external execution logic used within business processes usually follows the same invocation pattern. A business process sends a request in the form of a business event and receives a result in form of a business event. These are transformed and translated as discussed in binding processes as well as in interface processes. From a methodology viewpoint, it is suggested to build a process pattern for this request/reply case and bind the pattern to the respective events as needed.

7.4.4 User Interactions

In many business processes users need to be involved in the execution of business processes. These involvements are mostly of two forms. One is a notification whereby a user is notified about a specific execution state the business process reached or whether an unusual situation occurred. For example, sometimes the chief executive officer of an enterprise wants to be directly involved if a purchase order for more than US $10 Million is received. In other cases a vice president must authorize orders exceeding US $100,000. The notification or authorization can be implemented in different technologies. Examples are e-mail, web browsers, SMS messages and so on. The question arises how a business process implements the user interactions to either send notifications or obtain authorization.

The answer is, not surprisingly, the same as in earlier cases where B2B integration technology external application systems are invoked. Fundamentally, an e-mail system or a web browser (and its required infrastructure like a web/application server) are external execution logic from the B2B integration technology's point of view. As in all of these cases, interface processes and binding processes have to be modeled and adapters have to be put in place that can connect to the required technologies.

7.4.5 Business Rule

In general, business rules affect the processing of business events in business processes. Either the event instances are processed along different execution paths, or the contents of event instances are changed. For example, the tax computation example mentioned in Sect. 7.4.3 or the discount application to purchase orders are business rules that change the contents of a purchase order. Address resolution rules are a different form of business rules that determine the target endpoints that will receive business events.

An example of a business rule that affects the execution path within a business process is the following. Depending on the amount of a purchase order and the credit-worthiness of a customer, an authorization has to be obtained. The values might be different for each trading partner. The business rule evaluates the combination for each business event instance and indicates if an authorization is necessary or not. If it is, the branch of the business process is followed that contains an authorization step, otherwise the branch is executed that omits the authorization step.

In all cases the business rules can change without requiring changes in the business process. This is very important in deployment situations, where business rules change frequently but where the business processes are quite stable. The business process-independent change is achieved because the rules are not part of a business process, but are referenced by the respective process steps.

An important observation has to be mentioned here. Since business rules might change the contents of business event instances, they might change the contents in different ways depending on the target trading partner. For example, an announcement for a new product is sent out using the event broadcast functionality (several target endpoint identifiers in one business event). A business rule is defined that offers a discount to those trading partners that are good customers. Since not all customers are good customers, the business event contents are different for different trading partners. This makes it impossible to use the above mentioned event broadcast functionality because it replicates the business events without changing them. Instead, a separate broadcast for each form of discount must be modeled. In the example this might result in three different broadcasts if there are three different forms of discount.

However, this means that the business process is not a "change-resistant business process." A new form of discount would require revision of the business process to incorporate the fourth case. Instead, it would be better to replicate the business event within the business process for each target endpoint and apply the business rule to each business event instance. While this approach does not use the broadcast functionality, it makes the business process change resistant.

7.5 Binding Process

The binding process integration concept is the last process concept missing in order to achieve the general process layout as specified in Section 5.4.4. Binding processes bind interface processes and business processes so that clear text events are transformed into business events, and vice versa. Furthermore, they transform behavior, if necessary, as explained in the following.

7.5.1 Data and Data Flow

Binding processes can have clear text event types as well as business event types as parameters in addition to data types. Internally, either clear text events or business events are processed. Wire events are not used in binding processes at all.

The concept of binding processes introduces a new form of data flow. Process-external data flow has to be distinguished from process-internal data flow. Process-internal data flow is data flow that connects parameters within processes. All data flow discussions so far revolved around process-internal data flow, and binding processes like the other processes classes have process-internal data flow.

Process-external data flow is data flow between processes. There are two places where process external data flow can take place. First, this flow can occur between interface processes and binding processes. This external data flow connects input and output parameters of type clear text event of the interface and binding processes. One output parameter of an interface process is connected to one input parameter of a binding process, and vice versa. Second, flows occur between binding processes and business processes. These external data flows connect parameters of type business event. One output parameter of a binding process is connected with one parameter of a business process.

Figure 7.44 shows an example of a data flow between a binding process and a business process. In the external data flow specification the business process and the binding process have to be explicitly distinguished, since both have the same name. This is done by locally assigning proxy names to both and using them in the data flow specifications. Figure 7.45 shows the graphical representation. The binding process is represented as a dashed box.

business_process_type PO_POA
  parameter
    IN initiating be_PO: be_purchase_order;
    OUT be_POA: be_purchase_order_acknowledgment;
end_process_type

binding_process_type PO_POA
  parameter
    OUT be_PO: be_purchase_order;
    IN be_POA: be_purchase_order_acknowledgment;
end_binding_process_type

external_data_flow
  business_process a: PO_POA;
  binding_process b: PO_POA;
  data flow
    b.be_PO -> a.be_PO;
    a.be_POA -> b.be_POA;
end_external_data_flow

Fig. 7.44. Process-external data flow

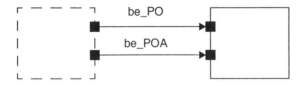

Fig. 7.45. Graphical representation

As Figure 7.44 shows, the business process, the binding process and the process-external data flow between both are three separate modeling constructs. This separation is chosen intentionally because it later allows dynamic process binding (Sect. 7.5.3). Besides, it enables the reuse of the three classes of processes because the process-external data flows can connect different combinations of the processes with each other. Process-external data flow between interface processes and binding processes are specified analogously.

To emphasize the point, processes are bound together by external data flow. The external data flow construct contains all data flow constructs that are necessary to connect two processes. The external data flow and the processes are themselves not part of a higher-level construct like a "integration process" or something similar. Otherwise the dynamic binding would be prohibited.

7.5.2 Intermediate Storing of Events

Binding processes have all process concepts available to them. This means that clear text events as well as business events can be stored intermediately. This is very important since, in many cases, event instances have to be stored in order to avoid the loss of data.

In the following, an example introduces the problem and its solution. It is kept simple, but can be generalized to more complex ones. An incoming message contains no only an endpoint identifier, it also contains the name of the endpoint, its network address (like a URL) as well as a complete ship-to and bill-to address. This message is represented as a wire event and translated into a clear text event. The corresponding business event, however, only contains the endpoint identifier. It does not require any of the other data like the network address or the bill-to or ship-to address. Transformation is therefore lossful and does not transform the unneeded data.

However, the message is not a one-way message but a round-trip message. This means that at some point in time a business event instance is returned from the business process, and it has to be transformed into the corresponding clear text event. The business event only contains the endpoint identifier, but the clear text event needs the complete description, like the network address as well as the bill-to and ship-to address. Since the business event does not contain this data, it has to be retrieved from elsewhere. The source can be the incoming clear text event, and the transformation can get the missing data from it. Of course, this requires that the incoming clear text event is stored in a process variable so that the transformation can access it.

7.5.3 Instantiation Model and Dynamic Process Binding

There is a triangular relationship between an endpoint, an interface process and a business process:

- The business process is bound through a binding process to the interface process as result of integration modeling.
- The endpoint is related to the interface process. The interface process implements the B2B or A2A protocol required by the endpoint.

- An outgoing business event instance is targeted to an endpoint at run time.

This triangular relationship selects the appropriate binding process (and therefore interface process) for a given outgoing business event instance by a particular business process. If the business process puts a business event instance on one of its output parameters, the target endpoint identifier is extracted. Based on the target endpoint, the B2B protocol for this type of event is selected and is implemented by the endpoint. Given the B2B protocol, the corresponding interface process is determined and with it the binding process. The appropriate external data flow is then instantiated, and the business event instance is flown to the initiating binding process parameter.

This instantiation model is executed at run time and hence represents the dynamic binding of binding processes. The binding of a binding process takes place at the latest point in the execution. Once the binding process has been instantiated, it will be used from then on. Subsequent event instances use this binding process instance.

Of course, one business process can have more than one binding process if several different interface processes have to be bound (Fig. 7.35). In this case the dynamic binding takes place twice.

Sometimes one endpoint implements more than one B2B protocol, and in some cases it is possible to send the same event over each of them. For example, RosettaNet as well as EDI both implement purchase order payloads. In this case the execution model might have to choose between the two for the actual binding and instantiation. A policy function might provide a priority scheme that performs the selection. However, another integration concept, endpoint agreement, comes into the play here (Sect. 7.8). An endpoint agreement states the agreement two endpoints have about which messages to exchange. Only if an agreement is in place is a message exchange allowed to happen. For the example at hand, this might result into only one B2B protocol if there is only an agreement in place for one of the two B2B protocol alternatives.

So far only the outbound case is discussed. In the inbound case the selection of the binding process is much more straightforward. For a given interface process there is only one process binding to a business process, which is instantiated as soon as the clear text event instance is available on the output parameters of the interface process. Also, a binding process is bound only to one business process from the inbound direction's viewpoint.

For a given business process there must be as many binding processes and interface processes as there are B2B protocols required by endpoints. For example, if 50 endpoints implement in total 10 different B2B protocols for a given business process, then 10 binding processes and 10 interface processes must be implemented.

7.5.4 Behavior Transformation

An interesting question is what happens if an interface process provides clear text events that the business process does not require and subsequently does not have input parameters for. That situation is a behavior mismatch in the sense that the number of events and their behavior in different processes do not correspond with each other. Another situation is when a business process requires events that are not provided by interface processes. Two cases can be distinguished: one case is a resolvable behavior mismatch, and the other case an unresolvable behavior mismatch (Fensel and Bussler 2002). A resolvable mismatch is one where the binding process can compensate for the mismatch. For example, an incoming event that cannot be passed to a business process can be consumed. The binding process receives the clear text event from the interface process but does not do anything with it. No transformation takes place, and therefore it is not passed on to the business process. And so the mismatch is resolved. The same works for the opposite case, where a business process provides a business event that is not necessary for the interface process.

If an interface process requires a clear text event that does not have a corresponding business event, then this type of mismatch can be resolved by the binding process creating the clear text event and passing it to the interface process. The creation of the event might require access to earlier events or back-end application systems.

An unresolvable behavior mismatch exists when missing events cannot be generated or superfluous events cannot be consumed. Such a situation most likely points to either a modeling mistake or, more significantly, to a mismatch in the business behavior of two enterprises.

7.5.5 Concurrent Processes and Process Coordination

From a more abstract viewpoint the different process classes are concurrently executed processes. As soon as an interface process, a binding process and a business process are instantiated, each of those three executes concurrently with every other one. The only synchronization points are parameters connected by external data flow. All other business logic within the processes can continue independently. of the process.

An integration modeler has to be aware of this behavior and has to make sure that concurrent execution is really possible. Otherwise, it has to be synchronized in order to implement the intended semantics. For example, a round-trip scenario that sends out a purchase order and receives a purchase order acknowledgment is usually synchronized in the sense that a purchase order acknowledgement can only be received once the purchase order has been sent out. The business logic requires this. In order to achieve this dependencies are specified within the processes that order the process steps accordingly.

However, in other situations it is perfectly possible that incoming events are executed concurrently. For example, a shipment notice and an invoice both can come at any point in time and need not come in a sequence. In this case the integration modeler can ensure that there are no dependencies that synchronize both.

Of course, it is easily possible to model processes that will deadlock or lifelock. A deadlock exists if two processes mutually wait for each other at the same time. For example, a business process waits for a clear text event from an interface process, and the same interface process waits for a business event from that business process. If this happens at the same time, these two processes will never finish without intervention.

A lifelock exists if two processes send events to each other forever. For example, a binding process and a business process both can have queued parameters and can both keep sending events to each other through two different external data flows. As soon as a process picks up an event it puts it to the other data flow. This way a never ending endless loop is modeled.

7.6 Process Layout Revisited

The general process layout was shown schematically in Sect. 5.4.4. In general each integration has one business process, one or more interface process and as many binding processes. An incoming message always is represented as a wire event, a clear text event and a business event.

A criticism of this integration model could be that for a simple one-way integration with no business logic this is overkill or "ove-engineered." This criticism requires an important discussion, and in the following alternative process layouts are discussed. If those are implemented in a given B2B integration technology is dependent on how flexible the technology wants to be or must be.

In general there are several different additional process layouts as follows:

- **No business process between binding processes**. In this layout each interface process has one corresponding binding process. However, the binding processes are directly connected with each other through external data flows, and no business process exists. The business events are exchanged directly between the binding processes.
- **No binding processes between interface processes and business process**. This layout consists only of interface processes and a business process. The interface processes are directly connected to the business process through external data flows. Each data flow has the transformation specified as part of data flow refinement (Sect. 7.3.3).
- **No binding processes and no business process**. In this case interface processes are directly connected with each other through external data flows. No transformation takes place, and therefore the clear text events are not represented as business events at all.

- **One binding process between interface processes**. In this layout all interface processes are connected to the same binding process, which coordinates the clear text events between them. It could transform the clear text events into business processes, however, it does not have to.
- **One overall interface process**. This is the minimal layout. All endpoints are connected to the same interface process. For a given integration only one interface process is in place. In this case it is possible that not even clear text events are generated, and wire events are passed between parameters unchanged.

The different alternative process layouts clearly show that the complexity of the integration metamodel increases since additional combinations of integration concepts are possible. For a user these additional possibilities might or might not make it easier to model integration. A uniform layout helps the user because the process layout does not have to be chosen at all; it is always the same. Furthermore, the additional benefit is that all properties, like a business event, are available, no matter what the user designs. On the other hand, more modeling has to be done because all constructs always have to be put in place. Alternative process layouts are easier because less modeling has to be done, which is often perceived by users to be much easier. Independent of these alternatives, the general process layout is used in all examples and explanations throughout this book to provide overall consistency.

7.7 Endpoint

An endpoint represents a source or a target of an event. Endpoints can be of different types like trading partners, users or back-end application systems, which all can be sources as well as targets of events. This section introduces the main properties of this integration concept, which is essential in order to receive and to send messages.

7.7.1 Type

Different types of endpoints can be identified. All these endpoints can be sources and targets of events and eventually messages. In order to exchange events with these types of endpoints, interface processes have to be available for each of them. All the different types of endpoints are alike from this perspective. What makes them different is what they represent in the real world. A user as an endpoint is definitely different from a back-end application system. For example, a user might not respond, while an back-end application system always does (except in an error situation). Consequently, the interface process design might be different. In the case of a user, a time out is implemented that awaits a response, whereas in case of a back-end application system a time-out is not necessary. The different types of endpoints are:

- **Hosted trading partners**. A hosted trading partner is the entity that implements the integration. All integration types are modeled from its viewpoint and under its control. Any endpoint agreement is between it and the other endpoint, the agreement refers. In the hosting integration scenarios there might be several hosted trading partners within one B2B integration technology installation. In nonhosted scenarios, the enterprise installing B2B integration technology is represented as the hosted trading partner in the installation.
- **Remote trading partners**. A remote trading partner represents another enterprise with which a hosted trading partner exchanges messages. A remote trading partner is a separately recognized entity (in many cases a different legal entity) that might have a structure in itself expressed through organizational units (see below). A remote trading partner is "across the wire" in the sense that the exchange of messages with a remote trading partner involves a network like the Internet.
- **Back-end application systems**. A back-end application system represents software that belongs to the hosted trading partner and is under its control. In many cases these are prepackaged software systems, like enterprise resource planning systems (ERPs).
- **User**. A user can be part of a hosted or remote trading partner. A user being defined as an endpoint means messages can be sent to it and received from it. This is important for notifications as well as authorizations.
- **Organizational units**. If it is necessary to recognize the internal structure of a hosted or remote trading partner, then it can be modeled as organizational units. An endpoint can consists of organizational units that themselves can be structured. Examples of organizational units are groups, divisions or task forces. An organizational unit can be addressable, i.e,. can be the source and target of events. This ensures that suborganizations of trading partners can engage in message exchange.

These types of endpoints are important to differentiate and to support in order to enable message exchanges and integration between them.

7.7.2 Trading Partner Community

A more advanced concept is the trading partner community. A trading partner community is a set of trading partners that have recognized communalities that make the communication between them more reliable as well as more efficient in terms of integration.

For example, a trading partner community might decide to use only one B2B protocol between themselves. Every trading partner that is part of the trading partner community is required to implement this B2B protocol. Therefore, a new trading partner joining the community does not impact the existing members of the community. In addition, the community might have its own conformance test to ensure that the trading partner's implementations of the B2B protocol are interoperable. The same approach might be taken for security requirements as well as endpoint agreement specifications. If all members are required to conform to the community's chosen standards then the intended efficiency is achieved.

Open trading partner communities can be distinguished from closed trading partner communities. An open trading partner community does not restrict new members from joining or existing members from leaving the community. Endpoints can choose to join or to leave at their discretion.

A closed trading partner community has a decision process that decides if a new endpoint should be allowed to join the community. There is also a decision process in case a trading partner leaves the community. Besides legal aspects that may potentially have to be enforced (like outstanding obligations), the decision process is necessary for bookkeeping purposes. This allows for updating of the community directory and removal of the leaving endpoint.

7.7.3 Property

Unique Endpoint Identifier

An endpoint has to be uniquely identified within the B2B integration technology. This means that each endpoint instance has a unique identifier, which the B2B integration technology assigns automatically when an endpoint is defined.

In addition to the unique identifier, within a B2B integration technology two trading partners that are exchanging messages need to agree on a common identification schema between them so they can recognize each other. A common identifier between trading partners that exchange messages is necessary. One example is the D&B D-U-N-S Number [DNB]. D&B D-U-N-S Numbers are unique identifiers that are managed by a separate enterprise named Duns and Bradstreet. Each enterprise can request a world wide unique identifier. When exchanging messages a D&B D-U-N-S Number can be used by trading partners to identify themselves. Another example is a private identification schema between two enterprises in which the two enterprises simply agree on the identifier used. In addition, specific B2B protocols might require a specific identification scheme. In this case new identification schemes might be introduced by different B2B protocols.

As this discussion reveals, trading partners may identify themselves in many different ways. Additionally, one enterprise might have several unique identifiers. Therefore a B2B integration technology must implement a trading partner identifier domain value map (Sect. 7.1.8) for trading partner identifiers. For each trading partner known to the B2B integration technology, the corresponding identifier used by that trading partner for exchanging messages has to be listed. In general there exist many different identifiers for trading partners.

Business events always use the identifier that is automatically assigned by the B2B integration technology when an endpoint is defined. Clear text events as well as wire events use the identifier as required by the B2B protocol or the trading partner. Therefore, transformation has to use the trading partner identifier domain-value map when transforming between clear text and business events in order to map the source and target endpoint identifiers accordingly.

Not only might B2B protocols have specific requirements for identifying trading partners but back-end application systems might also have their own way to identify trading partners. This means that each back-end application system might have a different identifier for a given trading partner. This also has to be recorded in the trading partner identifier domain value map. Section 9.3 discusses how these identifiers are synchronized.

Endpoint Property

In addition to unique identifiers, there are other properties of endpoints that are defined when an endpoint is defined, which might or might not be mandatory. The mandatory ones are necessary when defining integration. Examples are phone numbers for error handling, ship-to and bill-to addresses, headquarter address, time zones, country and so on.

Since it cannot be predetermined which of those properties are important for a given B2B integration deployment, an integration modeler must be able to add those properties as necessary for the different types of endpoints. For example, a trading partner might have a world headquarter address but a back-end application system will not have one. The integration metamodel must therefore be able to support the dynamic addition of properties. As usual, they can be added as data types, and since a data type system is available, adding more endpoint properties follows the data type model of the B2B integration technology architecture.

If properties are accessed by integration processes (for example, a conditional branching expression) then the property must have a value and is therefore mandatory. An integration modeler has to specify for each property if it is mandatory or optional when defining the endpoints. Through this specification, validation can ensure that mandatory endpoint properties have a value.

For each endpoint property a domain value map might be necessary if the properties have to be represented in clear text events according to an endpoint's definition. For example, an address in an endpoint specification might be normalized but in the clear text event is not normalized at all. One possibility is to make sure that transformation transforms between the two representations. Alternatively, a domain value map can be added to an endpoint that already specifies the representation. In the latter case the transformation only has to look-up the domain value map.

7.7.4 Organization Modeling

Endpoints can be viewed as black-box entities that have no internal structure. For example, a remote trading partner might be viewed as one entity, and all events are addressed to that trading partner with the same trading partner identifier.

However, some trading partners, while one legal enterprise, have an internal structure in terms of divisions or groups that are independent units from the viewpoint of integration. These units can be sources and targets of events. In those cases it might be necessary to exchange events directly with those units that are part of one remote trading partner. Events are addressed to the units of a trading partner. Therefore, the units are like trading partners themselves, except that they are not independent entities but part of remote trading partners.

The same might be true for the hosted trading partner. It itself might consist of units that autonomously exchange messages with remote trading partners or their units. These units also have to be explicitly recognized in order to allow the modeling of integration for the units.

Both scenarios, the explicit recognition of units in remote as well as hosted trading partners, require that there are integration concepts that support the modeling of these units. The integration concepts are organization modeling concepts.

Fundamentally, the organization modeling concepts are as follows. First, a concept is necessary to specify a unit. This concept is called an organizational unit. An organizational unit can be a group, a division, a task force or any other type of grouping concept in terms of an organizational structure. Since not all remote or hosted trading partners follow the same organization modeling concepts, it is not possible to predefine specific types of organizational units. An organizational unit therefore, when defined, needs to be specialized to one of those grouping concepts for a given trading partner. For example, a trading partner A might have divisions as grouping concepts that have to be modeled, while trading partner B might have groups. Each organizational unit is has to be specified if this organizational unit can send or receive events. This is important since only if an organizational unit can receive and send events can it be part of integration models.

The second concept necessary for organizational modeling is an organizational relationship. An organizational relationship supports the definition of relationships between organizational units. For example, it is possible to define that a remote trading partner has several divisions. This relationship between a trading partner and a division is an organizational relationship that might be called has_division in this example. Like in the case of organizational units, each trading partner might have different types of organizational relationships, and therefore it is not possible to predefine a set of organizational relationship types. Instead, when a trading partner is defined, it is necessary to define specializations of organizational relationship types in order to model the specific organizational structure of a trading partner.

Users are also part of an organizational structure, and they have to be included. A group might consist of several users, and in this case an organizational relationship has to be put in place that specifies which user belongs to which group.

In summary, with the two concepts organizational unit as well as organizational relationship any particular organizational structure of trading partners can be defined.

7.7.5 Endpoint Relationship

Organizational units as well as organizational relationships support the specification of an organizational structure within trading partners. However, sometimes it is necessary to define relationships between trading partners from a hosted trading partner's point of view. For example, a hosted trading partner might record the fact that three remote trading partners are competitors, and whenever a request for quotation is sent this knowledge can be used to make sure that the request is sent to all three of them.

Another example is that two trading partners are complementary and highly efficient in combination. For example, a supplier in conjunction with a specific shipper guarantees always next day deliveries. This knowledge can be used to ensure timely delivery, if necessary.

Therefore, it must be possible to model relationships between endpoints in order to express this knowledge in the integration model. Interendpoint relationships are the integration concept that specifies relationships between endpoints. Since there are many possible relationships, it is not possible to predefine a set of these up front. Instead, an integration modeler must be able to define them as required. The integration metamodel therefore has to allow for the specialization of interendpoint relationships so that an integration modeler can define them as required.

7.7.6 Capability

In addition to the unique identification of endpoints and their internal structure, their communication capabilities have to be specified in order to allow message exchanges. For each endpoint it must be specified which transports the endpoint supports (like HTTP or SMPT). A message exchange is only possible if there is a common transport protocol between a hosted trading partner and its endpoints.

In addition, for each endpoint it must be specified which type of security the endpoint requires and supports. This includes the encryption algorithms used, the key infrastructures as well as nonrepudiation schemes. Like in the transport case, a hosted trading partner and its endpoints need to have common security functionality available. Otherwise they cannot communicate securely.

Since each endpoint can decide on its own which B2B protocol it supports, those B2B protocols have to be specified for each endpoint. This enables the hosted trading partner to determine which B2B protocols are common between it and its endpoints. Again, only if a hosted trading partner and each of the endpoints is communicates with share a common B2B protocol is a message exchange possible.

All endpoints involved in a message exchange access components of the communication layer in the B2B integration technology architecture. They do not directly access the integration logic boundary, as defined in Sect. 5.1.2. However, some endpoints access the operations of the integration logic interface. For example, users need access in order to define integration types or monitor ongoing integration execution. For each endpoint that is allowed to access the integration logic interface, appropriate access rights have to be specified in the capabilities of this endpoint. For example, integration modelers have to be able to access operations that support the definition and management of integration types.

7.7.7 Hosting

In the case of hosting scenarios, the integration needs of several subscribers can be addressed within one installation of a B2B integration technology. Each subscriber is represented as a different hosted trading partner within the same B2B integration technology.

The B2B integration technology architecture ensures the total separation of hosted trading partners. The integration types one hosted trading partner models are completely separate from those another hosted trading partner defines. In addition, each hosted trading partner can specify its own endpoints, representing those trading partners and back-end application systems that it requires for its integration. Fundamentally, all hosted trading partners are completely autonomous and do not share any common types or instances, as if they were each installed on a separate B2B integration technology.

From a software technology viewpoint this is achieved by making sure that all data in the system are qualified by the hosted trading partner identifier. This ensures that no data are shared between the hosted trading partners.

However, someone still needs to manage the B2B integration technology itself. For example, backups have to be done or server processes have to be monitored. This system management is done by the enterprise that installs the B2B integration technology. In the hosted case, this is the application service provider. Since the application service provider has to have access to the B2B integration technology, it is itself a hosted trading partner. It is a specific one with administration rights to the B2B integration technology that no other hosted trading partner has.

A relatively rare case that requires special discussion exists where two hosted trading partners that are hosted on the same B2B integration technology installation exchange messages with each other. Given the fact that they cannot share any data whatsoever, how do they exchange messages? Their communication does not require them to share any data in the B2B integration technology installation. Each of the two hosted trading partners specifies the other one as endpoint. This includes the endpoint capabilities. One endpoint capability is the network addresses of the endpoint. For this, each of the two endpoint definitions contain the network address of the same B2B integration technology installation. Once one hosted trading partner sends out a message over a B2B protocol, the network address is resolved, and it points to the B2B integration technology installation itself. The message is sent and then received by the same B2B integration technology installation by the other hosted trading partner.

In summary, there is absolutely no difference if two trading partners are hosted in the same or in two different B2B integration technology installations.

7.7.8 Versioning

Even thought it was mentioned before, it is emphasized here that endpoints are singular versions, as discussed in Sect. 5.3.4. Endpoints represent real-world entities, like enterprises or back-end application systems, that are in only one state at any given point in time. Consequently, their representation inside a B2B integration technology architecture must follow this situation by ensuring that there is only one version of an endpoint valid at a given point in time.

Consider the example of a trading partner who upgrades a B2B protocol to the next version of that B2B protocol and says this is going to happen at a specific point in time and that the former version will be unavailable from that same point in time onwards. Then this trading partner's trading partners must ensure that they implement the same change in their B2B integration technology installations. This means that they have to change the respective endpoint specifications and therefore enforce the change.

7.8 Endpoint Agreement

Enterprises are protective in terms of the messages that they receive from endpoints or that they send to endpoints. An enterprise only wants to receive known messages from known endpoints. Any other message, either unknown message type or from an unknown endpoint, is usually treated with extreme caution. This is mainly the case because of the possibility of messages that are intended to disrupt the operations of the enterprise.

Message that are sent out are usually very carefully managed because messages in general should not reveal any competitive knowledge to competitors or should not create unintended obligations for an enterprise. Endpoint agreements are an integration concept that allows an enterprise to carefully manage the message exchange with external endpoints. An endpoint agreement fundamentally specifies which type of message can be sent or received from which specific endpoint.

7.8.1 Agreement

An endpoint agreement must be in place in order for endpoints to exchange messages. An endpoint agreement in this sense authorizes the B2B integration technology to send messages to an endpoint and to receive messages from an endpoint. Since not all types of messages should be received from any endpoint, an endpoint agreement must specify the details. An endpoint agreement contains the following:

- **Transport**. In case the involved endpoints can use several common transports, both have to agree on the particular transport they are going to use for exchanging messages according to this agreement. If the B2B protocol used prescribes a particular transport, then both endpoint need to be able to support it.

- **Transport addresses**. Since one endpoint might have several addresses for a given transport, the involved endpoints need to state which address to use for this agreement. This can be very detailed if a different transport address should be used for each different type of message exchanged.
- **Interface processes**. Each endpoint has to specify the interface process according to which the messages are exchanged. Indirectly, this defines the B2B protocol used in this endpoint agreement. The involved interface processes have to match in lockstep. This means that the message exchange order and direction have to be completely complementary. A message sent by one endpoint must be received by the other endpoint. An endpoint that waits for a message must eventually receive that message.
- **Security**. In order for all endpoints to be able to decrypt and to check the signature, both have to use the same security standards and algorithms.
- **Start date and time**. Endpoint agreements start at a given point in time. Any message sent before the start data and time is considered erroneous.
- **End date and time**. Endpoint agreements have an expiration date and a time after which messages are not accepted any more. This can be open-ended to be determined later on.
- **Initiating endpoints**. If the interface processes do not clearly specify which of the endpoints sends the initiating message then this has to be explicitly defined. If every endpoint can initiate then this has to be specified, too.
- **Responding endpoints**. Even though the specification of the initiating endpoint indirectly specifies the responding endpoints it can be specified explicitly, too.

In case two trading partners exchange messages both need an endpoint agreement. This is the case since both have their own B2B integration technology installed and therefore both need to configure their own system. There are two possibilities how to derive to two endpoint agreements. First, both can share the same endpoint agreement. This means that both B2B integration technology systems can understand the same textual representation and therefore both can import the same endpoint agreement. Chapter 20 discusses a standard proposal that could support this scenario.

Second, both endpoints have to create matching endpoint agreements within their B2B integration technology. This would be required if the two B2B integration technologies have different ways to specify endpoint agreements. For the latter case it is important to realize that some of the data in endpoint agreements is common, some complementary and some different. According to the above elements

- Transport is the same.
- Transport addresses are different since each endpoint has a different address.
- Interface processes are complementary since the interface process of one endpoint is the complement to the interface process of the other endpoint.
- Security is the same.
- Start date and end date are the same.

- Initiating and the responding endpoints are the same.

Not all endpoint agreements are always between exactly two endpoints (bilateral endpoint agreement). Some are between several endpoints (multiendpoint agreement), some are trading partner community agreements, some have to deal with anonymous endpoints and finally there are unilateral endpoint agreements. These different types are discussed in the following.

7.8.2 Unilateral Agreement

Endpoint agreements have to be established for each endpoint with which a hosted trading partner exchanges messages. This includes not only trading partners but also back-end application systems as well as users. back-end application systems and users are alike, since both endpoints are represented by a software package that is installed within the hosted trading partners enterprise and are under full control of the hosted trading partner.

In the most restrictive case back-end application systems can exchange messages through fixed interfaces. The message types are determined as well as the exchange sequences of messages. Messages can be sent and received at any point in time without restriction. If security is implemented at all by the back-end application system it might be predetermined, too. In summary, most of the elements of an endpoint agreement with this type of endpoint are predetermined by the endpoint and there is no choice. As outlined, there might be no choice at all when integrating with such a back-end application system.

This means that the endpoint agreement can only be enforced by the hosted trading partner, not by the back-end application system. For example, if the hosted trading partner only wants to receive purchase orders from the back-end system then it has to filter them. Other types of messages that are sent by the back-end application system are not received and processed.

In more flexible cases it might be that back-end application systems can be configured to some extent. For example, it might be possible to indicate to a back-end application system what message types a hosted trading partner wants to receive. In this case endpoint agreements can be enforced at both endpoints.

7.8.3 Bilateral Agreement

In bilateral agreements both endpoints are in full control over the elements of an endpoint agreement, and both can enforce the endpoint agreement by following the specification.

In bilateral agreements (and for that matter, in all agreements) one of the endpoints is always the hosted trading partner because agreements are always between a hosted trading partner and another endpoint.

There can be any number of endpoint agreements between the same set of endpoints. If there is no agreement then the two endpoints do not exchange any message. If there is one agreement, only those interface processes are executed. If there is more than one agreement, then all the specified interface processes can be instantiated and executed concurrently.

7.8.4 Multiendpoint Agreement

A multiendpoint agreement is an agreement between more than two endpoints. All endpoints are listed in the same endpoint agreement with the interface processes they are going to execute. It is possible that one endpoint can interact with an interface process of two or more other endpoints. If this is intended, no further specification is necessary. However, if this is not intended, then the interface processes with it should interact must be specified.

Multiendpoint agreements can be represented as bilateral endpoint agreements. For each pair of endpoints of a multiendpoint agreement, a bilateral agreement can be put into place instead that represents the interactions that are specified in the multilateral agreement. The difference is that in a multiendpoint agreement all endpoints are aware of each other and the interactions between all of them. In bilateral agreements this is not the case, since a bilateral agreement does not include the interactions of the other endpoints.

Another difference is that the interface processes might have to be changed. If one interface process sends events to several different endpoints, but only bilateral endpoint agreements are in place, then a mismatch exists because the interface process refers to endpoints that are not part of the bilateral endpoint agreement. In this case the interface process needs to be split so that events are only addressed to endpoints in the endpoint agreement.

If one endpoint has a multiendpoint agreement, then the other endpoints can have the corresponding multiendpoint agreements in their B2B integration technologies. However, if their B2B integration technologies do not support the specification of multiendpoint agreements, then they can specify bilateral agreements instead on their end. The exceptions to this rule are endpoints that are back-end application systems that cannot enforce endpoint agreements as discussed above.

The fact that a multiendpoint agreement is specified does not mean that every endpoint can see all messages. Each endpoint can only receive and send the messages as defined in the interface agreement. Furthermore, a multiendpoint agreement does not imply that each endpoint can inquire about the status of messages in other endpoints at any point in time. Status queries are implemented as messages themselves, and therefore only if they are included in interface processes can they be sent and received.

Finally, in addition to multiendpoint agreements, the endpoints can be part of other endpoint agreements, too. A multiendpoint agreement does not prohibit other endpoint agreements for other interaction purposes.

7.8.5 Trading Partner Community Agreement

As discussed in Sect. 7.7.2, trading partner communities might define specific standards that all members of the community have to follow, for example, specific types of security or B2B protocols. This means that the choices for endpoint agreements are limited. For example, if EDI is used as the B2B protocol of choice, then all endpoint agreements with community members need to specify EDI interface processes. Of course, community members can have endpoint agreements outside the community and in this case they are free to specify endpoint agreements as desired.

7.8.6 Agreement for Anonymous Endpoints

Anonymous endpoints pose an interesting problem. An anonymous endpoint is an endpoint that cannot be uniquely identified up front and is not known up front. An anonymous endpoint can claim to be whoever it wants to be, without the receiver having any possibility of verifying the claim up front. Still, it might be interesting to receive messages from anonymous endpoints because of the potential benefit. For example, a request for quote might be coming in for a large amount of goods. Rejecting the message based on the fact that the endpoint is not verifiable at the time of the message receipt might mean lost business.

One approach could be that these messages are flagged and a user gets involved to verify the endpoint. This can be done by examining the message and getting in contact with the sending endpoint, maybe by e-mail or phone. Serious messages will make it easy to get hold of the sending endpoint because the intent is to establish a business relationship. Once the endpoint is identified and regarded as trustable the message processing can be resumed. At the same time, the endpoint is specified in the B2B integration technology and is a known endpoint from then on. The next incoming message from that endpoint might no longer involve any user if the endpoint can be identified automatically.

The problem with unknown endpoints is, of course, that some endpoints have a malicious intent and try to interrupt operations. In this case, the endpoints try to make identification impossible. That might result in a lot of work for users since they have to filter out the malicious or frivolous messages. If it is possible to find similarities in messages from the same malicious endpoint, then those can be filtered out automatically based on the similarity. However, malicious endpoints try to avoid this, too.

7.8.7 Multi-Interface Process Agreements

It is possible to define endpoint agreements for single interface processes. In a given situation this might result in three different endpoint agreements for three different interface processes that are all bound through binding processes to the same business process. While this is a perfectly fine scenario, it requires manually ensuring consistency across the three agreements so that they establish a consistent specification. This is because all are bound to the same business process, and there must be consistency across the endpoint agreements in order to execute the business process successfully. For example, the start and end times might have to be the same for all of the three agreements.

A more convenient situation would be to have only one endpoint agreement for the three interface processes in this situation. Since there would be one start and one end date and time specified, these would apply to all three interface processes. This way this consistency is easier for an integration modeler to maintain.

7.8.8 Agreement Conflict Resolution

Since more than one endpoint agreement can exist between the same endpoints, it is possible to have conflicting endpoint agreements. Two or more endpoint agreements conflict if they state that a message exchange can happen and cannot happen at the same time. Alternative endpoint agreements are two or more agreements that allow the same message exchange. This means that two endpoint agreements allow the same interface processes for the same endpoints.

Conflicting endpoint agreements have to be avoided at specification time because a run-time error would happen at run time, forcing the resolution then. In the case of alternative endpoint agreements, a rule has to be provided, which endpoint agreement to follow if there is a choice between two or more endpoint agreements.

The question is what does it mean for an endpoint agreement to be conflicting or alternative. This depends on the interpretation of endpoint agreements. There are two interpretations that make the difference clear.

The first interpretation of an endpoint agreement is that the message exchange defined in the endpoint agreement is possible according to the endpoint agreement details, and no other agreement between the same endpoints with the same interface process and overlapping start and end dates is allowed. Alternatively expressed, the start and end date and time must not overlap for the same endpoints and interface process. Otherwise, the endpoint agreements conflict. For example, two endpoint agreements that are identical except the start and end date would be in conflict with each other if start and end dates overlap. For example, the second agreements starts before the first expires.

The second interpretation is that an endpoint agreement states that the message exchange as specified is possible but does not make a statement about what is not possible otherwise. In this case the same two endpoint agreements as in the previous example are alternatives and do not conflict because they state that there are two durations in which the interface processes can be executed. These durations happen to overlap, which makes them alternatives.

Both interpretations of endpoint agreements are possible. In the case of conflicting endpoint agreements the conflicts have to be resolved at design time, since at run time they would result in a run-time error. When endpoint agreements are specified it is possible to check if the start and end date and times conflict, and in this case the integration modeler is notified about the conflict. The conflict can then be avoided by changing the start and end dates and times.

In the case of alternative endpoint agreements, a rule has to be provided indicating which one to choose. For example, it could be always the one that has the earliest start time. In addition, the integration modeler could be warned about alternative endpoint agreements when specifying the endpoint agreements. The modeler then could choose to modify them, avoiding alternatives. But that is by choice and is not necessarily required.

7.8.9 Interface Process Instantiation Revisited

Endpoint Agreement Interpretation

The instantiation algorithm described in Sect. 7.3.2 ignored endpoint agreements completely when initiating interface processes with incoming wire events. The focus was on finding an input parameter that either instantiated an interface process or filled an input parameter of an already existing interface process.

However, endpoint agreements are the final authority in deciding if a message should be accepted or not before giving the corresponding wire event to an interface process. This means for an incoming message that first a corresponding endpoint agreement has to be found. An endpoint agreement applicable contains an interface process that can receive the incoming message from the particular endpoint from which the message comes. Only if an endpoint agreement is found for the message is the interface process either instantiated or continued. If no endpoint agreement can be found the message is rejected.

In the outbound case the same applies. Before an event instances is passed through external data flow from the binding process to an interface process, an endpoint agreement has to be found that allows sending this event to the target endpoint through the given interface process. If one can be found, the interface process is instantiated or continued. If not, a run-time error is generated.

This change in the algorithm establishes the endpoint agreement enforcement. Endpoint agreements are the only authority when deciding to accept an inbound message or to deny accepting an inbound message. In addition, endpoint agreements are the only authority that allows the sending of messages to endpoints.

Endpoint Agreement Expiration

One aspect of endpoint agreements requires a specific discussion, namely endpoint agreement expiration. Endpoint agreements have a start date and an end date. Before the start date no message exchange is allowed to happen. It is tempting to define the end date accordingly, that is, after the end date no message exchange is allowed to happen. However, integration processes are long-running and so it might happen that not all integration processes are finished if the corresponding endpoint agreements are expiring.

The question is how to deal with this case. One possibility is to let the integration finish despite the fact that the corresponding endpoint agreements expired. Only messages that are necessary to finish ongoing interface processes would be received or sent.

Another possibility is to interrupt the integration and to compensate it. In this case all involved process instances have to be interrupted. Error handling has to be invoked to undo the effects of these in order to leave a consistent system behind.

A third possibility is to interrupt the involved process instances and have an administrator decide how to react. The administrator could then either modify the endpoint agreement so that the process instances can continue. However, that might cause additional initiating messages to be accepted. To avoid this case it would be necessary to modify the endpoint agreement only for the ongoing integration processes but deny new ones to start. Or the administrator can compensate the processes manually. Also, the administrator could simply abort the processes without any error handling at all.

Another case regarding expiration can be that two back-to-back endpoint agreements refer to the same interface process. Back-to-back means that the end date and time of one is the start date and time of the other one. What happens if integration processes are not finished when the first endpoint agreement expires? Can they continue as if no expiration happened because the second agreement is in place? That only works if the only differences between the two agreements are the start and end times. However, if the transport changes then the messages would have to change the transport exactly at the expiration time. In the end, the particular implementation of a B2B integration architecture has to define the behavior of the endpoint agreement integration concept.

7.9 Error Handling and Compensation

Error handling is an important aspect of an integration metamodel. Failures of infrastructure as well as specification mistakes happen, and they ideally must not lead to an inconsistent state in one or several integration processes or object instances. This requires appropriate error-handling capabilities, which are discussed next.

7.9.1 Error Types

It is important to distinguish between two major types of errors in order to later introduce appropriate error-handling functionality. The two types are system errors and integration errors.

System Error

A system error is an error that occurs because of a fault in infrastructure or base components. For example, a network failure or a virtual machine failure leads to a system error. These errors can be transient or permanent. A transient system error disappears once the infrastructure component is reset or restarted. For example, a network failure no longer happens after the connection is reestablished.

A permanent system error does not disappear and can be reproduced. A failure of a virtual machine could be of this nature, where the virtual machine consistently fails in the same program execution context. This the requires the replacement of the virtual machine with a new version that contains the repairs of the failing code.

System errors must not affect the consistency of the integration object instances and integration types. If a business process cannot be continued because of a system error then it needs to be interrupted. Once the system error is handled and removed, the business process should be able to continue as if the system error never occurred. A system error might require manual intervention, like installing a new virtual machine, or can be handeled automatically, like reestablishing a network connection.

While a system error must not affect the integration objects in their consistency, it might change their execution paths. For example, a system error might occur when an interface process instance is waiting for an acknowledgment from a trading partner. At this point a time-out might be in effect that waits for two hours for the acknowledgment before resending the original wire event to the trading partner. If a system error occurs during the time-out and the time to remove the system error takes longer than the time-out duration, then a resend of the wire event will occur, even if the acknowledgment has been sent in the meanwhile (but not received due to the system error). Without the system error, the resend of the original wire event would have not occurred.

This example shows that the consistency of the interface process was not compromised at all. It executed as specified and did not fail. However, without the system error the execution would have been a different one. In the extreme case the time out during which the system error occurred could have been the last retry attempt. In this case the system error would have caused the business interaction to fail. For example, if the original wire event was a purchase order, the purchase attempt failed. However, this still would be a consistent behavior of the interface process, albeit an unintended one.

However, not all system errors are that "clean." Sometimes a system error affects the consistency of integration instances. For example, the contents of a message are accidentally modified during its transmission over a network, and that modification does not affect the header but only the message body. This modification is not detected until validation, if at all. If no validation rule checks the content of the message, then the subsequent content of the event elements might be inconsistent. This might lead to an integration error later on (see below) caused by a system error. For example, a transformation that tries to read the modified content might fail. This is an example of a system error that affects the consistency of integration instances. The only advice for this example is to make sure that there are complete validation rules in place for incoming as well as outgoing events.

Integration Error

An integration error is an error that results from either integration type-specification mistakes or from erroneous content of event instances (or a combination thereof). Integration type specification errors can occur, in general, in every type specification. For example, a transformation might contain a mistake in a transformation rule that later is detected by validation, causing the integration error. A validation might contain a mistake because it is missing one value of an enumeration. This might cause the failure of a transformation that has a special transformation rule for this enumeration value. Another example is a process type that contains a possible endless loop when one of the process variables has a specific value. Erroneous event instance content might cause integration errors when validation rules or parameter constraint rules are violated. The integration error in this case is caused by data type values, not specification mistakes.

No matter what causes an integration error the error must be raised as soon as possible. This requires that all components of the B2B integration technology architecture detect the error and raise it. Once the integration error is raised it has to be handled and repaired. After the repair, the affected integration instances must be in a consistent state again. After all, this is the goal of error handling in the first place.

Part of error handling is the assessment of the integration error itself. It has to be determined if the error occurred because of a specification mistake or because of faulty event instance content. In addition, it has to be assessed which of the integration types or integration instances caused the error. Based on this evaluation a second assessment takes place. This second assessment determines if the integration error is automatically repairable or if it requires manual intervention for repair. In cases where the integration error can be repaired automatically, an appropriate error repair function has to be executed. For manual intervention a user has to be notified who can take care of the error situation and has the ability to repair it.

A user can choose from two alternatives for manual error handling and repair: dynamic instance modification and resubmission, or integration abort. For manual and automatic error handling compensation is available. These three error handling and repair approaches are discussed in more detail in the following.

Before the discussion a brief note is important. In general, error handling and repair is sometimes referred to as error recovery. Two major types of error recovery are distinguished, namely forward error recovery and backward error recovery (Gray and Reuter 1993). Backward error recovery causes the system state in error to go back to a consistent state that has already been achieved and is known to the system. For example, a database abort does this by recovering to the last consistent state. The goal of backward recovery is to go back to the last known system state.

In contrast, forward error recovery establishes a consistent state that has not yet been established in the system. The goal is also to get to a consistent system state, however, by establishing a new one. For example, in a checking account, a wrong transfer is recovered by adding another transfer that compensates the first one. Instead of going back to the state before the first transfer (which would be backward recovery), another transfer is added to get to a new consistent state (forward recovery).

In the context of B2B integration, forward recovery is the choice of error recovery. Integration processes are long-running processes that externalize intermediate consistent states during execution. As soon as intermediate states are externalized, backward recovery becomes impossible.

For example, a purchase order event that is received is passed to two back-end application systems. In order to achieve this integration several process instances are executed. Every state change of the integration processes is externalized to the persistence layer. Achieving the delivery of the event is the final goal, but along the way intermediate consistent states are externalized. From the viewpoint of the integration processes, the externalized states are consistent.

If an integration error happens after the delivery of the purchase order to the first back-end application system, but before the delivery to the second back-end application system, then error handling has two choices. Either it has to ensure that the purchase order is delivered to the second back-end application system (the preferred approach), or the first back-end application system is told to ignore the purchase order and its sender is told that the integration failed. While the externalized states of the integration processes are consistent, the overall state from the viewpoint of the endpoints is inconsistent since the event has to go to both of the back-end application systems or neither.

In both cases, forward error recovery requires the execution of process steps in integration processes in order to achieve the desired results. Either the purchase order is sent to the second back-end application system after the error repair, or process steps have to be executed to send a cancellation to the first back-end application systems and an error notification to the sender of the purchase order.

7.9.2 Dynamic Instance Modification

Dynamic instance modification allows a user to modify an integration object in the error state and retry the execution that produced the error in the first place. The retry puts the objects in question out of their error state back into an execution state, so that the execution can continue as if the error never happened. If this retry does not produce the error again, the error is considered to be repaired. If the error happens again, the user can again modify the object instance and retry. At some point in time this strategy either works and the error can be repaired, or the user has to either compensate or abort the integration processes.

One example is a failed transformation because of a specification mistake in one of the transformation rules. If such an integration error happens, the transformation returns an error code that indicates that a transformation rule failed. The binding process instance that contains the transformation process step is halted and put into error state. The transformation step failed and because of this failure is put in error state, too. From the history of the system it is known which clear text event instance (or several) was involved in the transformation. The integration error assessment determines that the integration error was caused by a transformation failure, and it determines that the repair approach should be manual so that a user has the chance to repair the transformation.

Once this assessment happened a user is notified with a request to repair the error. The user has all object instances and types involved in the error availabl. Users can look at the transformation specification, the clear text event instances, the binding process instance as well as the error code that indicates what caused the error. Based on this information the user can change the transformation specification and create a new version of the transformation. It is the user who determines if this new version only applies to this instance or to all future uses of the transformation, as discussed in Chap. 5.

After the transformation is changed, the user starts a retry. This means that the binding process instance is put back into state in_execution. The same is done for the transformation step in the binding process. Once this happens the transformation step is executed again, and if the change to the transformation was correct the execution succeeds. If not, the same error happens again, and the user can again modify the transformation and restart the process. As the example describes, as soon as an integration error happens the relevant object instances have to be put in error state and halted so that a user can modify them and attempt a restart.

7.9.3 Compensation

From a user viewpoint, integration compensation is the most convenient error recovery approach. Once an error occurs that needs manual intervention, the user can just initiate the compensation to achieve a consistent overall state. While this is certainly convenient, this approach should be used as the last resort approach only when dynamic object instance modification and retry cannot achieve an error repair that allows the process instances to continue.

Compensation can be initiated automatically if the error-handling assessment comes to this result. In this case the error handling assessment will initiate the compensation. This requires, however, that compensation is defined in the integration process types, otherwise compensation would fail. Section 7.2.10 explains process or integration compensation in detail, and the reader is referred to that section for details.

7.9.4 Abort

Aborting integration processes is the most disruptive approach. Fundamentally, all integration processes are halted and put in aborted state. That means that they will never execute again, and consequently all the externalized states they left behind are the ones at the time of the abort. Needless to say that while the externalized states are consistent with the execution progress of the integration processes, the overall state from the viewpoint of the endpoints might be inconsistent. For example, not all events have been delivered yet that should have been delivered by the aborted integration processes. This puts the burden of achieving a consistent state across all endpoints completely on the user and requires a completly manual approach.

7.10 Complete Integration Model

7.10.1 Completeness

A user needs to specify one or more configurations so that endpoint integration can happen. A configuration needs to contain a complete set of types and instances. If one type or one instance is missing, the integration will either not start or fail along the way. Once the configuration is completely specified, it needs to be deployed so that messages and their corresponding events can be received and sent at run time (Sect. 16.6).

A complete configuration contains the following types and instances:

- **Set of integration processes**. For each endpoint that is going to be involved by the integration processes, one or more interface processes as well as their corresponding binding processes must be in place. All integration processes must be connected to each other by external data flow.
- **Compensation process steps**. Compensation is optional in the sense that integration processes can be executed without having compensation steps defined. However, if they are specified, they require defined event and data types.
- **Set of event types and data types**. All the event types and data types that are referenced by the integration processes have to be specified.
- **Transformations and translations**. All transformation and translation rules that are references by the translation and transformation process steps in the integration processes have to be specified.
- **Endpoints**. All endpoints that are going to be integrated with the configuration have to be defined.
- **Endpoint agreements**. For all endpoints that are going to be integrated with the configuration, the necessary endpoint agreements have to be defined. Only if the necessary endpoint agreements are in place will the integration execution succeed.

The completeness is automatically checked when a configuration is deployed so that no run-time error happens because of an incomplete configuration. Chapter 16 provides a detailed description of the deployment and configuration change methodology. One caveat follows: endpoints can be dynamically determined by integration processes at run time, therefore it is not possible to check the completeness of endpoints in the configuration. If an endpoint is not included in the configuration then this omission might result in a run-time integration error. However, with the ability to dynamically change and retry the execution such an integration error can be repaired.

7.10.2 Correctness

Completeness and correctness of configurations are related to each other. Only a complete configuration can be a correct configuration. Once a configuration is checked for completeness and it is complete, then its correctness is checked. This correctness is defined in the types and instances as part of the configuration. Semantic correctness is addressed later.

A very important part of a correctness check is the type check. A type check makes sure that all types and instances that refer to each other always refer to the correct type and that this type exists. In a typed system this is a very important check.

Beyond type checks more integration metamodel-specific checks can be applied. For example, whether a transformation produces a complete target event can be checked. All mandatory data types have to be populated. Another example is to check if the predicate in a conditional branch control flow construct only refers to known events and their elements. An important model check that is not caught by completeness is to check if interface processes connect to binding processes and that those connect to business processes.

The goal of a correctness check is to avoid run-time errors. If it were possible to have a complete correctness check the run-time execution would never produce an error. However, a complete correctness check is not possible due to the dynamic predicates that can be specified and that refer to data values that cannot be enumerated.

7.10.3 Semantic Correctness

Semantic correctness is defined as correct business behavior. A semantic correctness check would be able to determine if a configuration implements correct business behavior. For example, received purchase orders should result in more revenue. However, as is immediately clear from the example, this is impossible. Semantic correctness is mentioned here in order to contrast it with the completeness and correctness checks in terms of the integration metamodel and to show the clear limitation of any B2B integration technology in terms of the business.

7.11 Summary

This chapter introduced all integration concepts that are necessary to successfully specify and implement B2B integration. A complete and expressive set of integration concepts is essential for a good B2B integration technology architecture. The definitions of the integration concepts are very detailed in order to understand their meaning and usefulness.

Chapter 8 introduces integration functionality that is not reflected in integration concepts but has to be provided by a B2B integration technology architecture independent of the integration concepts. Chapter 9 introduces examples of integration processes that are used to maintain the B2B integration itself. This chapter not only applies the integration concepts but shows how several integration endpoints can be integrated in order to exchange definition data instead of business data in the form of events.

8 Additional Functionality

A complete B2B integration technology architecture has to provide functionality in addition to the integration concepts to make it accessible, useful and manageable. This chapter concentrates on the functionality a B2B integration technology architecture needs to expose that is required in addition to the integration concepts in Chap. 7.

8.1 History

In different situations it is very important to know how the B2B integration arrived at a specific state. Some of these are the following:

- **Audit**. An audit of a message requires determining in detail what happened to the message in terms of integration processes and which other events were sent out based on this message. For example, an incoming message was represented as a wire event, translated, transformed, processed in the business process and so on. An audit follows all these state changes in great detail and investigates wheter any errors occurred on the way. It follows the message and its corresponding events all the way from endpoint to endpoint. In case a message causes response messages, those will be included.
- **Business intelligence**. Business intelligence aggregates data for a given period of time. For example, it might summarize all purchase order amounts and compare them with the invoice amounts as well as payment amounts. This gives insight into the overall payment behavior of all endpoints involved in the message exchanges. In general, since it is not known up front what business intelligence aggregates, every integration object and all their state changes need to be available to it.
- **Status**. The status of a message or a business process is about the current state of these objects. For example, an event could be short before transformation or a business process can be in the state initiated. A status usually inquires for the current state of an integration object, not for a set of states as the previous two situations did.
- **Error**. If an error occurs then it is very important to see what happened to the integration objects involved in the error over time in order to figure out what causes the error and what can be done to repair the error. For example, a transformation error might be because of erroneous event content or a mistake in a

transformation definition. In order to find this out, the origin of the event (i.e., the incoming message) or the change history of the transformation itself (i.e., the changes to the transformation definition from the time it was created) might have to be investigated.

- **Repudiation**. In a repudiation case the sender or receiver of a message denies the sending or receipt of a message. In order to be able to prove that a message was sent or received, the messages that came in or left the system have to be recorded in such a form that later it can be proved that the message left the system or was received by the system, and that it did so unaltered.
- **Fraud**. In case of fraud, one of the investigations is who was involved and how much did those involved in the fraud know about it. In order to prove that an enterprise was not aware of a fraud scheme, it is important for the enterprise to provide nonrepudiation as well as audit data so that any investigation can determine that it was not involved at all.

All these different situations have in common that in all of them the history of the B2B integration is important. What is history? In a nutshell, the history is an explicit representation of past state changes of the objects in a system. Usually they are tied to the date and time that the state changes happened and the user who caused the state change. Furthermore, if several state changes happened together in one transaction, this set is identified with an unique identifier so later it is visible that all the state changes happened together. In B2B integration not only users can cause change but incoming messages, too.

In context of the B2B integration technology architecture this definition is followed and includes not only integration instances but also integration types. This means that which user changed which integration type at a given point in time is visible in history.

There are different types of history that can be implemented with different implications to the above situations that require history. One type of history is based on versions only. This type of history only records the versions of integration types, but not the changes that occurred between two versions. It is therefore impossible to find out which user was involved in the changes except the user who created the version itself and the state of the integration type at that time. Integration instances are not versioned and therefore do not show up in this type of history. Any situation requiring the history of integration instances therefore cannot use this type of history.

Another type of history records only specific states of integration objects. For example, only versions of integration types and only end states of integration instances. In this type of history certain states are visible and others are not. It depends on the situation that requires history if this type of history is useful or not. For example, in the error case, this type of history would show the wire event and the clear text event before and after the transformation. However, it would not show the individual transformation steps.

A more advanced type of history records specific states, too, but those are user configurable. This enables an integration modeler or integration administrator to specify the states that should be recorded. For the above example it would mean that a user can define that the results of the individual transformation rules should be recorded. However, the downside is that the user has to anticipate all possibly required states up front in order to be able to specify those that are relevant.

The ultimate type of history is the complete history. This type of history collects the full set of all state changes that occur in the complete B2B integration technology architecture. There is no state change anywhere that is not recorded. This type of history allows the complete replay of what happened at any point in time. No matter what the situation is that requires history, the history can provide whatever is recorded because it is complete. While this type of history is the most useful, especially when it is not clear which history details are relevant and to what extent, it is the most expensive type of history from a management point of view. All state changes have to be recorded without exception, and the resulting set of history data has to be stored and managed.

8.2 Consistency and Reliability

Like in database management systems, all committed changes that are caused by users are considered consistent. This means that if the state before the change was consistent, then the state after the change is consistent, too.

The same principle applies for the B2B integration technology architecture. Any change that happens because of user interaction or message exchange is considered consistent so that the resulting state is also consistent. Specified integration types in conjunction with endpoint definitions and endpoint agreement definitions restrict the changes that can happen when messages are incoming or outgoing, and therefore ensure the consistency. Integration types, endpoint definitions and endpoint agreements are enforced by the B2B integration technology architecture by allowing integration instances to only change according to the integration types, endpoint and endpoint agreement definitions. Therefore, any state change leads to a consistent overall system state. Any message exchange that would not result in a consistent state is rejected. The same applies for user interactions.

The reliability of a B2B integration technology architecture is achieved by enforcing every consistent state change to be a database transaction. The B2B integration technology architecture does not have to provide any functionality except to make sure that all consistent state changes are within a database transaction. If all state changes are encapsulated in this way, the reliability of the B2B integration technology architecture is achieved by the underlying database management system. No change should be recorded outside transactions or storage that does not participate in transactions (like, in most cases, file systems).

8.3 Security

Security in context of B2B integration is twofold. One area of security is related to the message exchange, and the other area is related to end users. Because security is a major concern of B2B integration, it is discussed in more detail in the following. A detailed discussion of security can be found in Sherif (2000) as well as many more references that are relevant for an even further detailed study of security.

8.3.1 Requirements

Security functionality revolves around a few major areas. Identification is the association of a unique token like a fingerprint with an endpoint, authentication uniquely identifies an endpoint, authorization establishes the access rights for an endpoint and integrity ensures that data send by an endpoint are in fact the ones it sent. Additionally, confidentiality ensures that no message is given to a nonauthorized third party and nonrepudiation ensures that neither a sender nor a receiver can deny having sent or received messages.

8.3.2 Identification

Despite newer methods around biometrical identifiers, like finger prints or voice prints, symmetric and private keys are the means of establishing the identity in B2B message exchange environments. In symmetric key situations both participants are identified by possessing the symmetric key. In public key situations a trusted certification authority issues a certificate that links an endpoint's public key with the uniquely identified endpoint itself. The certificate is signed with the certification authorities' private key. Through this mechanism the certification authority assures that the endpoint and the endpoint's public key belong to each other.

8.3.3 Authentication

Authentication tries to avoid allowing an endpoint to masquerade as another endpoint. In a symmetric key situation this is achieved by both communicating endpoints sharing a secret key. If the secret key is not in the open then the possession of the secret key proves the identity of an endpoint, because only two endpoints possess the secret key.

In a public key environment authentication is established as follows: an endpoint that is associated with a public key must be able to decipher a message encrypted with that public key. Since only that endpoint can possess the corresponding private key, it is the only endpoint that can decipher the encrypted message. If the encryption succeeds the authentication is established successfully.

Single Sign-on

In an environment where a user has to access several different user interfaces of several different back-end application systems, he must authenticate himself to each of those back-end application systems since each of them will challenge him for the token proving his identity. This is done through the sign-on process that asks for a user's identity as well as a token like a password to establish the identity.

A single sign-on environment relieves the user from signing on several times. This is achieved by the back-end application system trusting one sign-on authority. Once a user is initially signed on, every subsequent sign-on process is skipped since the back-end application can automatically verify that the user is already authenticated.

8.3.4 Authorization

Authorization determines if an authenticated endpoint can access a particular data element or invoke a particular operation. A well-known mechanism is access control lists that specify which authenticated endpoint has access to which operation. Multilevel access control is another approach that is used in military environments. Authorization is applicable when users are accessing the user interfaces of a B2B integration technology. Not all users have equal access to all functionality that is exposed through user interfaces. Hence, authorization rules have to be put in place and have to be enforced.

8.3.5 Integrity

Integrity is used to prevent any modification of a message on its way from its sender to its receiver. A method that senders can apply and receivers can verify is that of a signature. A signature of a message is a sequence of characters (signature) that is computed based on the message content. One possibility is a hash function that computes a hash value based on the message. The hash value is the signature. Any change applied to the message would change the contents of the sequence of characters and consequently the hash value.

If the signature is encrypted with a sender's private key, then the receiver possessing the sender's public key can decrypt the hash value. In addition, the receiver can recompute the hash value itself. Only if both hash values (signatures) are identical can the receiver be assured that the message was not modified. Other methods can be found in Sherif (2000).

8.3.6 Confidentiality

Confidentiality of messages can be achieved by encryption and decryption: the sender encrypts a message and the receiver decrypts it. The encryption of a message ensures confidentiality if the keys used for encryption are not public. In the symmetric key situation symmetric encryption takes place. The sender and receiver share the same symmetric key and hence the message is private to both. In the public key situation the sender encrypts the message with the receiver's public key. This ensures that only the receiver can decrypt the message with its private key.

8.3.7 Nonrepudiation

In context of message exchanges, the following types of repudiation can take place [Blixt and Hagstroem 1999]:

- **Repudiation of origin**. A party disagrees that a specific message with a specific content was sent by it.
- **Repudiation of submission**. The sender disagrees that it has sent a particular message.
- **Repudiation of delivery**. The receiver denies having received a particular message.
- **Repudiation of receipt**. The receiver denies having received a particular message with a particular content.

The corresponding nonrepudiation services are as follows:

- **Nonrepudiation of origin**. The receiver gets proof that a particular message with a particular content was in fact sent by the sender.
- **Nonrepudiation of submission**. The receiver gets proof that a particular message was in fact sent.
- **Nonrepudiation of delivery**. The sender gets proof that a particular messag was received by the receiver.
- **Nonrepudiation of receipt**. The sender gets proof that a particular message with a particular content was received by the receiver.

Glindin distinguishes one-way nonrepudiation from two-way nonrepudiation [Glindin 2000]. The latter involves a neutral trusted third party, while the former does not. Blixt and Hagstroem only discuss nonrepudiation involving a third party [Blixt and Hagstroem 1999]. Both references contain detailed descriptions of the services required to achieve nonrepudiation, and therefore these are not repeated here.

The significance of a third party comes into play because of key revocation. Keys are a sufficient means for a receiver to establish the identity of a sender. Using the mechanisms discussed above also allows a receiver to verify that the message was not altered during transmission. However, private or secret keys can be revoked if there is evidence or suspicion that the key is no longer private or secret, but in the open. As soon as a key is revoked it must not be used any more because it is in the open. It can therefore no longer be used to uniquely identify the owner. The assumption is that a key is valid up to the time the key is revoked and no longer valid after the key is revoked. If a sender's key is revoked, the sender can always claim that it took some time to revoke the key and any messages in that period of time are not from it. Furthermore, the sender can always claim that there are differences in the clocks of the sender and receiver and therefore can repudiate messages.

A trusted third party can help in these cases. First, a third party can establish the time and time stamp messages for the sender and the receiver. This means that neither sender nor receiver can repudiate time any more. Second, a third party can store the messages exchanged between sender and receiver. This way a trusted third party can provide evidence that specific messages were sent by specific senders and were received by specific receivers at given points in time.

When a key is revoked the third party knows the time of revocation, and it can be clearly established which messages were exchanged before the revocation and which were sent after the revocation. A third party is therefore very important for a reliable nonrepudiation scheme.

9 Recursive Application of Concepts to B2B Integration

The integration concepts introduced in Chap. 7 can be recursively used for managing B2B integration itself. This chapter applies the integration concepts to integration itself, making any B2B integration technology implementation very elegant in terms of its implementation. The focus of this chapter is to model the life cycle management of several integration objects in the context of B2B integration. All these integration objects can be managed manually using user interface tools. However, automating the management by modeling the corresponding integration processes makes it more reliable. Furthermore, once the management of the integration:objects is automated they can be audited, monitored, analyzed and secured like any other integration objects.

9.1 Graphical Notation

In order to avoid lengthy specifications in the pseudo-specification language introduced earlier, a graphical notation is used here to model the integration processes of this chapter. This graphical notation is complete and can be replaced by the pseudo-specification language. Figure 9.1 shows the symbols used.

Fig. 9.1. Graphical notation

9.2 Trading Partner Agreement Negotiation

Trading partners have to establish endpoint agreements in order to exchange messages. The two endpoint agreements, one at each trading partner's site, have to match and both have to come to an agreement about the endpoint agreement. Instead of using e-mail, fax or phone, the integration concepts themselves can be used to negotiate and to establish an endpoint agreement. This requires a business process that supports users in making endpoint agreement decisions. First, an initial set of endpoint agreement values have to be defined by a user and sent to the trading partner with whom an agreement should be established. Then, a user might propose changes to an endpoint agreement proposal. At some point in the process an endpoint agreement is accepted by a user, and the endpoint agreement becomes a valid endpoint agreement.

Figure 9.2 shows a simple endpoint agreement negotiation business process. It omits all the endpoint-specific processes, i.e., the binding processes and the interface processes. The business process is that of an endpoint initiating the endpoint agreement negotiation and accepting it.

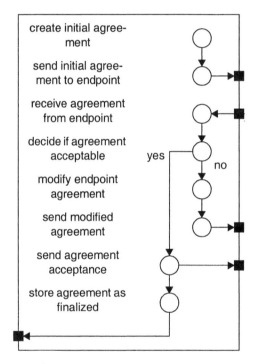

Fig. 9.2. Endpoint agreement negotiation business process

The endpoint initiates the endpoint agreement process by establishing a new endpoint agreement and filling in the initial values. Once this occurs the endpoint agreement is sent out as a business event to the endpoint with which the endpoint agreement should be established. The binding and interface processes with this endpoint are not shown in the figure.

At this point the endpoint has to wait for the other endpoint's response. At some point in time the other endpoint responds by sending back another endpoint agreement that contains its proposed changes, if any. A decision has to be made whether the other endpoint's proposal is acceptable or not. If it is, then an agreement acceptance event is sent and the endpoint agreement is stored as finalized. If it is not acceptable, then it is modified and the modification is sent back to the other endpoint. At this point a repetitive loop starts because it is expected that the other endpoint sends back another proposal.

The discussed business process is very simplistic. Many variations exist that make it more applicable to other situations and make it more robust. For example, it might be that the other endpoint accepts a specific endpoint agreement proposal. In this case it sends an endpoint agreement acceptance. The business process would have to be able to receive it. Furthermore, another endpoint might initiate the negotiation process, and therefore there must be a way to respond to initializations from other endpoints.

Of course, before an endpoint agreement can be exchanged there has to be an endpoint agreement in place that allows the exchange of messages containing an endpoint agreement. This leads to the B2B protocol "bootstrap" problem. At the heart of the bootstrap problem is the question how the exchange of endpoint agreements is enabled in the first place.

One possibility is that the first endpoint agreement that is put in place to exchange endpoint agreement messages is negotiated using e-mail or phone or fax. This is the manual approach, and it works just fine for that purpose. However, another alternative is to agree on a standard that says that by default every endpoint can exchange endpoint agreement messages with any other endpoint. By agreeing on such a standard, the first set of agreements for the exchange of endpoint agreements does not have to be negotiated manually every time a new endpoint is included.

9.3 Endpoint Identifier Synchronization

Since it is possible that the same endpoint defined in a back-end application system and in a B2B integration endpoint management component are identified by two different identifiers, a trading partner identifier domain value map has to put in place for these cases in order to establish that the two identifiers refer to the same endpoint. Not every endpoint that is known in a back-end application has to be known to the B2B integration technology. For example, if a message will never be sent by the back-end application to an endpoint, this endpoint does not have to be known by the B2B integration technology.

A trading partner identifier domain value map (or in general, an endpoint identifier domain value map) ensures that a B2B integration technology can relate the identifier of the endpoints known to it to the identifiers used by its endpoints, like back-end application systems. For example, if trading partner A is referred to as trading partner B by a back-end application system, then the endpoint identifier domain value map would state that A and B identify the same endpoint.

In the extreme case each endpoint identifies every other endpoint by a different identifier. Since this is possible an endpoint identifier domain value map has to be built and maintained so that the B2B integration technology architecture can map any external endpoint identifier to its internal ones.

There are two possibilities how a new endpoint is identified and defined. First, an endpoint is defined within the B2B integration technology. If this is the case, then a new endpoint exists in the B2B integration technology. Once this happens it must be determined if this endpoint that is new for the B2B integration technology is already known to one or more of the existing endpoints like back-end application systems. Each existing endpoint has to be asked to find out if the newly defined endpoint is already known to it. If it is known, an entry has to be inserted into the endpoint identifier domain-value map so that the mapping between the two identifiers is present. After all existing endpoints have been asked, the endpoint identifier domain value map is complete for this new endpoint. Figure 9.3 shows the business process for this case.

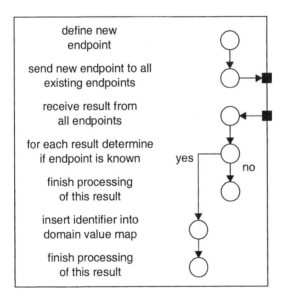

Fig. 9.3. New endpoint definition in B2B integration technology

Second, a new endpoint can be defined in a back-end application system. In this case the B2B integration technology has to be notified about this new endpoint addition. It adds the endpoint to its internal endpoints, and then asks all the other endpoints about their knowledge of this new endpoint (like in the first case). Figure 9.4 shows the business process for this case. The only difference is that the endpoint is not defined within the business process as the first step, but is received by a back-end application system and added to the B2B integration technology.

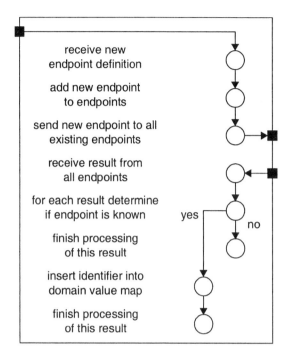

Fig. 9.4. New endpoint definition in back-end application system

An endpoint bootstrap problem also exists for endpoint management. If the B2B integration technology is installed into an environment where endpoints like back-end application systems already exist, the endpoints have to be synchronized. One approach for this is to define all existing back-end application systems as endpoints. Once this is achieved each endpoint is in turn asked for the list of endpoints is knows about. For each endpoint in every list all other endpoints are interrogated about this endpoint (like in the first case). This allows the system to bootstrap the endpoint synchronization. From this point forward, any new addition is handled as discussed above.

9.4 Endpoint Definition Update

Endpoint definitions of already existing endpoints might change. For example, a trading partner changes the delivery address or a support phone number. Instead of receiving the changes by phone and manually updating the changes through the user interface, it should be possible to send the changes of endpoint definitions as messages themselves. As soon as a corresponding business process of the hosted trading partner receives an update notification, it can notify all the endpoints it knows about of the particular update.

As in the case of defining new endpoints in Sect. 9.3 the change of an endpoint definition can originate at an endpoint itself or from the B2B integration technology. The business processes for the two cases are very simple (Fig. 9.5 and Fig. 9.6).

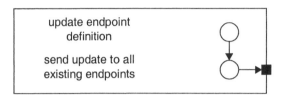

Fig. 9.5. Endpoint definition update in B2B integration technology

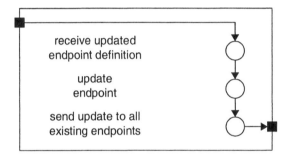

Fig. 9.6. Endpoint definition update in endpoint itself

9.5 B2B Protocol Change Management

So far the examples centered around endpoints and endpoint agreements. However, in general, all integration types and integration instances can be subject to automated management or supported by integration processes.

For example, B2B protocols that are defined and managed by standards organizations could be automatically updated upon their change. Whenever a standards organization approves a new version of an existing standard it can distribute the new version as messages. Messages would arrive at the B2B integration technology, and finally a business process could manage the introduction of the new standards version into the B2B integration technology.

The same approach applies for standards that are defined by a trading partner community. As soon as the community decides to update a community private standard, the update can be sent around as messages. And, again, the same approach applies to standards that are private to two endpoints.

Part III Business-to-Business Integration Technology Architecture

Integration concepts and functionality by themselves need a supporting architecture in order to derive a functioning B2B integration technology. A software architecture has to be in place that implements these concepts consistently. Part III introduces a B2B integration technology architecture as one example of how the introduced integration concepts can be implemented in various components and how the components interact in order to execute the modeled integration.

10 Architecture Overview

This chapter as well as the subsequent chapters in Part III continue the B2B integration technology architecture discussion from Sect. 2.3. Sect. 2.3 discusses the different layers of the B2B integration technology architecture as well as the individual components in the layers. The emphasis is on the structural properties of the architecture in terms of the various architecture layers and their internal components.

In contrast, this chapter and the subsequent chapters introduce the dynamic behavior of the B2B integration technology architecture in more detail. Fundamentally, it is shown how the different components of the different layers interact with each other in order to execute modeled integration processes. The emphasis is on the interaction between the different components and not on the internals of the components themselves. The goal is to give an overall description of the system behavior. All of the subsequent chapters use the integration example introduced at the end of this chapter in order to show the interactions between the individual components. In this chapter the fundamental architectural principles are introduced that are important in order to describe the behavior of the overall architecture.

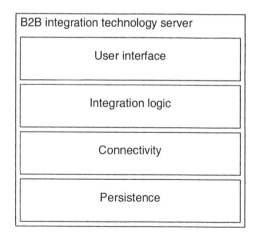

Fig. 10.1. Layers of the B2B integration technology architecture

10.1 Layered Architecture

Figure 10.1 gives an overview of the different layers of the overall B2B integration technology architecture. It is an exact copy of Fig. 2.28.

The interaction between the four layers is top-down. Each layer calls the directly underlying layer in order to access this layer's functionality. More precisely, components of one layer call components of the directly underlying layer. For architectural simplicity's sake no layer is skipped when an invocation takes place between layers. This means that an invocation from the user interface might indirectly reach the persistence layer, but never directly. The user interface layer calls the integration logic layer, which in turn calls the connectivity layer. Finally the persistence layer is invoked.

Figure 10.2 shows the general invocation pattern between the layers. The tips of the arrows point to the layers or components to be invoked. The other ends of the arrows point to the invoking layers or components. This convention is used throughout. In summary, each layer, if necessary, calls the next layer without skipping it. This applies for all layers except the persistence layer.

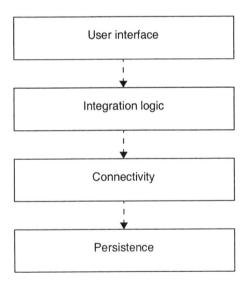

Fig. 10.2. Invocation pattern between layers

What happens if, for example, the integration logic layer wants to query for an instance of an object? This question is important since the connectivity layer does not provide a query interface but the persistence layer does. In more general terms, the question is how the functionality of lower layers is provided to upper layers. This is achieved by a default architecture principle as follows: each layer has to have an auxiliary component (not explicitly shown or discussed) that replicates certain operations from lower layers that are important to upper layers. For example, the connectivity layer could provide a query interface in the auxiliary component that is an exact replica of the query interface of the persistence layer. Through this mechanism the functionality from lower layers is provided to upper layers.

Why have this principle instead of allowing a direct invocation to lower layers bypassing intermediate layers? Fundamentally, these auxiliary components allow a layer to filter the operations of lower-layer components and possibly augment them. In this sense they help establish a very clear and concise overall architecture.

For optimization reasons in the implementation, layers can be skipped (see Chap. 15). The strict invocation patterns are in place for architectural reasons, which makes the architecture a lot easier to construct and to describe. In a specific implementation additional requirements come into play that have to be addressed, like performance and scalability.

10.2 Component Structure

10.2.1 Component Interface

Components in the different layers have a well-defined interface that they provide to other components for invocation. This is called the public export interface. The export interface is public so that the interface is visible to all other components in the same layer as well as the components in the layer directly above.

The interface of a component consists of a set of operations and the relevant parameters for the operations. For example, the interface to create an interface process type is create_interface_process_type(IN type_name: string, OUT identifier: integer), or something similar. Each parameter is either an input or an output parameter and is of a particular data type.

In addition to the public export interface, a component has an interface that is private to the layer. This means that although all components within this layer can invoke this interface, but none of the components of the layer directly above it can. This interface is called the layer private component interface. A component private interface contains operations that can be called only from within the component. This interface can be built in order to provide component internal abstractions.

10.2.2 Component Parts

Those components that are responsible for modeling data have to deal with type data and instance data at the same time. For example, the process management component of the integration logic layer manages the various process types as well as the process instances of those types.

In order to provide a better structure of the interfaces a component exposes, it can be further subdivided into those operations that operate on type data and those that operate on instance data. This division of the operations of a component helps build a clear structure and a clear invocation behavior within the overall architecture. This subdivision is not further detailed in the forthcoming descriptions since it is not relevant from the viewpoint of the architecture behavior.

Alternatively, two components could be defined instead of one component dealing with both type and instance data. One of the two could deal with type data and the other with instance data. The benefit is an even clearer separation. However, the downside is that both components could not easily share functionality that applies to both, type as well as instance data.

10.3 State-Based Architecture

The presented B2B integration technology architecture is state based. This means that integration instances as well as integration types have a life cycle model and are in one state of their respective models. For example, an event instance might be in state raised. Furthermore, type as well as instance data are stored in the persistence layer and can therefore be shared between several components, if necessary. At any point in time the persistence layer contains a consistent and complete set of integration types as well as integration instance data.

An alternative style is a queue-based architecture. In a queue-based architecture components do not share a common data model. Instead, data are passed between components in the form of queue elements (messages). Since in a queue-based architecture data only reside in queues, the queue elements must contain the complete type and instance data so that the various components can operate on those without additional data from anywhere else. No common state is available for the components, and objects cannot be shared between components through a shared persistent state. While this is certainly a possibility to define an architecture, the problems are immediately visible. If two components require access to the same object instance, it must be replicated and made available to both components. Any change to one of the two will not be reflected in the other, since queue messages are independent of each other.

In order to address the limitations of a pure queue-based architecture, a mixed form could be followed where both message as well as state are used where appropriate. While this is a possibility it does not result in a better architecture than a state-based architecture, only a different one. Since a state-based architecture is easier to introduce, the state-based architecture approach is followed in this book.

10.4 Coordinated Architecture

For each request originating at a user interface or for each incoming message, several components have to be invoked in a specific order.

10.4.1 User Interface Invocations

In the case of a user interface originating invocations, the user interface component invokes the necessary components of the integration logic layer in the correct order. A component in the integration logic layer that invokes components from the connectively layer does the same, and so do the components of the connectivity layer when invoking components from the persistence layer. If one component in a layer calls other components in the same layer, the same pattern is followed. The invoking component has to make the correct invocations in the correct order.

Invocations originating at the user interface are therefore hierarchical since each layer calls one or several components of the layer directly underneath it or within it. Components of the layer underneath do the same, and an overall hierarchical invocation pattern is followed.

10.4.2 Invocations Processing Incoming Events

An incoming message is received by the transport component of the connectivity layer. It receives the message and then has to invoke the security component to decrypt and nonrepudiate the message. The security component has to call the packaging component to unpack the wire message packaging. The packaging components have to call other components and so forth. Basically, a hierarchical invocation pattern originating at the transport component is followed.

This approach has several problems. First, since this invocation hierarchy starts in the connectivity layer, it will never be able to call those integration logic components that are necessary for the processing. That, however, is necessary to execute process instances and create event instances. Second, the transport component has to know about the security component, which has to know about the packaging component, and so on. However, the transport component should only focus on transport functionality and the security component only on security functionality.

Instead of one component calling the next one for message and event instance processing, the connectivity layer as well as the integration logic layer have a so-called coordinator component. A coordinator component coordinates the invocation of components within one layer in order to invoke and to execute them in the appropriate order. For example, as soon as the transport layer received a message, the coordination component takes over the invocation control and then calls the security, the packaging and other components.

This approach makes sure that each component focuses on its functionality, that the components do not have to know about each other, and that the necessary invocation sequences of the components are enforced. The execution coordination is completely the knowledge of the coordinator component.

The communication between the connectivity layer and the integration logic layer for this case is indirect. Once the connectivity layer is done processing an incoming message the message is stored in the persistence layer. The coordinator component of the integration logic layer is notified or checks periodically for messages that need to be processed, picks them up and continues processing them. Chaps. 11 to 14 explain the overall message processing in more detail.

10.5 Integration Example

The integration example that is used to explain the behavior of the integration architecture is a one-way notification. A trading partner that is obliged to ship a product sends a shipment notification, indicating that the product was handed over to a shipper and can be expected in a specific number of days. Once the notification is received, it is passed to a back-end application system, and the user that ordered the product is notified by e-mail.

Figure 10.3 shows the integration processes in more detail using the graphical notation introduced in Chap. 9. The incoming shipping notification is translated and transformed and then passed on to the business process. The business process splits the shipping notification business event and sends out one copy each to the user and the back-end application system through different process bindings and interface processes. This results in a transformation and one translation each.

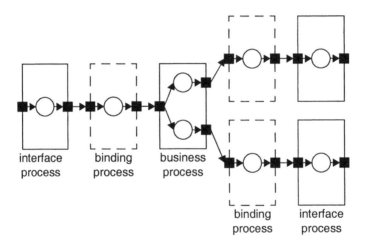

Fig. 10.3. Integration example used throughout the discussion of architecture part

The example is kept intentionally simple so that the behavior of the architecture and its components can be explained without unnecessary complication. In Chaps. 11 to 14 the invocation sequence between the components is shown based on the assumption that the above-mentioned example is executed.

11 User Interface

This chapter describes the user of the user interface components in more detail. A set of user types is introduced that can be generally distinguished when deploying and managing B2B integration technology. The tasks of the users are introduced and the ways users employ the user interface components to accomplish their tasks are discussed.

11.1 Overview

The user interface of a B2B integration technology architecture supports different types of users (user roles) in their various activities. The various user types and their tasks are as follows.

- **Integration modeler.** An integration modeler is responsible for the definition of integration types, including interface, binding and business processes, transformations, data types and event types. Once all the types for an integration are completely defined, the integration modeler tests the integration model by running instances in a testing environment like a debugger, a simulator or a performance test environment. Once the integration modeler is satisfied with the modeled integration, the integration modeler makes the types available for deployment in order to put them into production.
- **Integration manager.** The integration manager is responsible for the actual execution of integration with real endpoints. In order to achieve this an integration manager specifies endpoints and endpoint agreements and puts the necessary integration types into production. This allows endpoints to exchange event instances and message instances with each other. An integration manager monitors the ongoing event exchanges according to the deployed integration types at run time to detect major problems in advance. If an error occurs the integration manager attempts to address the error and provide error handling. The manager updates the endpoint specifications in the case of changes and deploys new integration types or new versions of existing integration types.
- **Integration analyst.** The integration analyst is not concerned too much about the ongoing event exchanges of various ongoing integration process and event instances. Instead, the integration analyst is interested in the analysis of finished integration processes and event instances based on a complete history of the integration processes. The integration analyst uses analysis tools like data ware-

house tools, reporting tools or business intelligence tools in order to provide insight into the execution patterns of integration.

- **Integration end user**. End users are involved in integration when they are notified about specific events (like a large purchase order or invoice) or when they are requested to perform the authorization of an event instance. In the case of authorizations, an end user has to reply with the authorization decision. Sometimes end users are asked to provide data that cannot be automatically retrieved. In these cases, too, they are expected to respond to the inquiry for input.
- **System administrator**. The system administrator manages the B2B integration technology from a system perspective. He makes sure that databases have enough disk space, that backups are done on a regular basis and oversees the operating system process structure in order to provide optimal performance and throughput. Depending on how much of the administration is done automatically by the B2B integration technology itself, the system administrator might not have to intervene often.

Figure 11.1 shows the different user interface components as discussed in Sect. 2.3.1. It is an exact copy of Fig. 2.29. These user interface components are available to users in order to accomplish their tasks.

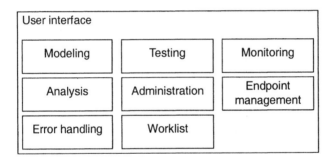

Fig. 11.1. User interface components

Table 11.1. Relationship between user roles and user interface components

User type	User interface component
Integration modeler	Modeling, testing
Integration manager	Endpoint management, monitoring, error handling
Integration analyst	Analysis, monitoring
Integration end user	Worklist
System administrator	Administration, monitoring

Each type of user employs a subset of the user interface components in order to achieve tasks (Table 11.1) This does not mean that a user in a particular role cannot access other user interface components, too. The table expresses the intended set for a particular user role. As shown, some user interface components are useful to several types of users, like the monitoring component. The association between user types and user interface components is followed in the next sections to describe how users can accomplish their tasks with the given user interface components.

11.2 Modeling Environment

11.2.1 Modeling Component

The modeling component provides user interfaces to introduce types into the B2B integration technology. Examples are processes, transformations or event types. For each integration concept a set of modeling windows is available that allows the integration modeler to specify integration types and their required details.

These user interfaces can have different forms, with "drag-and-drop" functionality being the most popular one. From the viewpoint of a hosting environment, an HTML-based user interface is preferable because subscribers could get access to their integration types without installing clients, but by only using their browsers.

11.2.2 Testing Component

Once an integration modeler has modeled all the integration types that need to be designed the modeled integration types can be tested. A testing component provides the necessary test tools in order to conduct the testing (Sect. 2.3.1).

While it is certainly important to test the complete integration as defined in Sect. 7.10, testing smaller units is important, too. For example, an integration modeler might want to test only a single process type or a transformation in isolation. Once the smaller units are tested, the integration modeler combines them into larger pieces like processes for continued testing. Only after those larger integration types execute satisfactorily will an integration modeler test a complete integration.

Usually, if after tests and modifications the integration types are stable, the integration modeler creates new versions of these in order to freeze the tested and satisfactory versions. Once versions are tested and frozen, the integration modeler makes them available to the integration manager for actual use with real trading partners.

Even though we have so far discussed testing as if it takes place in isolation, in reality this is not the case. Testing has to include all aspects of integration, including the transmission of events as messages. Trading partners usually agree on a test period or specific test messages that are really exchanged over networks. Only if those tests are successful are the integration types frozen.

The same applies to back-end application systems. Real exchanges of data are necessary to test the connectivity as well as the interoperation with back-end application systems. It is therefore important to either have known test scenarios within back-end applications that are in production or install test instances of back-end application systems so that testing is possible.

11.3 Management Environment

11.3.1 Endpoint Management Component

Once a complete set of integration types is modeled, an enterprise wants to put them into production so that message and event instances can be exchanged. However, in order to do this the endpoints as well as their endpoint agreements have to be specified. Only if trading partners or back-end application systems are defined is it possible to exchange messages with them. The functionality in this section has to be made available to the integration manager through the specific management user interfaces.

Endpoint

An integration manager specifies all endpoints that participate in different interactions. All types of endpoints are usually involved, like back-end application systems, users or trading partners. The integration manager has to specify all mandatory properties of endpoints in order to make sure that all necessary data about endpoints are provided. In addition, if domain value maps have to be defined for an endpoint, the integration manager has to set them up and fill in the endpoint-specific values according to the endpoint specific vocabulary. Only if those are specified correctly will transformation succeed. If trading partner identifier domain value maps exist they have to be updated with the specified endpoints, too. The same applies for properties of endpoints. Finally, trading partner capabilities have to be specified for each endpoint so that endpoint agreements can be specified based on them.

Endpoint Agreement

Endpoint agreements have to be specified for every endpoint that participates in integration. For each endpoint the messages have to be specified that are going to be exchanged with the endpoint. In addition, the direction of the messages, the security that has to be applied, the time-out, upper limit and retry values as well as which version of integration types (if several are available) have to be specified, too. Endpoint agreements are only valid for a specific duration; therefore the integration modeler has to specify start as well as end dates and times for endpoint agreements.

Endpoints, endpoint agreements and integration types have to match. This means that for a given endpoint, the integration processes have to be available for those

B2B protocols or A2A protocols that the endpoint requires (the endpoint capabilities).

Deployment and Redeployment

Once the integration types are specified, tested and frozen (a version is created), the endpoints are specified and the endpoint agreements are put in place, all these integration objects are deployed in order to make them available for actual production use. In general, each version of an integration type is only deployed once, since if the types are available they can be reused with different endpoints. Only when integration types are no longer be used must they be removed (undeployed) so that they are not available for use any more.

In contrast, endpoints can be deployed several times because endpoints are not versioned. Only a single version exists at any point in time. This means that a change in an endpoint results in a new version. However, upon its deployment the previous version is automatically undeployed (if a previous version exists at all). This ensures that only one definition of a single endpoint is in the system at any given point in time.

In case an endpoint is not used any more, its endpoint agreements are removed. Once all agreements are removed, the endpoint itself can be removed. Integration can be a long-running overall activity. Removing an endpoint agreement might take quite some time until the last message in an ongoing integration is received or sent. However, while this "shutting down" takes place, no new messages should be received to avoid the creation of new process instances that would continue to prolong the execution.

11.3.2 Error-Handling Component

Another management component is the error-handling component. This component becomes necessary when either an error occurs and the modeled error handling in the processes failed, or when no error handling is specified in the processes. In both cases the B2B integration technology cannot deal with the error itself and has to involve a user to address the error situation. In such a situation the integration manager is notified about the error, and the error-handling component is used to try to recover from the error.

The error-handling component must allow access to the content of event elements in order to modify them. This allows addressing of error situations where the contents of an event instance caused the error. Upon change the event instance is resubmitted, and its processing can continue.

In some cases the event instance content is correct, but translation or transformation maps have errors in their definitions. In this case the error component user interface must be able to create a new version, make the new version available to the process instance and resubmit the event instance to the new version of the translation or transformation map.

If it is not possible to repair an event, a process instance or other integration types then the integration manager can initiate the compensation for the processes. In this case the side effects are neutralized by compensation process steps and the error situation is resolved this way.

Two types of errors are not easily detected and are usually left to a user to detect. One is a deadlock and the other one is a lifelock. For example, a deadlock occurs in integration when two trading partners mutually wait for each other's events at the same time. This might lead to a situation where neither of the two can continue the processing. A lifelock exists if there is an endless loop executing that will never finish. An example is two process instances that keep sending event instances to each other without ever having the chance to get out of this situation. In both cases the integration manager uses the error handling component to break the lifelock or deadlock by either modifying the process instance structure or by starting compensation of the process instances.

11.3.3 Monitoring Component

Events are "faceless" in the sense that they are automatically processed by the B2B integration technology without involving user intervention. In order to view ongoing event processing and their states, a monitoring component is necessary. As already discussed, there are several different forms of monitoring. The most important forms are as follows.

- **Monitoring of a single event instance**. In this case the current status of a particular event instance is monitored at a specific point in time. The result of this event status is displayed in terms of an integration process instance, depending on where the event instance resides at this point in time. For example, if the event is in an input parameter that is not yet picked up for processing, the image would indicate the event in that particular input parameter with a specific symbol and color.
- **Monitoring of a set of related process instances**. In this case the current status of process instances is monitored, for example, two interface processes, two binding processes and one business process. At the time of the status request an image of all process instances and where current event instances reside are shown.
- **Aggregation of event instances**. If a user wants to see all event instances of a particular type, then more than one event instance has to be displayed. The different event instances can be in different execution states in different process instances. Therefore, an aggregation of the process instances and their event has to be shown. This is graphically achieved by having one set of process instances displayed, but all event instances from all processes instances of the same types. This means that all event instances are represented concurrently in one process instance representation.

- **History of an event instance.** While the monitoring so far only presented the current state of event or process instances, it is sometimes necessary to look at the history of an event instance. A history of an event instance is the list of all process states an event instance has, from its initial creation up to the time of the user request. If this time is after the event instance was finished processing, then the complete history is visible.
- **History of a set of related process instances.** Analogously, it is sometimes important to examine the history of a set of related process instances. This history shows all event instances and their different process states in the context of the process instances themselves. For example, if an event was received, translated and transformed so far, all these states are displayed. This means that the path of each event instance up to this point in time is shown.

An interesting question is how to identify an event instance in order to monitor its status. This becomes even more interesting in light of the fact that events are translated and transformed while being processed. A practical example is a trading partner calling and asking where its purchase order is. That usually translates into the trading partner wanting to know the status of the purchase order. The trading partner names the purchase order identifier and, based on this, the current status can be retrieved. However, this purchase order identifier is the identifier of the wire event. However, translation and transformation might already have taken place, possibly modifying the purchase order identifier. For the monitoring component this means that the user must be able to specify which class of event should be identified first (e.g., a wire event). Once the respective wire event instance is found, the corresponding clear text and business event instances can be found and their status shown.

11.4 Analysis Environment

In general, integration analysis in general asks questions about how long events require to be processed, what the maximum and minimum execution durations are, how many events were received by an endpoint and how many were sent back. Averages might be important, too, like the average number of events in the B2B integration technology.

In general it is not possible to enumerate all possibly interesting analysis questions because many might access the contents of event elements. Since event types are defined by the hosted trading partner, they can have any form and any content. Instead of trying to provide a set of analysis questions, a B2B integration technology can ensure that a complete history of all process instances and event instances is kept and made available in structured form. Based on this data set, analysis tools like reporting tools or business intelligence tools can load this complete data set and implement the analysis questions, as required by the particular enterprise running the B2B integration technology.

The benefit of the business event integration concept becomes very clear for this functionality. If all incoming wire events are translated and transformed into business events, then analysis tools only have to operate on business events in order to do content-based analysis. The analysis tools do not have to be aware of the different vocabularies and the different formats in which messages are sent and received. However, having the complete history data set available means that analysis tools can use all types of events, not just business events to retrieve information.

11.5 End User Environment

The worklist component is a means for users to access their notifications or pending authorizations. Also, any data entry request can be found there. A worklist is a user interface that has a similar behavior to an e-mail client. All notifications, authorizations or data entry requests assigned to a user (also called user tasks) are represented as a list of entries. A user who needs to execute authorizations selects one of the authorization entries, and in response a separate window is opened that show the user all the necessary details. The window also provides the necessary buttons to either authorize or deny the authorization. Once one of those buttons is selected the window and the entry disappear, and a wire event is sent to the connectivity layer delivering a response to the user task.

Workflow management systems have tasks lists like most systems requiring user interactions. Some systems do not provide a separate worklist interface but achieve the user interactions solely through an e-mail system. A user is notified by e-mail. In case an authorization or a data entry has to happen, a response e-mail is used to indicate the authorization decision or to capture the data entries. The response e-mail is then picked up, and a corresponding wire event is given to the connectivity layer.

11.6 System Administration Environment

The system administration environment depends to a large extent on the specific implementation of a B2B integration technology architecture. In general a system administration environment supports the management of technology concepts like operating system processes, database instances, queues, application servers and so on. Each of those requires management like starting and stopping of components, restarting components after failure situations, backup of persistent storages and tasks of this nature.

12 Integration Logic

This chapter introduces the behavior of the integration logic components and their communication with each other. Each of the components is introduced in the order an incoming event instance arrives at them for processing. The example introduced in Sect. 10.5 is used for these illustrations.

12.1 Overview

Figure 12.1 shows the components of the integration logic as discussed in Sect. 2.3.2. It is an exact copy of Fig. 2.30.

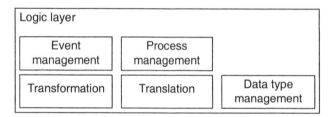

Fig. 12.1. Integration logic layer components

Every component in the integration logic layer has to manage type data as well as instance data. For example, the event management component provides operations to the user interface for creating, changing and deleting event type specifications. Whenever a user uses the modeling user interface and creates a new event type, the user interface invokes the event management component in order to create the event type. The same applies for changing or deleting event types. In the following the parts of the integration logic layer components that deal with type data are not further discussed, since these follow the same pattern for creating, changing and deleting types as well as other operations, like reusing types or creating versions. Instead, the focus of this chapter is to discuss the run-time behavior of the components in more detail that are related to the processing of event instances.

12.2 Integration Logic Component Coordinator

The components of the integration logic layer are coordinated by a coordinator as defined in Sect. 10.4. It ensures that for a given event instance in the context of a given process instance, the necessary components are invoked in the correct execution order. Figure 12.2 shows the coordinator and the invocation relationships between the coordinator and the components.

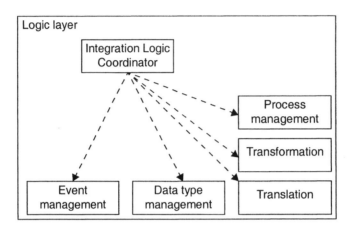

Fig. 12.2. Integration logic component coordinator

For presentation reasons, in this book the invocation relationships shown in Fig. 12.2 are not well suited for showing the flow of the event instances through the integration logic components. A more appropriate representation is the data flow between the components. For example, Fig. 12.3 shows an event instance passed between two of the components.

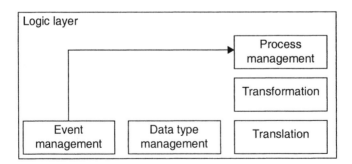

Fig. 12.3. Data passing between integration logic components

The representation in Fig. 12.3 is equivalent with the coordinator calling the event management component, first obtaining a reference to the event instance, and then invoking the process management component in order to hand over the event instance. The coordinator calls one operation on the event management component and one on the process management component in order to obtain the event instance and pass it along.

The representation in Fig. 12.3 is better than that in Fig. 12.2 since it explains the flow of events between the components more economically in a series of figures when explaining the example integration.

12.3 Initiating Event Processing

The example starts with a shipping notification message that is incoming from a trading partner endpoint. It is represented as a wire event by the connectivity layer. Once the wire event is in state raised, the event management component recognizes that a new wire event has arrived and awaits processing in the raised state. The event management component picks up the wire event (Fig. 12.4).

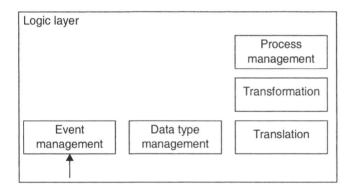

Fig. 12.4. Initiating wire event is picked up by event management component

Since the shipping notification is an initiating event instance, the next step in the processing is to pass the event instance to the process management component in order to instantiate the corresponding interface process instance. The incoming shipping notification wire event is the initiating event that causes an interface process to be instantiated.

If a correlated wire event had to be given to an existing interface process, the event management component would have found out by executing the correlation expression. The result of the correlation expression would have caused the selection of the right existing interface process instances as described in Sect. 7.3.2.

12.4 Interface Process Execution

Figure 12.5 shows the event being passed to the process management component, causing the creation of the interface process instance that takes the incoming shipping notification as the initiating input parameter. In order to better see the changes to the contents of the figures over time, the latest invocations are shown as dotted lines.

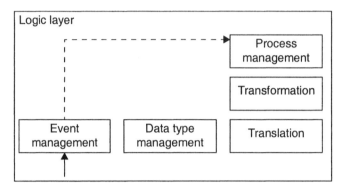

Fig. 12.5. Interface process instantiation

Once the interface process instance is created, the translation process step is executed. The wire event is passed to the translation component. It in turn translates the wire event instance into a clear text event instance. It creates the necessary data values and, based on those, the clear text event instance is created and transitioned in state raised. The wire event is consumed. Once this is accomplished, the clear text event is given to the interface process through the translation process step output parameter and the translation is accomplished. Finally, the clear text event is given to the output parameter of the interface process.

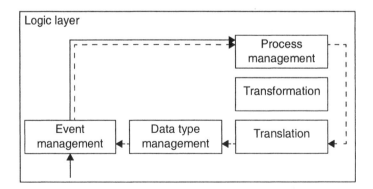

Fig. 12.6. Translation in the interface process

Figure 12.6 shows the data flow between the components. The process instance internal data flow is not further described here. However, it takes place and is executed by the process management component since it is a process aspect.

12.5 Binding Process Execution

Once the clear text event is available in the output parameter of the interface process, the external data flow is executed and the binding process is instantiated. The same pattern happens for the transformation step in the binding roles as happened for the translation step in the interface process. Once the business event instance is available, it is put into the output parameter of the binding process. Figure 12.7 shows the additional interactions between the components.

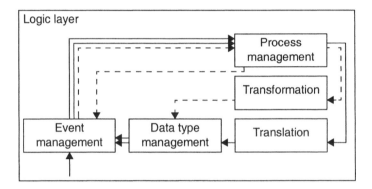

Fig. 12.7. Transformation in the binding process

12.6 Business Process Execution

Once the business event is available in the output parameter of the binding process, the external data flow is executed and a business process instance is created according to the business process type. As the example shows the incoming shipping notification business event is sent to two endpoints: one back-end application system and one end user (the one who ordered the product that is about to ship).

Since a separate business event is sent for each of the two trading partners, in order to achieve parallelism the shipping notification event is split into two business events. Each is put into a separate output parameter of the business process. No interactions take place for this functionality between the components. All execution happens within the process management component except for invoking the event manager component to split the event.

12.7 Outbound Binding and Interface Process Execution

For each of the two business event instances, a binding process and an interface process are instantiated with the corresponding translation and transformation steps. Figure 12.8 shows the additional component interactions between the components.

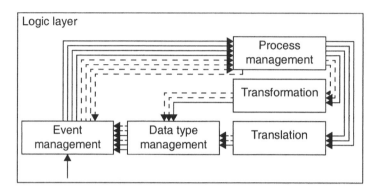

Fig. 12.8. Two business events, one for each endpoint

12.8 Outbound Wire Event Processing

Once the two wire events are ready to be sent to endpoints, the event management component passes them to the connectivity layer. It sends the wire events as messages to the endpoints. Figure 12.9 shows the final two interactions, this time with the next underlying layer.

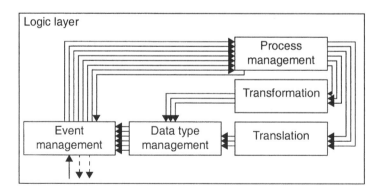

Fig. 12.9. Outgoing wire events

12.9 Summary

This concludes the discussion of the integration logic layer. As explained, its components always follow the same patterns when interacting with each other in order to execute integration process instances as well as event instances.

13 Connectivity

This chapter introduces the behavior of the connectivity layer components and their interactions. Like in Chap. 12 the components are introduced in the order an incoming wire message is processed by the components.

13.1 Overview

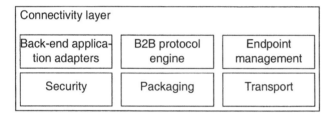

Fig. 13.1. Connectivity layer components

Figure 13.1 shows all connectivity layer components; it is a copy of Fig. 2.31. Like in the case of the execution layer components, the connectivity layer components deal with integration types as well as instances. In the following sections the discussion of the component's behavior is for the integration instance processing part only. And, as in the integration logic layer case, the connectivity layer components are also coordinated components that are coordinated by a connectivity layer component coordinator. The graphical representation follows that of Chap. 12 inasmuch as the flow of the data between the components is shown for brevity, but the invocation interactions based on the connectivity layer component coordinator are not shown.

13.2 Receiving a Message

A message is received by the transport component. It connects to various network and transport protocols like HTTP, SMPT, FTP, VANs and so on. Any incoming or outgoing message is processed by the transport component. Figure 13.2 shows the incoming shipping notification wire message.

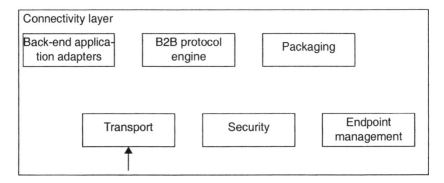

Fig. 13.2. Incoming message

13.3 Security Verification

After the incoming wire message representing the shipping notification message is received, it is forwarded to the security component. The security component (in the general case) decrypts the message and checks the message signature. In order to retrieve the correct private and public keys, it interrogates the endpoint management component for the required data. Once the message is decrypted and the signature is verified, the sending endpoint is identified, and from that point on the sender of the message is set to this endpoint.

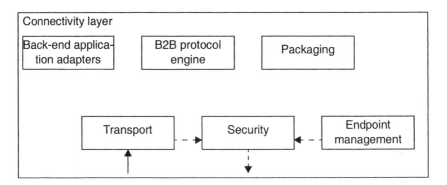

Fig. 13.3. Security verification of incoming message

Figure 13.3 shows the interactions between the connectivity layer components. As can be seen the security keys are given from the endpoint management component to the security component upon the security component's request. Also, the security component ensures nonrepudiation by ensuring the correct proofs are received as well as sent from and to the sender, depending on the agreed-upon type of nonrepudiation. If nonrepudiation has to be provided, the security component stores the message as received (fully encrypted), as shown in Fig. 13.3. If a trusted third party has to be involved for this purpose, the security component sends the appropriate messages to it (not shown in Fig. 13.3).

13.4 Endpoint Agreement Verification

Once the sender is identified and the message is verified from a security viewpoint, it has to be verified that an endpoint agreement is in place that authorizes the receipt of the message. In order to obtain verification, the message is sent to the endpoint management component that performs the endpoint agreement verification. Figure 13.4 shows the message flow.

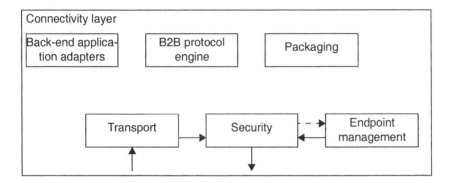

Fig. 13.4. Endpoint agreement verification

13.5 B2B Protocol Execution

Once it is verified that there is an existing and valid endpoint agreement that authorizes receiving the message, the message is forwarded to the packaging component in order for it to remove any specific packaging imposed by the corresponding B2B protocol. Once the packaging is removed the unpacked message is given to the B2B protocol engine.

The B2B protocol engine verifies the message further in case there are any B2B protocol-specific constraints. For example, it might check that the message is complete according to the B2B protocol-imposed syntax. Another constraint is that in case the message is a response message, it has to be in response to an existing message. Once the B2B protocol engine does its message processing, it constructs a wire event, which is stored in the persistence layer. From there it will be picked up by the event management component, and the flow as shown in Chap. 12 is executed in the given example. Figure 13.5 shows the additional message flow.

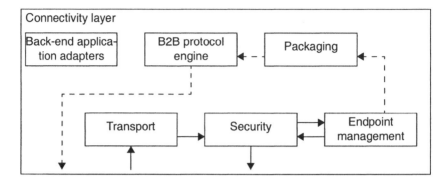

Fig. 13.5. Unpacking, B2B protocol verification and wire event construction

In order to create a wire event instance of the correct wire event type, the B2B protocol engine might have to consult an event map. An event map relates the particular message type to the corresponding wire event type. An event map ensures that external messages are mapped to the corresponding wire event types within the B2B integration technology. The event map might be based solely on a direct map between a message type and a wire event type. For example, a message in EDI version 4050 called 850 might have to be represented as a purchase order wire event instance. However, sometimes messages are not typed, and the event map cannot be based on its type. Instead, a predicate has to be specified that identifies a unique property of the message and that is related to a wire event type. For example, if the same message format is used for patient records and lab tests, then the predicate has to determine if a patient record or lab test is in the message. Depending on the case, a patient or lab wire event type instance is created for that message.

13.6 Outgoing Wire Event

The example business process creates two business event instances that are sent to a user and a back-end application system. Both are eventually represented as wire event instances to be sent out. In the following it is assumed that users are reached through e-mail, and back-end application adapters are connected through adapters.

In the case when a wire event is targeted to a user, the opposite flow through the connectivity components happens. The wire event instance to be sent out is picked up by the B2B protocol component. It reads the wire event contents and composes a message according to the rules of the B2B protocol use. That might involve an event map look-up to determine which message to construct for a given wire event instance of a particular wire event type. In the case of user notifications this might be a simple protocol based on SMTP. Once the B2B protocol component is done, the message is passed to the packaging component for transport-level-specific packaging. It is then passed to the endpoint management component to determine if there is an existing endpoint agreement authorizing the sending of the message. The security component signs and encrypts the message according to the endpoint capabilities and endpoint agreement specifications. If any proofs have to be provided for nonrepudiation, the security component provides them. In case nonrepudiation is necessary, the security component stores the fully encrypted message. Finally, the message is sent out through the transport component. Figure 13.6 shows the additional flow.

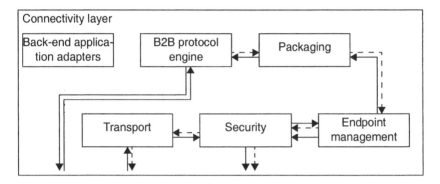

Fig. 13.6. Outgoing flow to user

13.7 Back-end Application System Adapter Execution

In the case when a wire event instance is targeted toward a back-end application system, the flow differs from the flow to a user. The back-end application adapter component picks up the wire event instance. It reads the contents and represents them in the form required by the back-end application system. This is determined by the particular back-end application adapter that is used to connect to the back-end application system (Apte 2002). The back-end application adapter component has adapters available that internally are required to connect to back-end application systems. If an adapter invokes the back-end application several times, then the wire event instance content has to be selectively given to the several invocations as input parameters. If, in another situation, the adapter enqueues a message for a back-end application, then the wire event instance has to be represented as one message in the queue dedicated to the back-end application system. No matter how the adapter interface requires the data, the back-end application adapter component has to represent the wire event instance content appropriately.

Figure 13.7 shows the additional flow for this case. The back-end application adapter component picks up the wire event instance. It checks whether for the given communication with the back-end application system, an authorizing endpoint agreement is available. If an agreement is available, the adapter invokes the back-end application system through one of the available adapters that it has and that is appropriate for the back-end application system in question.

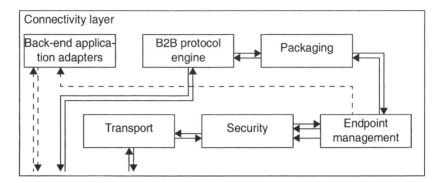

Fig. 13.7. Outgoing flow to back-end application system

Based on Fig. 13.7, the question arises if the communication with back-end application systems requires packaging, security or transports. In general, the communication with back-end application systems needs to be secured, and a transport is used to connect to it. Furthermore, in those cases where back-end applications are not invoked directly through remote invocations, packaging is also required in order to package the wire event instance content appropriately.

However, in reality the adapters are currently built as self-sufficient components that have all required functionality built in. They are not built to reuse existing components like security in order to avoid implementing security themselves. This might change over time as adapters become a commodity and as standardization in this area progresses.

14 Persistence

The persistence layer in principle does not have any B2B integration-specific functionality. Therefore it is discussed here only briefly.

14.1 Database

Without further discussion it is assumed that the main storage for integration types and instances is a central or a distributed database management system. It manages the integration types and integration instance in its schema. The layers above the persistence layer access the database when inserting, updating, deleting and selecting integration types and instances.

Depending on the particular B2B integration technology implementation, several different parts of the database schema can be distinguished:

- **Design-time data**. The design-time data contain the integration types and instances that are specified and defined through the user interface. The schema for this design-time data is optimized for user interface interaction. This usually means a highly normalized schema that is appropriate for model validation.

- **Deployment data**. When design-time data are made available for run-time execution, the schema can be optimized for run-time access. Usually this means fast access by reducing the amount of queries that are necessary to obtain the relevant data. In general this can be achieved by "denormalization," whereby more values are stored in tables than in normalized form. Also, data that are always selected together, like event type and data type data, are stored together in one table for fast access.

  This might result in the need for duplicate storage of certain integration type and integration instance data. However, this is not a problem since an explicit type and instance deployment makes sure that the duplication does not lead to an update problem.

- **Execution instance state**. Execution instance state captures the instance data that are instantiated and accessed at run time of the B2B integration technology. Again, this part of the schema is optimized for creating and retrieving instance data.

14.2 Persistent and Transactional Queues

In some cases instance data that are created and processed at run time exhibit a queuing behavior. For example, incoming wire events can be queued up using a persistent and transactional queue (Gray and Reuter 1993) so that the integration logic layer can retrieve incoming wire events by dequeuing them from a queue instead of selecting them from a database table. The latter has the issue that once the wire event is retrieved its state has to be changed and that costs an update. Dequeuing does not have this property and so update operations are saved.

14.3 Transactions and Distributed Transactions

The basic requirement that the B2B integration technology must execute consistently and reliably requires the use of transactions with the underlying database management system as well as persistent queues (if those are used).

In addition, external systems like back-end application systems are accessed. They themselves are in many cases transactional and manage their state in database management systems. When data is transferred from a back-end application system to the B2B integration technology or vice versa in form of message the question arises what happens in case of failures during the transmission.

For example, it might be that a back-end application system delivered a message to an adapter. If the back-end application system and the adapter use different transactions a window of failure exists. The back-end application system commits its internal state and notes that the message was delivered. However, the adapter failed before the message was committed to the B2B integration technology. This leads to an inconsistent state that needs to be avoided.

One possibility to avoid this type of failure is to use distributed transactions (Gray and Reuter 1993). A distributed transaction enables the update of two or more different database management systems in one atomic transaction. In the above example this would mean that the back-end application system cannot commit independently of the back-end application system. Both transaction commit or transaction abort leave both databases in a consistent global state. If the adapter fails the distributed transaction is aborted, and that means that the back-end application system will not store the fact that the message was delivered.

15 Implementation Principles

An implementation blueprint for a B2B integration technology would be another book altogether, because many design alternatives and implementation variations are possible. Many base technologies, like databases, application servers and persistent queues, are available and their particular use and combinations have different impacts on a B2B integration technology implementation.

This chapter therefore does not recommend a particular technology component selection or combination, nor does it try to discuss a particular B2B integration technology implementation. This chapter gives some ideas about a general approach as one example. However, many other alternative approaches are possible and justifyable.

15.1 Metamodel and Integration Execution Interpreter

15.1.1 Metamodel

In order to support the dynamic nature of a B2B integration technology in terms of integration types and instances, a metamodel approach is one possible avenue. An integration metamodel approach means that all integration types and instances are represented in the metamodel from which the schema of a database or a repository is derived. A database or repository with the particular schema for the integration metamodel is called an integration repository. An integration metamodel contains all integration types and instances as well as any configuration information that is not part of the integration metamodel. In addition, history as well as security rules are represented in the metamodel. In short, every piece of data in the B2B integration technology is represented in the metamodel, and consequently in the integration repository.

All data are stored fully normalized in the integration repository schema so that no change anomalies can occur when integration data are inserted, deleted or updated. All data are fully typed so that there is no type ambiguity at all at any time. Another benefit of the metamodel approach is that analysis tools like data warehouse tools or reporting tools can access the integration repository directly on the schema level in order to extract raw data for further analysis.

When integration type as well as integration instance data are explicitly represented in a normalized schema, then dynamic changes to types and instances can be supported. This is because any dynamic change is implemented as a series of changes to data representing type data or instance data or both. While consistency checks are still necessary when dynamically changing ongoing integration processes and events, a complete integration metamodel approach is a sound basis to enable dynamically changing types and instances.

An interesting development in the database field takes place that supports the multiple hosted trading partner model quite nicely. Databases start providing native hosting support as database functionality. For example, Oracle's 9i database has the virtual private database concept [Oracle VPD]. This concept separates data automatically in the database so that several hosted trading partners can be implemented without sharing any data. From a programming perspective a virtual database is like a nonvirtual one. The programmer does not have to distinguish the two cases at all. However, when the database is installed and the B2B integration technology is configured, several hosted endpoints are supported automatically.

15.1.2 Integration Execution Interpreter

Since all data that are necessary to define and to execute integration are explicitly stored in the integration repository, all integration functionality and business logic, in terms of process types, event types, data types, validation rules and so on, can be dynamically specified. No programming is required at all in any programming language in order to specify and execute integration. Fundamentally, the pseudo-language in this context as presented in earlier chapters is a declarative language, since it does not define how execution takes place but only what has to be executed. A compiler for this pseudolanguage would populate the integration repository. No executable code would have to be built or generated.

If all type and instance data are stored within the integration repository without exception, then one possibility for execution integration is to have an integration interpreter that reads from and writes to the integration repository. The integration types that are stored in the repository provide the specific execution directive to the interpreter. The interpreter creates, retrieves, modifies and stores instance data according to this. Dynamic changes are implemented by the interpreter by modifying the integration instance data accordingly. Since the execution is interpretative dynamic change is possible.

An integration execution interpreter is a very important aspect, since this approach makes the product migration a lot easier. No executable code has to be migrated, only data representing integration types and integration instances.

15.2 Centralized and Transactional Architecture

Despite the fascination of distributed architectures with heterogeneous and autonomous entities, it remains difficult to build one that is consistent. The major reason is that the state management and the state synchronization between the distributed entities requires special effort and extra care. System as well as network failures add another dimension of complexity to the design of a distributed system. While such a design is still a possibility, this approach is not addressed in the following. Instead, the focus is on a centralized architecture.

Centralized architectures center around a database with potentially several mid-tier components accessing the database. If these mid-tier components are stateless and do not have to be coordinated (share no state except through the database), they can be treated as fully independent components. This is beneficial since any number of mid-tier components can be started as well as shutdown without affecting the overall system state at all.

All operations of the mid-tier components are transactional with respect to database operations. This ensures overall consistency at all times. No failure compromises the database state if it is, in addition, well managed and backups are done correctly. Distributed transactions might be used when communicating with endpoints, especially back-end application systems. While this requires a distributed transaction manager in order to coordinate the different databases involved, it preserves the overall database consistency.

Some endpoints are nontransactional in nature. For example, B2B protocols are nontransactional as are back-end application systems not exposing any transactional interfaces. In these cases the communication can lead to inconsistencies when system failures occur. However, the state of the B2B integration technology is always consistent in itself, and is no ambiguous state at all. This is the best situation for determining if a communication failure left an inconsistent state behind with respect to the state of the endpoint. Fundamentally, a user can compare the state of the B2B integration technology architecture as well as the state of the endpoint and manually reconcile both.

Mid-tier components can be implemented in various ways. Currently, application servers are a preferred execution environment with thin clients (i.e., Internet browsers) as the user interface tier. In terms of the B2B integration technology architecture, the persistence layer is implemented by a database management system. The connectivity and integration logic layer correspond to mid-tier components, and the user interface layer corresponds to the user interface tier. If the mid-tier and the user interface tier are implemented with an application server as execution environment, then only those programming languages can be used that are supported by the application server.

While the B2B integration technology architecture emphasizes a clear separation of the layers, their invocation relationships as well as their interfaces at implementation usually need to deviate from this in order to achieve additional properties, like performance and throughput. Therefore, an implementation might allow components to invoke components from lower layers, bypassing a layer in between. Furthermore, a component from a lower layer might notify a component from an upper layer (in contrast to the top-down invocation direction). One such example is the B2B protocol management component notifying the event management component about the availability of a new wire event instance.

15.3 Integration Testing and Monitoring

While B2B integration functionality is mandatory in order to execute integration in the form of message exchanges, its development aspects must be addressed and should not be neglected. For example, an integration modeler must be able to test specified integration types. Therefore, the B2B integration technology implementation must enable an integration modeler to define and conduct test cases. Testing in the context of B2B integration technology has to overcome problems like simulating a trading partner. While an integration modeler specifies integration and fixes specification errors, the integration modeler might want to execute test integrations without really contacting a trading partner. In this case a trading partner must be simulated. This is true for any endpoint, therefore endpoint simulation is a very important test tool.

Another valuable test tool is the stepwise execution of integration processes. This is analogous a programming language debugger that steps through each line of execution code and can at any time introspect any parameter values and local variables. The equivalent tool for a B2B integration technology is to execute integration processes step by step and to allow the introspection of event instances as well as process parameters at any point in the process execution.

At some point the integration modeler will be satisfied with the specification of the integration types, and testing with real endpoints will start. In this situation events are generated from endpoints and are sent to endpoints. The integration processes and their steps involved execute on real test data as defined by the endpoints. In this case it is no longer feasible to have a step-by-step integration debugger investigate the state of the integration instances. Too many event instances and process instances are in the B2B integration technology concurrently and only the failing ones are interesting from a testing perspective.

An important tool for the integration modeler is a monitoring tool that selects specific integration processes and introspects them on demand in more detail. Such a monitoring tool would look at integration processes in several layers of abstraction. First, only the process instance names are shown. Then, the steps within the process instances as well as their execution state might be visualized. The next step in terms of details is to show the event instance contents as well as statistical data like execution times. With such a tool the integration modeler can pick the interesting processes for inspection during the test phases.

15.4 External Program Integration

In real implementations of B2B integration technology, there is a need to incorporate external program executables in order to provide B2B integration functionality. The reason for this external code is that the functionality cannot be declaratively specified for the general case. There are two specific areas that requires to bind to external code: application adapters and external data format interpreters.

15.4.1 Application Adapters

Application adapters have to be bound to the B2B integration technology architecture in order to establish the connectivity to back-end application systems. Adapters are executables that are build for the specific purpose of connecting with specific back-end application systems. For example, a SAP adapter connects to the SAP system, but to no other back-end application system.

Adapters (Apte 2002) bridge the difference in the interface of what a B2B integration technology requires and what a back-end application system provides. Since virtually every single back-end application system has a different interface with different behavior, different data types and different interaction patterns, as many adapters are required as there are back-end application systems to be integrated. From a B2B integration technology viewpoint, adapters provide an abstraction of back-end application interfaces. No matter how the interface of a back-end application is designed and implemented, the adapter abstracts from that and provides a homogeneous interface across all back-end application systems.

Recently, interfacing with adapters was greatly simplified with the emerging J2EE Connector Architecture standard [J2EE Connector Architecture], which standardized the interface to adapters. All adapters complying to this interface can be integrated with minimal effort if the B2B integration technology implements that same interface. And if all back-end application systems provide an adapter according to the standard then they can be integrated easily. This is important for back-end application systems since their integration becomes less difficult.

15.4.2 External Data Format Interpreter

There is a second area that usually requires external code. This area is concerned with the data formats that are external to the B2B integration technology. Wire messages and subsequently wire events can contain any data format that is conceivable. This is because endpoints can choose the data format that they use in order to communicate. For example, an endpoint can use XML but can also use a binary format. The concept of translation was introduced in order to convert the external data format in wire messages to the data format as defined by the data type system provided by the B2B integration technology. If this B2B integration technology internal format were XML, then an external data format has to be translated into XML. For example, if the external format is also XML, then this is not difficult at all since a copy is sufficient. However, if the external format is a binary, the binary content has to be represented as XML by the translation component.

Since binary format cannot be interpreted without access to the executable that produced the binary, the translation component needs to be extended in order to be able to interpret the binary and translate it to the B2B integration technology internal format. The opposite translation also has to be supplied, so that the B2B integration technology internal format can be translated to the binary format. This extension is external code that has to be written so that the translation component can invoke it at the appropriate times when translating wire event instances into clear text instances, and vice versa.

Since several external data formats are possible, and when dealing with many different endpoints it is most likely necessary to supply as many extensions in order to provide the necessary translation capability. An interface must be defined for this purpose, called the external data format interface. This interface extends the B2B integration technology over time as new external data formats are required because of new endpoints. This interface is not standardized and therefore is individually defined and built by different B2B integration technology implementations.

15.4.3 And Then There is Integration Reality

Even the best and most complete B2B integration technology is sometimes not sufficient to address all requirements in reality. For example, a request that can be found in many situations is that an enterprise wants to deploy a B2B integration technology, however, it also wants to keep the already deployed and running EDI translator for EDI-related translation and transformation. There is usually a significant investment in an EDI translator, and enterprises want to keep leveraging the investment in the context of the new B2B integration technology. The argument behind this is that if the EDI translator were to be removed, its translation and transformation maps would have to be reimplemented by the B2B integration technology. Furthermore, a stable and working environment would be replaced by one that is initially unstable due to the new specifications of translation and transformation that have to be tested and verified first.

While this is not a particularly appealing approach from an architecture perspective, it is a reality that has to be accounted for (or at least can be accounted for) by the B2B integration technology. One way to do this is to extend the component model. Components not only provide public and private interfaces but also implementations for these. One approach for integrating external execution logic is to have each component that provides its particular implementation of an interface also to provide a mechanism to add external execution logic that can replace its implementation in specific cases. Applied to the example, this means that in the case of incoming or outgoing EDI messages, the external EDI translator is invoked by the transformation components, whereas in case of non-EDI messages the native implementation would be taken.

Part IV Business-to-Business Integration Technology Deployment

Part IV of the book is focuses on deployment aspects of B2B integration technology. A very simple but nevertheless effective modeling methodology for B2B integration types and instances is introduced. Based on the results of modeling activities in the context of B2B integration technology, advertisement, negotiation and contract of B2B message exchanges is necessary. As soon as an enterprise can receive specific messages this has to be made known and agreed upon with specific trading partners. While messages are exchanged, the monitoring as well as the analysis of messages is performed in order to derive to information about the enterprise. And finally, a very important aspect of deployment is change management which support the enterprise in changing the definition of integration types and instances as well as their deployment.

16 Modeling Methodology

Not surprisingly, modeling methodologies are considered a "fuzzy art" by many. The main reason behind this is that there is no one single accepted and always effective way to modeling. This applies to B2B integration modeling as well. There are different modeling approaches to B2B integration type and instance modeling that are possible in the context of the introduced integration metamodel. Every integration modeler has to find the particular modeling approach to bring about success in the modeling tasks. Some basic and fundamental approaches can be distinguished that might serve as a starting point:

- **Top-down modeling approach**. The top-down modeling approach starts with those integration types that are the least detailed. These are business, interface and binding process, endpoints and endpoint agreements. Once these are established their details, like parameters or properties, are defined. Afterwards other integration types are defined that are necessary, like data types or event types. Finally, details are filled in, like validation rules, constraints or security attributes such as private and public keys.

  The top-down modeling approach lays out the overall processes first and fills in the details later. At a given point in time many integration types and instances are created, but their definitions are not complete until the end of the modeling task.

- **Bottom-up modeling approach**. The bottom-up modeling approach is to some extent the opposite of the top-down modeling approach. For example, data types are defined completely first before event types are introduced. All details in one endpoint are specified completely before another endpoint is defined. Over time more and more integration types and instance are available as building blocks and the processes are defined last, utilizing all of them.

  The bottom-up modeling approach results in an always consistent set of integration types and instances that are fully specified. At a given point in time only some of all necessary integration types are specified, and only at the end of the modeling task are all integration types and instances available.

- **Abstraction-based modeling approach**. While the top-down and bottom-up modeling approaches are generically applicable to any modeling environment, the abstraction-based modeling approach is specific to B2B integration. This modeling methodology models integration types and instances in an order that is suggested by the business abstractions provided by the integration metamodel.

16.1 Overview

The modeling methodology presented in the following sections follows the abstraction-based modeling approach. In brief, this methodology suggests the following steps and their order:

- **Business behavior.** First, the intended business behavior is modeled without taking the endpoints into consideration at all. The business behavior consists of a business process and the necessary business events. Both together define how the enterprise executes a particular integration process. For example, an enterprise might define that all sales require a credit check. This policy is implemented accordingly in a business process and therefor is applicable to all future endpoints.
- **Endpoint definition.** Once the business behavior is determined, the enterprise has to define all endpoints with which it is going to exchange messages. This might happen over a long period of time and can continue even while the enterprise is already exchanging messages, since new endpoints are incorporated and existing ones are deleted as trading partners agree to do business with each other. The interface and binding processes have to be defined for each endpoint and the hope is that not every endpoint requires its own interface process. Instead, the expectation is that endpoints share the specification of interface processes.
- **Endpoint agreement definition.** Once the endpoints are defined then appropriate endpoint agreements have to be put in place that authorize actual message exchanges. Only then can messages be exchanged with endpoints.

Modeling is an iterative long-lasting process in B2B integration. New endpoints might require modelers to revisit previous decisions in the business behavior if an endpoint exposes a very unusual behavior that has to be accommodated. New or changed requirements might require the modification of business process definitions to address these. Changes are discussed Chap. 19.

Testing and debugging as well as other tasks that are necessary in order to ensure that the modeled integration types and instances fulfill the requirements are not discussed here. Chapter 11 covered this aspect.

16.2 Business Behavior

Business behavior consists of two parts, the business process and the necessary business events. There can be as many business processes as the enterprise requires and they can be reused within each other. Business event definitions can be reused across business processes, too. In the following the description of the methodology is done from the viewpoint of modeling a single business process.

16.2.1 Business Process Modeling

The business process integration concept implements the necessary business logic in order to provide the desired enterprise behavior for a particular functionality. For example, in a selling business process a credit check of the buyer has to be performed before the sale is confirmed. If this credit check turns out to be not favorable, the purchase request can either be denied or the buyer can be asked to provide half of the purchase price up front. The purchase is acknowledged upon receipt.

Whatever the particular business logic might be, the only place to define it is the business process. The fundamental assumption is that the business behavior in general is the same for all involved endpoints. Therefore the business process is modeled so that it implements the business logic independent of specific endpoints and of specific endpoint properties and capabilities. In this sense the business process establishes the common behavior across all endpoints for the enterprise.

Of course, it might be that a business process has to implement a specific business logic for a specific set of endpoints if the enterprise requires it. For example, there might be a buyer who receives preferred treatment because it is a very special buyer. In this case the business logic has to implement the special case by either implementing a conditional branch within the business process that is executed only for the very special buyer, or the enterprise implements a whole new business process for this very special endpoint. No generally applicable recommendation can be given for this case. However, if there are many special cases, the business process might have to have many special branches inside it distinguishing all the different cases. This might result in a very complex business process because of the difference in the different execution paths through it. In such a case it might be better to have different business processes for the different cases in order to avoid the complexity. Common business process parts can always be implemented in a separate business process definitions and reused within the business processes implementing all the different execution paths.

16.2.2 Business Event Definition

A business process operates on data, which are represented as business events. A business event must contain all data that are required by a business process to implement its business logic as well as all data that are required by the endpoints.

Business event types are designed in two steps. The first step is to create the business event type and define all data necessary inside the business event that are necessary for the business process. For example, if a data value is necessary to implement the predicate of a conditional branching then this has to be part of one of the business events. As many business event types have to be creates as are required by the business process.

The second step comes later. It adds more data to the business event based on the data requirements from endpoints. These are all those data that an endpoint provides and another endpoint requires. All these have to be included in the business event and are subject to transformation later. However, they are not accessed by a business process at all, and therefore the change to the event type based on the endpoint requirements does not affect the business process specification at all.

In order for business event types to be consistent and business processes to be useful, the data required by business processes must be made available by the different endpoints through incoming events. If a data value required by a business process for a conditional branching predicate cannot be supplied by an endpoint then the business process will not be able to execute the predicate. Therefore, all data that are required by a business process for it to function must be available as data incoming from endpoints.

16.3 Business Partner and Endpoint Definition

Business partners are trading partners that want to engage in B2B message exchanges in order to do business with each other. An enterprise has to decide which trading partners it wants to exchange messages with and those with it does not want to do business. Those trading partners that participate have to be defined and have to be made available to the business processes. For the methodology discussion it is assumed that an enterprise knows its trading partners. In addition, an enterprise needs to know its available back-end application systems that implement part of the overall business logic and that also need to be integrated with the business processes.

16.3.1 Trading Partner Definition

Trading Partner

Each trading partner has to be defined separately. All its properties and capabilities have to be specified. That might require contacting a representative of the trading partner in order to obtain the necessary data. Probably a different contact person is in charge for trading partner identifiers than for obtaining public keys and network addresses for the message exchange.

Interface Process for B2B Protocol

For a given business process the trading partners that will participate in that business process have to be determined. In order to accomplish this, the interface process and the binding process have to be defined for each trading partner. In the general case this might require several interface and binding processes for each trading partner. For example, creating, updating and deleting purchase orders might very well be three different interface processes, which are all bound by binding processes to the same business process that implements the business logic for all three business events.

In the worst case each trading partner has its own message exchange requirements. This is the case if each trading partner involved implements a different B2B protocol with different message exchange sequences and different data formats. This means that for each trading partner a different set of interface processes as well as binding processes has to be modeled.

In the best case all trading partners follow the exact same B2B protocol, and therefore all share the same set of interface and binding processes. The reality may fall between these extremes. Several trading partners share the same B2B protocol, but not all. Several different B2B protocols are used by different trading partners.

For each interface process, the wire as well as clear text event types have to be defined. Furthermore, translation has to be put in place so that clear text events can be derived from wire events, and vice versa. Any required time-out and retry logic has to be modeled in the interface process. Correlation predicates have to be defined, if necessary, in order to relate the correct event instances to the interface processes at run time.

Once the interface processes are defined, they are related to trading partners as a capability. If several trading partners follow the same B2B protocol, then all have the same interface process capabilities.

Connectivity

It is assumed that all functionality in the connectivity layer is available that is needed to exchange messages with a particular endpoint. This includes network transport protocols, security functionality as well as packaging functionality. If this is not the case, then the connectivity layer has to be extended in order to support the required functionality for a given endpoint. Since this is endpoint specific, it belongs to this part of the methodology, even if integration concepts are not available for defining connectivity functionality.

Binding Process

Once an interface process is modeled it has to be bound to one or more business processes, depending on whether the same message exchange sequence is used in several business processes. A binding process is defined that relates the interface process to the business process. This means that external data flows have to be put in place as do transformation steps that perform the transformation from clear text events to business events, and vice versa. Any mismatch has to be mediated by either consuming events or creating events in order to fulfill the parameters of both interface as well as business processes.

16.3.2 Back-end Application System Definition

In principle, defining back-end application system endpoints is not different from trading partner definitions. An enterprise usually has several back-end application systems installed and in production that participate in business processes. In some cases a new back-end application is installed along with the B2B integration technology server. However, this is not different from the case where it already in place.

Back-End Application System

Each back-end application system that participates in business process execution has to be defined as an endpoint in the B2B integration technology. It has to be given a name, a unique identifier as well as properties and capabilities.

Interface Process for A2A Protocol

In general, each back-end application system exposes a different message exchange behavior. Except for the case when one application is installed several times, the interface processes are specific to back-end application systems. In contrast to trading partners that might share the same B2B protocol, A2A protocols are different for every back-end application system. Once the interface process for a back-end application system is defined, it is added to the back-end application system's capabilities.

Connectivity

Connectivity with back-end application systems is generally established through back-end application system adapters. Once the interface processes for a back-end application system are defined, the necessary adapter has to be put in place in order to enable the message exchange with the back-end application system. This step is put into the methodology at this point since the availability of the correct adapter is necessary in order to connect to the back-end application system.

Binding Process

As in the case of trading partners, the interface processes of back-end application systems have to be bound to the appropriate business processes through binding processes. The same rules apply, and there is no difference whatsoever from a modeling perspective.

16.3.3 Summary

At this point the necessary endpoints and all their properties and capabilities are defined for a given business process. As shown, the definition of trading partners and back-end application systems are alike in the modeling methodology, therefore the integration modeler does not have to follow different modeling approaches for them. It still remains to put the endpoint agreements in place and to deploy the integration types and instances.

16.4 Endpoint Agreement Definition

The final modeling task is to define the appropriate endpoint agreements for the endpoints that participate in a business process. For each endpoint one or more endpoint agreements have to be put in place that authorize the message exchange with the endpoint in the outbound as well as inbound directions. Besides specifying all the technical details, the start and end times are very important since those define when the message exchange can start and end. This is important from a business perspective, since the dates have to match the contracts between the involved enterprises.

One important aspect of endpoint agreement definition is that the endpoint agreements with trading partners cannot be defined in isolation. Each endpoint agreement has a matching one at a trading partner's site. If a message is sent it is going to be received by the trading partner, and vice versa. This means that the endpoint agreements have to match, which means that start and end dates have to match, too.

In advanced cases the best approach is that one of the trading partners specifies an endpoint agreement and sends it to the other trading partner for review. The other trading partner can change it and return the changes. Once the endpoint agreement is received it can be changed again and resent to the remote trading partner. This "back and forth" can continue until both parties agree on the contents. Once this is the case, both can incorporate the endpoint agreement into their B2B integration technology. Section 9.2 discusses the implementation of the negotiation process as integration processes themselves.

In less advanced cases this negotiation process is done manually over the phone, and each trading partner has to define a separate representation of an endpoint agreement. No matter what the particular negotiation process, in the end both trading partners must have a matching endpoint agreement in place, with matching start and end dates, so that business messages can be exchanged without any error, or failure.

16.5 Modeling Traps

The previous sections introduced the abstraction-based modeling methodology that leads to a working model when followed as intended. Sometimes, in specific situations, there seem to be "better" ways to model and this might very well be the case. However, some of the "better" ways might not be better at all, but just appear like it initially. These are usually modeling traps since they initially seem to be advantageous, but cause severe modeling and change management problems afterwards when changes have to be applied to the model. The modeling traps most often encountered are discussed next.

16.5.1 Point-to-Point Integration

In many real deployments of integration technology initially only two back-end application systems or one trading partner and one back-end application system are integrated. This initial integration is kept to a minimum because the enterprise has to learn and to get used to the newly acquired B2B integration technology first. So the initial integration is kept as minimal as possible. Usually, the long-term goal is to integrate all trading partners and all back-end application systems. In this case the overall number of endpoints goes well beyond two.

In this situation two mistakes can easily be made based on alternative process layouts, as described in Chap. 7.6:

- **Single transformation**. Since only two endpoints are integrated it is possible to introduce a single transformation for each clear text event type that originates at one endpoint and has to be sent to the other endpoint. The perceived benefit is that only one transformation has to be specified for each pair of clear text events in contrast to two when a business event type is introduced.
- **Copy transformation**. With the long-term goal of integrating more than two endpoints in mind an idea is to introduce a business event from the beginning, an "artificial" one, however. The business event is a copy of the clear text event from one endpoint and the transformation from this clear text event to the business event is a "copy." This means that there is only one real transformation: from the business event to the clear text event of the other endpoint.

Both approaches cause significant issues when more endpoints are added over time. In the single transformation case a point-to-point transformation happened. Every new endpoint requires another transformation between it and every already existing endpoint. As explained in Sect. 2.2.4 this will lead to a very high number of unnecessary transformations. Instead, a business event should be introduced to lower the number of transformations. This requires in this case that we remove the single transformation and add new ones to the business event instead. This causes additional, unnecessary work compared to the case where a business event has been introduced from the very beginning.

In the copy transformation case there are several issues. First, every time the endpoint changes from where the definition of the event was taken, the business event will change and subsequently all transformations related to it. This includes structural changes as well as vocabulary changes. This means that the isolation that could be achieved with an appropriate use of the business event is not achieved at all. Second, every new endpoint requiring additional fields or different fields cannot be accommodated until the business event is changed, departing from the "copy" approach. The same applies for vocabulary or domain value maps. The departure from the copy approach and the introduction of a real business event could have been done from the beginning, avoiding the change effort.

From the discussion it is very clear that defining real business events from the beginning is advantageous if the number of endpoints goes beyond two.

16.5.2 Split of Round-trip Behavior

When two endpoints have a conversation, in the sense that one sends an initiating event to the other that requires a response event sent back, then it is possible to model this within two sets of interface, binding and business processes. One set deals with one direction (the initiating event) whereas the other set deals with the other direction (the response event). The argument for this design is that no correlation has to be implemented; also the processes are easier since they only have to deal with one direction and one set of related event types.

There are several implications of this approach. First, it is not possible to get the overall status for one conversation since the two role sets are independent of each other. The same applies for the overall history. Second, it is not possible to transfer data from the initiating event to the response event during transformation. Third, it is impossible to guarantee that the order of response documents corresponds to the order of initiating events since both are decoupled. Fourth, no business logic in the business process can be defined spanning both events.

Any of these requirements that might be important at some point in time will require a redesign of the two sets of processes into one set.

16.5.3 No Business Process

Since binding processes can be directly connected through data flow it is possible to leave out business processes altogether. Instead, the binding process parameters are connected directly with each other to supply the right event instances to the right parameters. This approach is appealing since this removes the work of defining business processes altogether.

However, any business logic that might have to be implemented later on requires the addition of business processes since business logic cannot be implemented in binding processes that span the different endpoints.

16.5.4 No Real Business Events

Instead of designing business events that are able to capture all related clear text event contents in one body element, it is possible to define a separate event element for each clear text event that needs to be transformed. The appealing argument is that this is easy to design since the body elements correpond to clear text events.

As already discussed in Sect. 7.1.6, this implements really a point-to-point transformation case since a separate event element is used for different clear text events.

16.5.5 Inclusive Interface Processes

In many situations there are related events in the sense that they represent different operations on business objects like create, update or delete. If these different operations are all represented in the same event definition the temptation is big to have one interface process and subsequently one binding process deal with the different events. The perceived benefit is that the modeling effort is only put in once, since one set of processes can deal with several events at the same time. This would mean that there is only one set of processes dealing with the create, update or delete of an event.

The problem that easily arises with this approach is that as soon as processing is different for the different events, conditional branchings have to be modeled in the various processes as well as conditional transformation rules in order to distinguish the behavior. If there is a lot of difference this easily leads to a complex process and transformation design.

16.6 Deployment

Once all integration types and instances have been modeled (and tested), they have to be made available so that message instances can be received and processed accordingly by interface, binding and business process instances. Making integration types and instances available is sometimes referred to as deployment or releasing them into production. Fundamentally, this means that an explicit step is done by an integration manager whose responsibility comprises managing and deploying integration types and instances. Once integration types and instances are deployed, they can no longer be changed. Any required change has to be done in the modeling environment by introducing new versions of the type or instance in question. A subsequent deployment makes this change available for the run time. Once the deployment takes place, the change is picked up and the integration behaves accordingly.

As discussed in Sect. 7.10, the unit of deployment is a complete and consistent configuration. Only if a configuration is complete and consistent can major failures at run time be avoided.

16.7 Integration Project Management

In addition to modeling the integration processes and events as well as all the other relevant integration types and instances, a more project management-oriented aspect has to be considered and planned when deploying B2B integration technology. Requirements have to be gathered, the system size has to be determined, the appropriate vendor has to be found that offers a good B2B integration technology and so on. This aspect of B2B integration technology deployment is very important and significantly contributes to the success of an integration project. Yee and Apte (2001) describe some of the project management-oriented aspects in more detail.

17 Advertisement, Discovery and Agreement

The modeling methodology in Chap. 16 assumes that an enterprise defines its business processes and already knows all trading partners that it wants to integrate with those using B2B integration technology. This means that the enterprise either already conducts business with the trading partners or they agreed to do business with each other in the future, as soon as the business processes are specified.

However, once the business processes are modeled, the endpoints are defined, the endpoint agreements are put in place and the B2B integration technology is processing event and message instances the enterprise is not done with trading partner management. It will most likely continuously look for more potential customers as well as more possible suppliers and other types of trading partners in order to grow the business or make it more efficient.

An active way to this is to have staff that constantly looks for new customers and suppliers. While this is current practice, one can imagine an automated environment where an enterprise can search for customers and suppliers (using a search tool) as well as advertise its services and capabilities (using an advertisement tool). An enterprise that advertises its capabilities is called an advertising enterprise, and an enterprise that discovers advertisements is called a discovering enterprise. This chapter outlines briefly how searches (also called discovery) and advertisements fit with the B2B integration technology architecture approach.

17.1 Advertisement

By advertising, an enterprise can make its capabilities publicly visible to as-yet unknown discovering enterprises. This allows discovering enterprises to find out about the capabilities and to get in contact in order to explore potential business relationships.

The question is what to advertise in terms of integration concepts. In order for enterprises to determine a potential business relationship, they need to know what an advertising enterprise offers from a customer perspective or what it needs from a supplier perspective. Other types of trading partners, like shippers or banks, might also be interested, in order to offer their services. In all cases it is important to find out about the products and services that are offered or required. The integration concepts contain this information in te form of interface processes. An interface process describes the event types sent as well as received. Furthermore, domain value maps define valid values for the data types in the events. The valid values define the possible business content.

For example, an interface process might send out a purchase order and expect a purchase order acknowledgment. From this it can be derived that the enterprise engages in buying products. The domain value map for these event types indicates that valid values for products are T-shirts in particular sizes and particular colors. From this it can be determined that the enterprise buys T-shirts in the sizes and colors as enumerated for the appropriate fields in the event types.

In order to automate the search for these enterprise capabilities, a formal advertisement language as well as a place where the advertisements can be stored are required so that potential business partners can find out about them. Since advertisements have to be understood by potential business partners some form of standard language is required in order to advertise the capabilities. Not surprisingly, the same formalisms can be used that are provided by B2B standards that define the B2B protocols. For example, RosettaNet has a formalism that defines the various interface processes suggested by the standard. This formalism can also be used by an enterprise to announce which of the interface processes it supports and what the event types and domain values are. Newer developments like Web services can be used in the same way, and this applies to all standards (see Chap. 20). Since enterprises understand the various B2B standard formalisms they support in their B2B integration technology, they can search among advertised interface processes in these languages.

There are several places where advertisements can be made available:

- **Home page**. The most direct way to advertise is the enterprise's home page on the World Wide Web. An advertising enterprise can make its interface processes visible and accessible on its Web site for discovering enterprises.
- **Registry**. A public registry is a publicly accessible repository or database where advertising enterprises can store their interface processes. Since these registries are public, any discovering enterprise can access and search them. An example is UDDI [UDDI].
- **Broker**. An enterprise can give its interface processes to a broker that in turn knows discovering enterprises and what they are looking for. The broker tries to match both. The broker is not fully public but restricted, since only the enterprises that are represented by the broker are considered in the search and match.
- **Trading partner community**. A trading partner community also represents a restricted set of enterprises to which advertisements are visible. If interface processes are advertised to the trading partner community, only the participating trading partners can search them.

All these different places are external in the sense that they are accessible by discovering enterprises that are potential business partners. Advertisements are therefore enterprise external advertisements. However, sometimes it is necessary to advertise capabilities only within the same enterprise. This is true especially for large enterprises that consist of several distributed divisions. In this case internal divisions or groups can also look at advertisements and supply the necessary products or services. These are called enterprise-internal advertisements and are used to increase the efficiency within enterprises.

17.2 Discovery

If all enterprises advertise their capabilities, then this is not helpful unless there is a discovery process that supports the search for matching advertisements. A search mechanism has to be in place that can search for advertisements and that can access the various places where advertisements have been made available. Various search mechanisms can be envisioned:

- **Advertisement crawler.** An advertisement crawler is like a Web crawler that visits as many Web sites as it can and retrieves interface process advertisements from them. In the case where such a crawler is configurable, a discovering enterprise could configure the crawler in such a way that only the interesting interface processes and their advertising enterprises are selected. In the more general case, an advertisement crawler searches for all advertisements and makes them available to a search engine, operating much like popular Internet search engines.
- **Registry search engine.** Advertisements that are stored in a registry can be searched by search functionality provided by the registry. The more fine grained the search criteria, the easier the search will be.
- **Broker notification.** Brokers are like registries inasmuch as they possess advertisements from advertising enterprises that are their clients. Discovering enterprises that work with brokers will be notified by their broker if a new advertisement is given to it that might fit the discovering enterprises' interests. In this case the search is performed within the broker, and the broker sends the research results as notifications to the discovering enterprise.
- **Broadcast.** A more direct and intrusive mechanism is to eliminate the search by the advertising enterprise broadcasting its advertisement to all known trading partners. This is like mass mailing, where the receiver does not really ask for the letters but receives them anyway. Each receiving trading partner has to evaluate the advertisement in this case to determine whether it is of interest. However, trading partners can guard themselves from unwanted advertisements by not establishing an endpoint agreement that authorizes their receipt.

In addition, a matching service has to be implemented that can, for a given advertisement, determine if the products or services that are advertised can be supplied or can be bought. From an integration concept point of view this matching service has to match interface processes. Namely, the advertised interface process has to be matched by an interface process in the discovering enterprise. For example, if one enterprise requests shippers to ship goods, then the other enterprise matches only if one of their interface processes can receive requests for shipment.

The ideal situation is the precise match, where both interface processes match without a single mismatch. This can only be expected when enterprises implement B2B standards without modification or extension. A less ideal situation is when parts of the interface processes match, but other parts do not fit with each other. In these cases, one or both of the involved trading partners have to modify their interface processes in order to make them fit perfectly. The integration concepts certainly allow for this case, and therefore this case can be addressed. As soon as new interface processes are defined, the two trading partners can start negotiating the endpoint agreements. And, of course, the new and modified interface processes can be advertised, too.

The same enterprise can be an advertising and discovering enterprise at the same time, of course. An advertising enterprise does not have to wait for discovering enterprises to contact it. It can itself discover potential business partners. At the same time enterprises can also only advertise or only discover. Of course, they can do neither, too. What strategy to follow (if any) is completely in an enterprise's discretion.

17.3 Agreement

In the optimistic case, the searching and the matching of interface processes through advertisements is fully automatic. Once a matching pair of interface processes is found (or several, for that matter), the enterprises involved have to decide if they want to engage in a business relationship. If so, they need to negotiate an endpoint agreement.

Based on the matching service, an initial endpoint agreement can be proposed to the two enterprises involved. Since the matching service knows the interface processes as well as the enterprises involved, it can try to gather all the required data necessary for an endpoint agreement. Once the draft of an endpoint agreement is established, the integration managers of the two enterprises are notified. The managers can then manually either sign off or refine the draft agreement (Sect. 16.4).

The most optimistic case of agreement negotiation is that the whole process is fully automatic, that is, it occurs without any human user involvement at all. After the search was successful and the matching service determined matching interface processes, an automatic endpoint agreement process is executed that performs the negotiation steps fully automatically by following predefined negotiation rules. Once the negotiation process is successful, the endpoint agreement is put in place and the two enterprises start doing business with each other.

While it is easy to have this vision, its implementation is rather remote in the general case since rules of engagement for trading partners are quite complex. In addition, complex legal aspects are usually involved. However, in specific cases for specific services or products, automatic endpoint agreement negotiation might be quite feasible.

18 Monitoring and Business Intelligence

An important aspect of B2B integration technology deployment in an enterprise is the ongoing monitoring of the deployed integration processes in order to ensure that these are running smoothly and that any errors are detected as early as possible. This allows them to be repaired as soon as possible in order to avoid future execution disruption.

In addition to error detection and handling, the streamlining of processes in order to make them more efficient is a very important activity of an enterprise. Streamlined processes require less resources, provide faster responses to trading partners and have fewer possibilities of errors since they have fewer process steps. Observing processes and analyzing them for inefficiencies is therefore very important. Status monitoring as well as analyzing finished process instance executions are two fundamental approaches to observing integration processes.

18.1 Status Monitoring

In principle, it is possible to monitor the status of any integration instance without exception. However, some of them are more interesting to monitor than others. For example, to monitor a data instance and its value over time is only interesting when an error occurred and this data instance is the source of the error. In order to determine error repair possibilities, its status and history are very relevant. In contrast, it is much more important to be able to monitor the progress of a purchase order event that is of high value to the enterprise to prevent any problem that might be caused by its delay or by an error during its processing.

Section 11.3.3 lists the most important integration instances that are generally monitored and how a user interface presents their observed state. These are repeated here briefly:

- Monitoring of a single event instance
- Monitoring of a set of related process instances
- Aggregation of event instances
- History of an event instance
- History of a set of related process instances

As soon as complete and consistent configurations are deployed and message instances are exchanged with endpoints, any of the above-listed ways of monitoring are available for the user in the role of integration manager. The user can look at event instances as well as integration process instances in order to find out their state and progress, independently of whether an error happened or not. If an error happened, the monitoring tool allows the user to find out where the error occurred and why. In this case the integration modeler can address the error case by using the error-handling user interface to repair the error.

In many cases the end user want to get access to the monitoring user interface, too. The reason for this request is that from a business viewpoint a user who issued a purchase order is interested in the progress of this purchase order and all subsequent messages related to it. If end users have access to the monitoring user interface then an additional benefit is that end users monitor the ongoing integration processes, too, and can give warnings if they see any particular process causing problems or encountering errors. The monitoring load is distributed across a larger set of users, which allows earlier problem detection.

Observations made during status monitoring might cause changes in the integration type definitions. For example, an occurring error might be repaired for a given instance. However, to avoid the future appearance of this error one or several integration types might be changed, too. Chapter 19 addresses change management issues in more detail.

18.2 Business Intelligence

Enterprises striving for transparency and business process improvement are in all cases interested in aggregated information about their business operations. Aggregation is usually performed on current operational data as well as historical data describing the past process executions. Based on the aggregated data, enterprises can compare their current performance with the targeted performance. In case there is a deviation, enterprises can implement changes in order to improve. Typical aggregations might be: how many purchase orders have been sent out but have not yet been confirmed as of noon today? What is the average, shortest and longest response time for each of my trading partners in the last 6 months excluding acknowledgement messages?

The characteristic of these types of queries is that they aggregate information about integration instances across integration processes and for specified periods of time, usually extending into the past. Both are possible since the B2B integration technology provides a complete history for all integration instances. In order to not lose the ability to aggregate data, this complete history should be maintained and kept for the necessary periods of time. Then business analysis questions like those mentioned above can be implemented based on the complete history.

The best basis for data warehouse tools is a fine-grained and normalized schema providing the raw, not yet aggregated data. This foundation paired with completeness provides all possible data that can be used by data warehouse technology. From an operational perspective the deployment of a data warehouse technology in an enterprise can decide when to extract the raw data from the B2B integration technology and how to store it, and for which period of time.

18.2.1 Querying the Correct Integration Concepts

Since the questions to be answered are different for each enterprise and since the number of possible questions is quite high, no attempt is made here to even try to enumerating them. Technologies like data warehouse technologies (Kimball 1996) are possible tools for the implementation of analysis queries and their answers.

Instead of trying to enumerate possible aggregations, a qualitative analysis is made of which integration instances to use and which should not be used in order to avoid wrong conclusions based on inappropriate query results. The following example shows the potential problems. The first of the two analysis questions stated above was: how many purchase orders have been sent out but are not yet confirmed as of noon today? In order to answer this question the following elements of the query have to be clarified:

- **Purchase orders**. The term purchase orders is very vague. It is not clear if create, update or cancel purchase order is meant. In order to avoid this ambiguity it would be best to refer to event types in the query: how many instances of the create purchase order event type have been sent out but are not yet confirmed?
- **Confirmation**. The term confirmation is vague, too. Confirmations are usually sent as purchase order acknowledgment instances. So, to further clarify the query, it should look like: how many instances of the create purchase order event type have been sent out for which the correlated instance of the event type purchase order acknowledgment has not yet been received?
- **Class of event type**. The query could be on business event types. However, in this case it might be that the native event purchase order acknowledgment has been received, but has not been translated and transformed yet into its corresponding business event type. In this case the query would return the fact that the acknowledgment has not yet been received when it really has. The same difference would exist for the outgoing create purchase order event type. Therefore, the query would look like: how many instances of the create purchase order native event type have been sent out for which the correlated instance of the native event type purchase order acknowledgment has not yet been received?

Fundamentally, each query that represents a business intelligence question must be rephrased in terms of the precise integration concepts. Otherwise, it will be ambiguous and therefore subject to the interpretation of whoever constructs the query. As a consequence, the results might be misinterpreted.

18.2.2 Taking Event Behavior into Account

Another example is the question: what is the sum of the values of all invoices that were sent out last month? First, the query has to be rephrased in terms of the integration concepts. It would look like: what is the sum of all total amounts (given that this is the name of the field) of the instances of the business event invoice that were sent out last month? This query accesses the business event instances, retrieves the total amount and then sums them up.

However, there is a big problem with this query. The query sums up all invoices that were sent out to remote trading partners. It does not account for any invoice cancellations or updates that might have been made. In general, for a given event instance there can be additional ones that contain modifications of the original intent. Examples are updates and cancellations. In order to accommodate this case, the query has to only sum up the sums of those invoices that have neither been cancelled or updated. Cancelled ones are not allowed to be included, and in the case of updates, the last update value has to be included. This is important since an invoice might have been updated several times.

As can be seen in this example, several different event types relate to each other, and the business objects they are derived from implement a specific behavior, like update or cancellation. This has to be taken into account for accurate results. Otherwise, the results do not represent the state of the system correctly.

19 Change Management

As is often said, change is the most stable constant in today's business world. This observation applied to B2B integration fundamentally says that any integration type or instance definition is not built to last but is built for change. While changes occur more or less frequently, the integration types and instances have to be stable and consistent between changes. When changes occur, they have to be performed with ease to avoid being a burden for the integration modeler. Since changes cannot be avoided but have to be carefully planned for, change management is key to maintaining a consistent B2B integration technology.

Changes will be distinguished in integration type and integration instance changes. Integration type changes in general result in a new version that requires deployment. The same applies for integration instances like endpoints or endpoint agreements (the singleton instances). Possible changes are updates as well as deletions of integration types and instances. The introduction of new types and instances has been discussed in Chap. 16.

19.1 Reasons for Change

Changes can come from within hosted trading partners or are requested by remote trading partners because of a change within their environment. Internally caused changes are therefore distinguished from externally caused changes.

19.1.1 Internally vs. Externally Caused Changes

An internally caused change might or might not affect endpoints. A change in a data type might require a change in the transformation rules that access data of this type, but no endpoint is affected by this change. An endpoint is affected by a change if its interface processes, wire event types, endpoint definitions or endpoint agreement definitions change. If one of these integration objects changes, a corresponding change within the endpoint's B2B integration technology has to take place if the endpoint is a trading partner. This causes a renegotiation of the endpoint agreements to agree on the changes.

A trading partner is an external endpoint. External endpoints can be distinguished from internal endpoints, like back-end application systems or users. An internal endpoint is local to the hosted trading partner. A change that can be limited to affecting internal endpoints is preferable over a change that affects external endpoints, since internal endpoints are not visible from outside the enterprise and such a change does not require negotiation of external endpoint agreements. Affected internal or external endpoints constitute the scope of a change.

Independent of the scope of the changes there can be different reasons for change. The most common are:

- **Business behavior of hosted trading partner.** A hosted trading partner decides to change internal business processes, for example, to become more competitive. This in turn might change interface processes, requiring negotiation of internal and external endpoint agreements.
- **Business behavior of remote trading partners.** Conversely, a remote trading partner can change its internal business behavior, which requires a change in the interface processes. This potentially affects its business partners and their interface processes. Compared to the previous case, the change is initiated by a remote trading partner of a hosted trading partner.
- **Behavior of endpoints.** Internal endpoints can change, for example, when a new version of a back-end application system is installed. In this case its interface might change requiring, a change in the corresponding interface processes.
- **Existence of endpoints.** New endpoints appear, for example, a new trading partner or a new back-end application system. Also, endpoints can disappear. For example, a supplier change or the decommission of a back-end application system might cause the removal of an endpoint.
- **Regulations.** Regulations that enterprises must follow might change. For example, it might be that from a specific point in time onwards all nonrepudiation has to include an impartial third party for time stamping as well as message observation purposes. That requirement might be a legal requirement imposed by legislation in order to enforce nonrepudiation.
- **Optimization and streamlining.** Independent of a particular business need an enterprise might optimize a business process, removing specific steps. That in turn might cause changes outside the business process.
- **Errors.** Nontransient error situations might occur. In order to avoid these in the future, several integration types and instances might have to be changed. Such a change might stay within the enterprise or affect remote trading partners.
- **New products.** An enterprise might introduce new products, and as a consequence, the domain value maps might have to be changed so that the new product names become valid values. Remote trading partners need to become aware of the new product so that they can adjust their internal domain value maps, too.
- **New version of standard.** A B2B standard might evolve and a standards organization may release a new version of it. An enterprise supporting this standard has to prepare itself to support this new version if one or more of its remote trading partners wants to upgrade to the new version, too.

- **New standard**. In addition to new versions of existing standards, entirely new standards are developed. Recently, many new standards appeared and, if adopted, might require support by an enterprise.

No matter what specific reasons causes a change, in general several integration types and instances have to be changed as a consequence. The change management aspects are discussed in the following in more detail.

19.1.2 Compatible and Incompatible Changes

When does a change of an object cause a change propagation? This is the case whenever one or several objects refer to the changed object. For example, a conditional branching expression accesses an element of the event contents. Any change in the element definition causes the conditional branching expression to change, and thus change propagation happens. Changes that affect other objects are called incompatible changes.

Compatible changes are those that do not affect other objects at all. For example, changing the order of two process steps can be done without affecting other objects. Even though compatible changes are preferable, in reality most changes are incompatible because the object structure in B2B integration is highly connected.

Given this situation another question is whether incompatible changes can be made compatible by allowing the system to be "change tolerant." For example, a business process does not require a specific input parameter anymore. Instead of removing it, the process simply does not use it anymore. If supplied at run time, it is not used. The related object does not have to be changed.

However, this is far from ideal. For example, if the same business process is reused in another situation, the input parameter must be connected and so the integration modeler has to supply it. He does not necessarily know that the input parameter is not relevant anymore. He makes sure that the input parameter is supplied unnecessarily. From this perspective, incompatible changes should be avoided and the change propagation dealt with. This results in a consistent set of modeling objects and that is very important.

19.2 Business Behavior

19.2.1 Business Process Type Change

Business behavior is implemented by business process types and business event types. All business process types and all business event types are in a specific version. Any change of these will cause the creation of a new version. Changes are then implemented as a new version (or several, if several types are affected) that does not affect the existing versions at all.

A new version might cause a version change propagation (Sect. 5.3.2). A new version of a business process might have two different forms of impact. First, if the previous version of the business process was reused in another business process, then this one might be affected, too. An example is the interface of the business process changed. An interface change is a change in the input and output parameters of a business process. A new parameter as well as a change in an existing one have to be supported. If a parameter is deleted, the deletion also has to be recognized by the reusing business process since it must not supply a value any more.

Second, binding processes can be affected if some or all of the parameters of a business process change. New versions of the binding processes have to be implemented that in turn might cause further changes to other integration types.

19.2.2 Business Event Type Change

The same principle applies to business event type changes. A new version of a business event type might affect all business processes that reuse this business event type. Parameters might have to be changed to the new version of the business event type. Transformations might have to be changed as would business process internal business logic, like conditional branching predicates that access the changed content of the changed business event type.

Business event type changes do not only happen because of changes within business processes but also because an endpoint sends more or less data because of the change. That in turn affects the business event type definition because the changes in the messages eventually have to be reflected in the business event types. This type of change typically happens if a trading partner is going to use a new version of a B2B protocol, or a back-end application system is upgraded to a new version of a software release.

19.3 Business Partner and Endpoint Definition

A change in an endpoint affects at least four integration objects: the endpoint definition itself, its interface processes, the related binding processes and connectivity functionality. These topics are addressed in detail in the following.

19.3.1 Endpoint Definition Change

The definition of an endpoint can change like its properties or capabilities. Properties can be local changes that do not cause any version change propagation. An example is the update of a contact phone number or a bill-to address. Some of those changes are time sensitive in the sense that they cannot be issued independently of the ongoing process or event instances. For example, the exchange of a public key has to be done at a specific point in time, since not only the endpoint itself has to change but also the remote trading partner's endpoint definition. Changing a public key means that both trading partners have to use the same public key starting at the same time. Changes that are not local to the endpoint definition itself have to be coordinated with all the affected endpoints. Setting a specific date and time when the changes are effective is a good approach.

Another good approach is the explicit sending of change messages between the endpoints. In this case every endpoint can prepare for the change by creating new versions of the affected types and instances. However, these new versions are not put in place manually or automatically at a specific point in time. Instead, change messages are sent between trading partners that indicate when to deploy the new versions. This is like a two-phase commit protocol that coordinates the deployment of changes across endpoints. The benefit of the latter approach is that the change does not rely on clock synchronization and manual intervention. Instead, the change is coordinated by messages themselves, making sure that all changes are deployed at the correct point in the overall processing between the endpoints.

However, change messages require modelling of the corresponding event types representing the change messages and the process types that process these events. In addition, the necessary endpoint agreements must be in place. The initial effort to set this approach up is higher compared to the case where changes are manually coordinated, but the benefit is substantial because of the reduced manual change management effort and the reduced error possibilities due to automation.

The removal of endpoints must not automatically cause the removal of interface processes since these might be used for other still-existing endpoints. Even if there were not any endpoints left that use an interface process, later a new endpoint might require this interface process again since it follows the corresponding B2B protocol. Since interface processes implement B2B protocols they are generally valid, even without a specific endpoint in place that uses it.

19.3.2 Interface Process Type Change

If an endpoint changes its behavior, like sending additional events or changing the order in which events are sent, the interface process type has to be modified accordingly. Internal as well as external endpoints can exhibit this type of change. If an internal endpoint changes its behavior, the interface processes in the B2B integration technology have to be modified accordingly. If an external endpoint does this, the corresponding interface processes in the B2B integration technology have to change and the endpoint agreements have to be renegotiated.

The B2B integration technology itself represents the hosted trading partner, and its interface processes can change, too. In this case the remote trading partners have to be notified that are affected by the modification so that they can change their internal B2B integration technology configuration.

19.3.3 Binding Process Type Change

A binding process usually has to adapt to business process or interface process changes. If one or both change, the binding process has to mediate the change. That means that changes in parameters have to be accommodated as do changes in the behavior.

Transformation changes are sometimes necessary, too, if event types change. A change in event type structure requires transformation rules to be added or removed. Sometimes the existing transformation rules need be modified. Data type changes usually result in changed transformation rules.

19.3.4 Connectivity Change

Changes in the connectivity layer are rather seldom, since transport functionality is stable in most environments. However, it might stil happen, and therefore changes have to be possible. New transport functionality might be added, or existing ones might be changed. In the case of a change, it is important that the changes are applied at the correct moment in time to avoid miscommunication on a transport layer when the sender uses a different transport specification then the receiver expects.

19.4 Endpoint Agreement Definition

Any change in an endpoint agreement requires that all endpoints referenced in the endpoint agreement need to agree on the change and need to change their corresponding endpoint agreements, too (if they want to continue to exchange messages, of course). However, since only one version of an endpoint agreement can be valid at a given point in time, a change in an endpoint agreement usually includes a change in the start and end times so that the change can be deployed before its former version expires.

Endpoint agreements consist of several parts that can be changed. These are:

- **Transport**. An endpoint agreement refers to the transport used. It can be changed if the transport has to be switched. An example is a switch from SMTP to HTTP.
- **Transport addresses**. Reconfigurations might result in a change of network addresses on the transport level. A change can be reflected by updating the endpoint agreement accordingly. Once the change is deployed the message are sent to the new network addresses.
- **Interface processes**. If interface processes change, the new versions have to be referenced in an endpoint agreement before they can be used for the actual message exchange. This is typically the reason to change an endpoint agreement.

- **Security**. Security is an area that generally does not change often, if at all. Once an enterprise has decided on the form of security, the security algorithms and the form of nonrepudiation, it usually keeps them for long periods of time. However, security keys change much more often. Public keys have to be made available then, which causes change.
- **Start date and time**. Changes have to be applied at some point in time and the start date and time are usually changed to the date and time when the changes have to be effective. A new start date and time is adjoining to the previous version of an endpoint agreement. In this case no overlap exists. If it is later, then there is a "gap" that prevents message exchange with the trading partners during that time. If it is earlier, then the new version overlaps with the previous version of the endpoint agreement.
- **End date and time**. End dates and times can also be changed if, for example, the cooperation with a trading partner is extended or shortened.
- **Initiating endpoints**. Initiating endpoints are usually stable. It is rarely the case that another endpoint becomes the initiating one for a given interface process. However, this can also change, of course.
- **Responding endpoints**. Like initiating endpoints, responding endpoints are stable, too, and a change cannot be expected often.

Any change that affects an endpoint automatically requires a change in the corresponding endpoint agreements. Otherwise, the change cannot be deployed. This ensures that changes are coordinated with the affected endpoints, and no mismatches in message exchanges happen.

19.5 Deployment

No change will become effective unless the new version of the changed integration types and integration instances are deployed. Deployment is the only way to make new versions of integration objects available for run time so that the new versions of the objects are used at run time.

There are several different scenarios that can happen when a new version of an integration object is deployed. These different scenarios are distinguished by the impact a change has on existing instances of integration objects that are not yet finished. The question is what should be done with existing instances once a new version of their corresponding types becomes available through deployment. The scenarios are as follows:

- **Stop and abort ongoing instances**. The easiest approach is to stop and abort instances once new versions of one or more of their types become available. While this approach is the easiest from a B2B integration technology perspective, it most likely leaves an overall inconsistent state behind. For example, if an event needs to be sent to several back-end application systems and the integration processes for this are aborted, only some of the back-end application systems receive the event. In general this leads to an inconsistent state among the back-end application systems.

- **Stop and compensate ongoing instances**. This approach recognizes the fact that aborting ongoing instances results in an inconsistent state. Consequently, compensation is initiated to ensure that no inconsistencies are left behind. After compensation occurs, the deployment of the new versions takes place and message and event processing can start again.
- **Allow ongoing instances to finish**. This approach, like the previous one, also recognizes the fact that inconsistencies should not happen. However, instead of initiating the compensation of ongoing instances, they are allowed to finish according to their existing versions of their types. The new versions do not affect existing instances at all. New initiating messages are processed according to the new version of the types, and existing instances are executed according to the former versions of the types.
- **Stop and move ongoing instances to new version**. This is the most complicated approach. This approach stops the ongoing instances, creates new instances according to the new version of the types and transfers the data from the existing to the new instances. This is effectively a type change that ongoing instances undergo during their lifetime. In order for this approach to work, it must be possible to transfer the instances between different versions of types. An example problem is a value in an instance that does no longer has a corresponding value in the new type. This value can be dropped or aggregated with other values, depending on what constitutes consistent handling.

Deployment in conjunction with the handling of existing instances is done in stages. First, the instances are managed, and then deployment takes place. During this time no new instances should be started of those types that are affected by the deployment of the new versions. For the duration of the new deployment, the creation of new instances has to be blocked, and new messages are accepted only after deployment.

19.6 Self-Service Changes

Since trading partners can communicate with each other using messages, the question arises whether this ability can be used to communicate any changes to each other that relate to interface processes, message definitions, transport changes, endpoint agreement changes and so on. A self-service change is one where the changing endpoint notifies all other endpoints about the change directly. This means that the changing endpoint initiates the change on its own initiative and therefore causes the change to happen automatically. The hosted trading partner might not be involved at all or might only authorize the automatic changes.

In Sect. 9.4 an example business process is defined that supports the example of updating the endpoint definition. This can be extended to include not only endpoint definitions, but also endpoint agreements or even interface processes. The new definitions are represented in messages and sent to the appropriate trading partners for update. The receiving trading partner updates the definitions, thereby creating new versions and deploying them. Once deployed, an acknowledgement message is sent back to confirm the changes. Once the confirmation is received all trading partners involved know that they can start executing according to the new definition.

Standards organizations can use the this mechanism to let every endpoint know about a new version of a standard. Endpoints interested in receiving electronic updates through messages have to sign up with the standards organization. Once this takes place, the standards organization can notify the subscribers about changes. The subscribed endpoints can then deploy the changes to support the new version.

An alternative way of self-service changes is to allow endpoints to use modeling tools directly. In this case the tools are invoked at an endpoint's site with the B2B integration technology of the hosted trading partner as the target environment. This means that the hosted trading partner does not use the tools to update its B2B integration technology, but uses a remote trading partner to convey its changes. As in the case of sending the update through messages, the remote trading partner initiates the change on their own and the hosted trading partner is not involved at all, or maybe only to authorize changes.

Part V Integration Standards, Products, Research and the Future of Integration

Part V embeds B2B integration concepts as well as B2B integration technology architecture into a wider context. Integration standards are introduced and they are related to the defined B2B integration technology architecture. Since B2B integration is an area with considerable history, many commercial products exist. Some of these products are introduced. Since not all the problems in this space are solved by far, some research efforts are introduced that contribute to B2B integration. And finally, everything has a future, and so does B2B integration. Some speculation about the future of integration concludes the fifth part of the book.

20 Standards

According to Robin Cover [Robin Cover], there are several hundred standards related to integration. To be precise, there are several hundred standards as well as standard proposals. Only time will tell which of the proposals or existing standards will be adopted widely enough to be relevant and to exist for a significant amount of time.

Since this vast number is impossible to cover even remotely, a selected subset of the standards is briefly introduced here to give an impression of the variety. The references given allow readers to study the standards in more detail, independently of this book.

The selection of the standards is solely based on the contribution to this book and the presented B2B integration concepts and architecture. The selection is not a statement from the author about the viability of a standard, the probability of wide adoption, its quality, significance or any other judgement whatsoever.

20.1 Standards in Today's World

The two categories of standards that are relevant in the context of B2B integration are those that standardize the communication either with back-end application systems or trading partners. In the following the focus is on these two types and other standards are only touched on briefly, if at all.

20.1.1 Portability and Interoperability Standards

One important distinction that can be made about standards is that of portability standards and interoperability standards. Portability standards are those that allow an executable program to run in a different system context. For example, a program accessing a database might use the SQL standard in order to be able to run on different relational database management systems (i.e., being ported to different database management systems). The same program can then access the databases of different vendors. This way portability is achieved. The same holds true if the program is implemented in a portable programming language like Java. The same program can run in the context of several operating systems and is hence portable across those.

Interoperability standards in contrast allow a program to communicate with another program without specifically knowing its implementation or its implementation technology. Only the interface has to be known, not its implementation. A standard defining the interface is called an interoperability standard. Any program that implements the interoperability standard can be contacted and can be communicated with. The particular implementation is hidden and is not of interest as long as it achieves the communication. Any implementation technology used is invisible.

While portability standards are important from a vendor perspective in order to be able to sell the product in many different configurations of hardware and infrastructure software, for B2B integration interoperability standards are very relevant. Otherwise, it cannot be assured that an enterprise installing a B2B integration technology can exchange wire messages with its trading partners. Therefore, the focus is on interoperability standards in the following.

20.1.2 Current Situation in Context of B2B Integration Standards

Even though standards should be very static and should seldom change in order to allow products to be compliant for an economically significant amount of time, standards actually do change. Controlled processes have to be in place so that changes do not affect existing products too much, and so that all products can adjust to standard changes at the same pace in order to maintain interoperability. Different standards have different processes for modifying the standards through new versions and revisions and release processes to make the change available.

This is the operational aspect of managing a standard, and it is not discussed further. A much more important aspect of standards has to be discussed in the context of this book. An interoperability standard is only valuable if the majority (if not all) B2B integration technology products comply with the standard. Only then is the standard beneficial to the users of the products. For example, if every B2B integration technology product implements EDI, then all users of the various B2B integration technology products can interoperate using EDI. On the other hand, a product not implementing EDI would not allow an enterprise to communicate using EDI. In this case an alternative standard would have to be found that is implemented by the trading partners of this enterprise. This in turn means that there must be at least one B2B integration technology product that implements two standards, EDI and the alternative one. Furthermore, the user of this product has to implement the transformation between EDI events and events of the alternative standard. It becomes immediately clear that the more standards that are available, the greater the implementation and configuration work be for some of the trading partners. The optimal (albeit unrealistic case) is to have only one standard, since in this case all B2B integration technologies would have to implement only one standard and all would be interoperable. Since this is a quite unrealistic case, it is not discussed further here.

What happens if there are many interoperability standards that standardize the same concepts? Or, to ask the question the other way around, what is the benefit for users if a product is compliant to different standards that cover the same concepts? To even further emphasize the question, what would be the benefit of having several interoperability standards in the same application domain (like health care)? These questions make clear that standards by themselves are not that beneficial if there are several that "compete" or are at least equivalent. In this case a choice has to be made by the vendor of a B2B integration technology product of which interoperability standard to implement (if not all of them). And the users of a B2B integration technology product have to determine which of the products support the standard they require in order to select a B2B integration technology product that addresses their requirements. With luck, there is one product that implements all the standards the user needs.

In summary, for interoperability standards to be effective, it is important that not too many equivalent standards are available. Otherwise, they all have to be implemented by at least some of the B2B integration technology products, and users of these have to provide the costly transformation between the events of the different standards.

However, even if the "academic" discussion hints strongly at having as few standards as possible, there is an interoperability boom happening right now, as discussed by Robin Cover [Robin Cover]. Not only are there many interoperability standards proposed in different application domains, but also within application domains. This is in part caused by the perceived ease of defining a standard through XML as well as by the many standards organizations, consortia and companies proposing standards independently of each other.

While this situation is surely fascinating because of the problems the huge number of interoperability standards creates, it is not the main focus of the book. Hence, the situation is taken as is, and the focus is put on the interoperability standards themselves in the following.

20.1.3 Elements of Interoperability Standards

Not all relevant interoperability standards provide standardization in all necessary areas. For example, some standards only define the content of messages like purchase orders, whereas other standards also define the permissible vocabulary or the messaging infrastructure in order to send messages across networks. Therefore, the first discussion in the following is about the important elements of interoperability standards:

- **Process**. Processes describe the message or event sequence on a business level as public processes. For example, a purchase order acknowledgment has to follow a purchase order. This type of dependency is described through processes.
- **Payload**. The payload defines the business content of messages and events. For example, a payload definition defines the structure of address or line items.

- **Security.** Security defines what particular signature or encryption standard is to be used for securing messages or the transport connection.
- **Endpoints and agreements.** Endpoints have to be defined as well as agreements between endpoints. A standardized representation of both is preferable because in this case both can be exchanged between trading partners.
- **Packaging and transport.** While transport is an element that defines which particular transport technology to use, packaging defines how a business payload is represented during message transmission.
- **Transactions.** Messages transmitted over unreliable networks are also unreliable. A specific effort has to be made in order to make the transmission reliable and exactly-once. Transactions are a general mechanism for this so that every standard does not have to come up with its own way.
- **Adapter.** Adapters provide the connectivity to back-end application systems and are an important element to provide the necessary abstractions that make the invocation of back-end application systems possible.

20.1.4 Domain-Specific and Domain-Neutral Standards

Not all standards arae actually application domain specific in the sense that they specify concepts from application domains like the health care industry, high tech industry or food industry. Some are independent of a particular application domain, i.e., domain neutral. Therefore, a distinction is made between domain-specific and domain-neutral standards.

Domain-Specific Standards

Domain-specific standards contain the specification of concepts of a particular application domain like healthcare or banking. Applying these standards in another application domain would not make sense since this would result in a concept mismatch. The domain specificity is expressed in a few aspects:

- **Payload definition.** The definition of payloads defines the structure of the data contained in messages. Addresses, unique identifiers, product descriptions or engineering data definitions are some examples. These definitions carry the semantics of the particular application domain.
- **Vocabulary.** While all payload definitions define the structure of the data contained in messages, only a few define the permissible values that can be used for particular fields. For example, the value of the data type city should be restricted to a valid city name, i.e., a name of a city that really exists, or if a data type contains a measure, then all possible measures need to be defined that can be used as a value for this data type.
- **Validation rules.** While all elements of a message can contain valid values, it is not given that their combination is consistent. For example, not every combina-

tion of product identifier and price is correct. The price depends on the particular product, the quantity ordered and so on.

Domain-Neutral Standards

Domain-neutral standards are applicable in all application domains since they do not implement particular domain-specific concepts, but concepts that are in principle applicable across all application domains. These are (Sect. 20.1.3):

- Process
- Security
- Endpoint and agreements
- Packaging and transport
- Transactions
- Adapter

Of course, it might be that in some application domains, specific standards are preferred over others. For example, in the health care industry specific security requirements are implemented that could be implemented in other industries, too, but they are not.

20.1.5 And Where Does XML fit?

XML is a means to an end. XML is a metalanguage (metasyntax) that allows users to represent hierarchical data structures in XML syntax. In some payload standards XML is used to define the payload structure. Sometimes XML schema or Document Type Definition (DTDs) are also used to describe valid values of payload elements or consistency rules. Establishing an XML schema (XSD) to describe a particular message is defining a syntax for that particular message. While XML schema and DTDs have some provision for this, it is usually not enough to capture the particular constraints in a business content.

The question if XML is an appropriate means for defining payloads is not discussed here. Opinions vary widely about this specific topic, depending on the viewpoint.

20.1.6 Standards Compliance

A very interesting observation is that standards compliance is not seen as an integral part of the standards definition activity by most standard organizations. Only for some of the standards is a process defined that tests whether products implementing the standard or a particular revision of it are compliant and interoperable. While this is not the focus of this book, a selection is provided in the following:

- **ebXML message services v2.0** [ebXML]. The compliance of the ebXML message services version 2.0 is tested by the Drummond Group, Inc. [Drummond Group], a vendor-neutral consultant group. It is based on a full matrix test so that every vendor has to exchange messages with every other vendor. This ensures that all software products can interoperate.

- **EDIINT** [EDIINT]. EDIINT is a standard defined by the Internet Engineering Task Force [IETF]. The compliance test is performed by the Drummond Group, Inc. [Drummond Group]. Two separate types of interoperability are specified by EDIINT called Applicability Statement 1 (AS1) and Applicability Statement (AS2). Each is tested separately.

- **RosettaNet** [RosettaNet]. RosettaNet, in contrast to other standardization organizations, provides a set of software tools and program code that allow developers to test their software for interoperability. This is called RosettaNet Ready. Everyone who implements the RosettaNet standard can use RosettaNet Ready to test their software. However, no specific event is set up where software vendors have to participate in order to test there software directly with each other.

- **Web Services Interoperability Organization (WS-I)** [WS-I]. This organization is specifically created in order to ensure interoperability between web service implementation providers. The organization is working toward a set of specifications for interoperability tests as well as interoperability test software that will be used to test interoperability of software implementing Web services.

20.1.7 Standards Organizations

There are many so-called standards organizations and consortia that are preparing standard drafts and that are issuing "standards." These might be de facto standards as well as real standards as issued by the official international and national standards organizations. In the following only some of the organizations are listed and are briefly introduced without further classification:

- **ebXML**. The Electronic Business XML Initiative (ebXML) was announced in 1999. UN/CEFACT [UN/CEFACT] and OASIS [OASIS] established this noncommercial initiative with the goal to develop a comprehensive technical framework for using XML to exchange business data. The initiative was limited to a duration of 18 months, and its results are publicly available [ebXML]. Project teams for the following areas are established: ebXML Requirements, Business Process Methodology, Core Components, Technical Architecture, Security, Transport/Routing and Packaging, Registry and Repository, Quality Review, Proof of Concept, Trading Partner Profiles, Marketing/Awareness and Education. In May 2001 the ebXML specifications developed in the 18-month period were formally approved.

    After the first 18 months it was decided to continue the work, however, the standards were distribute to two organizations for further development. One is OASIS (see below) and the other is eBTWG (eBusiness Transition Ad-Hoc

Working Group) [eBTWG]. The eBTWG was created by the UN/CEFACT Steering Group in July 2001. The group is chartered to continue and complete the ebXML Business Process Specification Schema and the Core Components. The eBTWG has an internal structure comprised of chairs and vice chairs, an executive committee, a steering committee and a plenary. The group is transitional with the Steering Group planning to establish a single permanent organization for UN/EDIFACT and ebXML work.

OASIS is responsible for the Messaging, Registry and Repository, Collaboration Partner Profile (CPP) and Collaboration Partner Agreement (CPA) as well as security and conformance work.

- **IETF**. The Internet Engineering Task Force (IETF) [IETF] is a self-organized noncommercial group without a board of directors, without formal membership and without dues. Its focus is on the engineering and evolution of Internet technologies. The first IETF meeting took place in 1986, and since then three meetings have been held every year to coordinate the standards work. Until 1992 the IETF was an independent organization. In 1993 the Internet Society (ISOC) [ISOC] (a nonprofit organization) was founded, and the IETF proposed to work under its auspices. The IETF has a Internet Engineering Steering Group (IESG). It is responsible for managing technical activities as well as the standards process. It has an internal structure (according to areas like security, transport and the like) and voting rules for the standardization process.

    Another group inside the IETF is the Internet Architecture Board (IAB). Its goal is to do long-range planning and ensure consistency across all activities. The IAB also sponsors the Internet Research Task Force (IRTF) with long-range research tasks. The standards of the IETF are published as Request for Comments (RFCs). Not every RFC is a standard, though; it might be just a note. There is a process in place telling how to start developing a standard and how to finally publish it as one.

- **ISO**. The International Organization for Standardization (ISO) [ISO] is a worldwide federation of national standards bodies from 140 countries (ISO is not an acronym, but the name of the organization). ISO was established in 1947 as a nongovernmental organization with the goal to develop standards, thereby facilitating the exchange of goods and services. The results of ISO are published as international standards.

    ISO is a membership organization, and its members fall in three categories. A Member Body of ISO is the national body that is the most representative of its country. One body per country is admitted. It has full voting rights, represents the country and has to pay membership fees. A Corresponding Member is an organization of a country that does not have a fully developed national standards activity yet. A Subscriber is specifically made for small economies that only can pay reduced membership fees.

    The work of ISO is achieved in 2850 technical committees, subcommittees and working groups with about 30,000 participants. National standards bodies have the major responsibility for the committees and are working toward achieving consensus within the committees. A Central Secretariat provides administrative support.

ISO covers all technical fields except electrical and electronic engineering standards (covered by the International Electrotechnical Commission (IEC) [IEC]) and information technology (done by JTC 1 [JTC 1]).

Standards are developed following the principles of consensus, being industry-wide and voluntary. The standardization process has three phases. First, the technical scope of a future standard is defined. Second, countries negotiate the detailed specifications. Third, the standard is formally approved. Afterwards, periodic revisions are conducted for published standards. So far, 12,000 international standards have been published.

- **OASIS**. OASIS (Organization for the Advancement of Structured Information Standards) [OASIS] is a non-profit consortium. Its goal is to drive the development, convergence and adoption of e-business standards. OASIS has 500 corporate and individual members from 100 countries. OASIS was founded in 1993 with the name SGML Open. Its name was changed in 1998 to reflect its wider scope.

  OASIS has a board of directors and its members are elected for a specific period of time. OASIS also has staff providing administrative, technical and marketing support for OASIS. OASIS has established a Technical Committee Process to govern the technical work. Several technical committees exist that work on specific standards.

  In 2002, OASIS joined several international standards organizations in a Memorandum of Understanding on Electronic Business. The standards organizations are the International Electrotechnical Commission (IEC) [IEC], the International Organisation for Standardization (ISO) [ISO], the International Telecommunication Union (ITU) [ITU] and the United Nations Economic Commission for Europe (UN/ECE) [UN/ECE]. The goal of the memorandum is to join efforts and to coordinate the various standards activities related to electronic business.

- **W3C**. The World Wide Web Consortium (W3C) [W3C] was founded in 1994 by Tim Berners-Lee. It is represented by two W3C hosts in Europe and Asia. Worldwide offices ensure the international presence. W3C's mission is to lead the technical evolution of the Web. It contributed a large number of technical specifications as Recommendations in order to achieve its mission. The principle tasks of W3C are to provide a vision of the future of the Web, to provide designs for Web technologies to implement the vision and to standardize Web technologies (standards are called "Recommendations"). W3C's guiding design principles are interoperability, evolution and decentralization.

  W3C's long-term goals are to make the Web universally accessible by anybody, to provide the semantic web to allow users to make the best use of the Web and to provide a Web of trust considering legal, commercial and social issues.

W3C is a membership organization. W3C organizes itself in various entities. The Team is a group of about sixty researchers and engineers that lead the technical activities from a management viewpoint. The Advisory Committee consists of one member representative from each member organization (like vendors, laboratories or standards bodies) and reviews proposals for new activities and proposed recommendations. It is the official link between the Team and the member organizations. The Technical Architecture Group was put in place to provide architectural guidance and to resolve architectural conflicts. The Advisory Board was founded to provide the Team with guidance related to strategy, management, legal matters, process and conflict resolution. Working groups are established for technical developments, interest groups for general work and coordination groups for ensuring communication between groups.

20.2 Process Standards

There are many process standard proposals suggested by various organizations as well as individual companies. Some are discussed here and references are provided for others.

20.2.1 BPEL4WS

The newest process definition standard proposal is Business Process Execution Language for Web Services (BPEL4WS) [BPEL4WS] brought forward by BEA [BEA], IBM [IBM] and Microsoft [Microsoft]. BPEL4WS tries to achieve two goals. First, it wants to be the process definition language for public processes that define the message exchange behavior between trading partners. Second, it also wants to be the process definition language for the private processes within trading partners to define enterprise internal behavior. For both it provides a set of modeling constructs that are available to define the processes. Besides providing the basic necessary modeling elements, it also provides advanced concepts like compensation and correlation.

BPEL4WS is applicable only in the context of Web services since it is layered on top of WSDL [WSDL]. For example, it uses the concept of WSDL operations. BPEL4WS supersedes XLANG [XLANG] and WSFL [WSFL], which were proposed earlier by Microsoft and IBM, respectively.

20.2.2 DAML-S

The DARPA Agent Markup Language (DAML) [DAML] effort is put in place in order to provide a language for constructing formal ontologies. It extends the Resource Description Framework (RDF) [RDF]. The US effort joined forces with the corresponding European effort in a joint US/EU committee and proposed

DAML+OIL [DAML+OIL] as the joint language. DAML is sponsored by the DARPA Information Exploitation Office [DARPA IXO].

The DARPA Agent Markup Language for Services (DAML-S) [DAML-S] is a specialized ontology for defining composite web services. It is very feature rich including concepts for resources, actors or location in addition to the basic process modeling constructs.

20.2.3 ebXML BPSS

ebXML's Business Process Specification Schema (ebXML BPSS) [ebXML BPSS] is a process definition language defined by ebXML as part of the set of ebXML standards [ebXML]. The goal of BPSS is to provide a language for defining collaborations between trading partners. In order to define these, it provides a set of concepts like business transactions, business collaborations, business signals, choreography and patterns. Business documents that are sent back and forth between trading partners are not defined within processes themselves. They are defined outside through Core Components [ebXML Core Components] and referred to by the processes. BPSS is therefore a language that implements public processes of trading partners. BPSS is layered on top of the ebXML Message Service Specification [ebXML MSS] in order to transmit messages reliably between trading partners.

BPSS recognizes the fact that collaborations between trading partners might be binary collaborations (i.e., between two trading partners) and multiparty collaborations (i.e., between more than two trading partners). Multiparty collaborations are composed of binary collaborations. The processes defined in BPSS are represented in XML Schema [XML Schema].

20.2.4 RosettaNet

RosettaNet [RosettaNet] was founded in 1998 as a nonprofit consortium to develop standards for the IT supply chain industry. RosettaNet has published several versions of its standards and recently announced the merger with the Uniform Code Council, Inc. (UCC) [UCC].

RosettaNet in contrast to the other process standards, does not define a language for defining processes, but defines domain-specific processes themselves. The domain chosen is the IT supply chain industry. The processes are called Partner Interface Processes (PIPs) and are categorized as public processes between partners (trading partners). PIPs are represented as UML diagrams and specify the message exchange sequence on a business level. An example is the exchange of a create purchase order message and a purchase order acknowledgment message. PIPs are either one-way message exchanges or request/reply message exchanges. Every PIP follows one of the two patterns. Error handling is provided by a special PIP called 0A1. This special process was introduced to allow for asynchronous error message communication. An underlying message transmission infrastructure was developed that supports the exactly-once message transmission semantics. This is called the RosettaNet Implementation Framework (RNIF).

A significant number of PIPs have been defined, and this approach relieves trading partners from the need to define and agree on those themselves. Instead, the trading partners only have to name the PIP they want to implement. In addition, RosettaNet defines payloads (as discussed below) that are used in the PIPs.

20.2.5 Other Process Standards

Other standards and proposals for process definitions are BPML [BPML], WSCL [WSCL], WSCI [WSCI], and PDL [PDL]. Standards XLANG [XLANG] and WSFL [WSFL] are superseded by BPEL4WS. However, a version of XLANG is implemented in Microsoft's BizTalk Server as part of the Orchestration Engine. The site for ebPML [ebPML] lists many of the process standards and also provides comparisons and analysis of them to some extent.

20.2.6 Future Process Standard?

In January 2003 the W3C initiated the Web Services Choreography Working Group. The charter of the group is "to create the definition of a choreography language(s) for describing a choreography, as well as the rules for composition of, and interaction among, such choreographed Web services." Before the first official meeting of this group there were several discussion threads on the public mailing list that showed that the members of the working group are going to be very engaged. Only time will tell if this group is going to be successful in establishing a web service choreography standard.

20.3 Payload and Vocabulary Standards

Presumably every industry has one or several standards defined in order to support the definition of payloads for message exchanges. Robin Cover [Robin Cover] lists an impressive number of these. And this site clearly indicates that it is impossible to cover even a small percentage in the following. Still, some payload standards are briefly discussed.

20.3.1 ACORD

ACORD [ACORD] is a nonprofit organization with the goal to facilitate the development of standards in the insurance industry and related financial industry. ACORD has been operating since 1970. ACORD's vision is to have one global standard for the insurance industry. The areas that are supported are Life & Annuity, Property & Casualty, and Reinsurance.

Over the years the standards supported by ACORD underwent evolution. Several different standards are available. A forms standard provides standard forms that meet the required regulations so that insurance companies do not have to print their own forms.

Payload standards are available for message exchange and an XML-based version is provided, too. In addition to the structural definition, type code lists are specified that provide the list of permissible values for many of the elements. An example is address type, whereby the codes stand for home address, business address, residence address, vacation address and so on.

20.3.2 EDI

Electronic Data Interchange (EDI) is standardized in two major standards, ANSI [ANSI] ASC X12 [ASC] and UN/EDIFACT [EWG]. ASC X12 is the organization that defines EDI within the USA as a national standard; it came into existence in 1978.

UN/CEFACT (United Nations Centre for Trade Facilitation and Electronic Business) [UN/CEFACT] is the international standards organization that defines the international EDI standard called UN/EDIFACT (United Nations Directories for Electronic Data Interchange for Administration, Commerce and Transport) [UN/EDIFACT] through its subgroup UN/EDIFACT Working Group (EWG) [EWG]. This group was established in 1988.

DISA (Data Interchange Standards Association) [DISA] is the organization that distributes the official X12 standard versions as defined by Accredited Standards Committee (ASC) [ASC]. Anybody who is interested in receiving the standard can do this through DISA.

In the X12 standard, documents are called transaction sets. A transaction set has a number (e.g., 813 for Electronic Filing of Tax Return Data) and has a specific version (e.g., 4050, the latest version). Several hundreds of transaction sets are defined across multiple industries like transportation, supply chain, retail or automotive industry.

Transaction sets are represented in a line-based structured format (non-XML) with delimiters. Transaction sets have an internal structure comprised of segments and elements. A segment is a named line of data. PID, for example, stands for product/item description. A segment ends with a segment terminator. An element is an item within a line. Elements are the most detailed items and are separated by the delimiters. Each trading partner involved can define the delimiters it expects.

A transmission unit (i.e., message) in EDI has a higher level structure that contains transaction sets. Each transaction set is enclosed in a transaction set header and a transaction set trailer. The transaction sets that are addressed to the same group or department within a trading partner are further grouped into functional groups. Each functional group has a header and a trailer, too. All functional groups that are sent to a trading partner are further grouped into an interchange. An interchange has an interchange control header as well as an interchange control trailer. At the minimum, each EDI message has one interchange, one functional group and one transaction set. Messages are acknowledged by so-called functional acknowledgments. A functional acknowledgment is itself a transaction set numbered 997.

VANs (value added networks) are networks specifically designed and operated for EDI. Each trading partner has a mailbox within a VAN. An EDI message sent to a trading partner is put into its mailbox. The trading partner can receive messages from there. Several VANs exist, and not every trading partner has a mailbox on every VAN. In order to support the communication between any pair of trading partners, the VANs are connected with each other so that any trading partner on any VAN can reach any other trading partner on any other VAN.

20.3.3 EPISTLE

The European Process Industries STEP Technical Liaison Executive (EPISTLE) [EPISTLE] started informally in 1993 and was formalized in 1994. EPISTLE is a liaison to ISO TC184/SC4 ("Industrial Data"). The focus of EPISTLE is the development of specifications that manage data in te context of process plants. EPISTLE specifications are standardized as ISO standards.

EPISTLE's most important standards are a core model, a reference data library and templates (all can be found on EPISTLE's Web page). The core model is an upper ontology [SUO] of the terms needed to later on describe process plants and their parts. It contains terms like class, UPC_representation_of_time, activity, axis_of_coordinate_system or class_of_composite_material. The core model is standardized as ISO 15926-2.

The reference data library provides process plant specific definitions as subclasses of the core model. Contents described are valves, means of transport, or instrumentation of various types. The reference data library makes the core model process plant-specific is therefore the equivalent to a domain-specific ontology.

The core model in conjunction with the reference data library allow users to model the same fact in several ways. An implication of this is that if two or more plants have to interoperate, a mismatch might exist in the representation of the same fact. In order to minimizing this situation, the concept of templates is introduced.

A template is a way to specify a unique way of representing a fact. For example, in order to define the protection of a physical object, a template is built whereby the template relates all core model elements necessary to define protecting a physical object. The only two parameters the template leaves unspecified are the object that needs protection and the protective device itself. In order to state the fact that a motor is protected by a cover the template has to be instantiated with motor and cover. Anybody having the need to specify the protection of a physical object can use the same template, leading to the same use of the core model for this case.

20.3.4 HL7

Health Level 7 (HL7) [HL7] is a national standards organization accredited by ANSI. It's focus, as the name says, is the health care industry. More specifically, the definition of messages used to connect health care entities across the entire health care organization.

Over time, HL7 developed several versions of the HL7 standard, with Version 3 being the latest in development. Version 3 is based on a reference information model (RIM) that relates all health care concepts with each other, independently of the message structure and message definitions. It provides a common data model across the health care domain from which the message structures are constructed. The six main concepts modeled are Act, Entity, Role, Participation, ActRelationship and RoleLink. Other concepts like Patient or Employee are subclasses or subordinate concepts of the six basic concepts.

In addition to the RIM, a vocabulary is developed that lists the valid values the concepts in the reference information model can have. Since messages are constructed based on the reference information model, the vocabularies also apply to the messages, making message exchange more reliable. In addition, HL7 allows for the use of existing vocabularies that are not necessarily developed by HL7.

Another concept of Version 3 are templates. Templates are constraints against Version 3 definitions. For example, the value of a field can be constrained to a particular range. This allows templates to be used for message validation.

The last ANSI approved version of HL7 is version 2.4, and it was approved in October 2000. In addition to the message standards, HL7 developed a document architecture called Clinical Document Architecture Framework (CDA). This ANSI-approved standard defines how documents are structured as well as their properties, like protection. The CDA relies on the RIM to describe the schema of documents. Documents can contain medical data and can be sent between different health care organizations.

20.3.5 OAGI

The Open Applications Group, Inc. (OAGI) [OAGI] was founded in 1995 as a nonprofit organization. The goal of OAGI is to create payload standards in order to enable and support the integration of back-end application systems. In the meanwhile, the focus includes interenterprise message exchange in addition to intraenterprise integration.

The OAGI released many versions of its payloads standards over time. The latest version of the Open Applications Group Integration Specification (OAGIS) [OAGIS] is version 8.0. While initially not specified using an XML schema language, OAGI has now embarked on this approach. The payloads are called business object documents (BOD) and more than 200 are specified.

A BOD has a control area and a business data area. The control area holds metadata about the actual BOD instance, like date and time, sender as well as business service request. These three elements together form a unique global identifier. The business data area contains the business data.

It is noteworthy that OAGIS has a well-defined methodology supported by the BOD structure to extend the definitions of the content of a BOD so that they can be modified to satisfy specific needs of particular trading partners. Since OAGI only defines payload data the remaining elements necessary to transmit these payloads have to be from other standards. For example, it has been demonstrated that ebXML can be used to transport BOD instances (OAGI Extension 2001). In addition, OAGIS defines business processes scenarios between endpoints. However, these are informally defined and for illustration purposes only.

20.3.6 RosettaNet

RosettaNet defines not only Partner Interface Processes, but also specific business document types for particular business data, like purchase orders or invoices. The definitions are accomplished using XML. Two distinct business documents are defined for communication management. One is the Receipt Acknowledgment to acknowledge messages and one is the Exception to indicate error situations.

In addition, RosettaNet provides several dictionaries that define the valid content of the business data in the business documents. These are the Business Dictionary defining business data and entities, IT Dictionary defining IT products and properties and the EC Dictionary defining components and their properties. Validation rules are also specified that make use of the dictionary data in order to establish the correctness of a transmitted RosettaNet document. RosettaNet supports the D&B D-U-N-S Number, GTIN as well as UN/SPSC codification standards.

In addition to the business documents, RosettaNet defines the message structure for sending business documents to trading partners. This structure contains three headers called Preamble, Delivery and Service Header and is followed by the payload and any number of attachments. The payload is the area where a business document is located.

20.3.7 SWIFT

The Society for Worldwide Interbank Financial Telecommunication (SWIFT) [SWIFT] was founded about 30 years ago with the goal to provide message exchange between financial institutions. It is a company owned by enterprises in the financial industry. SWIFT provides not only business document adventitiousness for the financial world, but also provides the necessary network and software infrastructure for participants to exchange messages.

SWIFT has developed a methodology for developing standards called SWIFT-Standards Modeling and it has three layers. The business layer describes the particular business independent of any technology support. The logic layer describes the necessary business data exchange and the physical layer provides the particular syntax necessary.

Since SWIFT started so long ago, initially a non-XML syntax was used and deployed for quite some time in order to transfer financial business data. Recently, SWIFT started acknowledging XML as an alternative syntax by proposing swiftml as XML-based definition of financial business data.

The business data element definitions are stored in the SWIFT Standards Repository. From there the business documents can be generated in different syntaxes while sharing a common business model, ensuring interoperability. Therefore, SWIFT did not have to develop the business documents using XML from the very beginning, but devised a generation scheme from the existing repository. This common business model is defined using UML as design methodology. UML class diagrams are the means for representation.

Fix Protocol, Ltd. (FPL), developed a public domain protocol called Financial Information Exchange Protocol (FIX) [FIX] targeted for the real-time exchange of securities transactions. SWIFT and FPL agreed to join efforts and to converge their protocols. This is done in the ISO Working Group 10, and the result of this convergence effort is the Securities Standard ISO 15022 XML. Once this is accomplished the standard will allow seamless message flow across the pretrade/trade and post-trade domain.

Several more specific XML standards have been developed in the financial industry. As in the case of FIX, the financial industry attempts to unify the standards to prevent a costly divergence. In [Robin Cover] these standards are introduced, starting from the swiftml description.

20.3.8 Other Payload Standards

It is impossible to even remotely list a significant number of payload standards. In order to get an impression of the high number of proposed and released standards the reader is referred to [Robin Cover].

20.3.9 Vocabulary Standards

Vocabulary standards are standards defining a set of values for a given concept. Examples are names of countries or currencies. When defining a payload standard it can refer to a vocabulary standard to specify the valid values some of its elements can have.

UCC

The Uniform Code Council (UCC) [UCC] provides a number of keys as follows:

- **GIAI (Global Individual Asset Identifier).** This identifier is used for identifying assets of an enterprise. The GIAI has a structured format consisting of three parts. The first part is the fixed number 8004. This fixed part indicates that the identifier is a GIAI. The second part contains a company identifier. This identifier uniquely identifies the company to which the asset belongs. The third part contains the individual asset reference. This number is created by the enterprise and is meaningful within it. This identifier can be used as a reference to more data describing the asset.
- **GLN (Global Location Number).** This identifier identifies functional entities like departments, physical entities like rooms or legal entities like trading partners. It contains three parts. The first part is a company identifier. The second part is a location reference. This identifies a location within the company. The third part is a check digit computed to ensure the integrity of the GLN.
- **GRAI (Global Returnable Asset Identifier).** This identifier is used to identify returnable assets like railroad cars or kegs. It consists of four parts. The first part is a fixed number 8003 that identifies the identifier as GRAI. The second part is a company identifier of the company that owns the asset. The third part is the asset type, and the fourth part is an optional serial number of the asset.
- **GSRN (Global Service Relation Number).** The GSRN is an identifier that relates a recipient of a service to a service, for example, a student to a library. This identifier does not contain the student identifier so that the student cannot be identified based on the GSRN alone. The GSRN is introduced to ensure privacy by means of an indirection.
- **GTIN (Global Trade Item Number).** The GTIN identifier is used to uniquely identify products and services a company sells. The GTIN identifier comes in a variety of data structures, from 8 digits to 14 digits. No matter what the specific form looks like, it always contains the company identifier and the unique reference number within the company. This uniquely identifies a product or a service of a particular company.
- **SSCC (Serialized Shipping Container Code).** The SSCC identifier identifies logistics units, which are items like containers or pallets. The SSCC consists of the company identifier followed by a unique reference number that the company assigns. This ensures uniqueness.

UN/LOCODE

UN/LOCODE (code for trade and transport locations) [UN/LOCODE] is a database of location codes that can be used to define locations like countries and cities. The newest issue of the list is called 2002-2. Besides the name of the location, additional attributes are listed like a change indicator from previous versions, a LOCODE column with the unique identifier or geographical coordinates.

UN/SPSC

UN/SPSC (United Nations/Standard Products and Services Code) [UN/SPSC] is a classification used to classify products and services (product classification scheme). It is based on a hierarchical numbering scheme five levels deep. The highest level is called segment. The next is a family, then class and finally, a commodity.

D&B D-U-N-S Number

The D&B D-U-N-S Number (Data Universal Numbering System) is issued by a company called D&B [DNB]. Each corporation in the world can request a D&B D-U-N-S Number in order to uniquely identify itself. Many standards require these numbers as the means to uniquely identify the trading partner.

20.4 Security Standards

Many security standards exist. Recently, many have been proposed around XML as the fundamental syntax used for describing messages. Some of the existing standards and some of the new proposals are discussed in the following.

20.4.1 SAML

The Security Assertion Markup Language (SAML) [SAML] focuses on an interchange format for exchanging authentication and authorization information. It is the deliverable of the XML-Based Security Services Technical Committee (SSTC) of OASIS. Version 1.0 was delivered on May 31st, 2002, as a set of specifications including assertions and protocol, bindings and profile, security and privacy considerations and conformance program specification.

SAML is a XML dialect for exchanging security information, more specifically, assertions about subjects. A subject is an entity, like a user or a computer, that has an identity in a security domain. Assertions are statements about subject authentication, attributes of subjects or authorization decisions that have been made. In addition, a protocol is defined that defines how requests and responses are structured in order to obtain assertions from SAML authorities that are able and trusted to make assertion statements.

An example of using SAML is SSO (single sign-on). Single sign-on support means that users authenticate themselves only once and any subsequent authentication required can obtain an assertion that the users are already authenticated. Consequently, no additional authentication has to take place.

It is important to note that a separate specification is developed that defines a conformance process based on use cases in order to achieve interoperability.

20.4.2 SSL

The Secure Socket Layer protocol (SSL) [SSL] was originally developed by Netscape Communications [Netscape]. The IETF standardized the Transport Layer Security (TLS) protocol based on SSL [TLS]. SSL is a layer on top of TCP/IP [TCP/IP]. It serves two purposes. First, it allows a client to authenticate itself to a server, and vice versa. Second, it allows both client and server to establish an encrypted connection between each other.

SSL consists of two protocols. The SSL handshake protocol is used to establish a connection between a server and a client. The SSL record protocol is used to format and to transmit data between client and server. SSL involves trusted certificates issued by trusted certificate authorities (CA). In addition, several different ciphers can be used in order to achieve the encryption and decryption necessary.

20.4.3 XACML

XML Access Control Markup Language [XACML] is a deliverable of OASIS' XACML Technical Committee. The committee was founded in 2001 in order to deliver XACML, an XML schema for representing authorization and entitlement policies. XACML builds a comprehensive set of concepts to define authorization. Evaluation rules are defined that specify when a request for authorization is to be granted or denied.

In addition, a protocol is defined to transmit requests for authorization as well as results of authorization decisions based on policies.

20.4.4 XKMS

XML Key Management Specification [XKMS] is a W3C working draft published on March 18th, 2002. It provides a protocol for distributing and registering public keys. It consists of two parts, the XML Key Information Service Specification (X-KISS) and the XML Registration Service Specification (X-KRSS).

X-KISS defines a protocol to retrieve public keys so that anybody requiring public key information can obtain it without managing the public key values itself. This means that the public key management task can be outsourced. X-KRSS defines a protocol to register public keys so that they can be accessed later on by the X-KISS protocols. Methods for revoking public keys are available, too.

20.4.5 XML Encryption

XML Encryption [XML Encryption] is a W3C-proposed recommendation issued on October 3rd, 2002, that defines how to encrypt a whole XML instance or only parts of it. This is in contrast to, for example SSL, that always encrypts the complete message ,since through SSL the complete transport channel is encrypted.

20.4.6 XML Signature

XML Signature [XML Signature] is a W3C recommendation issued on February 12th, 2002, that defines the syntax for signatures in context of XML documents. It includes the algorithms for computing and verifying the signatures. According to the recommendation it is possible to sign only a portion of the XML instance (a subtree) so that a subset rather than the whole instance has to be signed. The signature itself can be part of the XML instance, the XML instance can be part of the signature or the signature is separate from the XML instance.

20.5 Endpoint and Agreement Standards

Endpoints have to be defined and described. Based on these, agreements have to be put in place to enable integration. Some of the standards for these areas are discussed next.

20.5.1 CPP

Collaboration Partner Profile (CPP) [ebXML CPP] is part of the ebXML's set of standards. A CPP is a description of a trading partner's profile or capabilities. The major elements in a CPP are data about the trading partner (called PartyInfo) and the message packaging requirements called Packaging. The packaging specification defines how message headers and payloads are configured. It also includes security specifications and packaging requirements like MIME.

PartyInfo is a complex structure defining details in several parts about the trading partner the CPP describes. The most important part are:

- **PartyId**. This element defines the unique identifier of the party described. An example is the D&B D-U-N-S Number.
- **PartyRef**. This is a link to some other data about a party, like a Web page or a UDDI entry.
- **CollaborationRole**. This element defines in which business process specifications the party can participate and what role it plays in these.
- **Certificate**. This element describes the security certificates used for encryption and signatures.
- **Delivery Channel**. This element enumerates all transports a party can use to transmit messages. Furthermore, it enumerates document exchanges that define which encryption to use if nonrepudiation has to be ensured or how the messages are encoded.

A CPP defines all properties necessary to support message exchanges between trading partners. In that sense, it describes the capabilities of a trading partner. If a message is really exchanged based on these capabilities, is described in the collaboration partner agreement that is discussed next.

20.5.2 CPA

Collaboration Partner Agreement (CPA) [ebXML CPA] is also part of ebXML's set of standards. Its purpose is to be able to define the agreements between trading partners that are necessary to enable the exchange of messages. This includes not only transport prescriptions but also the selection of the appropriate public processes as well as security measures from the trading partner's CPPs to be applied.

The CPA acts as an authorization to send or to receive a message. If a message arrives and there is no corresponding agreement, then it will be rejected. The same applies if a message is to be sent out without an agreement. In this case, too, the message cannot be sent.

The elements of a CPA are:

- **Status**. This element describes the life cycle state of an agreement like proposed or agreed.
- **Start** and **end**. These are two dates, one for the date when the agreement becomes effective and one for the end date when the agreement becomes ineffective. In addition, what must happen to message exchanges under way when the agreement expires can be specified.
- **ConversationConstraints**. The number of message exchanges that can happen under one agreement can be limited. The same is true for the number of concurrent ongoing message exchanges.
- **PartyInfo**. This element refers to a party. This element is the same as the one used in the CPP.
- **Signature**. This element contains a signature that signs the CPA. When the signature fails the agreement is considered invalid.

With these elements a B2B integration technology can find out at run time if an incoming message should be received or an outgoing message should be sent, in the sense that the receipt or sending is in compliance with a CPA that is valid at that point in time.

20.5.3 ebXML Registry

The ebXML registry (Kotok and Webber 2002) serves as a global place for trading partners to store properties about themselves as well as to search for matching trading partners (like UDDI, see below). The ebXML registry specification provides two interfaces, one for submitting objects like DTDs, XML schemas or CPPs and one for querying these objects.

Each submitted object goes through a lifecycle of submission, approval, depreciation and removal. This means that the registry is not only a passive store but is used to manage its contents. In addition, metadata are attached to submitted objects like classifications in order to ease the management as well as the retrieval of the objects contained in the registry.

Several interfaces are defined for retrieving objects that allow users to "drilldown" on the contents. It is possible to query the list of all top-level classifications. For each of these, the next layers can be queried. Finally, the objects classified under this classification can be retrieved. Filtered queries are possible, too, in order to perform a more focused access.

Based on the submission and query capabilities, trading partners can submit information about themselves (advertisement) and can search for other trading partners (discovery) they might want to do business with.

20.5.4 EDI 838

EDI's transaction set 838 (Trading Partner Profile) was introduced in order to allow trading partners to send each other messages about updates of their profile information. This transaction set can contain segments containing address information, employer identification numbers or phone numbers. This transaction set enables a trading partner to send changes about its own data to its trading partners, making a manual update of this information unnecessary.

20.5.5 UDDI

Universal Description, Discovery and Integration (UDDI) [UDDI] is a standard defining a registry structure for storing and discovering services provided by organizations. The organization behind UDDI is called UDDI.org, or UDDI for short. It was founded in 2000 and contains several hundred software vendors.

The UDDI standard (the latest version is 3.0) defines a structure with which organizations can describe their offered services. These descriptions are stored in so-called UDDI Business Registries that can be searched. The underlying idea is that organizations publish their offered services in searchable registries. An organization in need of a service can search the registries and find potential service providers or even business partners. Some public business registries exist that are accessible by any organization. In addition, private business registries exist within organizations' boundaries in order to register organization internal services.

An organization can register itself by means of specifying a businessEntity. A businessEntity contains the name, contacts, description, identifiers and categories of the organization. The businessEntity forms the top-level construct. In addition, it contains a set of businessServices. A businessService is a set of services and business processes that belong together from a domain semantics. For example, purchasing services would be described in a businessService.

Within a businessService so-called bindingTemplates are stored. A bindingTemplate contains the network address used to invoke the service. A bindingTemplate, however, does not contain enough information to understand the behavior of the service, i.e., possible responses upon invocation. Each bindingTemplate can therefore point to a tModel that contains the specific definition of the service.

Access to registries is defined as a set of services itself, in this case Web services based on SOAP. A publication interface defines how to enter data into a registry whereas an inquiry interface defines how to extract data from a registry. Early in 2001 RosettaNet announced the support of UDDI by registering its process standards (PIPs) in UDDI so that trading partners can specify their support of PIPs in UDDI.

20.6 Packaging and Transport Standards

Transport technologies are used to transport messages between network nodes. Messages have to be packaged according to the transport protocols, and several packaging standards exist. Standards in both areas are discussed next.

20.6.1 ebXML MSS

ebXML's Messaging Service Specification (MSS) [ebXML MSS] is defined to support secure transfer, routing and packaging of MIME-packaged messages. Early in 2001 RosettaNet announced the support of ebXML MSS in its RNIF development so that RosettaNet partners can choose to use ebXML standards for sending and receiving messages. ebXML in turn decided to use SOAP (see below) as underlying infrastructure for message transmission.

ebXML MSS provides services to process the following elements that make up an ebXML message. An ebXML message consists of the following nested elements (from outside to inside):

- **MIME envelope**. A MIME envelope is used to structure all the different parts of an ebXML message. The first MIME part contains a SOAP header and a SOAP body. The other MIME parts contain payloads.
- **SOAP header**. The SOAP header contains the ebXML MessageHeader with addressing-specific data like sender and recipient address, the identifier of the CPA that governs this transmission, the conversation identifier that identifies the conversation in which the messages are transmitted, unique message identifier or a sequence number. The next element contained in the SOAP header is the ebXML TraceHeaderList. In case the message should be sent along multiple intermediaries, the list is given in this part. Another part is the ebXML Signature, which signs the message allowing users to check whether the message was modified since it left the sender's infrastructure.

- **SOAP body**. The SOAP body contains the ebXML manifest. The manifest is like a directory of payloads contained in the message.
- **Payload**. An ebXML message can contain many payloads. Each payload is a separate MIME part. The contents of the payload are not predefined by ebXML but have to be chosen by the sender and receiver.

An ebXML message can be sent over several different transports, like FTP or SMTP. Each transport mechanism has its own particular headers and trailers in order to achieve the transmission. Once an ebXML message has to be sent it will be enveloped, with the transport specific headers and trailers making up the outermost envelope of the unit of transmission.

20.6.2 EDIINT

The IETF introduced EDI over the Internet (EDIINT) [EDIINT] in order to enable the sending of EDI documents in their native syntax over the Internet. This effort allows trading partners to send EDI messages to each other independent of VANs. The proposed value is that a trading partner can save the cost it incurs by using VANs.

At the same time, the processing model changed. VANs provide a mailbox for every trading partner. Messages sent to a trading partner are stored in its mailbox, and the trading partner can pick it up from there. VANs enforce authentication and authorization before a trading partner can send or receive messages. In addition, VANs provide tracing so that a trading partner can find out what happened to a message.

The Internet does not provide any of this functionality. In contrast to a VAN, the Internet does not provide an intermediate storage functionality. Trading partners have to communicate in a true peer-to-peer model, where trading partners send message to each other directly without any intermediary. This requires that security, tracking and auditing have to be done by the trading partners themselves.

A good source for understanding the requirements is Harding et al. (2001). Harding et al. (2002) define the IETF standard for transporting EDI securely over SMTP. It builds on EDIINT and focuses on providing security and nonrepudiation. Moberg et al. (2002) describe a draft of how to transport EDI messages over HTTP.

20.6.3 FTP

The File Transfer Protocol (FTP) [FTP] is a user-level transport protocol that allows the transfer of files between computers independently whether they are inside or outside an organization's firewall. FTP has been standardized by the IETF over time through a series of RFCs.

20.6.4 HTTP

The Hypertext Transfer Protocol (HTTP) [HTTP] is a stateless protocol to exchange messages between different computers. Originally, it was targeted toward use in collaborative hypermedia systems. However, over time its use extended beyond hypermedia information, and today it most likely transports any data that can be transported, such as business data, streams or photographs. HTTP was standardized in form of several RFCs of the IETF, and the latest version is HTTP/1.1.

20.6.5 MIME

The Multipurpose Internet Mail Extensions (MIME) standard defines the structure of e-mail messages. Originally, only text messages of limited length were addressed. Over time the need for supporting larger text as well as nontext messages like audio files arose and was taken into consideration. A series of RFCs specify the latest version of the MIME standard. These RFCs are [MIME 1], [MIME 2], [MIME 3], [MIME 4] and [MIME 5].

20.6.6 SMTP

The Simple Mail Transfer Protocol (SMTP) [SMTP] is defined to provide reliable and efficient mail transport between computers. The protocol does not assume a particular underlying transport like TCP/IP and can be bound to many different ones.

20.6.7 SOAP

SOAP (Simple Object Access Protocol) [SOAP] is a packaging standard that relies on underlying transport standards for the actual exchange of messages. SOAP is based on XML and defines a message structure. In addition, it defines encoding rules for the representation of data values. Finally, it describes how messages are bound to transport protocols, specifically HTTP.

SOAP messages are one-way transmissions that can be combined into more complex patters like a request/response pattern. A SOAP message consists of an envelope, a header and a body. The header has a series of attributes that are necessary for managing a message. The body contains the payload, i.e., the data that are transmitted through the message.

The encoding of data values is organized into the encoding of simple types like strings and compound types like array. Both, the sender as well as the receiver of a SOAP message are required to follow the encoding rules in order to achieve interoperability.

The binding to HTTP defines how a SOAP message is represented as a HTTP request. This ensures that all senders and recipient of SOAP message can follow the same message representation to achieve interoperability.

20.6.8 WSDL

The Web Service Description Language (WSDL) [WSDL] is a W3C Note published in March 2001. Its purpose is to define the call interface of a server in terms of operations with input and output data called messages. The actual network endpoints are defined as ports, and a binding takes place between each operation and a port so that it is defined which network endpoint provides which operation.

WSDL is strictly an interface definition since it does not define the implementation of the operation at all. Furthermore, WSDL only describes operations in isolation. No sequencing between operations can be defined with WSDL in order to describe any invocation constraints. Process standards would have to be used for this. While not mandatory, WSDL operations are invoked with SOAP messages at run time. WSDL and SOAP constitute what is called Web services. Alonso et al. (2003) give a detailed introduction into WSDL as well as how it is used in practical examples.

20.7 Transaction Standards

The Internet is nontransactional in the sense that a network failure does not cause the message transmission to be set back to the last consistent state. The communicating programs have to reestablish consistency themselves after a failure. In order to make message exchanges transactional, some standards are proposed. Some of these are discussed in the following.

20.7.1 BTP

OASIS' Business Transactions Technical Committee released version 1.0 of the Business Transaction Protocol (BTP) in May 2002 [BTP]. It proposes a protocol to implement long-lasting transactions across multiple enterprises. In order to achieve this, several types of transactions are introduced. The main design point is the fact that enterprises want to retain the control on their resources event though they participate in a transaction. This is in contrast to distributed transactions (Gray and Reuter 1993).

In addition, commitments take place in stages in interenterprise coordination. For example, reserving a hotel room can result in a committed hotel room, however, it is still possible to cancel it (even though it was committed). This meaning of commitment is different from a committed database transaction and has to be taken into consideration in the transaction protocol.

20.7.2 WS-Coordination and WS-Transaction

WS-Coordination [WS-C] defines a general protocol that allows users to define arbitrary coordination types between two or more entities. The goal of WS-Coordination is to provide the infrastructure for defining different distributed transaction protocols (coordination types) in order to provide transactional behavior across different enterprises across the Internet. The basic elements provided by WS-Coordination are an activation service, a registration service and coordination types containing coordination protocols.

The activation service is used to start a coordination and to create a coordination context (or coordination instance). This coordination instance is shared by all entities that participate in a particular coordination. It is passed along when applications invoke each other. It contains the address of the registration service of the coordinator that executes the particular coordination.

The registration service is used by applications to register for coordination protocols that are part of a coordination type. At run time, entities participating in a coordination register at a registration service so that it can coordinate the participation of the entity according to the protocol passed along in the coordination context.

Coordination protocols belonging to coordination types are used to participate in a particular coordination in order to coordinate the actions of entities. Each participant might play a different role, and according to its role in the coordination, it executes according to a specific coordination protocol. New coordination types and protocols can be added in order to accommodate new requirements.

WS-Transaction [WS-T] defines two coordination types, Atomic Transactions and Business Activity, using the elements WS-Coordination provides. Atomic transactions implement functionality in the sense of ACID transactions in databases (Gray and Reuter 1993). They either commit successfully or abort. Business Activities implement long-running transactions that require compensating activities in the case of business exceptions. Each side effect along the way is externalized, hence the term long-running, and hence the need for compensation.

20.8 Complete Standards

Some of the standards and standard proposals have chosen to implement all elements that are required for message exchanges, i.e., the whole "stack." Some of these complete standards are discussed in the following.

20.8.1 ebXML

The specifications of ebXML cover all aspects of a B2B protocol except the payload definitions themselves [ebXML]. In terms of message transport, security, process modeling, trading partner management and agreement, all areas are covered by the ebXML specifications. In that sense it is a complete standard. ebXML, however, does not define payload structures like purchase orders. ebXML realizes that many payload standards are available and acknowledges that another payload standard would not contribute to advancing the field. It therefore allows trading partners to use their preferred payload standard.

Kotok and Webber (2002) provide a complete overview of all aspects of ebXML with extensive references to related work relevant for ebXML.

20.8.2 RosettaNet

RosettaNet is a complete standard in the sense that it defines all aspects of message exchange that are necessary to securely and reliably transmit a message. This is achieved through the RosettaNet Implementation Framework (RNIF) in conjunction with PIPs and the definition of business documents. In contrast to ebXML, general process definition language is not provided by RosettaNet. Instead, already modeled processes are available. This greatly reduces the interoperability effort since trading partners do not have to develop and agree upon process definitions themselves.

20.8.3 SWIFT

SWIFT is a complete standard since it provides the business document definitions as well as the network functionality necessary for secure and reliable message transmission. No additional implementation work has to be done when deploying SWIFT since all aspects are covered. SWIFT also provides connectivity software to its clients so that they can connect more readily without necessarily writing their own software for exchanging SWIFT messages.

20.8.4 Web Services Architecture

The W3C issued a working draft outlining the Web Services Architecture [WSA]. While the document it is still a draft, it clearly shows the authors' intent to define a complete architecture for Web services implementation. All areas starting at the transport level up to business and service level agreements are covered. As in ebXML, the definition of business content is not part of the architecture. Instead, any definition of business data in a schema language is supported by the Web Services Architecture.

20.9 Adapter Standard J2EE Connector Architecture

In the context of back-end application adapters only one single standard is proposed and implemented. This standard is called the J2EE Connector Architecture [J2EE Connector Architecture]. It receives wide support from almost all adapter vendors. Version 1.0 was released in 2001, and currently the next version is under design and review.

The J2EE Connector Architecture standard defines an application programming interface to connect a J2EE environment with back-end application systems (called enterprise information systems (EIS) in the standard terminology). Application servers are hosting J2EE environments. Any numbers of adapters conforming to the J2EE Connector Architecture can be added to an application server without requiring any programming. This achieves the "pluggability" of adapters based on the standardized interface defined by the J2EE Connector Architecture. Once adapters are made available to the application server, they are available for invocation from the J2EE environment (as are the EIS connected by the adapters).

The J2EE Connector Architecture standard defines four interfaces, three of which are called System Contracts, and the fourth is called Common Client Interface (CCI). System contracts are defined between the adapter and the application server. The CCI is the interface a client of an adapter (located in the J2EE environment) uses to exchange data with the back-end application system. The interface between the adapter and the back-end application systems is not defined (of course), since this interface is already defined and given by the back-end application system. An adapter has to adjust to this situation, which is precisely one of the fundamental goals of an adapter. The other four interfaces provide an abstraction across all back-end application systems in terms of the interfaces (not in terms of the data passed back and forth). That abstraction is the value and supports the pluggability.

The system contracts are:

- **Connection management**. This contract provides connection pooling to the back-end application system. Consequently, the client accessing a back-end application system does not have to deal with managing connections and connection pooling itself.
- **Transaction management**. Through this contract transactions between the application server and one or more back-end applications systems are managed. Depending on the requirements, back-end application system-local as well as distributed transactions across various back-end applications can be managed.
- **Security**. The security contract secured the access to a back-end application system. This is an important aspect because the availability of an adapter should not allow any client to access any of the connected back-end application systems.

The Common Client Interface (CCI) is a set of operations that allow a client to exchange data with back-end application systems through the adapter. The main data structure are interaction specifications and records that contain the actual data values at run time. Since this API is standardized, all back-end application systems look alike in context of adapters from the viewpoint of the interfaces. However, the data structures and contents passed back and forth are not standardized, and the client has to deal with these as defined and provided by the adapter. Two books are describing the standard and adapters in more detail: Apte (2002) and Sharma et al. (2001).

20.10 Application of Standards in B2B Integration Architecture

In the following it is briefly shown where the various standards apply to the overall B2B integration technology architecture. The discussion is based on the various layers that were introduced earlier.

- **Process**. Process definition languages like BPEL4WS or predefined processes like in RosettaNet have to be mapped to interface processes (public processes). These define the enterprise-external message exchange behavior. The process languages are developed for the purpose of public process definition. Once a public process is defined in a process definition standard, it has to be mapped to a definition in the B2B integration technology in order to be executed.
- **Payload**. Payload definitions play a role for the wire event definitions as well as clear text event definitions. These represent the business data as received according to the particular standard. Business document definitions like those of OAGIS can be used as a starting point for the definition of business events, too.
- **Vocabulary**. The vocabulary is relevant in two places. One is the validation of incoming or outgoing clear text events. Vocabularies that are defined by standards organizations are used to validate the business document values so that only applicable values are used.

  The other places vocabularies are important are domain value maps that have to map the vocabulary from the clear text events (i.e., the particular B2B standard) to the business event vocabulary and back. The domain value maps must be loaded with the particular vocabulary of the B2B protocol.
- **Validation rules**. When a B2B standard defines validation rules, then they have to be implemented as event validation. This ensures that only those events successfully enter or exit the B2B integration technology that are consistent with the validation rules.
- **Security**. Security standards apply in two areas. One area is user authentication and authorization. In this area users have to provide credentials like passwords to gain system access. This applies for modeling tools as well as other user interface tools like administration.

  The other area is the message security area. In this area the standard security functions and protocols have to be implemented to secure messages according to the B2B standard requirements for message transmission. Message security standards are implemented in the connectivity layer.

- **Endpoints and agreements**. Standards for endpoint and agreement definition are applicable in the trading partner management components, where agreements and endpoints are defined. Standards define a particular way to represent the endpoint and agreement definitions. These have to be mapped to the one provided by the B2B integration technology.
- **Packaging and transport**. Packaging and transport standards have to be implemented in order to support the message transport. These standards are implemented in the transport component for use by any other higher level B2B standard.
- **Transactions**. Transactions like packaging and transport are relevant in the context of message transmission to ensure exactly-once and reliable message transmission. Standards in this space have to be implemented by the transport component, too.
- **Adapter**. Finally, the adapter standard standardizes the interface between adapters and the B2B integration technology. In order for a B2B integration technology to connect to adapters implemented according to this standard, it has to implement the standard itself. Once this is the case, adapters can be added to the B2B integration technology as required or available.

As can be seen from the brief discussion of the different layers, all play an important role and are essential when implementing interoperability in all areas of a B2B integration technology.

21 Products

One indication that B2B integration is not yet founded on a commonly agreed-upon set of integration concepts is that no product consolidation has yet taken place. Journals like eAI Journal [eAI Journal] or eBizQ [ebizQ] continuously report on an astonishing array of established and new integration products from different vendors. In addition, mergers and acquisitions of integration product vendors change the product landscape continuously.

Characteristic for a maturing domain is that the number of products first increases and then decreases to at most a handful, which own the lion's share of the market. B2B integration is not yet at this maturity level, and so many products are offered today. However, the consolidation of integration products can be expected to happen over time.

It is difficult to cover most products in this space even briefly because of their high number. In addition, it is difficult to obtain enough technical information about the products to provide a meaningful description. Only a few vendors make their technical information available on their web pages. Therefore, only a few products are characterized that are highly visible in the marketplace. Their selection is based on the availability of technical resources in the form of product manuals and accompanying technical white papers. Their descriptions are intentionally brief and mainly focus on the core concepts, since any elaborate discussion will be immediately outdated with the next version of the product.

The fact that a product was selected or not does not make any statement about its quality or any other characteristic, like its current or potential market share. In addition, no quality assessment is implied, since the evaluation of an integration product must always take place in the context of a specific integration problem at hand that needs a technical solution. Evaluating an integration product outside a particular deployment context would leave out many important aspects relevant in the context of the particular problem.

The descriptions of the individual products only address the concepts that the respective product implements. Implementation technology details, like particular programming languages, database management systems or operating systems, are not addressed at all since this information is readily available from vendor Web sites and collaterals.

21.1 BEA's WebLogic Integration

BEA's WebLogic Integration 7.0 [WebLogic Integration] is a workflow-based integration environment. The core of the architecture is a workflow system that allows to define processes (also called workflows). Three areas of functionality, namely B2B integration functionality, application integration functionality and data integration functionality, are added to the workflow system through a plug-in framework that allows the workflow system to communicate with the implementation of these three areas by means of workflow steps. The different components are discussed in turn in the following.

The workflow management system provides user interface tools for the design, monitoring, and run-time interactions (like user interactions) with the system. In addition, application programming interfaces are provided for configuration clients, design clients, run-time management clients and monitoring clients. These APIs support the access outside the provided user interface tools. The workflow system supports the definition of flowcharts (also called process flow) that use predefined modeling elements like start, decision or join in order to define sequences of workflow steps. Defined flowcharts are stored as templates ready for instantiation at run time. Instantiation of workflow instances can happen through several means: explicit call by an application or another workflow, manual invocation triggered by the arrival of a XML instance message or started automatically through a timer. At run time, data are represented as XML instances. Interaction with workflow-external components during workflow execution is achieved through either Enterprise Java Bean (EJB) methods or XML instances as messages on Java Message Server (JMS) queues. External communication is achieved through actions that are implemented within workflow steps.

The distinction of private and public processes can be made in WebLogic Integration. Private processes are implemented in the workflow system. Public processes (also called collaborative processes) are implemented in the B2B integration plug-in.

The B2B integration component supports several concepts for B2B integration: conversations, trading partner configurations, business protocols, collaboration agreements and security. Collaborations are exchanges of XML and non-XML messages. The message transmission is secured, and the sequence of business messages is supervised by conversations. Conversations are implemented through collaborative or public processes. A conversation describes a process for each interacting trading partner. Each partner has a conversation role associated with it (like buyer or shipper), and this relates the partner to a specific process of the conversation. Through this, it is defined which trading partner executes which public process and therefore exhibits a specific message exchange behavior. Trading partner configurations define individual trading partners. For example, a unique name is provided as well as the connectivity information like network addresses. A trading partner configuration also refers to the B2B protocols a trading partner supports for integration.

Some business protocols (also called B2B protocols) are supported by WebLogic Integration out of the box. Amongst them are RosettaNet, ebXML and EDI. Collaboration agreements are necessary to relate all concepts necessary to conduct message exchanges. Conversations, roles, collaboration processes, trading partners and network connectivity are related by collaboration agreements. Only then does WebLogic Integration a complete configuration to allow message exchanges.

Security functionality is provided as required by B2B protocols. This includes a SSL-based platform for conversations, certificate verification, digital signatures, nonrepudiation of origin and receipt and data encryption.

The application integration component provides a framework to integrate adapters to back-end application systems through the J2EE Connector Architecture standard. Each back-end application that needs to be integrated must have an associated adapter installed in WebLogic itself. WebLogic Integration defines the concept of an application view as an additional abstraction on top of adapters. An application view of an adapter represents the data going into an adapter and coming from an adapter as XML instances, independent of the particular representation the adapter needs. From an integration viewpoint, all adapters take and produce XML instances through this approach. In addition, an adapter development kit is provided to support the building of custom adapters that are not provided out of the box by any adapter provider.

The final component is the data integration component. It consists of translation and transformation functionality. Translation translates any format into XML and vice versa, thereby allowing legacy data formats to be represented in XML for processing in WebLogic Integration. It is metadata driven and the particular transformation rules are modeled through a user interface. As soon as data are represented in XML format, WebLogic Integration can interpret its contents. Data transformation is provided in the form of a transformation tool that transforms XML instances to XML instances. It is based on XSL style sheets that are defined through a graphical tool.

21.2 IBM's CrossWorlds

IBM acquired CrossWorlds in 2002. With the acquisition, IBM inherited CrossWorlds' product with the same name [CrossWorlds]. Technical information is readily available on the IBM Web site for CrossWorlds. A good overview is provided in IBM CW (2002).

IBM CrossWorlds V4.1.1 implements collaborations and business objects as the core concepts. Business objects are equivalent to the integration concept of events (not business objects). Two classes of business objects are implemented. Generic business objects are equivalent to the integration concept of business events. And application-specific business objects are equivalent to the integration concept of clear text events. Business objects implement not only the structure of the data exchanged, but also verbs that correspond to the integration concept action. Example verbs are create, retrieve or delete.

Collaborations are used to describe business processes and are equivalent to the integration concept of business processes. Collaborations have the equivalent to process parameters. This is called ports in CrossWorlds. Through ports business objects are given to collaborations and returned from collaborations. Ports are accessible from the internal of collaborations in order to implement the business object flow, implementing the business logic in collaborations.

Collaborations can be aggregated into collaboration groups. Collaborations that are part of a collaboration group can pass business objects to each other. This accomplishes not only the reuse of collaborations but also the building of complex processes based on simpler building blocks.

Collaborations have an internal structure if the integration modeler chooses to define it. A collaboration can consist of scenarios, where each scenario implements a different process. For example, instead of one collaboration implementing the processing for create, update and delete a customer, a collaboration can be built with three scenarios, one for create, one for update and one for delete customer. This allows users to separate the processing within a collaboration, depending on the business object and its verb coming in. At run time, when a create customer business object is received, the appropriate scenario is executed.

Collaborations can be transactional. In the transactional case collaborations implement long-running processes that provide compensation functionality. For each transactional substep of a collaboration that requires compensation, a compensation step has to be defined by the integration modeler. At run time, when an error occurs, the system automatically initiates compensation, and the compensation steps are executed in the reverse order of the original collaboration steps. Various data isolation levels are implemented that assure that collaborations execute in various degrees of isolation in order to avoid data inconsistencies through concurrent updates.

Maps are provided that are the equivalent to transformation. Maps are used to map generic business objects to application-specific business objects, and vice versa.

CrossWorlds is a metadata-driven system that stores all modeling data in a relational repository. A large set of adapters is provided (in CrossWorlds lingo, called connectors) that allows connectivity to a whole range of back-end application systems. A connector consists of two parts, a controller and an agent. The controller is the part of a connector that connects to the CrossWorlds' hub part of the product. The agent is responsible for connecting to the back-end application system. The agent produces the application-specific business object in the inbound case, or receives the application-specific business object in the outbound case. Translation is not an explicit modeling concept in CrossWorlds, however, the functionality is implemented through program language code by so-called data handlers.

In addition to accessing data of back-end application systems through connectors, CrossWorlds allows access to itself through a synchronous server access interface. A component like an application server can access CrossWorlds directly without going through a connector. The server access interface allows the external component to send data to CrossWorlds and to receive data from CrossWorlds. Through this additional interface homogeneous access can be implemented where the external component does not have to have a connector associated with it. CrossWorlds provides a range of tools for the integration modeler in order to set up, define and monitor the execution of integration.

21.3 Microsoft's BizTalk Server

Microsoft's Biztalk Server 2002 [Biztalk Server] consists of two parts. One part is the business process execution engine, called Biztalk Orchestration Engine. Its user interface is called Biztalk Orchestration Designer. The other part provides the base functionality for integration that does not require business process management. It is called Biztalk Messaging Services and is discussed first in the following.

The base messaging concepts provided by the Biztalk Server are receive functions, channels and messaging ports. In addition, documents can be validated as well as correlated in order to detect acknowledgements corresponding to already processed documents. Receive functions are the entry point for documents submitted to the Biztalk Server. There are several ways through which documents can be submitted to receive functions. These are the Internet, e-mail attachments, message busses, message queues, adapters or programmatically. Receive functions receive documents and deliver them to the different available channels. A Component Object Model object called Interchange is also supplied by the Biztalk Server to submit documents directly to a channel without going through receive functions.

Channels modify the document structure, if necessary, through transformation. For example, if the incoming document structure does not conform to the one expected by the target, then transformation is used to transform it. In addition, channels provide functionality for encryption/decryption, digital signatures as well as logging. Incoming documents can be logged in their entirety or only partially.

Messaging ports connect the Biztalk Server to schedules (see below), trading partners or applications (through adapters). Messaging ports represent the target or recipient of documents processed by the Biztalk Server. Messaging ports are the outbound interface of the system, and they deliver the documents. Different channels can send documents to the same messaging port. This allows a target to receive documents from many different sources.

Schedules are the processes implemented by the Biztalk Orchestration Engine and are connected through the messaging ports to channels. A document delivered to a schedule through a messaging port becomes available in this schedule. It processes the document according to the process definition as built by the Biztalk Orchestration Designer. A schedule can receive documents from different messaging ports and can deliver documents to multiple channels. This allows routing of messages from different sources to different targets.

Schedules consist of process steps that are connected by decisions, loops, actions (like receiving or sending documents), parallel branching and synchronization as well as other process execution elements. A schedule in turn can deliver documents to channels. This means that a schedule can deliver documents to targets. In addition, it is possible to deliver documents through channels to other schedules, allowing a decomposition and reuse of schedules.

Schedules separate the interface of a business process from its implementation. Fundamentally, sources and targets of documents like message queues or COM objects are separated from the business process through ports. Ports are like input and output parameters of schedules that are bound to the sources and targets of documents (and are different from messaging ports, which are connected to channels). This means that a designer specifying a schedule has to specify ports, however, without necessarily knowing how the documents are delivered or provided to ports. Later on, once the schedule with its ports is defined, a developer can link the ports to the various technologies like message queues or COM objects to receive document from or to deliver documents to the schedule. Within a schedule, ports can be accessed by actions (specific process steps). An action that is part of the processing flow can either read or write to a port.

Schedules can implement different types of transactions. One type are long-running transactions that externalize intermediate execution states in order to support long lifetimes of schedules, like weeks or years. In addition, compensation handling is possible by specifying compensation transactions in case a schedule requires compensation in error cases. In addition to long-running transactions, schedules can also implement short-lived transactions, when specified as those by a user. In this case the complete schedule is executed as one (database) transaction. Furthermore, sets of process steps within a long-lived schedule can be specified as being short-lived. This groups process steps within schedules together as short atomic transactions. For these, compensation transactions can be specified that are executed in case of failures. And finally, timed transactions are available that run up to a specified time. Once this time is reached and the transaction is not committed successfully, compensation is initiated automatically.

In addition, Biztalk Adapters as well as Biztalk Accelerators are available that connect the Biztalk Server to B2B protocols and to back-end application systems. The Biztalk Server provides native adapters as well as adapters provided by third parties to the Biztalk Server.

Biztalk Server provides a large array of tools. These are Biztalk Orchestration designer, Biztalk Editor, Biztalk Mapper, Biztalk Messaging Manager, Biztalk Server Administration, Biztalk Document Tracking and Biztalk SEED Wizard.

21.4 Oracle's 9iAS Integration

Oracle's offerings for integration are 9iAS Integration 9.0.4 and 9iAS InterConnect 9.0.2. The latter is the preceding version of the former. Therefore, only 9iAS Integration is discussed in more detail [9iAS Integration].

9iAS Integration provides an integrated set of concepts for processes and data. The handling of data is implemented through the concept of events. An incoming message from a back-end application system or trading partner (through a B2B protocol) is represented as a native event that contains the data format as received. A native event is converted into an application event through translation. The application event is in the common syntax of 9iAS Integration, but the values are still the same as in the native event. The application events are transformed into business events through transformation. Business events are in the common syntax and common terminology of 9iAS Integration. Business events are user defined and provide a common view or common representation of all application events of all B2B protocols or back-end application systems (both subsumed under the concept party). For example, if three different parties can send purchase orders, then the business event purchase order would be a common representation into which every party's purchase order can be transformed. Business events that are sent to parties go through the same conversions. First, they are transformed into application events, and then they are translated into native events.

Native events are created and consumed by the adapter framework of 9iAS Integration. The adapter framework allows for the connection of adapters that are J2EE Connector Architecture compliant. Native events are converted into the representation as required by the adapter interface (i.e., records according to the connector standard) and sent out as messages. Messages received by adapters are given to the adapter framework according to the adapter's interface. 9iAS Integration provides back-end application system adapters as well as B2B protocol adapters. Native events can be correlated to determine related events. Various security mechanisms are provided according to B2B protocol requirements so that 9iAS Integration can participate in secure B2B interactions.

Process management is provided through several concepts. For each class of event a corresponding process has to be defined. This is called a role (the term role indicates behavior like seller or buyer). Native events are processed in native roles, application events are processed in application roles and business events are processed in business roles. For example, a RosettaNet partner interface process (PIP) is modeled as a native role. This constitutes the public process. After translation the application events are processed in application roles in order to define the behavior of application events. Since native roles are different from application roles, it is possible to build an abstraction. For example, it is possible to not pass acknowledgments on to application roles from native roles. This means that application roles do not have to deal with acknowledgments any more. The same applies to duplicate checks or time-out behavior. After transformation of the application events, the resulting business events are given to business roles. These define the enterprise's behavior, like seller, buyer, shipper and so on. Business logic is implemented in an additional concept called business process. Business roles are connected to business processes and therefore connect to parties through this approach. For example, a request for quotation-based buying would connect to two different business roles, one for handling the request for quotation exchange and one for handling the purchase order exchange.

Events are passed back and forth between roles through role parameters called ports. Ports are like input and output parameters and bind event instances at run time. Process steps are available within roles and business processes for process modeling, like conditional steps and other constructs. Roles and business processes implement long-running transactions since intermediate processing states are externalized in the database.

A party management component manages back-end application systems as well as trading partners. Agreements are managed to define which events are accepted from which party, and which event can be sent to a party.

9iAS Integration is a modeled environment where all aspects of integration are modeled. All definition data is stored in a database as values. At run time the execution of events, roles and processes is interpreted based on one holistic database schema.

21.5 Further Products

Of course, there are more integration products offered for A2A and B2B integration. Some of them are listed in Table 21.1 with a reference to the company's web site for more information. Since technical information like product manuals is not readily available the products are not discussed in detail here.

Table 21.1. Additional integration roducts

Integration Product	Reference
Cyclone Commerce	[CycloneCommerce]
eXcelon	[eXcelon]
IONA	[IONA]
Modulant	[Modulant]
SeeBeyond	[SeeBeyond]
SUN	[SUN]
TIBCO	[TIBCO]
Vitria	[Vitria]
WebMethods	[WebMethods]

22 Research

B2B integration is very complex, as this book clearly shows. In addition, no commonly accepted set of integration concepts has been developed so far, and no standard architecture is accepted throughout the industrial or research community, either. For example, an area where both are available is relational database management systems. In this particular field the relational model as well as a standard architecture are both accepted by the industry and research community.

A consequence of the lack of a commonly accepted set of integration concepts and a missing standard architecture is that research projects have a very different focus and propose vastly different solution approaches to common problems. In addition, because of the complexity of the subject, no research project addresses all areas of B2B integration completely. Instead, research projects focus on particular aspects of the B2B integration domain.

In the following some of the research projects in the area of B2B integration are characterized briefly by area of integration functionality. This is not a complete set of research efforts, and their discussion is not meant to be a judgement of their quality or impact. An attempt is made to cover the various areas of B2B integration and list relevant research projects and results.

22.1 Event Definition and Transformation

Fensel (2001) introduces the transformation problem in context of ontologies. The scaling problem is recognized, and the intermediate representation is proposed as a solution to reduce the number of necessary transformations from an exponential to a linear order. The transformation sources and targets are defined in terms of ontological concepts (instead of data types), elevating the level of formal representation of business concepts. Sources and targets that are not represented as concepts are brought on the concept level before transformation and reduced after transformation. However, transformation rules have to be written by the integration modeler.

The IEEE Bulletin on Data Transformations (1999) is a collection of brief articles from various research groups and companies outlining different approaches to the data transformation problem. This bulletin gives a good overview of the state of the art.

Madhavan et al. (2001) propose a transformation approach based on heuristics in conjunction with linguistic-based and structure-based matching. This approach is fundamentally based on the assumption that the metadata description and names of the source and target event types and data types contain enough information to determine whether two data values might be related. The approach suggests certain transformation rules to the integration modeler that have to be confirmed or changed by an integration modeler.

Rahm and Bernstein (2001) provide a categorization of schema-matching (transformation) approaches as well as a survey of existing work that is organized according to the categorization. An overview of the matching problem is provided as well as a high-level architecture of a potential solution.

Wiederhold and Genesereth (1997) outline the fundamental concepts and an architecture for mediation. They observe that mediators are components by themselves that act as intermediary between applications and information sources. The task of mediators is to access the information sources and provide the information as required by applications. This means that mediators need to have an understanding of the schemas and ontologies of the data sources and the ability to transform those into information according to the applications' schemas. The important statement is made that total automation of mediation is not possible but human work is required to make mediation possible.

22.2 Web Services and Web Service Composition

Benatallah et al. (2001) and Sheng et al. (2002) define Web service composition based on elementary services. An elementary service is an invocation of an operation with input and output parameters. Elementary services can be grouped into service communities that constitute a collection of equivalent services. The flight reservation service of different airlines belongs in a flight management service community. Complex services are the invocation of several elementary services. The invocation sequence is expressed as state charts. In addition, an execution model is provided for the distributed execution of composite services. It is not assumed that there is only one central site that manages and executes the definition of composite services. Instead, a composite service can be partitioned, and the partitions can be distributed to several computer nodes. Each node executes its partition of the composite service. This requires that the different partitions synchronize with each other in order to achieve a consistent execution.

Cardoso and Sheth (2002) describe semantic e-Workflow Composition. The fundamental idea is that parameters of workflow tasks are associated with ontologies. Based on this association, the workflow modeler has a clear understanding of the input and output parameters and their meaning. When a task is added to a workflow, the modeler has to manually assign the input and output parameters to workflow variables. However, since the output and input parameter are associated with concepts from ontologies, an automatic match is attempted and the result suggested to the human workflow modeler. The modeler can then decide to accept a suggestion or overwrite it manually with a better match.

Casati and Shan (2001a, 2001b) define e-services and their composition in the context of workflow management. E-services are operations that can be invoked with input as well as output parameters. A composition language allows for the invocation of several e-services in sequence, and the composition itself is a service that can be invoked. The execution of the composite service is mapped to a workflow management system as the execution environment. The invocation of e-services is achieved by a separate component that is able to handle all the protocols necessary for remote e-service invocation. Therefore, the workflow management system, while executing a composite service, interacts with the e-service component. It is recognized that during the execution of composite services changes might be necessary, and dynamic changes to the executing composite service are required. Once composite services have been defined and are executing, enterprises generally ask for the ability to optimize the execution to reduce cost or speed up the execution time. Business process intelligence functionality can be used to analyze the execution of composite Web services and suggest changes to them in order to improve their execution.

Casati et al. (2001) introduce the concept of a meta e-service for the composition of e-services. The idea is that not every service requester is willing or able to buy or build the infrastructure required for service composition. Instead, a service can be envisioned that allows users to compose services. The benefit of such an approach is that service requesters can register composite services and execute them without having to have a composition environment themselves. A comprehensive model and language for this purpose is presented that defines a composite service and passes it to the meta e-service. A prototype providing the meta e-service functionality is described.

Casati and Shan (2002) introduce the notion of events and event nodes into the concept of composite services. Events are published or subscribed to by composite services. Events can be used for notification of occurrences (like the successful execution of a service) or synchronization of different composite services. Several types of events are introduced: state change events, error events, application-specific events and temporal events. Temporal, state change and error events are detected automatically by the system. Application-specific events have to be explicitly raised. An architecture is introduced that outlines one possible implementation of events in the context of composite service execution.

Dogac et al. (2002) recognize that Web service definitions based on WSDL and SOAP are not based on a semantic definition language, but only on a syntactic definition language (XML). Furthermore, syntactically defined Web services advertised in UDDI cannot be discovered based on their semantic meaning. Therefore this work extends Web service definitions with RDF-based definitions that capture the semantics. Furthermore, if Web service definitions based on RDF are stored in UDDI, a semantics-based discovery is possible due to the formal definition using RDF. With this type of extension of UDDI contents, higher fidelity Web service composition is possible.

Florescu and Kossmann (2001) describe XL (XML Programming Language), a XML-based programming language that implements programs solely based on XML. The fundamental rational behind XL is to avoid the paradigm mismatch that currently exists when using relational databases, Java and Web browsers. Each of those technologies follows different language models. XL tries to unify the model across all layers required to implement application logic. XL is therefore very comprehensive, since it not only allows to write down program logic but also has language constructs for user interaction, persistence layer interaction as well as transaction boundary definition.

Maedche and Staab (2003) propose the combination of Web services, the Semantic Web and ad-hoc information exchange in conjunction with peer-to-peer technology. The combination enables the location of services dynamically based on a precise semantic definition. Once located, the services can be executed.

22.3 Quality of Service

Cardoso et al. (2002) discuss quality of service in context of workflow management. The work described is based on four dimensions: time, cost, fidelity and reliability. Analytic as well as simulation models are developed in the context of a workflow management system in order to compute the quality of service.

Klingemann et al. (1999) provide an approach to derive a model of a service based on its external observable behavior. The fundamental problem is that an enterprise outsourcing a task to a service provider has to control the service execution in order to assess its quality. However, the enterprise cannot introspect the service implementation at the service provider because the service provider is a separate and autonomous enterprise. The introduced approach allows an enterprises to derive the model of a service and compare it with the advertisement of a service provider. This allows for the comparison of the promised and the actual behavior and therefore enables the service-requesting enterprise to do quality-of-service monitoring and control.

Zeng et al. (2001) introduce the concept of dynamic binding of Web service providers to composite Web services at run time. A discovery agent is responsible for discovering and selecting Web services that implement the functionality required by a composite service. Execution rules added to a composite service specify the acceptable cost as well as the maximum execution time. These quality of service requirements dictate the specific execution plan. Based on past performance, appropriate Web service providers are selected to complete the execution plan. In case a Web service provider fails, exceeds the cost or execution time, alternative execution plans might have to be chosen, since they might stay within the specified boundaries of cost and execution time.

22.4 Process

In van der Aalst and Weske (2001) the notion of private and public processes are discussed in terms of specific Petri nets called WF-net. Public processes define the enterprise-external visible behavior. Private processes define the enterprise-internal behavior, which is invisible from the outside. Private processes are subclasses of public processes. Through this relationship between private and public processes consistent behavior is ensured, guaranteeing that the private processes behave as the public processes externalized. Since Petri nets are used as the underlying model, various aspects like data, transformation, trading partner management and so on are not considered at all and are not part of the discussed results. The distinction of private and public processes are discussed in more detail by van der Aalst (2002), who provides a methodology for designing sound public processes that do not exhibit behavior anomalies.

Alonso et al. (1999a) introduce the notion of virtual business process as a process that is executed across several organizations and not within only one. A company that only has virtual business processes is called a virtual enterprise. The set of organizations involved in a virtual business process is called a trading community. It is argued that the process support system WISE is an ideal platform for executing virtual business processes. Alonso et al. (1999b) and Lazcano et al. (2000) provide a more detailed architecture of the WISE system in context of virtual enterprises and virtual business processes.

Fensel and Bussler (2002) introduce a comprehensive framework for modeling and executing semantic Web services called Web Service Modeling Framework (WSMF). This framework introduces a comprehensive conceptual model required to model public behavior by considering the semantic aspect of integration. Ontologies are used to define the meaning of services, and the notion of mediation is introduced to support the mediation across different ontologies. In addition to mediating data, the framework introduces the mediation of behavior. Behavior mediation is introduced in order to allow enterprises exposing different message exchange behavior to communicate with each other. WSMF addresses all aspects of interenterprise integration and is complete compared to the current state of Web services.

Bussler (2002a) discusses current workflow technology and its inability to deal with concurrently executing and cooperating workflows. This is due to the fundamental assumption that one single workflow is the unit of execution. It is argued that cooperating workflows are required in order to provide the different execution abstractions as introduced in this book in form of the interface, binding and business processes. The article provides a rationale why concurrently executing workflows are advantageous and discusses various examples outlining this in the B2B integration context.

Dogac et al. (2000) introduce a workflow system composed of cooperating agents that is targeted toward the execution of workflows between enterprises across the Internet. In addition, the workflow system can invoke applications within an enterprise. In order to ensure necessary security, a security service is implemented that provides confidentiality, authentication as well as signatures. Failure handling as well as error handling are explicitly required in order to provide the means for recovering from mistakes or system failures.

Johannesson and Perjons (2001) introduce a process modeling language in the context of A2A integration. This process modeling language has a fairly small set of modeling constructs that allow for the integration of back-end application systems through a methodology based on different types of processes like synchronization processes, request processes or release processes. These can be integrated with each other through a view mechanism to implement an integration process. The paper points out why point-to-point relationships between back-end application systems cannot achieve more complex integrations as well as why integration brokers are not sufficient for implementing process integration. Instead, it introduces the notion of a process broker that executes the introduced process modeling language.

22.5 Adapter

Chiang (2001) describes an architecture and provides algorithms to integrate back-end application systems with distributed object technology. The approach proposes a dispatcher that can handle synchronous as well as asynchronous invocation of back-end application systems. The approach is limited to a client calling the back-end application system. Invocations originating from the back-end application systems are not considered.

Troya and Vallecillo (2001) introduce the concept of controller with a variety of functionalities in order to achieve the integration of components. The communication between components is asynchronous based on a mailbox model, whereby each component has a mailbox for incoming and a mailbox for outgoing messages. A controller can capture and modify messages from a component (e.g., back-end application system). A controller can split, reorder, join or reply to messages. Furthermore, the controller can interact with the component it controls and reconfigure itself to a changing environment.

22.6 Ontology

Cyc [Cyc] establishes an upper ontology that attempts to define common concepts that are perceived as constituting our world. Hundreds of concepts have been captured and thousand of constraints have been placed on the concepts in order to restrict their combinations. Domain-specific extensions of Cyc have to be built in order to define proper domain-specific concepts. This is necessary before they can be used for automatic transformation between domain-specific concepts. Cyc has also established an open source effort called OpenCyc [OpenCyc].

The Karlsruhe Ontology and Semantic Web Framework (KAON) as described in Motik et al. (2002) is a sophisticated framework for the management of ontologies. A multilayer approach is taken that successively abstracts from representation toward the semantics of data. It is based on the Resource Description Framework (RDF) [RDF]. KAON is programatically accessible through well-defined application programming interfaces implemented as Web services using SOAP and HTTP.

The Stanford Information Network (SIN, Genesereth 2002) is an Internet service providing access to structured information. SIN does not restrict the specific domain of the information sources. Furthermore, the information is coming from multiple sources containing structured data, and only sources with structured data can be part of SIN. Since the data sources have different schemas, SIN provides a mechanism for integrating heterogeneous data sources. SIN's underlying data model, are semantic nets and integration rules operate on those. SIN can be queried for information, but SIN can also notify about changes in data sources. Furthermore, updates in the data sources can be performed through SIN.

Standard Upper Ontology (SUO) [SUO] is an IEEE standards activity with the goal to develop a standard upper ontology. As such, the ontology will be limited to concepts that are meta, generic, abstract and philosophical. The reason for this restriction is the goal for SUO to be applicable to as many domains as possible.

22.7 Integration Architecture

Chen et al. (2001) describe a high-level architecture of a B2B integration technology server (called business server in the technical report). It outlines basic architectural components like collaboration manager and message manager. On a conceptual model the need for a peer-to-peer interaction model is recognized, and a collaborative process model based on process roles is provided based on this interaction model. Chen et al. (2000a, 2000b) discuss the underlying collaborative process model in more detail including an execution model.

Cingil and Dogac (2001) describe a comprehensive high-level architecture for supply chain automation. This architecture supports business-to-business interactions as well as business-to-consumer interactions. It consists of two main elements. One element is the management of catalogs that store product information. A dedicated component called Electronic Catalog is responsible for this management, and a catalog agent provides access to it. The other element implements technologies for managing the supply chain processes. This consists of a workflow management system in conjunction with wrappers to access back-end application systems. The workflow management system also implements the message exchanges between the companies.

22.8 Business Process Monitoring

Sayal et al. (2002) address business process monitoring in the context of a service architecture. The approach allows end users to define their own metrics through taxonomies. For example, a negotiation outcome taxonomy includes categories like success and failure. A duration taxonomy includes fast, acceptable, slow and very slow as possible categories. A visualization tool is described that allows for the review of existing process instances according to focus points. These are processes, resources and services. The focus point is the center of the representation. For example, the services focus point displays information related to the invoked services. This combined with the taxonomies allows a user to see the information in the needed way. For example, the duration taxonomy would display the duration of services. An architecture is shown that explains the implementation strategy for such a business process monitoring approach.

22.9 Agreements

Ludwig and Hoffner (1999) introduce cross-organizational workflow as a means to outsource tasks in form of services. Workflow management systems are brought forward to execute the outsourced requests. However, it is recognized that enterprises engage in a formal relationship before executing common processes. The approach therefore introduces the notion of establishing a contractual basis first. This is accomplished by an enterprise searching for suitable service providers. Once a provider is found a contract establishment phase is entered whereby the involved companies come to an agreement of how to interact. Once an agreement is found, their information systems (in the form of workflow management systems) are configured accordingly, and the execution can take place. Once the contract ends the relationship between the enterprises is finished. The whole process of search, establishment, execution and ending is system supported. Jonker et al. (1999) and Damen et al. (2000) show a detailed example of several enterprises coordinating their cross-organizational processes with workflow technology.

23 The Future of Integration

23.1 Why Integration?

Why is integration necessary in the first place? In the context of B2B integration this question has two answers based on two cases that are addressed separately: back-end application systems that are integrated with each other without any external trading partner communication, and back-end application systems that are integrated with one or more external trading partners through B2B protocols. Integrating back-end application systems is necessary since there is no one single back-end application system that implements all (!) required functionality for an enterprise completely. Only in this case would one back-end application system be sufficient for all needs and requirements of an enterprise (and so no integration with any other back-end application system would be necessary). This is a philosophical answer to some extent, since there will be no back-end application system with this functionality really soon.

Instead, an enterprise has to install several back-end application systems or has them hosted at one or more ASPs to cover all the required functionality. Their selection is based on various criteria, one of which is the best-of-breed criterion whereby the best solution is selected from the set of all alternative back-end application systems. Of course, this selection is very subjective. Multiple back-end application systems generally implement the same business concepts or a subset of these in different ways. In addition, business activities of the enterprise are supported by different back-end application systems at different times. Therefore these have to be integrated so that the necessary business data can be exchanged between the back-end application systems. Based on the exchange, they can support the execution of business activities.

This constitutes the need for integration. The introduced integration concepts support the common understanding of business concepts between different back-end application systems through the concept of business objects, which are a common representation across the different back-end application systems.

Integrating back-end application systems with external trading partners is necessary, since enterprises are autonomous entities that intentionally do not operate on data shared between them. Consequently, there is no common semantics and no common shared state across enterprises. This situation requires explicit integration through messages if enterprises want to exchange business data. In addition, different enterprises might have different back-end application systems, which have different representation of business concepts, as discussed above.

In summary, integration is necessary due to the autonomy of enterprises as well as heterogeneity and functional limitations of back-end application systems. Integration technology, while existing for a significant amount of time, still changes and evolves. No standard architecture or standard set of integration concepts are emerging. And so one interesting question is where integration technology will go in the future in terms of its functionality.

23.2 Integration, Quo Vadis?

Instead of asking where is integration going (on its own, so to speak) the real question is: where should integration go? A possible answer was given in the form of Chap. 6: integration technology should strive to provide the ideal integration world for enterprises.

This can be achieved in two ways. One way was outlined throughout this book. Fundamentally, a B2B integration technology is to be built that implements different layers of abstraction, giving enterprises the feeling that they operate in an ideal integration world that is homogeneous in all its aspects. Network, communication, data and behavior heterogeneity are abstracted from through concepts like interface processes and semantic transformation, providing an ideal integration world inside an enterprise. As a consequence, the enterprise can concentrate on defining its world-class business processes. This is what a business should do since these processes represent and implement the core expertise of enterprises and are, in the end, the revenue generators.

The other way that was indicated in Chap. 6 was an unlikely alternative. Networks are becoming reliable and transactional, communication is fully trusted since enterprises are fundamentally honest and there is one world ontology defining the semantics of data and behavior to which every single enterprise subscribes. While this is in principle possible to achieve, it will not be accomplished any time soon. It is probably easier to have enterprises use B2B integration technology that accepts heterogeneity and provides the abstraction functionality rather than to restrict the heterogeneous world to such an extent that a homogeneous world emerges from it. Enterprises would look suspiciously at having no alternatives to choose from on their own to make the best choice from their viewpoint. This leads to two challenges lying ahead: the grand challenge and the "grander" challenge.

23.3 The Grand Challenge

The grand challenge poses the question if it is possible to build integration technology based on sound integration concepts that allows the integration of heterogeneous and autonomous back-end application systems, as discussed in Sect. 23.1. This book precisely addressed this requirement and outlines a potential approach. However, more specifically, the grand challenge as outlined in Brodie (2002) poses the more narrow question if the semantic integration problem can be solved inasmuch as back-end application systems can "contain" enough semantics so that they are semantic aware and that their integration is semantically correct.

The semantic integration problem consists of two parts, data semantics as well as behavior semantics. Both are discussed in the following.

Data Semantics and Ontologies

Transformation rules and maps as introduced in Sects. 2.2.3 and 2.2.4 provide a mechanism to map concepts in one event into the concepts of another event by mapping data values of specific data types. Transformation is characterized as a mechanism since transformation does not rely on any attempt to formally define data semantics or any inference rules that support the automatic inference of concept equivalence. Transformation rules are designed by a human integration modeler, and the quality of the transformation rules completely depends on the skills of the human integration modeler. If the integration modeler consistently achieves semantic equivalence by modeling transformation rules appropriately, then this is great. However, the transformation toolset has no ability to check if the integration modeler really achieved to construct the correct rules or not.

Madhavan et al. (2001) propose a transformation approach based on heuristics. This approach is fundamentally based on the assumption that the metadata description and names of the event types and data types contain enough information to determine if two data values might be related or not. The approach suggests certain transformation rules to the integration modeler that have to be confirmed or changed by an integration modeler. While this approach is very helpful, it still requires human involvement and therefore has ample opportunity for errors caused by integration modelers.

More formal approaches like in Fensel (2001) attempt to solve the transformation problem based on the representation of a formal ontology. Concepts are defined instead of data types, elevating the level of formal representation of business concepts. However, transformation rules still have to be written by the integration modeler. To achieve completely automatic transformation without human involvement more expressive representations have yet to be found.

Cyc is an example of an upper ontology that attempts to define common concepts that are perceived as constituting our world. These common and general concept definitions can be used as a starting point to formally define the semantics of business objects. Domain-specific extensions of Cyc have to be built in order to define proper domain-specific concepts. This is necessary before they can be used for automatic transformation between domain-specific concepts.

In summary, establishing a formal semantics description of business domain concepts is a precondition for automatic transformation between them. If the semantics is established, the chance of a solution for automatic transformation emerges that does not require a human integration modeler. Automatic transformation based on strictly formal business concept representations would be the answer to the grand challenge.

Process Semantics

In addition to the data transformation problem the behavior problem has to be solved. The behavior problem (also called process semantics) is the question if two communicating interface processes match so that their execution results in a consistent state after their execution is finished. For example, an interface process representing seller behavior and an interface process representing buyer behavior have to match in order for two enterprises, one executing the seller interface process and one executing the buyer interface process, to flawlessly exchange messages resulting in a series of correct intermediate states and a consistent end state.

Recent standards recognize the need to explicitly define interface processes in B2B integration. Examples are RosettaNet, ebXML and WS-Coordination. If both the data semantics problem and the process semantics problems are solved, then the grand challenge is addressed. Once these results are available it is possible to integrate any number of back-end application systems and any number of trading partners so semantic mismatches no longer occur.

23.4 The Grander Challenge: Self-Forming Virtual Enterprises

If the ideal integration world is seen as a means to an end instead of the goal itself, and if the grand challenge is met, the interesting question arises what would be the next greater goal? This is termed the grander challenge: how to achieve self-forming virtual enterprises.

The term virtual enterprise is to some extent a misnomer. First of all, enterprises are not virtual, they must be real, if only for legal or accounting reasons. Second, enterprises might exist for a short time only or only until a specific outcome is achieved (i.e., for a specific purpose). The fact that an enterprise does not have set an explicit date or reason to terminate does not mean that it exists forever. The lifetime of an enterprise does not make it virtual or real either. Third, the amount of outsourcing an enterprise chooses to do does not make it virtual. An enterprise having many assets is not more real than one having only a few assets.

The term virtual enterprise is used in the following to characterize an enterprise that has most of its operations outsourced to service providers and those are contracted automatically without any human involvement. A human is only involved when there is an exceptional case that requires problem-solving skills that cannot be provided in automated form. The automated detection of service providers as well as their contracting is called self-forming. Some of the problems that have to be solved to achieve self-forming virtual enterprises are as follows, and those characterize the meaning of virtual enterprise in more detail.

- **Capability.** Every enterprise that wants to be part of one or more self-forming virtual enterprises has to announce its capabilities so that other enterprises know what it can provide. This includes services as well as real products.

- **Availability.** An enterprise must announce the availability of the services or products it advertises.
- **Revenue expectations and cost model.** An enterprise must be financially sound, which requires that it can pay its bills and make some profit. Whenever it is part of a virtual enterprise it must maintain its financial stability, and so it must be able to announce its financial requirements.
- **Default compensation.** If an enterprise that is part of a virtual enterprise defaults because it cannot deliver the services or products as agreed, a compensation scheme has to be in place that can compensate the default. That might be a deposit of funds in an escrow account, an alternative enterprise, an insurance that can pay for the damage and so on.

  The same applies if the enterprise asking for a service or goods does not accept them as negotiated and defaults payment for those. In this case also compensation mechanisms have to be in place.
- **Guarantee and support time frames.** Enterprises usually provide guarantees for their services or products as well as announce availability of support time frames to repair errors or supply spare parts. An enterprise must announce the time frames for guarantees and support. Nobody would buy a car from a car manufacturer that is not likely to exist as long as the car is in operation or if spare parts were not readily available.
- **Goal and risks.** The goals of an enterprise must be clear so that a match-making environment can determine if it makes sense to engage. For example, an enterprise migt want to grow its customer base and hence does not want to engage in large contracts. In order to achieve the goal an enterprise might accept a certain risk, and so the goal and risks must be known.
- **Contract negotiation.** Enterprises must negotiate a contract that includes the obligations to deliver services or goods, guarantees, default compensation, legal statements and so on.
- **Trust.** Before engaging, enterprises would like to determine past performance of their potential partner, including quality of delivery, dependability, flexibility, reliability and so on. It must be possible to find this out about an enterprise, which becomes interesting if the enterprise is a virtual enterprise itself.

All these areas need to be addressed so that virtual enterprises can be formed automatically. The goal is no human user involvement in the discovery and the subsequent contract negotiations at all. Also, during execution or even closure of the virtual enterprise, no human is required to be involved except to solve problems. Only in exceptional cases that cannot be addressed automatically must a human be involved.

To paint the picture even more clearly (and too futuristically one might say) the CEO of a virtual enterprise only has to found the company, define its goal and then the enterprise starts forming itself. From inception, to finding customers, suppliers, paying the salaries and preparing the tax return statements: all is done automatically and only in exceptional situations the CEO has to engage.

While this is very clearly a far-out vision it provides a clear direction for research and advanced development. Some of the problem areas like finding services are addressed already today through public registry efforts like UDDI [UDDI].

Solutions to the listed problems can be seen as extensions to a B2B integration technology architecture with a component that manages the formation of virtual enterprises. That component can use the existing B2B integration technology components and add its functionality on top of it.

Meeting the grander challenge has a severe social impact since it changes the way enterprises operate and the skill-set enterprises require. However, since self-forming virtual enterprises do not appear overnight, society in all its aspects will have a chance to adjust if this vision ever becomes true.

Part VI References and Index

Part VI contains a list of references as well as an index to allow fast access to specific topics throughout the book.

References

Many resources on the World Wide Web (WWW) are not available in printed form. While these resources are very valuable, their content can change any time on the Web, they can move to a different location or disappear altogether. This is the reason why WWW resources are listed separately from printed publications below. Printed publications are referenced with name and year of publication throughout the book, while WWW resources are referenced with brackets [ ].

Printed Publications

W. van der Aalst: Inheritance of Interorganizational Workflows to Enable Business-to-Business E-Commerce. Electronic Commerce Research, Vol. 2, No. 3, 2002

W. van der Aalst, M. Weske: The P2P Approach to Interorganizational Workflow. In: Proceedings of the 13th International Conference on Advanced Information Systems Engineering (CAISE'01), Interlaken, Switzerland, 2001

W. van der Aalst, K. van Hee: Workflow Management: Models, Methods and Systems. MIT Press, 2002

G. Alonso, C. Mohan, R. Guenthoer, D. Agrawal, A. El Abbadi, M. Kamath: Exotica/FMQM: A Persistent Message-Based Architecture for Distributed Workflow Management. In: Proceedings of IFIP WG8.1 Working Conference on Information Systems for Decentralized Organizations, Trondheim, Norway, 1995

G. Alonso, C. Hagen, A. Lazcano: Processes in Electronic Commerce. In: Proceedings of the ICDCS Workshop on Electronic Commerce and Web-Based Applications. Austin, Texas, 1999a

G. Alonso, U. Fiedler, C. Hagen, A. Lazcano, H. Schuldt, N. Weiler: WISE: Business to Business E-Commerce. In: Proceedings of the IEEE 9th International Workshop on Research Issues on Data Engineering. Information Technology for Virtual Enterprises (RIDE-VE'99), Sydney, Australia, 1999b

G. Alonso, F. Casati, H. Kuno, V. Machiraju: Web Services. Springer Berlin Heidelberg New York, 2003

A. Apte: Java Connector Architecture. Building Enterprise Adapers. Sams Publishing, Indianapolis, IN, 2002

B. Babcock, S. Babu, M. Datar, R. Motwani, J. Widom: Models and Issues in Data Stream Systems. In: Proceedings of 21st ACM Symposium on Principles of Database Systems (PODS 2002), 2002

B. Benatallah, M. Dumas, Q. Sheng, A. Ngu: Declarative Composition and Peer-to-Peer Provisioning of Dynamic Web Services. In: Proceedings of the IEEE Conference on Data Engineering, San Jose, California, 2002

A. Bouguettaya, B. Benatallah, A. Elmagarmid: Interconnecting Heterogeneous Information Systems. Kluwer Dordrecht, 1998

The Grand Challenge of Information Technology and The Illusion of Validity. Keynote presentation, CAiSE 2002, Toronto, Canada, May 2002

C. Bussler: B2B Protocol Standards and their Role in Semantic B2B Integration Engines. Bulletin of the Technical Committee on Data Engineering. Vol. 24, No. 1, IEEE Computer Society, 2001

C. Bussler: The Application of Workflow Technology in Semantic B2B Integration. Distributed and Parallel Databases. An International Journal. Kluwer International Publishers. Volume 12, Issue 2-3, 2002a

C. Bussler: Process Inheritance. In: Proceedings of The Fourteenth International Conference on Advanced Information Systems Engineering (CAiSE 2002), Toronto, Ontario, Canada, 2002b

J. Cardoso, A. Sheth: Semantic e-Workflow Composition. Technical Report. LSDIS Lab, Computer Science Department, University of Georgia, Athens, 2002

J. Cardoso, A. Sheth, J. Miller: Workflow Quality of Service. Technical Report. LSDIS Lab, Computer Science Department, University of Georgia, Athens, 2002

F. Casati, M.C. Shan: Definition, Execution, Analysis and Optimization of Composite E-Services. In: IEEE Data Engineering Bulletin, Vol. 24, No. 1, 2001a

F. Casati, M.C. Shan: Dynamic and Adaptive Composition of E-Services. In: Information Systems, Vol. 6, No. 3, 2001b

F. Casati, M.C. Shan: Event-based Interaction Management for Composite E-Services in eFlow. Information Systems Frontiers, Vol. 4, Issue 1. Kluwer, Dordrecht, 2002

F. Casati, M. Sayal, M.-C. Shan: Developing E-Services for Composing E-Services. In: Proceedings of the 13th International Conference on Advanced Information Systems Engineering (CAISE'01), Interlaken, Switzerland, 2001

Q. Chen, M. Hsu: Inter-Enterprise Collaborative Business Process Management. Software Technology Laboratory. HP Laboratories Palo Alto. HPL-2000-107, 2000a

Q. Chen, M. Hsu, I. Kleyner: How Agents from Different E-Commerce Enterprises Cooperate. Software Technology Laboratory. HP Laboratories Palo Alto. HPL-2000-108, 2000b

Q. Chen, M. Hsu, U. Dayal: Peer-to-Peer Collaborative Internet Business Servers. Software Technology Laboratory. HP Laboratories Palo Alto, HPL-2001-14, 2001a

C.C. Chiang: Wrapping Legacy Systems for use in Heterogeneous Computing Environments. Information and Software Technology 43, Elsevier Science, Amsterdam, The Netherlands, 2001

I. Cingil, A. Dogac: An Architecture for Supply Chain Integration and Automation on the Internet. Journal of Distributed and Parallel Databases, Vol. 10, No. 1, 2001

Z. Damen, W. Derks, M. Duitshof, H. Ensing: Business-to-Business E-Commerce in a Logistics Domain. In: Proceedings of the CAISE'00 Workshop on Infrastructure for Dynamic Business-to-Business Service Outsourcing. Stockholm, Sweden, 2000

A. Dogac, Y. Tambag, A. Tumer, M Ezbiderli, N. Tatbul, N. Hamali, C. Icdem, C. Beeri: A Workflow System through Cooperating Agents for Control and Document Flow over the Internet. In: Proceedings of the International Conference on Cooperative Information Systems (COOPIS'00), Israel, 2000

A. Dogac, I. Cingil, G. Laleci, Y. Kabak: Improving the Functionality of UDDI Registries through Web Service Semantics. In: 3rd VLDB Workshop on Technologies for E-Services (TES-02), Hong Kong, China, 2002

A. Elmagarmid, M. Rusinkiewicz, A. Sheth: Management of Heterogeneous and Autonomous Database Systems. The Morgan Kaufmann Series in Data Management Systems, Morgan Kaufmann, San Francisco, CA, 1998

D. Fensel: Ontologies: A Silver Bullet for Knowledge Management and Electronic Commerce. Springer, Berlin Heidelberg New York, 2001

D. Fensel, C. Bussler: The Web Service Modeling Framework WSMF. Electronic Commerce Research and Applications, Vol 1, No. 2. Elsevier Science, 2002

D. Florescu, D. Kossmann: An XML Programming Language for Web Service Specification and Composition. In: IEEE Data Engineering Bulletin, Vol. 24, No. 2, 2001

M. Genesereth: Stanford Information Network. Center for Information Technology, Stanford University, 2002

J. Gray and A. Reuter: Transaction Processing: Concepts and Techniques. Morgan Kaufmann, 1993

T. Harding, R. Drummond, C. Shih: Requirements for Inter-operable Internet EDI. Internet Draft draft-ietf-ediint-req-09.txt. EDIINT Working Group, IETF, 2001

T. Harding, R. Drummond, C. Shih: MIME-based Secure Peer-to-Peer Business Data Interchange over the Internet. Request for Comments 3335. Network Working Group, IETF, 2002

IBM CW 2002: Technical Introduction to IBM CrossWorlds. WebSphere software. IBM, Armonk, NY, 2002

IEEE Bulletin of the Technical Committee on Data Engineering. Special Issue on Data Transformations. Vol. 22, No. 1, 1999

S. Jablonski, C. Bussler: Workflow Management: Modeling Concepts, Architecture and Implementation. International Thomson, London Boston, 1996

P. Johannesson, E. Perjons: Design Principles for Process Modelling in Enterprise Application Integration. Information Systems 26. Elsevier Science, 2001

W. Jonker, W. Nijenhuis, Z. Damen, M. Verwijmeren, W. Derks: Workflow Management Systems and Cross-Organizational Logistics. In: Proceedings of the WACC Workshop on Cross-Organizational Workflow Management and Co-Ordination. San Francisco, CA, 1999

R. Kimball: The Data Warehouse Toolkit. Wiley, New York, NY, 1996

J. Klingemann, J. Waesch, K. Aberer: Deriving Service Models in Cross-Organizational Workflow Management. In: Proceedings of the IEEE 9th International Workshop on Research Issues on Data Engineering. Information Technology for Virtual Enterprises (RIDE-VE'99), Sydney, Australia, 1999

A. Kotok and D. Webber: ebXML: The New Global Standard for Doing Business over the Internet. New Riders, 2002

A. Lazcano, G. Alonso, H. Schuldt, C. Schuler: The WISE approach to Electronic Commerce. International Journal of Computer Systems, Science & Engineering, 2000

F. Leymann, D. Roller: Production Workflow: Concepts and Techniques. Prentice Hall, 1999

H. Ludwig, Y. Hoffner: Contract-Based Cross-Organizational Workflows–The CrossFlow Project. In: Proceedings of the WACC Workshop on Cross-Organizational Workflow Management and Co-Ordination. San Francisco, CA, 1999

J. Madhavan, P. Bernstein, E. Rahm: Generic Schema Matching with Cupid. Proceedings of the 27th International Conference on Very Large Databases. Rome, Italy, 2001

Services on the Move–Towards P2P-Enabled Semantic Web Services. In: Proceedings of the Tenth International Conference on Information Technology and Travel & Tourism, ENTER 2003, Helsinki , 2003

J. Miller, D. Palaniswami, A. Sheth, K. Kochut, H. Singh: WebWork: METEOR's Web-based Workflow Management System. Journal of Intelligence Information Management Systems, Vol 10, No. 2, 1997

D. Moberg, D. Brooks, R. Drummond, D. Fisher: HTTP Transport for Secure Peer-to-Peer Business Data Interchange over the Internet. Internet Draft draft-ietf-ediint-as2-11.txt, EDIINT Working Group, IETF, 2002

B. Motik, A. Maedche, R. Volz: A Conceptual Modeling Approach for Semantics-Driven Enterprise Applications. In: Proceedings of the Confederated International Conferences DOA, CoopIS and ODBASE. Irvine, CA, 2002

P. Muth, D. Wodtke, J. Weissenfels, G. Weikum, A. Kotz-Dittrich: Enterprise-wide Workflow Management Based on State and Activity Charts. NATO Advanced Study Institute on Workflow Management Systems and Interoperability, ACM Press, New York, NY, 1997

OAGIS Extensions: Exploring Extensions. White Paper. Document Number 20010301. Open Applications Group, Inc., Marietta, GA, 2001

E. Rahm, P. Bernstein: A survey of approaches to automatic schema matching. The VLDB Journal, Vol. 10, 2001

M. Sayal, F. Casati, U. Dayal, M.C. Shan: Business Process Cockpit. In: Proceedings of the 28th Very Large Database Conference, Hong Kong, China, 2002

H. Schuldt: Process Locking: A Protocol Based on Ordered Shared Locks for the Execution of Transactional Processes. In: Proceedings of the ACM Symposium on Principles of Database Systems (PODS'01), Santa Barbara, CA, 2001

R. Sharma, B. Stearns, T. Ng: J2EE Connector Architecture and Enterprise Application Integration. Addison Wesley Professional, Essex, UK, 2001

Q. Sheng, B. Benatallah, M. Dumas, E. Mak: SELF-SERV: A Platform for Rapid Composition of Web Services in a Peer-to-Peer Environment. In: Proceedings of the 28th Very Large Database Conference, Hong Kong, China, 2002

M. Sherif: Protocols for Secure Electronic Commerce. CRC, Boca Raton, 2000

J.M. Troya, A. Vallecillo: Controllers:Reusable Wrappers to Adapt Software Components. Information and Software Technology 43, Elsevier Science, Amsterdam, The Netherlands, 2001

H. Waechter, A. Reuter: The ConTract model. In: A.K. Elmagarmid (ed.): Transaction Models for Advanced Applications. Morgan Kaufmann, San Francisco, CA, 1992

G. Wiederhold, M. Genesereth: The Conceptual Basis for Mediation Services. IEEE Expert, Vol. 12 No. 5, 1997

A. Yee, A. Apte: Integrating Your e-Business Enterprise. SAMS Publishing, 2001

L. Zeng, B. Benatallah, A. Ngu: On Demand Business-to-Business Integration. In: Proceedings of the 12th International Conference on Cooperative Information Systems (COOPIS'01), Trento, Italy, 2001

World Wide Web Resources

[9iAS Integration] Oracle Corporation. otn.oracle.com/products/integration/content.html

[ACORD] ACORD Corporation. www.acord.org

[ANSI] American National Standards Institute. www.ansi.org

[ASC] The Accredited Standards Committee (ASC) X12. www.x12.org

[BEA] BEA Systems, Inc. www.bea.com

[Biztalk Server] Microsoft Corporation. www.microsoft.com/biztalk/default.asp

[Blixt and Hagstroem 1999] K.F. Blixt, A. Hagstroem: Adding Non-Repudiation to Web Transactions. www.it.isu.liu.se/~asa/publications/NonRepudiation.html

[BPEL4WS] Business Process Execution Language for Web Services, Version 1.0. www-106.ibm.com/developerworks/webservices/library/ws-bpel/

[BPML] Business Process Modeling Language. www.bpml.org

[BTP] Business Transactions Protocol. www.oasis-open.org/committees/business-transactions

[CrossWorlds] IBM CrossWorlds. www.ibm.com/software/integration/cw/

[Cyc] Cycorp, Inc. www.cyc.com

[CycloneCommerce] Cyclone Commerce, Inc. www.cyclonecommerce.com

[DAML] DARPA Agent Markup Language. www.daml.org

[DAML+OIL] DAML+OIL. www.daml.org/2001/03/daml+oil-index

[DAML-S] DAML Services. www.daml.org/services/

[DARPA IXO] DARPA Information Explotation Office. dtsn.darpa.mil/ixo/

[DISA] Data Interchange Standards Association (DISA). www.disa.org

[DNB] Duns & Bradstreet. www.dnb.com

[Drummond Group] Drummond Group, Inc. www.drummondgroup.com

[eAI Journal] eAI Journal. www.eaijournal.com

[ebizQ] ebizQ. www.ebizq.net

[ebPML] ebPML. www.ebpml.org

[eBTWG] UN/CEFACT Electronic Business Transition Working Group (eBTWG). www.ebtwg.org/

[ebXML] Electronic Business using eXtensible Markup Language (ebXML). www.ebxml.org

[ebXML BPSS] ebXML Business Process Specification Schema Version (BPSS) 1.01. www.ebxml.org/specs/index.htm

[ebXML Core Components] ebXML Core Components. www.ebxml.org/project_teams/core_components/core_components.htm

[ebXML CPA] ebXML Collaboration Protocol Agreement (CPA) Version 1.0. www.ebxml.org/specs/index.htm

[ebXML CPP] ebXML Collaboration Protocol Profile (CPP) Version 1.0. www.ebxml.org/specs/index.htm

[ebXML MSS] ebXML Message Service Specification (MSS) Version 2.0. www.ebxml.or/specs/index.htm

[eXcelon] Excelon. www.exceloncorp.com

[EDIINT] D. Crocker: MIME Encapsulation of EDI Objects. Network Working Group. Request for Comments 1767, Internet Engineering Task Force, March 1995. www.ietf.org/rfc/rfc1767.txt

[EPISTLE] European Process Industries STEP Technical Liaison Executive (EPISTLE) www.btinternet.com/~chris.angus/epistle/

[EWG] UN/EDIFACT Working Group (EWG). www.edifrance.org/edifact-wg/

[FIX] Financial Information Exchange (FIX) Protocol. www.fixprotocol.org

[FTP] A. Bhushan, B. Braden, W. Crowther, E. Harslem, j. Heafner, A. McKenzie, J. Melvin, B. Sundberg, D. Watson, J. White: The File Transfer Protocol. Network Working Group. Request for Comments 172, Internet Engineering Task Force. June 1971. www.ietf.org/rfc/rfc172.txt

[Gindin 2000] T. Gindin: Internet X.509 Public Key Infrastructure Technical Requirements for a Non-Repudiation Service. www.ietf.org/proceedings/01aug/I-D/draft-ietf-pkix-technr-03.txt

[HL7] Health Level 7. www.hl7.org

[HTTP] R. Fielding, J. Gettys, J. Mogul, H. Frystyk, L. Masinter, P. Leach, T. Berners-Lee: Hypertext Transfer Protocol -- HTTP/1.1. Network Working Group. Request for Comments 2616, Internet Engineering Task Force. June 1999. www.ietf.org/rfc/rfc2616.txt

[IBM] Internation Business Machines Corporation. www.ibm.com

[IBM MQ] WebSphere MQ Series. www.ibm.com/software/ts/mqseries/

[IEC] International Electrotechnical Commission. www.iec.ch

[IETF] Internet Engineering Task Force. www.ietf.org

[IONA] IONA Technologies. www.iona.com/

[ISO] International Organization for Standardization (ISO). www.iso.ch

[ISOC] Internet Society. www.isoc.org

[ITU] International Telecommunication Union. www.itu.int

[J2EE Connector Architecture] J2EE Connector Architecture. java.sun.com/j2ee/connector/

[Java] Java. java.sun.com

[JTC 1] JTC 1. www.jtc1.org

[Microsoft] Microsoft Corporation. www.microsoft.com

[Microsoft MSMQ] Microsoft Message Queuing. http://www.microsoft.com/msmq/

[MIME 1] N. Freed, N. Borenstein: Multipurpose Internet Mail Extensions (MIME) Part One: Format of Internet Message Bodies. Network Working Group. Request for Comments 2045. Internet Engineering Task Force, November 1996. www.ietf.org/rfc/rfc2045.txt

[MIME 2] N. Freed, N. Borenstein: Multipurpose Internet Mail Extensions (MIME) Part Two: Media Types. Network Working Group. Request for Comments 2046. Internet Engineering Task Force, November 1996. www.ietf.org/rfc/rfc2046.txt

[MIME 3] K. Moore: MIME (Multipurpose Internet Mail Extensions) Part Three: Message Header Extensions for Non-ASCII Text. Network Working Group. Request for Comments 2047. Internet Engineering Task Force, November 1996. www.ietf.org/rfc/rfc2047.txt

[MIME 4] N. Freed, J. Klensin, J. Postel: Multipurpose Internet Mail Extensions (MIME) Part Four: Registration Procedures. Network Working Group. Request for Comments 2048. Internet Engineering Task Force, November 1996. www.ietf.org/rfc/rfc2048.txt

[MIME 5] N. Freed, N. Borenstein: Multipurpose Internet Mail Extensions (MIME) Part Five: Conformance Criteria and Examples. Network Working Group. Request for Comments 2049. Internet Engineering Task Force, November 1996. www.ietf.org/rfc/rfc2049.txt

[Modulant] Modulant Inc. www.modulant.com

[Netscape] Netscape Communications, Inc. www.netscape.com

[OAGI] Open Applications Group, Inc. www.openapplications.org

[OAGIS] Open Applications Group Integration Specification. www.openapplications.org/services/designdocument.htm

[OASIS] Organization for the Advancement of Structured Information Standards. www.oasis-open.org

[OpenCyc] OpenCyc.org. www.opencyc.org

[Oracle AQ] Oracle Advanced Queuing. otn.oracle.com/docs/products/oracle9i/doc_library/release2/appdev.920/a96587/toc.htm

[Oracle VPD] Virtual Private Database. otn.oracle.com/docs/products/oracle9i/doc_library/release2/network.920/a96578/toc.htm

[PDL] XML Process Definition Language (XPDL). www.wfmc.org/standards/docs/TC-1025_10_xpdl_102502.pdf

[RDF] Resource Description Framework. www.w3.org/RDF/

[Robin Cover] R. Cover, Cover Pages. www.oasis-open.org/cover/sgml-xml.html

[RosettaNet] Rosettanet. www.rosettanet.org

[S/MIME] S/MIME Mail Security. www.ietf.org/html.charters/smime-charter.html

[SAML] Security Assertion Markup Language (SAML). www.oasis-open.org/committees/security/

[SeeBeyond] SeeBeyond Technology Corporation. www.seebeyond.com/

[SMTP] J. Klensin: Simple Mail Transfer Protocol (SMTP). Network Working Group. Request for Comments 2821. Internet Engineering Task Force, April 2001. www.ietf.org/rfc/rfc2821.txt

[SOAP] Simple Object Access Protocol (SOAP) 1.2. www.w3.org/TR/soap12-part1/ and www.w3.org/TR/soap12-part2/

[SSL] A. Freier, P. Karlton, P. Kocher: The SSL Protocol, Version 3.0. Transport Layer Security Working Group. Internet Draft. Internet Engineering Task Force, November 18th, 1996. wp.netscape.com/eng/ssl3/draft302.txt

[SUN] Sun Microsystems, Inc. www.sun.com

[SUO] IEEE P1600.1 Standard Upper Ontology (SUO) Working Group. suo.ieee.org

[SWIFT] Society for Worldwide Interbank Financial Telecommunication (SWIFT). www.swift.com

[TCP/IP] M. Rose, K. McCloghrie. Structure and Identification of Management Information for TCP/IP-based Internets. Network Working Group. Request for Comments 1155. Internet Engineering Task Force. May 1990. www.ietf.com/rfc/rfc1155.txt

[TIBCO] TIBCO Software Inc. www.tibco.com

[TLS] T. Dierks, C. Allen: The TLS Protocol, Version 1.0. Network Working Group. Request for Comments: 2246. Internet Engineering Task Force, January 1999. www.ietf.org/rfc/rfc2246.txt

[UCC] Uniform Code Council Inc. (UCC). www.uc-council.org

[UDDI] Universal Description, Discover and Integration. www.uddi.org

[UN/CEFACT] United Nations Centre for Trade Facilitation and Electronic Business (UN/CEFACT). www.unece.org/cefact

[UN/ECE] United Nations Economic Commision for Europe (UN/ECE). www.unece.org

[UN/EDIFACT] United Nations Directories for Electronic Data Interchange for Administration, Commerce and Transport (UN/EDIFACT). www.unece.org/trade/untdid/welcome.htm

[UN/LOCODE] Code for trade and transportation locations. www.unece.org/locode

[UN/SPSC] United Nations Standard Products and Services Code (UN/SPSC). www.un-spsc.net

[Vitria] Vitria Technology, Inc. www.vitria.com

[W3C] World Wide Web Consortium. www.w3c.org

[WebLogic Integration] BEA WebLogic Integration. www.bea.com/products/weblogic/integration/index.shtml

[WebMethods] webMethods, Inc. www.webmethods.com

[WSA] Web Services Architecture. W3C Working Draft 14 November 2002. www.w3c.org/TR/ws-arch/

[WSCI] Web Service Choreography Interface (WSCI) 1.0 Specification. wwws.sun.com/software/xml/developers/wsci/

[WSCL] Web Services Conversation Language (WSCL) 1.0. www.w3.org/TR/wscl10/

[WSDL] Web Service Description Language (WSDL) 1.1. www.w3.org/TR/wsdl

[WSFL] Web Services Flow Language (WSFL 1.0). www.ibm.com/software/solutions/webservices/pdf/WSFL.pdf

[WS-C] Web Services Coordination (WS-Coordination). www.ibm.com/developerworks/library/ws-coor/

[WS-T] Web Services Transaction (WS-Transaction). www.ibm.com/developerworks/webservices/library/ws-transpec/

[WS-I] Web Services Interoperability Organization. www.ws-i.org

[XACML] OASIS eXtensible Access Control Markup Language (XACML). Committee Specification 1.0, October 8th, 2002. www.oasis-open.org/committees/xacml/

[XKMS] XML Key Management Specification (XKMS). www.w3c.org/TR/xkms2/

[XLANG] XLANG. www.gotdotnet.com/team/xml_wsspecs/xlang-c/default.htm

[XML Encryption] XML Encryption Syntax and Processing. www.w3.org/TR/xmlenc-core/

[XML Schema] XML Schema. www.w3.org/XML/Schema

[XML Signature] XML-Signature Syntax and Processing. www.w3.org/TR/xmldsig-core/

Index

Symbols

2n 41

A

A2A integration 17, 91
A2A protocol 219, 220
abstract architecture component 59
abstract data type 124
abstract software component 58
abstraction layer 139
abstraction-based modeling approach 307
access control lists 257
access rights 256
access rights management 64
acknowledgment message 133
ACORD Corporation 349
actual message 37
adapter 18, 106, 296
adapter error handling 217
adapter standard 367
address resolution 12, 221, 222
address resolution step 55
administration user interface 61
administrative rights 30
advanced business process 55
advertisement 319
advertisement crawler 321
advertising enterprise 319
after-production phase 68
aggregation of events 61
aggregation query 61
agreement 319, 322
agreement conflict resolution 243
agreement for anonymous endpoints 242
alternative endpoint agreements 243

alternative process layouts 230
analysis environment 281
analysis user interface 61
anonymous endpoint 242
API 31
application clear text message 33
application of standards in the B2B integration architecture 368
application programming interfaces 31
application service provider 16, 81
application wire message 34
architectural view 66
ASC X12 350
ASP 16, 81
ASP aggregation 84
ASP aggregator aggregation 85
ASP connector 16, 24
ASP integration 17, 91
ASP protocol 24
ASP protocol component 24
asynchronous behavior 127
asynchronous communication 6, 9
asynchronous invocation 126
asynchronous send step 127
attachment 143
audit 61, 253
auditing 32
authentication management 64
authorization 224, 256, 257, 282
authorization management 64
automated supply chain integration 3
automatic buyer/seller matching 76
automatic error handling 247
automatic repair 247
automatic replication 222

B
B2B clear text message 33
B2B integration 3, 17, 91
B2B integration architecture 269
B2B integration technology architecture 18
B2B integration technology deployment 29

B2B message 33
B2B protocol 3, 31, 219, 236
B2B protocol bootstrap problem 263
B2B protocol change management 266
B2B protocol engine 18, 64
B2B protocol execution 293
B2B protocol standard 22, 31
B2B wire message 33
back-end application adapter 295
back-end application system 3, 29, 57, 232
back-end application system adapter 31, 64, 106
back-end application system adapter execution 295
back-end application system definition 312
backward error recovery 247
basic data type 145
batch 143, 217
batch acknowledgement 143
batch identifier 218
batch integration 97
batch message 217
batch processing 217
batch wire event 218
behavior 46, 126
behavior error 46
behavior mismatch 229
behavior of an endpoint 205
behavior status 46
behavior transformation 229
behavioral definition 110
behavioral process change 196
behavioral semantics 110
behavior-aware integration 95
behavior-unaware integration 95
bilateral agreement 240
bilateral communication relationship 74
bilateral endpoint agreement 240
binding model 111
binding of real type 197
binding process 181, 225, 310

binding process execution 287
binding process type change 332
black-box entity 234
BOD 352
BPEL4WS 347, 349
BPML 349
broadcast 222, 321
broadcast steps 57
broker 320
broker notification 321
browser technology 16
BTP 364
business activities 3
business behavior 308, 329
business concept abstraction/subsump-
    tion 162
business concept equivalence 162
business data 18
business data aware integration 93
business data awareness 93
business data heterogeneity 137
business data unaware integration 93
Business Dictionary 353
business event 40, 155, 171, 308
business event definition 309
business event type 221, 225
business event type change 330
business event type change manage-
    ment 165
business intelligence 33, 61, 253, 323,
    324
business intelligence tool 276
business intelligence user interface 18
business logic 12, 14, 15, 50, 220
business object 171
business object document 352
business object instance 173
business partner definition 310, 330
business process 32, 46, 50, 124, 149,
    181, 220, 308
business process execution 287
Business Process Execution Language
    for Web Services 347
business process improvement 324

business process modeling 309
business process type change 329
business rules 24, 224
Business Transaction Protocol 364
business-to-business integration 3
business-to-consumer 89

C
CCI 367
CDA 352
central coordinator 129
central storage 12
centralized communication 129
certificate 256
change in place 118
change management 327
change message 331
change propagation 115, 118
change-resistant business process 225
changing an existing clear text event
    type 167
classes of events 62
classes of processes 181
clear text event 50, 151, 153, 155
clear text event transformation 164
clear text event type 225
client/server behavior 126
Clinical Document Architecture
    Framework 352
closed endpoint support 94
closed trading partner community 233
code for trade and transport locations
    355
coherent B2B integration architecture
    25
coherent set of integration concepts 25
Collaboration Partner Agreement 359
Collaboration Partner Profile 358
Common Client Interface 367
common version 121
communication between enterprises
    129
communication within enterprises 129
compensating event instance 204

compensation 130, 202, 245, 247, 249
complete configuration 250
complete history 32, 61, 255
complete integration functionality 16
complete integration model 250
complete replay 255
complete standard 365
complete type 110
complex data type 144
complex dynamic multinational supply chain 3
complex event 219
complex event relationship 217
complex message sequence 10
complex transformation 36
complex type 145
component interface 271
component invocation model 66
component parts 271
component private interface 271
component structure 271
concept classifier 163
conceptual model 108
concurrent execution 229
concurrent parameter binding 184
concurrent processes 229
concurrent specialization 121
concurrently executed processes 229
concurrently valid version 121
conditional branch 14, 193
confidentiality 256, 258
configuration 114, 115
configuration information 65
conflicting endpoint agreements 243
conflicting specification 193
connectivity 63, 291, 311, 312
connectivity change 332
connectivity layer 18
consistency 255
consistency check 177
consistency rules 178
consistent event instances 177
constant parameter 186
constant value 186

contact information 58
content-based analysis 282
content-based routing 93
contents-based routing 11
context-dependent event validation rule 190
context-dependent validation 180
context-dependent validation rule 192
control flow 192
control flow rule 181
conventional workflow management system model 184
conversation 128
coordinated architecture 272
coordinator 63
coordinator component 273
Core Components 348
correct configuration 251
correctness 251
correlation 205
correlation predicate 175
CPA 359
CPP 358
CRM 21

D

D&B D-U-N-S Number 353, 356
DAML 347
DAML+OIL 348
DAML-S 347, 348
DARPA Agent Markup Language 347
DARPA Agent Markup Language for Services 348
data 35
data and data flow 183
data aspect 183
data entry request 282
data flow 183, 186
data flow aspect 183
data flow between processes 225
data flow rule 181
data format 30
data integration 95, 96, 131
Data Interchange Standards Associa-

tion 350
data interface of process 183
data loss 159
data model 135
data transformation 6, 10, 13, 30
data type 35, 37, 144
data type conversion 160
data type management component 63
data type mismatch 164
Data Universal Numbering System 356
data warehouse 61
data warehouse tool 275
database schema 297
database system 6, 10, 65
database tables 31
data-centric integration approach 131
de facto standard 344
deadlock 230, 280
deadlocked integration process 62
declared integration 94
decomposition 181
decomposition hierarchy 182
decryption 64
dedicated B2B protocol back-end application system adapter 75
dedicated integration model 93
dedicated queues 9
default output parameter 184
delimitation character 38
delimited representation 38
deployment 279, 316, 333
deployment data 297
depth of the decomposition 182
design-time data 297
design-time repository 19
direct addressing 10, 12
direct communication 128
direct data transfer 6
direct event addressing 221
direct transformation 41
direct version relationship 115
direct vs. indirect communication 128
DISA 350
discovering enterprise 319

discovery 319, 321
discovery process 321
discrete event 131
discrete pieces of data values 142
distributed database management system 297
distributed transactions 202, 298
divide-and-conquer 50
divisions within enterprises 29
domain value list 168
domain value map 31, 168, 234, 278
domain-neutral standard 342, 343
domain-specific standard 342
drag-and-drop 60
D-U-N-S Number 233
duplicate check step 211
dynamic addition of properties 234
dynamic and idempotent domain value map 169
dynamic and nonidempotent domain value map 169
dynamic arrays 161
dynamic behavior 269
dynamic change 118
dynamic determination of endpoints 57
dynamic domain value list 168
dynamic domain value maps 31
dynamic instance modification 247, 248
dynamic process binding 227
dynamic process model 196
dynamic type change 111

E
early A2A integration 20
early and late binding 110
early B2B integration 20
early binding 111
early combination of A2A and B2B integration 22
early instantiation 111
eBTWG 344
ebXML 15, 22, 344, 365
ebXML BPSS 348

ebXML message services v2.0 344
ebXML MSS 361
ebXML Registry 359
ebXML's Business Process Specifica-
    tion Schema 348
ebXML's Messaging Service Specifi-
    cation 361
EC Dictionary 353
EDI 15, 38, 350
EDI 838 360
EDI over the Internet 362
EDI translator 15, 20
EDIINT 65, 344, 362
electronic business message 3
Electronic Data Interchange 350
elements of interoperability standards
    341
encryption 64
end date and time 239
end user environment 282
endpoint 29, 231, 278
endpoint agreement 57, 58, 238, 278
endpoint agreement definition 308,
    313, 332
endpoint agreement enforcement 244
endpoint agreement expiration 244
endpoint agreement interpretation 244
endpoint agreement negotiation busi-
    ness process 262
endpoint agreement verification 293
endpoint and agreement standard 358
endpoint attribute 57
endpoint behavior 46
endpoint behavior awareness 95
endpoint bootstrap problem 265
endpoint capability 57
endpoint definition 58, 308, 310, 330
endpoint definition change 330
endpoint definition update 265
endpoint external event 131
endpoint identifier domain value map
    263
endpoint identifier synchronization 263
endpoint management component 64,
    278
endpoint management user interface 61
endpoint property 234
endpoint relationship 236
endpoint state awareness 95
endpoints, types of 29, 231
enterprise external advertisements 320
enterprise-internal advertisements 321
EPISTLE 351
ERP 21
erroneous content of event instance 247
error handling 245, 247, 279
error recovery 247
error types 245
error-handling component 279
error-handling user interface 62
ETL 6
European Process Industries STEP
    Technical Liaison Executive 351
event 30, 35, 141
event address resolution 221
event addressing 148
event addressing process step 221
event and process boundary 105
event and vocabulary 167
event broadcast 222
event classes 151
event correlation 174, 175
event elements 144
event header 144
event instance 62, 181
event integration 131
event interface 105
event life cycle 146
event management component 62
event map 294
event property 145
event state 61, 146
event state transitions 147
event status 280
event type 62, 144
event validation and data type valida-
    tion 177
evolution of integration technology 19

EWG 350
exactly-once message transmission 133
exactly-once semantics 97
execution cycle 201
execution instance state 297
execution logic 182
execution model 215
explicit representation of past state
    changes 254
extensionally defined data type 168
external endpoint 327
external execution logic 223
externally caused change 327
extraction process 7
extract-transform-load 6

F
failed transformation 62
FIFO 65
file system 6, 10, 31, 65
File Transfer Protocol 362
final authority 244
final destination 128
firewall 34
first-in first-out 65
Fix Protocol, Ltd. 354
flow of event instance 284
formal parameter 183
forward error recovery 247
FPL 354
FTP 23, 65, 362
full set of all state changes 255
function integration 130, 202
fundamental architectural principles
    269
future of integration 387

G
GIAI 355
GLN 355
Global Individual Asset Identifier 355
Global Location Number 355
Global Returnable Asset Identifier 355
global schema 131

Global Service Relation Number 355
Global Trade Item Number 355
GRAI 355
graphical notation 261
GSRN 355
GTIN 353, 355

H
hash function 257
hash value 257
Health Level 7 352
heterogeneous data source 96, 131
heterogeneous endpoint 139
heterogeneous environment 21
heterogeneous integration 95
heterogeneous public business behav-
    ior 137
heuristics 60
hierarchical decomposition 181
hierarchical invocation pattern 273
history 32, 61, 253, 254
history of an event 61, 146
history of B2B integration 3
history query 61
HL7 352
holistic B2B integration architecture 19
homegrown integration 5
homogeneity 94
homogeneous communication and in-
    teroperation 138
homogeneous integration 94, 139
homogeneous integration behavior 137
homogeneous logical data schema 96
homonyms 171
hosted application integration 24
hosted application model 24
hosted application system 16
hosted back-end application system 16
hosted data 24
hosted integration 87
hosted integration model 94
hosted trading partner 30, 57, 232
hosting 237
hosting paradigm 93

HTTP 23, 65, 66, 363
hub 10, 76
hub-and-spoke integration 10
human action 62
Hypertext Transfer Protocol 363

I

ideal integration concepts 137
ideal integration world 133, 137
identification 256
IDL 100
IEC 346
IETF 345
immediate and delayed behavior 127
impact analysis 111
implementation component 59
implements relationship 113
inconsistency 118
inconsistent type definition 119
indefinite compensation 204
indefinitely executing loop 204
independent message 12
indirect communication 128
indirect configuration 118
indirect event addressing 222
indirect version relationship 115
individual employee 29
information hiding 124
inheritance 121
inheriting validation rule 178
initiating endpoints 239
initiating event processing 285
initiating process parameter 184
input parameter 183
insertion process 7
instance 108, 109
instance consistency 111
instance-based integration 93
instance-of 108
instance-specific configuation 118
instance-specific integration type 119
instance-type-metatype hierarchy 108
instantiation model 205
integration analysis 281

integration analyst 275
integration architecture 18, 29
integration behavior 136
integration broker 22
integration buffer 7
integration compensation 249
integration concept requirements 29
integration concepts 18, 29, 108, 141
integration end user 276
integration error 247
integration failures 62
integration functionality 131
integration instance change 327
integration instance representation 93
integration interpreter 300
integration logic 62, 283
integration logic boundary 107
integration logic component coordina-
    tor 63, 284
integration logic layer 18, 62
integration manager 275
integration metamodel 299
integration modeler 275
integration patterns 14
integration point 31
integration problem 6
integration process 52
integration project management 317
integration repository 299
integration requirement specification
    68
integration requirements 29
integration scenarios 69
integration technology architecture 58
integration technology deployment 66
integration type change 327
integration type modification 114
integration, quo vadis? 388
integration, three forms of 18
integration, three types of 91
integration, types of 69
integrity 256, 257
intended semantics 110
intent of the sender 171

intentionally defined data type 167
interaction between enterprises 126
interaction scope 128
interaction within enterprises 129
interactive application 78
interendpoint relationships 236
interenterprise communication 129
interenterprise integration 83
interenterprise interaction 126
interface change 330
interface definition language 100
interface layer 18
interface process 50, 122, 124, 181,
    204, 219, 239, 310
interface process execution 286
interface process instantiation 244
interface process type change 331
interface process-specific process steps
    211
intermediary 3
intermediate storage 5, 6
intermediate storing of events 227
internal endpoint 327
internal security attacks 34
internal structure 235
internally caused change 327
International Electrotechnical Com-
    mission 346
International Organization for Stan-
    dardization 345
international standards organization
    344
International Telecommunication
    Union 346
Internet 16
Internet Engineering Task Force 345
Internet Society 345
interoperability standard 339, 340
intra-enterprise communication 129
intra-enterprise integration 79, 88
introspection 129
inverse broadcast 223
inverse operation 203
invocation 126

invocation paradigm 96
invocation pattern 270
invocation relationship 284
invoker is blocked 126
ISO 345
ISO TC184/SC4 351
ISOC 345
isolated transmission 46
isolation of back-end application sys-
    tem 9
IT Dictionary 353
ITU 346

J
J2EE Connector Architecture 367
JTC 1 346

K
key management 64
key revocation 258

L
late binding 111, 118
layer component invocation model 66
layer private component interface 271
layered architecture 270
legacy applications 21
lifelock 230, 280
list of endpoints 150
local process data variable 183, 186
local schema 131
local variable 181
long-running process 184, 201
long-term trends 33
loss of information 163, 164
lossless and unambiguous conversion
    135
lossless transformation 165
lower layer 59, 66

M
management environment 278
management user interface 18

mandatory fields 178
manual error handling 247
manual intervention to repair 247
manufacturing resource planning 21
mapping 154
marketplace integration 75
matching advertisements 321
matching endpoint agreements 239
matching service 321
mature B2B integration 24
mature B2B integration technology 17
message 33, 106, 131, 141
message acknowledgments 14
message body 11
message contains references 142
message duplicates 133
message duplication detection 133
message encryption 133
message exchange behavior 204
message exchange protocol 14
message exchange sequence 46
message exchanges 122
message format 141
message header 10, 143
message injection 133
message instance 37
message introspection 133
message loss 133
message modification 133
message receipt time-out 133
message reordering 133
message resend retry counter 133
message resend upper limit 133
message resending 133
message signature 133
message structure 143
messages are self-contained 143
messages with multiple parts 154
metadata synchronization 71, 72
metatype 108, 110
metatype constraints 110
metatypes in Java 112
microprocesses 202
MIME 65, 363

modeling component 277
modeling concepts 18
modeling environment 277
modeling methodology 307
modeling the endpoint behavior 50
modeling user interface 18, 60
monitoring 61, 323
monitoring component 280
monitoring user interface 61
MRP 21
multiendpoint agreement 240, 241
multi-interface process agreements 242
multilevel access control 257
multipoint integration 70
Multipurpose Internet Mail Extensions 363
multistep integration 12, 13
mutual trust 134
my instance is your type 112

N
n*(n-1) 40
naive B2B integration 15
national standards organization 344
network failure 246
network of queues 93
network protocol 126
nonauthorized third party 256
nonhosted trading partner 30
nonoverlapping 115
nonrecoverable 202
nonrepudiation 38, 64, 256, 258
nonrepudiation of delivery 258
nonrepudiation of origin 258
nonrepudiation of receipt 258
nonrepudiation of submission 258
NOOP process step type 183
NOOP process type 183
normalized representation 38
notification 224, 282

O
OAGI 352
OAGIS 22, 352

OASIS 344, 346
OASIS' Business Transactions Techni-
    cal Committee 364
observing integration processes 323
one-way integration 12
one-way nonrepudiation 258
Open Applications Group Integration
    Specification 22, 352
Open Applications Group, Inc. 352
open endpoint support 94
open trading partner community 233
optimistic case of agreement negotia-
    tion 322
optional fields 178
order criteria 216
order of change 115
ordering of sub-process execution 192
organization aspect 195
Organization for the Advancement of
    Structured Information Standards
    346
organization modeling 234
organization modeling concepts 235
organizational relationship 235
organizational unit 232, 235
origin endpoint 148
OUT 184
out-of-order event 215
output parameter 183
outside components 105
overwriting the target address 149

P

packaging 33
packaging and transport standard 361
packaging component 64
parallel branch 193
parameter constraints 184
Partner Interface Process 348
part-of relationship 110
pattern 197
payload definition 342
PDL 349
peer-to-peer communication 128

peer-to-peer exchange of messages 3
pending authorization 282
performance test 60
permanent system error 246
persistence 65, 297
persistence component 65
persistence layer 19
persistent intermediary states 201
persistent queue 9, 31, 298
persistent queueing system 10, 65
PIP 348
pluggability 64
point-to-point integration 6, 70
point-to-point limitations 9
point-to-point pairwise transformation
    158
policy function 206
policy on external communication 81
portability standard 339
postcondition 184
postproduction phase 68
potential business relationship 319
preceding version 115
precise match 322
precondition 184
predicates over formal process parame-
    ter 184
preproduction phase 68
prescriptions for execution 181
private keys 57
private process 123
process 180
process binding 52, 124
process compensation 203
process compensation step 203
process context 106
process coordination 229
process execution 200
process execution cycle 200
process execution model 198
process instance 109
process integration 96
process management 12
process management component 63

process metatype 109
process parameter 183
process pattern 197
process standard 347
process state 198
process state transitions 199
process step type 181, 182
process type 109, 181
process type reuse 182
process variable 181
process-based integration 12
processes, three classes of 63
process-external data flow 225
processing incoming events 273
process-internal data flow 225
production 275, 278
production phase 68
public and private behavior 121
public export interface 271
public keys 57
public process 121, 122, 204
public registry 320
publication 11
publish/subscribe addressing 10, 11, 12
publish/subscribe technology 99

Q

queue-based architecture 272
queued parameter 189
queueing model 93

R

RDF 347
real standard 344
reasons for change 327
receiving a message 291
recoverable process state 201
recoverable state 201
redeployment 279
reference information model 352
refinement of data flow 208
registry 320
registry search engine 321
related message 46

reliability 97, 255
reliable integration 97
reliable relationship 134
remote back-end application system 74
remote communication 65
remote procedure call 100
remote trading partner 30, 57, 232
removing an endpoint agreement 279
removing an existing clear text event
    type 167
renegotiation of endpoint agreement
    327
repeating fields 161
replace endpoint 219
replacement event type 198
replacement of validation rules 178
replacement type 197
replica of business event instance 222
report generation 12
reporting tool 276
representation of a query 141
representation of a state change 141
repudiation 254
repudiation of delivery 258
repudiation of origin 258
repudiation of receipt 258
repudiation of submission 258
request/response invocation 128
resolvable behavior mismatch 229
Resource Description Framework 347
responding endpoints 239
resubmission 247
resubmitting a changed event 62
reuse relationship 110
reverse hosting 88
rewriting queries 131
RIM 352
RNIF 349
RosettaNet 15, 22, 344, 348, 353, 366
RosettaNet Implementation Frame-
    work 349
run-time engine 18
run-time repository 19
run-time system of Java 112

S

S/MIME 65
SAML 356
schema integration 131
schema integration problem 96, 131
schema transformation 131
schematic overall process layout 125
secret key 256
Secure Socket Layer protocol 357
security 64, 236, 239, 256
Security Assertion Markup Language
    356
security component 64
security services 64
security standards 356
security verification 292
selection 68
selection process 68
self-contained type definition 124
self-service change 334
semantic correctness 251
semantic heterogeneity of business
    concepts 162
semantic mismatch 155
semantic preserving transformation 31
semantic superset 155
semantics 110
sender and recipient of messages 142
sending spoke 10
sequence number 133
Serialized Shipping Container Code
    355
set of all metatypes 108
set of event addresses 222
set of transformation rules 37
share same endpoint agreement 239
short-running process 201
shutting down 279
signature computation 64
signature of a message 257
Simple Mail Transfer Protocol 363
Simple Object Access Protocol 363
single network 134
single point of management 85

single secure and reliable network 133
single semantic data model and integra-
    tion behavior 134
single set of integration concepts 19
singular one-way invocation 128
singular version 120, 238
small trading partners 74
smallest integration scenario 71
SMTP 23, 65, 363
SOAP 65, 66, 361, 363
Society for Worldwide Interbank Fi-
    nancial Telecommunication 353
source address 149
source event 31, 37
specialization 162
specializations of integration type or in-
    stance 121
spectrum of integration use cases 69
split 160, 161
split batch message 217
spoke 10
SSCC 355
SSL 357
standard compliance 343
standards 339
standards organization 344
start date and time 239
state based architecture 272
state of the process 61
state-aware integration 95
state-based architecture 272
state-unaware integration 95
static and dynamic process 195
static and idempotent domain value
    map 168, 169
static domain value list 168
static process model 195
static type change 111
status 253
status of the overall communication
    129
status query 9, 61, 241
stream-based integration 93
streaming query 98

streamlining of processes 323
structural definition 109
structural process change 196
structural semantics 110
sub-process type 182
subscribers 16
subscriptions 11
subsequent version 115
subtyping 121
superfluous event 229
superset 163
superset of meaning 163
superset of structure 163
superset of the business data 159
supply chain 74
supply chain integration 72
supply chain topology 73
SWIFT 15, 353, 366
swiftml 354
symmetric and private key 256
symmetric encryption 258
symmetric key 256
synchronization point 183, 229
synchronous behavior 127
synchronous communication 6
synchronous invocation 126
synchronous send step 127
synchronous vs. asynchronous invoca-
    tion and behavior 126
synonyms 171
syntax 38
syntax conversion 154
system administration environment
    282
system administrator 276
system behavior 269
system error 246
system or power failures 61

T

target address 149
target endpoint 148
target event 31, 37
target spoke 10

TCP/IP 357
test function 186
test scenario 278
testing component 277
testing user interface 60
the grand challenge 388
the grander challenge 390
the integration problem vi
threshold 62
time-out 193
time-out attribute 211
time-out step 211
time-stamping service 78
TLS 357
top-down 66
top-down invocation relationship 59
top-down modeling approach 307
top-level process type 182
total separation of hosted trading part-
    ners 237
trading partner 3, 15, 23, 29, 57
trading partner agreement negotiation
    261
trading partner capability 278
trading partner community 232, 266,
    320
trading partner community agreement
    242
trading partner definition 310
trading partner identifier domain value
    map 233, 263
trading partner information 23
trading partner management compo-
    nent 23
trading partner mock-up 60
Trading Partner Profile 360
transaction 201, 298
transaction processing monitor 65
transaction standard 364
transactional adapters 32
transactional communication 129
transactional message transmission 134
transactional queues 298
transformation 37, 154, 155, 160

transformation component 63
transformation hub 77
transformation map 162
transformation mismatches 162
transformation of data 7
transformation rule 37, 162
transformation step 55
transient system error 246
translation 37, 38, 151, 153, 154
translation component 63
transport 238
transport address 239
transport component 65
transport header 33
Transport Layer Security 357
transport of a message 126
transport protocol 236
transport-specific data 36
tribal knowledge 220
trusted certification authority 256
trusted communication 134
trusted third party 258
two-way nonrepudiation 258
type 108, 109
type change in place 118
type definition interface 62
typecast 164
type-specification mistake 247

U
UCC 348, 354
UDDI 360
UN/CEFACT 344, 350
UN/ECE 346
UN/EDIFACT 350
UN/EDIFACT Working Group 350
UN/LOCODE 355
UN/SPSC 353, 356
uncorrelated out-of-order event 215
Uniform Code Council, Inc. 348
unilateral agreement 240
unique endpoint identifier 233
unique meaning 135
unique token 256

United Nations Centre for Trade Facilitation and Electronic Business 350
United Nations Economic Commission for Europe 346
United Nations/Standard Products and Services Code 356
Universal Description, Discovery and Integration 360
unreliable and insecure network 133
unreliable integration 97
unresolvable behavior mismatch 229
upper layer 59, 66
user 232
user interaction 29, 224
user interface 60
user interface component 275
user interface integration 97
user interface invocations 273
user roles 275
user task 282
users, types of 275

V
validation rules 177, 178, 342
value added network 351
value-added networks 20
VAN 20, 351
variant 114, 121
version 114
version change propagation 117, 330
version number 114
versioning 60, 238
views on business objects 173
virtual machine failure 246
vocabulary 278, 342
vocabulary transformation 168

W
W3C 346, 366
Web Service Description Language 364
Web Services Architecture 366
Web Services Interoperability Organization 344

why integration? 387
wire event 50, 106, 141, 151
wire event type 152
workflow management system 12
worklist user interface 62
world ontology 135
world ontology of business behavior
  136
World Wide Web Consortium 346
WSCI 349
WSCL 349
WS-Coordination 365
WSDL 347, 364
WSFL 347, 349
WS-I 344
WS-Transaction 365

X

XACML 357
X-KISS 357
XKMS 357
X-KRSS 357
XLANG 347, 349
XML 38, 66
XML Access Control Markup Lan-
  guage 357
XML Encryption 357
XML Key Information Service Specifi-
  cation 357
XML Key Management Specification
  357
XML Registration Service Specifica-
  tion 357
XML Signature 358
XML-formatted messages 3

Druck: Strauss Offsetdruck, Mörlenbach
Verarbeitung: Schäffer, Grünstadt